Advance Praise for *America, the Owner's Manual: You Can Fight City Hall—and Win*

"When it comes to the state of American democracy, are you a doer or a complainer? Bob Graham and Chris Hand are concerned we've become a nation of complainers and forgotten how to be effective citizens. In *America, the Owner's Manual*, Graham and Hand don't just urge more Americans to be better citizens, they provide the instructions on how to do it. And I can think of no better person whom I'd like to see teach the country about civics and citizenship than Bob Graham. His thoughtfulness and intellect comes through in this important manual, and I hope it becomes essential reading for anyone looking to make a difference in our grand experiment that is the United States of America."

—Chuck Todd (@chucktodd), *Meet the Press* Moderator
and NBC News Political Director

"Now, as much as any time in our history, Americans need to be reminded of the importance of their role in our democracy. We are the only ones who can change the direction of our country, and *America, the Owner's Manual: You Can Fight City Hall—and Win* provides just the road map to achieve those changes. Real-world examples of how citizens have effected change, along with examples of what hasn't worked, make this book an important read for every concerned citizen."

—Christine Todd Whitman, Former Environmental
Protection Agency (EPA) Administrator and Governor of New Jersey

"Bob Graham and Chris Hand's book, *America, the Owner's Manual: You Can Fight City Hall—and Win*, is an exciting, energizing, and hope-giving guide to effective citizenship. It could (and should) play an important role in our 2016 election and well beyond. The authors remind us that the keys to better government come not from electing parental figures who will make others do what we want, but from citizens engaging their passions and learning the skills to bring about change."

—Donna Brazile (@donnabrazile), Democratic Political Strategist,
Columnist, Commentator, and Former Presidential Campaign Manager

"Senator Bob Graham belongs to that now practically endangered breed of public servant who puts country above politics. He did not live in a Blue world or a Red world, but tried to make this a better world for all. Graham was part of a Washington where 'compromise' was not a bad word, where policies were debated civilly and national issues were actually addressed. In *America, the Owner's Manual*, Bob Graham and Chris Hand provide an important read for those of us who want to see citizens restore those governing values in American democracy."

—Ana Navarro (@ananavarro), CNN and ABC Political Commentator

"In *America, the Owner's Manual,* Senator Bob Graham and Chris Hand honor the ideal of a government of, by, and for the people by preparing citizens with the skills they need to hold public officials accountable. This book tells compelling stories of Americans who have flexed their citizenship muscles, overcome special interest influence, and broken gridlock to make government respond. When you finish reading, you'll be ready to make a real difference in the governmental and political process."

—Joe Lieberman, Former Vice Presidential Nominee, United States Senator, Connecticut Attorney General, and State Senate Majority Leader

"Combining expert advice with relevant and timely examples, *America, the Owner's Manual* is a straightforward and accessible 'how-to' guide to working for change in any political system. Bob Graham and Chris Hand have provided the civics lessons one would want if civics were still routinely taught."

—Annise Parker (@AnniseParker), Former Houston Mayor, Controller, and Councilmember

"Bob Graham's durable bipartisan appeal shines through in *America, the Owner's Manual* by reminding Americans that engagement with our government is a central duty of citizenship. This road map for citizen involvement isn't about party or politics. It's about getting results locally, in the states, and nationally. Senator Graham and Chris Hand have provided a how-to manual complete with clear examples, simple rules of the political road, and smart strategies for Americans ready to get off the couch and get results from their government."

—Rick Wilson (@TheRickWilson), Republican Political Strategist, Media Consultant, Author, and Commentator

"Senator Bob Graham and Chris Hand have produced an invaluable primer on how American citizens can be involved in politics and affect policy change. *America, the Owner's Manual* offers their real-world insights on how to influence policy makers, points that are often overlooked in other books. If you want to know how to be an engaged and effective citizen, read this book."

—Russell J. Dalton, Founding Director, Center for the Study of Democracy, University of California, Irvine

"*America, the Owner's Manual* is the only book that comprehensively explains how to be effective in American politics and civic life, and it does so brilliantly. It's consistently practical, realistic, accessible, and inspiring. It's perfect for anyone who wants to improve the world."

—Peter Levine (@peterlevine), Associate Dean for Research and Lincoln Filene Professor of Citizenship & Public Affairs, Jonathan M. Tisch College of Civic Life, Tufts University

America, the Owner's Manual

New Edition

SAGE was founded in 1965 by Sara Miller McCune to support the dissemination of usable knowledge by publishing innovative and high-quality research and teaching content. Today, we publish over 900 journals, including those of more than 400 learned societies, more than 800 new books per year, and a growing range of library products including archives, data, case studies, reports, and video. SAGE remains majority-owned by our founder, and after Sara's lifetime will become owned by a charitable trust that secures our continued independence.

Los Angeles | London | New Delhi | Singapore | Washington DC | Melbourne

America, the Owner's Manual

You Can Fight City Hall—and Win

New Edition

Senator Bob Graham

and

Chris Hand

FOR INFORMATION:

CQ Press
An Imprint of SAGE Publications, Inc.
2455 Teller Road
Thousand Oaks, California 91320
E-mail: order@sagepub.com

SAGE Publications Ltd.
1 Oliver's Yard
55 City Road
London EC1Y 1SP
United Kingdom

SAGE Publications India Pvt. Ltd.
B 1/I 1 Mohan Cooperative Industrial Area
Mathura Road, New Delhi 110 044
India

SAGE Publications Asia-Pacific Pte. Ltd.
3 Church Street
#10-04 Samsung Hub
Singapore 049483

Printed in the United States of America

Library of Congress Cataloging-in-Publication Data

Names: Graham, Bob, 1936– author. | Hand, Chris, 1973– author.

Title: America, the owner's manual : you can fight City Hall—and win / Bob Graham, Chris Hand.

Description: Revised edition. | Los Angeles : SAGE/CQ Press, [2017] | Includes bibliographical references and index.

Identifiers: LCCN 2016008152 | ISBN 978-1-5063-5058-5 (pbk. : alk. paper)

Subjects: LCSH: Political participation—United States. | Politics, Practical—United States.

Classification: LCC JK1764 .G71 2017 | DDC 322.40973—dc23
LC record available at https://lccn.loc.gov/2016008152

This book is printed on acid-free paper.

Senior Acquisitions Editor: Michael Kerns
Editorial Assistant: Zachary Hoskins
Production Editor: David C. Felts
Copy Editor: Karen Taylor
Typesetter: C&M Digitals (P) Ltd.
Proofreader: Eleni-Maria Georgiou
Indexer: Wendy Allex
Cover Designer: Gail Buschman
Marketing Manager: Amy Whitaker

SUSTAINABLE FORESTRY INITIATIVE
Certified Chain of Custody
Promoting Sustainable Forestry
www.sfiprogram.org
SFI-01268

SFI label applies to text stock

16 17 18 19 20 10 9 8 7 6 5 4 3 2 1

For our families

And, to borrow from President Theodore Roosevelt, for the men and women who are actually in the arena, whose place shall never be with those cold and timid souls who knew neither victory nor defeat.

About the Authors

 Following 12 years of service in the Florida Legislature, **Bob Graham** was elected governor of Florida in 1978. During two successful terms as governor, Graham was nationally recognized for reforms in education, environmental protection, and economic diversification. Upon concluding his two terms as governor, Graham had an 83 percent approval rating from the people of Florida.

Graham was elected to the United States Senate in 1986, serving three consecutive terms. As a member of the Senate Finance, Environment and Public Works, and Veterans Affairs Committees, he was a leader on health, trade, tax, water and infrastructure issues.

One of Graham's most important contributions came during his last Senate term, when he was named chairman of the Select Committee on Intelligence. As Senator he cosponsored the bill to create the Director of National Intelligence position and co-chaired the Joint Inquiry into Intelligence Community Activities Before and After the Terrorist Attacks on September 11, 2001. In 2016, Graham received international attention for urging President Obama to declassify and make public 28 pages redacted from the final Joint Inquiry report. Graham also authored the 2004 book *Intelligence Matters* and the 2011 novel *Keys to the Kingdom*, both revealing serious faults in the U.S. national security system.

Graham may be best known for his workdays. During the nearly 30 years that he campaigned for or served as Florida's Governor and U.S. Senator, Graham worked at more than 400 jobs alongside Floridians. His first workday was teaching citizenship at Carol City High School in Miami Gardens, Florida. Graham wrote of these experiences in his first book *Workdays: Finding Florida on the Job*.

Since leaving the Senate in early 2005, Graham has led national commissions on weapons of mass destruction, the BP oil spill, and financing public higher educations. He spent the 2005–2006 academic year at Harvard University's Kennedy School of Government as a senior fellow. Graham continues his work in environmental protection as chair of the Florida Conservation Coalition. The former Governor and U.S. Senator leads efforts to enhance citizen engagement and train the next generation of public leaders through the Bob Graham Center for Public Service at the University of Florida.

Chris Hand is an attorney with a long record of public service. He previously served as speechwriter, press secretary, and campaign press secretary for Senator Graham and as campaign manager for Florida's former statewide elected chief financial officer, Alex Sink. In 2008, Hand served as one of 27 Florida electors in the United States Electoral College.

In 2010, Graham and Hand authored the original version of this book, entitled *America, the Owner's Manual: Making Government Work for You.*

From 2011 to 2015, Hand served as Chief of Staff at the consolidated City of Jacksonville, Florida—the largest city by area in the contiguous United States and the 12th largest by population in the entire nation—during the administration of Mayor Alvin Brown. As Chief of Staff, Hand managed the Mayor's Office team, with oversight for policy, advocacy, communications, outreach and scheduling. He also led the advancement of strategic initiatives, including efforts to achieve comprehensive pension reform for taxpayers and public safety employees. Those efforts culminated in the enactment of a landmark agreement in 2015.

Hand graduated with honors from the Woodrow Wilson School of Public and International Affairs at Princeton University and the Fredric G. Levin College of Law at the University of Florida. At Princeton, Chris was honored with the *Daily Princetonian* Award for his successful efforts to reform the university's then century-old Honor Code. At the University of Florida, the law school student body elected Hand as president of the student bar association. He also served as a research assistant to former Florida Governor and U.S. Representative Buddy MacKay.

Contents

Preface

When we started to write the new edition of *America, the Owner's Manual* in 2015, Donald Trump topped early Republican presidential polls but was seen by most experienced observers as a fad that would ultimately pass. But as we finish our book in June 2016, Trump has accumulated the delegates required to secure the Republican nomination and received the endorsement of party leaders like the Speaker of the United States House of Representatives.

Though there are countless political lessons to be learned from the 2016 presidential contest, our focus is on what it says about the state of citizenship in the United States. The fact that so many voters have responded to the increasingly bombastic rhetoric and vitriolic tone of the campaign suggests a serious lack of confidence in American political leaders and institutions. In a January 2016 online poll of approximately 3,000 respondents, the RAND Corporation found that likely Republican primary voters were "86.5 percent more likely to prefer Donald Trump as the first-choice nominee relative to all the others if they 'somewhat' or 'strongly agree' that 'people like me don't have any say about what the government does.'"[1] RAND also found that "this increased preference for Trump [was] over and beyond any preferences based on respondent gender, age, race/ethnicity, employment status, educational attainment, household income, attitudes towards Muslims, attitudes towards illegal immigrants, or attitudes towards Hispanics."

Those survey results reinforce the existence of a long-standing national ailment: limited knowledge of what it truly means to be a citizen in our democracy, including the power to engage government directly and move it in a different direction. The truth is that Americans don't have to pin their hopes for greater participation on any one candidate. They do have a say about what the government does—if they learn, master, and practice the skills of effective citizenship. We strive to describe and exemplify those skills in this book.

Perhaps a health analogy best puts our goals in perspective. In recent years, doctors, scientists, and fitness experts have decried our nation's increasingly sedentary lifestyle and made clear its negative effects on our health. Research shows that people who regularly exercise and engage in other physical activity are much less likely to suffer from heart disease, diabetes, premature aging, and other serious medical conditions than are those who are inactive. The fact that many Americans do not lead active lives accounts for alarmingly high rates of dangerous health conditions—and the biggest concern is for children.

---

[1] Michael Pollard and Joshua Mendelsohn, "Rand Kicks Off 2016 Presidential Election Panel Survey," *The Rand Blog*, January 27, 2016, www.rand.org/blog/2016/01/rand-kicks-off-2016-presidential-election-panel-survey.html

This book addresses another health crisis in which activity produces beneficial effects and inactivity poses unacceptable risks, particularly for our youngest generation. Although the hubbub surrounding every presidential election temporarily obscures concerns about our civic health, American democracy suffers from a pervasive lack of active participation among our citizens. For a variety of reasons, many of our fellow Americans see civics as a kind of spectator sport—something to be viewed from afar through the filters of media outlets and personalities, or to be ignored altogether. Since my retirement from the U.S. Senate in 2005, I have become increasingly involved in the effort to transform civics from a spectator sport into a participatory sport—one in which citizens directly engage in democracy and shape local, state, and federal policies to the betterment of their families and communities. Through my involvement in this effort, I have become convinced that many Americans would embrace active citizenship if they just knew how.

Thus the title of this book: *America, the Owner's Manual: You Can Fight City Hall—and Win*. In order to realize the benefits of citizen engagement, we must understand more than just the structure or history of American democracy. Our goal is to help citizens interact directly with their government and make it respond to their hopes and concerns.

We finished the first version of this manual as President Obama was taking office in 2009. Though that was fewer than eight years ago, much has changed in that time. Some of it is not so good. According to The Center for Information and Research on Civic Learning and Engagement (CIRCLE), youth voting rates dropped to a 40-year low in November 2014.[2]

But much of the change is encouraging and empowering. While turnout hit a nadir at the end of the 2014 election cycle, youth voting in the 2016 presidential nominating contests was a very different story. States such as Florida, Michigan, Mississippi, Missouri, New Hampshire, South Carolina, and Wisconsin saw youth voting rates achieve record levels of participation for one or both major political parties.[3] Younger Americans have also taken up other nonvoting forms of political engagement, especially direct action using technology.

---

[2] CIRCLE, "2014 Youth Turnout and Youth Registration Rates Lowest Ever Recorded; Changes Essential in 2016," civicyouth.org/2014-youth-turnout-and-youth-registration-rates-lowest-ever-recorded-changes-essential-in-2016/

[3] See CIRCLE, "Young People in Wisconsin Vote in Record Numbers, Posting Second-Highest State Turnout in 2016," April 7, 2016, civicyouth.org/wp-content/uploads/2016/04/WisconsinPressRelease.pdf; CIRCLE, "Young Voters Break More Participation Records; Youth Support for Frontrunners Still Lagging," March 16, 2016, civicyouth.org/wp-content/uploads/2016/03/March15PressRelease.pdf; CIRCLE, "Young People in Michigan and Mississippi Vote in Record Numbers; Tremendous Youth Support for Sanders Propels His Upset Win in Michigan," March 9, 2016, civicyouth.org/wp-content/uploads/2016/03/MIandMSPressRelease.pdf; CIRCLE, "Young Republicans Participating in Record Numbers in 2016, Youth Only Age Group Trump Does Not Win in Nevada," February 24, 2016, civicyouth.org/wp-content/uploads/2016/02/FinalNevada2016PressRelease.pdf; CIRCLE, "Youth in New Hampshire Vote in Record Numbers; Tremendous Youth Support for Sanders Continues, February 10, 2016, civicyouth.org/wp-content/uploads/2016/02/2016NHPrimary_Release.pdf; CIRCLE, "South Carolina Marks 3rd Contest in a Row with Record-Setting Republican Youth Participation; Young South Carolinians Prefer Cruz to Trump," February 21, 2016, civicyouth.org/wp-content/uploads/2016/02/NV-D-and-SC-R-Press-Release.pdf

We're also writing this new edition because the toolbox for effective citizen engagement has grown considerably in the last seven years. Social media has exploded, fundamentally changing the way we think about communicating and collaborating with others who share our interests. More governments are providing open data for citizen use. Traditional telephone polling now shares the public opinion research space with newer options like leadership polling and Internet and interactive voice response (IVR) surveys. Business interests and citizen advocates who were once on opposite sides are joining together to advance common social and economic policy goals. New media tools, including social media sites, online journalism, and podcasting, have altered the face of journalism. Budget austerity has motivated citizens and decision makers to find innovative ways of financing policy initiatives.

In the planning stages of both the previous version of *America, the Owner's Manual* and this version, we drew on the expert advice of many civic advocates as well as on our own experiences in public and civic service to identify the skills most critical to effective citizenship. Each of the ten chapters in this book provides instruction on a different skill: defining the problem to which you want government to respond; gathering the facts you need to generate solutions and influence public officials; identifying which level of government and which agencies and officials are authorized to act on your concerns; determining public opinion; persuading decision makers; using deadlines, trends, and cycles to your advantage; building coalitions; engaging the media; raising or identifying funds; and capitalizing on victory and rebounding from defeat. Most of the chapters include valuable practice tips—"Tips from the Pros"—from professionals with expert knowledge of these skills and experience using them.

One of the biggest roadblocks to participation in democracy is the perception that it isn't possible—that privileged citizens and special interests command the levers of power, that bureaucracy makes change impossible, and that everyday Americans can't fight City Hall. And, if they try, they lose. In writing this book, we didn't expect readers to simply take our word that they can make a difference. That's why we provide case studies that show what a single person or a group of people can accomplish. The prologue and each chapter contain stories about citizens who used their skills to make democracy respond to a problem they had identified and wanted to solve. If reading these stories of citizen participation inspires you to share your own, or others of which you are aware, please follow and talk to us on Twitter and Periscope (@USAownersmanual). Like and engage us on Facebook (facebook.com/USAownersmanual). Share photos and videos of citizenship in action at instagram.com/USAownersmanual, or e-mail us at USAownersmanual@sagepub.com. Stay tuned for more information on a possible America, the Owner's Manual-related podcast.

Although the case studies provide meaningful examples of citizens who have made a difference, they still represent learning by reading. We believe in learning by doing and we encourage you to take that approach while exploring this book. After completing chapter 1, define a community problem you would like to address. As you learn additional citizenship skills in chapters 2 through 10, incorporate each skill into a step-by-step advocacy plan to solve the challenge you have identified. By the end of *America, the Owner's Manual*, we hope you will have the necessary knowledge and enthusiasm for citizen engagement to put down the book, iPad, Kindle, Nook, or other electronic reader and implement that plan with success. Your journey to effective citizenship won't truly begin until you are in the arena, flexing your citizenship muscles in pursuit of a just cause to move government in your direction.

Keep three caveats in mind as you explore the pages of this book. First, we have provided multiple links to help you access resources and real-life examples that may assist you in your own citizen engagement. If you find that one of these links has changed since this book was published, use a search engine to track down the source. Second, though we list numerous social media sites, please remember that new tools emerge all the time in our dynamic digital world. Third, the law is subject to change and often does. You would be wise to check the status of any of the local, state, or federal laws or regulations referenced in *America, the Owner's Manual.*

This book would not have been possible without the help of many people who share our passion for civic engagement. We want to acknowledge them here.

The inspiration to teach participatory democracy came early in my political career when I taught a semester of twelfth-grade civics at Miami Carol City Senior High School. My colleague, the late Donnell Morris, was one of the most effective and passionate educators I have ever known. Together with our students, we learned what committed and trained citizens of any age can do to make their community a better place.

The idea for the first version of this book took root during the fall of 2005 when I was a senior fellow at the Institute of Politics Kennedy School of Government at Harvard. During that fall semester, I led a group of undergraduates in a weekly seminar about effective citizenship. Hayley Fink, Matt Greenfield, Rachel Johnson, Steven Johnston, Richard Krumholz, Nicholas Melvoin, John Oxtoby, Baruch Shemtov, Zak Tanjeloff, and Jarrett Zafran were highly motivated students who helped me understand the skills required to take a citizen from a seat in the audience to the arena floor.

During that Harvard experience in 2005, several members of the Kennedy School faculty—including Professors Archon Fung, David King, and Robert D. Putnam—greatly facilitated the task of putting concepts onto paper. I was fortunate to have the support of remarkable people at the Institute of Politics, including Eric R. Andersen, Sarah Bieging, and Amy Howell. Professor Graham Allison, director of the Belfer Center for Science and International Affairs and Douglas Dillon Professor of Government at the Kennedy School, has been for many years a mentor.

No officeholder could survive without an effective staff. I've been blessed to work with dedicated staff members for my entire career, including the two who worked with me during the writing of this new and improved version of *America, the Owner's Manual.* April Bolet and Kendall Graham Elias played critical roles in the completion of this project. They kept me on schedule, provided research assistance, and performed the many other tasks that have enabled me to stay actively engaged in local, state, and national issues following my retirement from public office.

Since 2007, I have chaired the board of advisors of the Bob Graham Center for Public Service at the University of Florida. I have received generous guidance from its director, David Colburn, the superb colleagues he has recruited, and Graham Center students in bringing the objectives of this book to my alma mater.

We are very grateful to the citizen leaders who helped in crafting the eleven case studies in this book that powerfully illustrate democracy in action. Former Georgia legislator Jeff Chapman, State Representative Mike Dudgeon, Debbie Dooley, Colleen Kiernan, Jason Rooks, and Georgia Public Service Commissioner Bubba MacDonald were instrumental in telling the story of the Green Tea coalition in the prologue. When we first wrote the chapter 1 case study, Roger Turner and Bob and Susan Leveille, members of the Jackson County Smart Roads Alliance, and Walter Kulash, the Smart Roads Alliance's consultant, generously gave of their time and materials in narrating this saga. This time, Sarah Thompson, director of planning and development for the Southwestern Commission, helped us update the story. The chapter 2 case study was expertly written by Nick Maynard, Brian Gilmore, and Mariele McGlazer of the Doorways to Dreams (D2D) Fund. Later in the chapter, we again used the Florida Keys case study previously written with the help of Cindy DeRocher, a leader of the successful initiatives for fair insurance rates in Monroe County, and Heather Carruthers, a Monroe County commissioner.

When we first wrote the Barbara Capitman case study for chapter 3, we had the help of South Florida's leading historian—Arva Parks McCabe—and one of its most distinguished civic leaders, Ruth Shack, both of whom lived through and were invaluable sources on the revitalization of South Beach. Historic Preservation Officer Daniel Ciraldo of the Miami–Dade Preservation League was helpful when we updated the case study for this new edition of the book. Dr. Cyndy Simms, Bob Maddox, and Dr. David Hill, three of the principal figures in the educational reform initiative in Steamboat Springs discussed in chapter 4, explained how confrontation evolved into highly successful consensus. Thanks also to Hill Research Consultants for allowing us to display part of the Steamboat Springs poll at the end of chapter 4. In chapter 5, the story we wrote for the first edition benefitted greatly from the insights of Karolyn Nunnallee, former president of Mothers Against Drunk Driving (MADD). Current MADD Executive Director Debbie Weir provided invaluable assistance as we updated the case study for this new and improved version of *America, the Owner's Manual.*

We are grateful to the *Huffington Post* for permission to use its article entitled "Why the Mizzou Football Protests Are a Watershed Moment in Sports Activism" as our chapter 6 case study. The unnamed (but known to me) university professor in chapter 6 refreshed my memory and added details to his lesson in clock management. We also owe thanks to Professor Burdett Loomis of the University of Kansas for his counsel on the importance of deadlines, trends, and cycles in the political process. Telephone conversations with him when we wrote the first edition, as well as the wisdom in his book *Time, Politics, and Policies: A Legislative Year*, greatly assisted in the development of chapter 6. In Chapter 7, Nadine Smith provided the compelling case story of LGBT advocates and business leaders coalescing in support of equality, while Gaby Pacheco helped us understand her efforts to build a coalition of support for undocumented immigrant youth on the "Trail of Dreams."

For more than three decades, I have maintained a friendship with Tom Fiedler, former *Miami Herald* reporter and editor and now dean of the College of Communications at Boston University, because we always have understood the boundaries and standards of a relationship between a journalist and a politician. His willingness to contribute the story of the Boston Health Care for the Homeless Program, as well as substantial advice on engaging the media, for chapter 8 is but the latest expression of that friendship. When we wrote the first edition, Rick Reilly and Elizabeth Gore of the United Nations Foundation were as generous with their contributions to chapter 9 as supporters of Nothing But Nets have been in reducing deaths caused by malaria. Mr. Reilly graciously took time from his busy schedule to assist our update to the Nothing But Nets story in this new version of *America, the Owner's Manual*. Jersey City Mayor Steven Fulop shared his community's innovative use of crowdfunding to finance needed transportation options. Public finance expert Jonathan Trichter took us to the coastal town of Newburyport near the Massachusetts–New Hampshire border for the story of how citizens earned financial credibility and used it to secure the approval of needed athletic fields.

We also greatly appreciate the assistance of George Deukmejian, former governor of California, and his former chief of staff, Steve Merksamer, with the East L.A. case study when we prepared it for chapter 10 of the first edition. That story remains intact here. We also owe enormous thanks to the President and Fellows of Harvard College and the John F. Kennedy School of Government's Case Program. Two Harvard Kennedy School case studies written by Pamela Varley were also important sources for the case study in chapter 10: "No Prison in East L.A.! Birth of a Grassroots Movement" (C14-00-1541.0) and "No Prison in East L.A.! Birth of a Grassroots Movement Sequel" (C14-00-1541.1).

Many expert professionals generously shared their practical advice in the "Tips from the Pros" segments, showing citizens how they can maximize their effectiveness. We are grateful to Congressman Derek Kilmer of Washington State; former Indianapolis Mayor Stephen Goldsmith; Mike Rice, president of VR Research; Avi Green, executive director of the Scholars Strategy Network; Alyce Robertson, executive director of the Miami Downtown Development Authority; former Idaho Governor, U.S. Senator, and U.S. Secretary of the Interior Dirk Kempthorne; Karen Feather, former chief of staff to Congressman Paul Kanjorski of Pennsylvania; Leon County, Florida, Commissioner and 2016–2017 National Association of Counties President Bryan Desloge; Michael Meyers, president of Target Point Consulting; Dylan Sumner, senior partner at Mack Sumner; Mike Bocian, founding partner of GBA Strategies; Jeff Boeyink, partner at LS2group and former chief of staff to Iowa Governor Terry Branstad; Geoff Garin, president of Hart Research; David Hill, director of Hill Research Consultants; Maine RSU 71 School District member Caitlin Hills; public policy leaders Annabel R. Chang, Laura Bisesto, and Felipe Pereira of Lyft; Mark Block, founder and chairman of Block By Block Productions, LLC; former Congressman Jason Altmire of Pennsylvania, now senior vice president for public policy and community engagement at Florida Blue; Southeast Regional Director Randall Reid from the International City/County Management Association; former Chattanooga Mayor Ron Littlefield; Chris Lehane, head of Global Policy and Public Affairs at Airbnb; public education advocate and former television anchor Deborah Gianoulis; former radio reporter, editor, and news director Judith Smelser; broadcast host and columnist Michael Smerconish; new media journalist Sarah Rumpf; Laura O'Shaughnessy and Ben Weiss of SocialCode; Steve Ziff, vice president of marketing and digital media for the Jacksonville Jaguars of the National Football League; Margie Omero and Kristen Soltis Anderson, cohosts of podcast *The Pollsters*; J.J. Balaban and Pia Carusone, partners in the media consulting firm The Campaign Group; Chris Talbot, founder of the digital marketing firm Talbot Digital; Paul Anderson, senior vice president for integrated communications and marketing at the American Association of Retired Persons (AARP); Taryn Rosenkranz, founder and chief executive officer of New Blue Interactive; former Rhode Island Auditor General Ernie Almonte; Tom Greene, director of budget and management for the City of St. Petersburg, Florida; and innovative financing expert LeAnna Gutierrez Cumber.

Several civic leaders graciously reviewed chapters of this new version to help us ensure accuracy and completeness: David Draine, a senior researcher at Pew Charitable Trusts, and Mike Rice, president of VR Research, provided expert advice on research strategies and tools for chapter 2; pollsters David Beattie of EMC Research and Michael Bocian of GBA Strategies assessed our public opinion discussion in chapter 4; Political and legislative strategist Steve Schale helped our explanation of why timing matters in chapter 6; Ryan Smart, president of 1000 Friends of Florida, applied his environmental coalition-building know-how to chapter 7; Media expert David DeCamp used his journalism background and corporate/governmental communications experience to help us describe the media in chapter 8; Greg Goddard offered counsel from his service as a fundraiser in mayoral, gubernatorial, U.S. Senate, and presidential elections for chapter 9; Kevin Cate, Ryan Clarke, and James Croft supplied invaluable social media insights for the book.

We have been very pleased to work on the new version of *America, the Owner's Manual* with the same publisher that produced the original book: CQ Press, an imprint of SAGE. You are reading these pages thanks to the efforts of editors Charisse Kiino, Matthew Byrnie, Michael Kerns, David Felts, and associates Zachary Hoskins and Janae Masnovi; senior marketing manager Amy Whitaker and senior marketing associate Jade Henderson; and other CQ Press employees. We are also very grateful to Karen Taylor for her excellent copyediting. Karen repeatedly improved the quality of our work.

Five women who have long influenced my life and work played critical roles in this project. My four daughters—Congresswoman Gwen Graham, who demonstrated that she practices what this book preaches when *CQ Roll Call* ranked her in February 2016 as the most independent-voting member of the Florida congressional delegation, the sixth most independent Democrat in the House, and the ninth most independent representative of either party; Cissy McCullough; Suzanne Gibson; and Kendall Elias—have not only provided love, support, and eleven wonderful grandchildren but also helped me by suggesting ideas and reviewing chapters.

Throughout this process, as she has been for nearly sixty years, my wife, Adele, was an invaluable source of inspiration, encouragement, and—drawing on her decades of experience as a teacher and civic activist—advice on the skills of participatory citizenship. Without her, this project would long ago have lost momentum.

Chris Hand greatly appreciates the many people mentioned above for their contributions of time, insights, and advice to the new version of *America, the Owner's Manual*, particularly Kendall Graham Elias and others who were on the receiving end of his frequent telephone calls and e-mails.

Chris is especially grateful to his three favorite redheads—wife Heather and children Garland and Graham—for their patience during this writing and editing process. He has been motivated to write this book by the hope that his children—and all young people—will decide to live their lives as engaged citizens who actively work to make the world a better place.

He also deeply thankful to the other family members and friends whose encouragement made his participation possiblehis parents Jack and Grace Hand; Mike, Sarah, Liam, Connor, Brody, and Ronan Hand; Bill Hand; Sam and Missie Leprell; Lamar Sarra Jr.; J.J. Balaban and Daphne Hasbani; Dave and Jennifer DeCamp; Steve and Jennifer LaSota; Mario Decunto; Jon Leonard; Paul Lutz; Stephen Schmier; Matt Strong; and Paul Tibbits Jr.

Last but not least, Chris appreciates the civic leaders and advocates who have encouraged or facilitated his interest in citizen engagement and participation in public service: Former Florida Governor and U.S. Senator Bob Graham, and Mrs. Adele Graham; attorney and Florida legal community leader Wayne Hogan; former Florida Governor, Lieutenant Governor, and Congressman Buddy MacKay; former Florida Chief Financial Officer Alex Sink; former Speaker of the Florida House of Representatives Jon Mills; former Jacksonville Mayor Alvin Brown; nonprofit leader and housing advocate Bill Lazar; Northeast Florida community trustees Deborah Gianoulis and Audrey Moran; the dedicated public servants with whom Chris served as a staff member in the United States Senate and at the City of Jacksonville, Florida; his teachers, school administrators, and friends at Seabreeze Elementary, the Jacksonville Beach Sixth Grade Center, Duncan U. Fletcher Junior and Senior High Schools; professors and classmates at Princeton University, including the Woodrow Wilson School of Public and International Affairs, and at the Levin College of Law at the University of Florida; the Leadership Jacksonville Class of 2014; and all of the citizen advocates who have inspired his strong belief that men and women in the arena can make a difference.

Prologue

Green Tea[1]

Joeff Davis

Debbie Dooley (left) and Colleen Kiernan (right) pose for *Creative Loafing Atlanta*'s "Best Odd Couple" award in 2012, after forming an unlikely political coalition to defeat Georgia's proposed T-SPLOST tax increase. They would continue their alliance to promote solar energy.

Mention the last name Dooley in the state of Georgia, and most residents are likely to think of the legendary University of Georgia football coach and athletic director who led the Bulldogs to six Southeastern Conference (SEC) titles and their only national college football championship. Vince Dooley's teams were known to be conservative, relying on strong defense to stop other teams and powerful running backs like Heisman Trophy winner Herschel Walker to move the chains. But as tough as his teams could be on Saturdays, Coach Dooley was equally known for his good sportsmanship. No matter how much he won, Vince Dooley was the consummate gentleman.

Though not related to Vince Dooley, Debbie Dooley shares his last name. Her political ideology matches his coaching philosophy: she is conservative. But the similarities end there. On the playing field of politics and government, Debbie Dooley has been as risk-taking and as offensive-minded as Vince Dooley was cautious and defensively oriented. Her adversaries will not accuse her of being too nice or polite. But Debbie Dooley's willingness to challenge the status quo, face down entrenched powers, and build coalitions across partisan and ideological lines have become a model for effective citizen advocacy, just as Vince Dooley's teams were once a standard for college football success.

Against all odds, Dooley's efforts—and those of other grassroots organizers, renewable energy advocates, and interested elected officials—succeeded in overcoming corporate giant Georgia Power and turning the Peach State into a national leader in the use of solar energy.

The economic collapse of 2008 was the clarion call that summoned Debbie Dooley to engage governmental decision makers in new ways. A 55-year-old housewife from Buford, Georgia, Dooley had been involved in politics for most of her

[1] Our thanks go to Jeff Chapman, Debbie Dooley, Mike Dudgeon, Colleen Kiernan, Bubba McDonald, and Jason Rooks, who granted interviews and provided information and insights for this story. Any quotations without citations come from those interviews.

adult life as an active member of the Republican Party. "I loved Ronald Reagan and Margaret Thatcher," she said. But the financial crisis marked a turning point for her political participation.

Dooley was already disappointed by what she saw as overspending and "big-government Republicanism" in the presidential administration of George W. Bush. Disappointment turned to outrage when President Bush proposed, and Congress ultimately passed, a bailout of the same Wall Street financial institutions that had precipitated the crisis. She associated herself with every word of CNBC commentator Rick Santelli's "epic rant" on February 19, 2009 from the floor of Chicago Board of Trade:

> The government is promoting bad behavior. . . . This is America. How many of you people want to pay for your neighbor's mortgage that has an extra bathroom and can't pay their bills? . . . We're thinking of having a Chicago tea party in July. All you capitalists that want to show up to Lake Michigan, I'm going to start organizing it . . . and we're going to be dumping in some derivative securities.[2]

The video of Santelli lashing out at the federal government went viral, cascading across the Internet and social media as well as the television and radio airwaves. People like Debbie Dooley saw Santelli's shouting spree and took his suggestion to heart. On February 19, 2009, Dooley found herself on a conference call with 21 other Americans who shared her frustration with the state of politics in the United States—a call that concluded with the creation of the Tea Party. Just over a week later, on February 27, Dooley and 300 of her Georgia allies ignored a pouring rain and gathered on the steps of the Georgia State Capitol to join the Tea Party's first national day of protest against what its advocates saw as massive federal spending and irresponsible corporate bailouts.

A new political movement had been founded, and Dooley was its acknowledged leader in the eighth largest state in the nation.

Since its creation in 2009, the Tea Party movement has been associated nationally with its anti-Washington, populist brand of conservatism. Many political analysts credited Tea Party members with helping Republicans achieve a majority in the United States House of Representatives in 2010—and subsequently blamed the Tea Party–affiliated members for pulling the GOP caucus so far to the right that it could not govern effectively. Even casual observers remember breathless media coverage of fervent rallies denouncing newly elected President Obama and highlighting notable Tea Party champions, such as former Alaska governor and 2008 Republican vice-presidential nominee Sarah Palin.

As is often the case with political identity, the Tea Party's image was simultaneously accurate and incomplete. Many members did conjure up the old movie scenes of angry townspeople storming the castle with pitchforks and torches. But that stereotyping missed the work that some Tea Party leaders were doing to hold state and local governments accountable, regardless of which party was in control.

Debbie Dooley was a prime example of the latter—a Tea Party leader abiding by former U.S. House Speaker Tip O'Neill's sage observation that "all politics is local." Unlike many of her peers, Debbie was not as focused on the White House and

---

[2] "CNBC's Rick Santelli's Chicago Tea Party," The Heritage Foundation YouTube Channel, uploaded February 19, 2009, www.youtube.com/watch?v=zp-Jw-5Kx8k

Congress. Her efforts to fight the power were local—and became literal when she joined solar power advocates and environmentalists in challenging Georgia Power, the state's preeminent utility.

AN 800-POUND GORILLA

Georgia Power, a subsidiary of the Southern Company, is an investor-owned utility. As of late 2015, the company served nearly 2.5 million customers in 155 of Georgia's 159 counties.[3] In 2015, Georgia Power reported nearly $8.4 billion in annual operating revenue and over $32 billion in total assets.[4] The company employs nearly 8,000 Georgia workers.

Due to its massive economic presence, Georgia Power has long been an entity that wields considerable influence, which it has not been afraid to demonstrate. In 2008, the president of the Georgia American Association of Retired Persons (AARP) chapter wrote an op-ed for the *Savannah Morning News* describing one such show of strength: "[W]hen the PSC was deciding how much Georgia Power could raise electric rates for fuel costs, an army of skilled attorneys and company representatives and boxes of documents descended on the Commission in white, 15-passenger vans—all in the defense of Georgia Power."[5]

If the power of billions of dollars in economic activity and a well-oiled lobbying machine weren't enough, the Georgia Legislature voted in 2011 to lift a decades-old ban on utilities contributing directly to political campaigns.[6] In the first year following the end of the prohibition, elected officials received nearly $200,000 in political contributions from utilities.[7] A July 2012 report in the *Atlanta Journal-Constitution* found that during the previous five years, elected Georgia utility regulators received 70 percent of their campaign contributions "from companies and people that may profit from the agency's decisions"—including more than $52,000 from current and former employees of the Southern Company, Georgia Power, and a law firm representing Georgia Power.[8]

Georgia Power's economic and political prowess has long given it great sway on matters before state decision makers. That influence has translated into numerous policy victories over time. But two of those wins would ultimately prove to be costly— because they turned Debbie Dooley and other Tea Party–affiliated, libertarian-leaning conservatives against Georgia Power.

---

[3] Georgia Power, "Facts & Figures," www.georgiapower.com/about-us/facts-and-financials/facts-and-figures.cshtml; Georgia Public Service Commission, "Electric," www.psc.state.ga.us/electric/electric.asp

[4] Georgia Power Company, 2015 Annual Report (Atlanta: Georgia Power Company, 2016), 84, georgiapower.com/docs/about-us/2015GPCAnnualReport.pdf

[5] Cas Robinson, "Georgia Consumers Lose Voice, *Savannah Morning News*, September 18, 2008, savannahnow.com/opinion/2008-09-18/robinson-georgia-consumers-lose-voice

[6] Senate Research Office, "2011 Session of the Georgia General Assembly: Legislation Passed," Senate Research Office, May 2011, www.senate.ga.gov/sro/Documents/Highlights/2011Highlights.pdf

[7] Associated Press, "Utility Firms Pour Money into Candidate's Coffers," *Online Athens: Athens Banner-Herald*, April 20, 2012, onlineathens.com/local-news/2012-04-20/utility-firms-pour-money-candidates-coffers

[8] AJC, "Donors Have Stake in PSC Decisions," *Atlanta Journal-Constitution*, July 21, 2012, www.ajc.com/news/news/local/donors-have-stake-in-psc-decisions/nQXQQ/

The first occurred in September 2008, when then-Governor Sonny Perdue defunded the state Consumers' Utility Counsel (CUC), a branch of the Governor's Office of Consumer Protection that, for more than three decades, had advocated for residential ratepayers in Public Service Commission proceedings. Perdue announced the move—to save $150,000—as necessary budget cutting in a global financial crisis. The deprivation of funding was unpopular with many consumer advocates, some of whom suggested that the governor's chief of staff, who had spent the previous four decades working for Georgia Power, was behind the move.[9] Even some members of the Public Service Commission raised questions:

> When the counsel was de-funded, Commissioner Doug Everett said, "They were the main voice of the consumer and small business. Now they won't have anyone representing them directly anymore."
> Commissioner Stan Wise observed that, "At different times, the (counsel) was very effective in the process."
> Commissioner Robert Baker said, "There's a giant void there. There's no third-party representation for small consumers."[10]

Although the abolition of the CUC in September 2008 left Dooley suspicious, the governor's action occurred a few months before organization of the national and Georgia versions of the Tea Party Patriots. But 2009 brought an even bigger Georgia Power triumph—one that committed Dooley and her allies to the path of opposing the state's biggest utility.

By 2005, Georgia Power had analyzed future population growth and determined that its current infrastructure would not support long-term customer needs, especially as the company might have to close up to 15 of its coal-fired plants to comply with federal clean air standards. In cooperation with other utilities, Georgia Power launched plans to build two new nuclear power reactors in the existing Alvin W. Vogtle Electric Generating Plant in Burke County, south of Augusta—home of golf's legendary Masters Tournament. Those units would come to be known as Vogtle 3 and 4.

The project posed a significant economic dilemma for Georgia Power, particularly in light of the financial damage wreaked by the recession. Georgia Power's share of Vogtle 3 and 4 construction would be expensive—an initial certified cost of $6.133 billion, which by February 2016 would grow to nearly $8 billion.[11] And the collapse of Wall Street made financing more costly to obtain. Even worse, it would be many years until the units generated both electricity and the revenue necessary to pay down any debt incurred on the new plants.

---

[9] Walter Jones, "One Fewer Voice to Speak Up on Utility Matters," *Savannah Morning News*, March 29, 2010, savannahnow.com/walter-c-jones/2008-09-14/analysis-one-fewer-voice-speak-utility-matters

[10] David Markiewicz, "Consumers Lack Voice at PSC as Big Utility Cases Loom, Advocates Say," *Atlanta Journal-Constitution*, February 20, 2010, www.ajc.com/news/news/local/consumers-lack-voice-at-psc-as-big-utility-cases-l/nQchJ/

[11] Kristi E. Swartz, "Georgia Power Defends 'Every Dollar and Every Day' Spent on Reactors, *EnergyWire*, April 8, 2016, http://www.eenews.net/stories/1060035284; David Williams, "Lawmakers Reject Bill Aimed at Plant Vogtle Overruns," *Atlanta Business Chronicle*, March 5, 2013, www.biz journals.com/atlanta/news/2013/03/05/lawmakers-reject-bill-aimed-at-plant.html

Georgia Power looked for alternative solutions and learned that utilities in Florida and North Carolina had won regulatory approval to have customers prepay the cost of new nuclear power plants. On February 26, 2009, the Georgia Legislature overwhelmingly approved SB 31, which authorized Georgia Power to impose a monthly surcharge on utility bills until the funds had been raised to pay for Vogtle 3 and 4, plus an 11 percent profit margin for Georgia Power shareholders.[12] Just over two weeks later, in mid-March 2009, the Public Service Commission certified Georgia Power's plans to build Vogtle 3 and 4 and obtain prepayment from ratepayers.[13]

When the prepayment proposal encountered opposition from consumer activists, nuclear power opponents, and some legislators, Georgia Power left nothing to chance in the approval process. As the Associated Press reported in the aftermath of the final vote in February 2009,

> Lobbyists are a mainstay under the gold dome. But Georgia Power's full court press this year has raised eyebrows, even among some legislative veterans. In recent weeks the powerful utility has hired a pricey fleet of the most sought-after lobbyists. The minimum price tag for the hired help is $50,000, according to lobbying registration documents. Additionally, Georgia Power's chief executive officer, Michael Garrett, registered with state ethics officials this month to officially lobby on the bill.
>
> "It's been the lobbyist employment act of 2009," said state Sen. Steve Thompson, a Marietta Democrat who voted against it. . . . .
>
> Besides the lobbying drive, Georgia Power has been lavishing meals and sports tickets on lawmakers in recent months, according to state lobbying disclosure reports. In January alone, Georgia Power spent $497 on a dinner for House Republican leadership, $996 on a lunch for House Democrats and $565 for the executive committee of the Georgia Legislative Black Caucus. And the utility coughed up $520 worth of hockey tickets for House Speaker Pro Tem Mark Burkhalter. Mr. Burkhalter wrote an op-ed piece in October calling on Georgia officials to cut the red tape to build nuclear facilities.[14]

Georgia Power's successful effort to pull out all the stops did not go unnoticed by legislative opponents, good government groups, and members of the media. Another person was also paying close attention: Debbie Dooley. The episode solidified a viewpoint she would repeat many times in the years to come. "These giant monopolies are trying to protect their profit margin," Dooley told a media outlet in 2014. "They are no longer looking out for the best interests of their utility customers. They are looking

[12] Shannon McCaffrey, "House OK's Georgia Power Plan to Raise Power Bills," *Covington News*, February 26, 2009, www.covnews.com/archives/6013/

[13] Georgia Public Service Commission, "PSC Approves Agreement to Allow Construction of New Units at Vogtle Nuclear Power Generation Plant [news release]," March 17, 2009, www.psc.state.ga.us/newsinfo/releases/2009/20090317-b.pdf

[14] Associated Press, "Lobbyists Push Hard on Rate Bill," *Augusta Chronicle*, February 23, 2009, chronicle.augusta.com/stories/2009/02/23/met_512392.shtml

out for the best interest of their stockholders."[15] As she would later explain, "I like choice and competition. Georgia Power was all about control and monopoly."

THE ODD COUPLE[16]

The prepayment legislation—and the lobbying and gift-giving strategy to secure its passage—touched a nerve with Dooley. Motivated by Vogtle 3 and 4, the CUC defunding, and an unrelated ethics scandal involving the Speaker of the Georgia House of Representatives, Dooley championed the cause of ethics reform. In her activism, she encountered a variety of advocacy groups with whom the life-long conservative had never previously worked—such as the ACLU, NAACP, and Common Cause. By January 2011, Dooley and the Tea Party were charter members of the newly formed Georgia Alliance for Ethics Reform, a coalition that also included consumer watchdogs and good government advocates.[17]

The ethics reform effort, which culminated in the passage of legislation sponsored by Columbus Senator Josh McCoon in 2012, convinced Dooley of the value of coalitions. She became a firm believer that allies "may disagree on some issues and work together on others. The important thing is to trust each other." Her new coalition-building approach soon resulted in the unlikeliest of allies—Colleen Kiernan, the director of the Sierra Club's Georgia chapter.

To put it mildly, the Tea Party was not exactly a bastion of environmental activism. A *New York Times*/CBS poll conducted in October 2010 found that "only 14 percent of Tea Party supporters said that global warming is an environmental problem that is having an effect now" and "[m]ore than half of Tea Party supporters said that global warming would have no serious effect at any time in the future."[18] Those survey results aligned the Tea Party with "oil, coal and utility industries" that according to one analysis "collectively spent $500 million" between January 2009 and October 2010 "to lobby against legislation to address climate change and to defeat candidates . . . who support it."

Yet, to their great surprise, Kiernan and Dooley found they had more interests in common than either could believe or might publicly admit. Kiernan took notice of these common interests when the Tea Party unexpectedly joined unions and various progressive organizations in opposing proposed legislation that would outlaw some forms of political and economic protest and turn other forms into felony offenses.[19]

[15] Robert Trigaux, "Tea Party Leader Roils the Far Right with Clean Energy Stance," *Tampa Bay Times*, October 30, 2014, www.tampabay.com/news/business/energy/tea-partys-debbie-dooley-roils-far-right-with-clean-energy-stance/2204416

[16] Joeff Davis, "Best Odd Couple: The Sierra Club's Georgia Director Colleen Kiernan and Debbie Dooley of the Atlanta Tea Party," *Creative Loafing*, December 2012, clatl.com/atlanta/best-odd-couple/BestOf?oid=6380126

[17] Aaron Gould Sheinin, "'Culture of Corruption' Leads to Calls for Ethics Reform," *Atlanta Journal-Constitution*, January 20, 2011, www.ajc.com/news/news/local-govt-politics/culture-of-corruption-leads-to-calls-for-ethics-re/nQptB/

[18] John M. Broder, "Climate Change Doubt Is Tea Party Article of Faith," *New York Times*, October 20, 2010, www.nytimes.com/2010/10/21/us/politics/21climate.html?_r=0

[19] Mike Hall and Jennifer Kauffman, "Tea Party Joins Fight against Georgia Anti-Picketing Bill," *AFL-CIO Now*, March 19, 2012, www.aflcio.org/Blog/In-The-States/Tea-Party-Joins-Fight-Against-Georgia-Anti-Picketing-Bill

She subsequently called Dooley and invited her to lunch. They met just a few days before Earth Day in April 2012.

At lunch, Dooley and Kiernan discovered a mutual exhaustion with "business as usual" and a joint desire to leave the nation better for future generations. They also shared distaste for what Dooley called "crony capitalism"—the prioritization of special interest-backed corporate interests over those of everyday citizens. Or, as Dooley put it more bluntly, "good ol' boys getting rich and the taxpayers getting the shaft."[20]

Kiernan was pleasantly surprised when she learned that Dooley vehemently opposed the Vogtle nuclear reactor prepayment plan. Dooley banged the table in joy when she heard that Kiernan and the Sierra Club opposed a ten-year sales tax increase to build transportation infrastructure—known as T-SPLOST—because it represented "business as usual." For Dooley, the business as usual was asking taxpayers to foot the bill for an initiative that she believed mostly helped big businesses like profitable road builders. Kiernan saw more road building that would ultimately create more gridlock and air pollution rather than a truly meaningful commitment to mass transit. They came from different perspectives but agreed on the bottom line.

Thus began an unusual alliance that fought multiple electoral battles together in 2012. The main contest was the overwhelming defeat of T-SPLOST in the July 31, 2012, general primary election.[21] Though T-SPLOST had been strongly backed by the business community, governor, state legislative leaders, and elected mayors and commissioners from all ten counties in the Metro Atlanta area, grassroots groups like the Georgia Tea Party, Sierra Club, and the NAACP opposed the initiative.[22] Despite T-SPLOST supporters spending at least $8 million to tout the proposal, voters agreed with the opponents by a more than two-to-one margin.

The other joint political effort was over the membership of the Georgia Public Service Commission (PSC). Though in some states the governor selects utility regulators subject to confirmation by the state legislature, Georgia voters directly elect PSC members to six-year terms.[23] Commissioner Stan Wise—known as the strongest Georgia Power supporter on the PSC—was on the 2012 ballot.

Wise had come under particular scrutiny. In 2010, an *Atlanta Journal-Constitution* investigation determined that Wise had showed up at his PSC office on only 58 percent of working days between June 2008 and November 2010.[24] During a challenging Republican primary contest, it was reported that Wise received more

---

[20] Jon Terbush, "The Green Tea Coalition: Why the Sierra Club and the Georgia Tea Party Keep Teaming Up," *The Week*, November 20, 2013, theweek.com/articles/455976/green-tea-coalition-why-sierra-club-georgia-tea-party-keep-teaming

[21] Ariel Hart, "Voters Reject Transportation Tax," *Atlanta Journal-Constitution*, August 1, 2012, www.ajc.com/news/news/state-regional-govt-politics/voters-reject-transportation-tax/nQXfq/

[22] Mike Owen, "NAACP, Sierra Club Hold Press Conference Opposing T-SPLOST," *Ledger-Enquirer*, July 26, 2012, www.ledger-enquirer.com/news/local/article29236027.html

[23] Georgia Public Service Commission, "The PSC: An Introduction to Your Georgia Public Service Commission," www.psc.state.ga.us/pscinfo/pscintro.asp

[24] John G. Perry, AJC, and Channel 2 Action News, "Highly Paid PSC Officials not Showing Up at the Office," *Atlanta Journal-Constitution*, November 18, 2010, www.ajc.com/news/news/local-govt-politics/highly-paid-psc-officials-not-showing-up-at-the-of/nQm82/

than 90 percent of his campaign contributions from people associated with utilities.[25] His son worked for a law firm that represented Georgia Power.[26] Wise also came under fire for accepting $10,000 in campaign donations from attorneys who represented Georgia Power before the PSC. The donations were received just two days before Wise voted to allow Georgia Power to pass on $3.2 million in expenses from nuclear plant service outages to ratepayers.[27] He skipped debates with both his primary and general election opponents.[28] More to the point, Wise was the staunchest opponent of solar power on the PSC.

One of the reasons Kiernan had originally invited Dooley to lunch in April was to sound her out about backing Stan Wise's opponent in the July 31, 2012, Republican primary. Dooley agreed to help, though both she and Kiernan would ultimately focus much of their attention on the effort to defeat T-SPLOST on the same day. While that opponent—Pam Davidson—mounted a respectable challenge to Wise, she was underfunded and ultimately lost 57 percent to 43 percent. But Dooley and Kiernan were not done trying to focus attention on Stan Wise and working to impact the public dialogue about the PSC.

No Democrat had filed for the seat, so on October 12, 2012, the duo endorsed a little-known Libertarian candidate named David Staples. Staples had almost no chance of unseating Wise, an incumbent Republican who was from Georgia's third-biggest county and who had previously been elected statewide in 1994, 2000, and 2006. In addition to the name identification that came from his long service, Wise had raised nearly $200,000 in campaign contributions. Staples, 31 years old, had never before run for office and ultimately raised less than $9,000. No third-party candidate had ever won or even come close to winning a seat on the PSC. On paper, the contest was over before it started.

Dooley and Kiernan were political veterans who did not operate under illusions. They knew that electoral victory was next to impossible, and they did not mount a serious campaign challenge to Wise. But success at the ballot box was not their goal. They backed Staples for the same reason they backed Pam Davidson in the Republican primary: the duo wanted to send a message to those commissioners who would be on the ballot in 2014 and 2016—Doug Everett, Bubba McDonald, and Tim Echols—that Tea Party supporters and Georgia conservationists would be watching. So Dooley and Kiernan did not mince words in their endorsement of Staples:

---

[25] Eric Stirgus, "GA Candidate Questions Incumbent's Donor List," *Politifact Georgia*, June 5, 2012, www.politifact.com/georgia/statements/2012/jun/05/pam-davidson/ga-candidate-questions-incumbents-donor-list/

[26] Tow Crawford, "GA Politics is Greased by Dollars," *Gainesville Times*, June 27, 2012, www.gainesvilletimes.com/archives/69315/

[27] Tom Crawford, "Wise Voted to Okay $3.2 Million for Georgia Power Two Days after Receiving Contributions from Utility's Law Firm," *Georgia Report*, July 17, 2012, gareport.com/story/2012/07/17/wise-voted-to-okay-3-2-million-for-georgia-power-two-days-after-receiving-contributions-from-utilitys-law-firm/

[28] Walter C. Jones, "Pam Davidson Blasts Absent Stan Wise in PSC Debate," *Rome News-Tribune*, July 23, 2012, www.northwestgeorgianews.com/rome/pam-davidson-blasts-absent-stan-wise-in-psc-debate/article_f3eb753a-ef43-5ed9-9c3a-26ec461beca7.html; Walter C. Jones, "GA PSC Candidate Ducks Debate," *Augusta Chronicle*, October 2, 2012, chronicle.augusta.com/news/government/elections/2012-10-02/ga-psc-candidate-ducks-debate

"A lot of activists don't like the closeness that Stan Wise appears to have with lobbyists for the utilities that are regulated. I think that's a problem," said Dooley.

Dooley noted a significant amount of Wise's campaign contributions have come from people affiliated with the utilities he helps regulate.

It's why Dooley and Kiernan are backing the libertarian candidate in November.

"David Staples pledged not to take gifts from lobbyists and is in favor of developing renewable resources," said Kiernan. "He thinks public health needs to be a consideration in thinking about the appropriate mix of power generation sources." [29]

In the end, Staples lost. But even in losing, he garnered a higher share of the vote than any third-party PSC candidate since at least 1990. He also made solar power part of the public dialogue. During the campaign, Staples suggested "numerous ideas to boost clean energy and encourage Georgia Power to start investing in wind, solar, and biomass." He also pledged to "use the PSC's bully pulpit to push state lawmakers to pass legislation encouraging homeowners to use solar power."[30]

Commissioners Everett, McDonald, and Echols were on notice, and at just the right time. In 2013, the PSC would review Georgia Power's plans to meet energy needs over the next 20 years—including what energy sources it would use to meet those needs.

THE RIGHT LEVEL AT THE RIGHT TIME

It was Lauren "Bubba" MacDonald who answered the call. At first glance, McDonald seemed to be an unlikely champion for innovative thinking on the Public Service Commission. McDonald won election as a state representative in 1978, when Georgian Jimmy Carter was president. He served 20 years in the Georgia Legislature, including 5 years as chairman of the Industry Committee and 8 years as the chairman of the Appropriations Committee. After 20 years in the Georgia House of Representatives, McDonald left in 1998 to join the PSC. Four years later, while running as a Democrat, he lost his PSC seat by less than .5 percent of the vote in the November 2002 general election. McDonald switched parties and was reelected to the PSC in 2008 as a Republican.

Given that history, and his strong support of nuclear power as a state legislator, McDonald was one of the last people that solar power advocates would expect to champion their cause. But if anything, McDonald was a realist and pragmatist who understood energy economics. He knew that Georgia relied on coal for nearly half of its energy needs. He knew that the federal government was intent on reducing

---

[29] Jonathan Shapiro, "PSC Challenger Attracting Support from Both Sides of Aisle, *90.1 FM: WABE*, October 12, 2012, news.wabe.org/post/psc-challenger-attracting-support-both-sides-aisle

[30] Tom Wheatley, "Turn Up the Heat on the Public Service Commission," *Creative Loafing*, November 1, 2012, clatl.com/atlanta/turn-up-the-heat-on-the-public-service-commission/Content?oid=6788808

environmentally damaging carbon emissions from power plants. He knew that Georgia Power would decommission 15 coal-fired power plants in the next decade. And he knew that solar technology had improved, panel prices had dropped 40 percent since 2011, interest rates were down, and an Arizona State University study had concluded Georgia was one of the five best states for solar energy. [31]

Some source of energy would have to fill the gap. Why not solar? Though McDonald could not predict the future, he knew that "the sun will come up, and it's free. It's not owned by Georgia Power, it's not owned by Bubba McDonald, it's not owned by the Public Service Commission." [32]

McDonald was known as an effective horse trader with a keen sense of timing. Those qualities served him well on the PSC, when he saw—and seized—a unique moment in time to make Georgia Power more solar friendly.

Like many other states, Georgia requires its utilities to submit an integrated resources plan (IRP) for approval every three years. The IRP process required Georgia Power to determine the demand for electricity in its service area over the next 20 years and specify the types and percentages of energy sources to be used in meeting that demand.

When Georgia Power proposed its IRP early in 2013, the utility did not include solar power in its recommended energy mix. Bubba McDonald was appalled but undeterred. Using the skills learned in two decades as a state legislator and committee chair, and despite fervent opposition from the utility, McDonald secured three votes on the five-member PSC—his and two others—for a plan to add solar energy to the Georgia Power IRP.

McDonald was not alone in his fight. He had reinforcements, including Dooley and Kiernan. In the month before the final PSC vote on the Georgia Power IRP, the conservative activist group Americans for Prosperity (AFP) fought publicly against the McDonald plan. Pro-solar grassroots activists checked them at every turn. When AFP blasted mass e-mails to its Georgia subscribers denouncing the inclusion of solar as a hidden tax on consumers, Dooley and other Tea Party Patriots fired back with e-mails of their own questioning the veracity of the AFP claims.[33] When AFP organized a lightly attended State Capitol press conference shortly before the vote, pro-solar forces staged a much larger rally across the street.

On July 11, 2013, the PSC reviewed Georgia Power's IRP in a meeting that *Atlanta Journal-Constitution* political columnist Jim Galloway described as "surreal." Though Georgia Power had been criticizing McDonald's plan for months, its representatives could count votes and knew they were beaten. Not wanting to alienate the regulatory body that would later in the year review utility rates, they had earlier agreed to accept additional solar in the energy mix and that solar power would be

---

[31] Mary Landers, "Solar Has Bright Future in Georgia," *Savannah Morning News*, September 2, 2013, savannahnow.com/news/2013-09-02/solar-has-bright-future-georgia#

[32] Jim Galloway, "In Georgia, Solar Power Finds a Respected Place in the GOP Vocabulary," *Atlanta Journal-Constitution*, July 6, 2013, www.ajc.com/weblogs/political-insider/2013/jul/06/georgia-solar-power-finds-respected-place-gop-voca/

[33] Jim Galloway, "Your Daily Jolt: Solar Power Divides Two Georgia Tea Party Groups," *Atlanta Journal-Constitution*, July 2, 2013, www.ajc.com/weblogs/political-insider/2013/jul/02/your-daily-jolt-solar-power-divides-two-georgia-te/

procured through competitive bidding. Publicly, Georgia Power reversed course and capitulated:

> One of the most surreal moments of today's state Public Service Commission sessions—and there were many—came when Kevin Greene, the lead attorney for Georgia Power, walked to the front and, under orchestrated questioning by PSC chairman Doug Everett, denied every objection that the utility had ever expressed about the solar requirement about to be imposed on it.
>
> No, this was not a mandate, Greene said.
>
> No, there would be no upward pressure on power bills, the attorney said.
>
> No, PSC member Lauren "Bubba" McDonald's requirement that Georgia Power incorporate 525 megawatts of solar power by 2016—an unprecedented development in Georgia utility history—posed no threat to the territorial monopolies laid out by the Legislature, Greene said.[34]

The end result was unprecedented. With solar energy skeptic Stan Wise protesting until the final vote, the PSC voted 3–2 to support McDonald's plan to have Georgia Power bring online 260 megawatts of solar power by 2015 and an additional 265 megawatts by 2016—in total, 525 megawatts.[35]

FRAMING THE PROBLEM AND THE SOLUTION

McDonald's historic victory was a testament to his shrewd understanding of success in a collegial body like a legislature or commission. But he was also a skilled messenger. Knowing he had to convince the majority on an all-Republican PSC, he subtly blamed President Obama for his plans to reduce carbon emissions at coal-fired power plants—an action that would force more use of natural gas and raise the price of that energy source. "When the president finishes his war on coal, he'll come after fracking, and gas prices will go up," McDonald said. "We have to be ready."[36] McDonald also portrayed solar energy as a potential savior of jobs that would be lost when Georgia Power closed coal-fired facilities. Why let those generating stations sit empty when the existing infrastructure and transmission lines could be converted for use as job-providing solar arrays?

Those same communications skills would be needed as solar power advocates worked to channel the momentum from their PSC triumph into success at the Georgia Legislature. Fortunately, one of the principal leaders had what he described as a "Jerry Maguire moment."

---

[34] Jim Galloway, "Counterpoint: Stan Wise's Blistering Criticism of PSC's Solar Decision," *Atlanta Journal-Constitution*, July 11, 2013, www.ajc.com/weblogs/political-insider/2013/jul/11/counterpoint-stan-wise-blistering-criticism-psc-so/

[35] Georgia Public Service Commission, "PSC Approves Agreement to Resolve Georgia Power 2013 Integrated Resource Plan and Expands Use of Solar Energy [news release]," July 11, 2013, www.psc.state.ga.us/GetNewsRecordAttachment.aspx?ID=250

[36] Jim Galloway, "In Georgia, Solar Power Finds a Respected Place in the GOP Vocabulary," *Atlanta Journal-Constitution*, July 6, 2013, www.ajc.com/weblogs/political-insider/2013/jul/06/georgia-solar-power-finds-respected-place-gop-voca/

Some advocates, like Debbie Dooley, are right-out-of-central-casting characters born for the spotlight. "The media loves Debbie, and she's great at it," said solar advocate Jason Rooks. Others, like Rooks, operate more effectively behind the scenes. As he explained, "When I get into political fights, I am not in it to raise money or to be on television. I just want to win."

Rooks had been on the forefront of solar advocacy in Georgia since the beginning. He was a Georgia native who practiced law in the North Georgia town of Gainesville before moving to Silicon Valley to launch a technology start-up. In 2002, he returned home to serve as executive director of Georgia Conservation Voters. Six years later, in 2008, he founded Clean Energy Strategies, so he could focus specifically on building support for solar and other renewable power sources.

"I thought Republicans and Democrats in Georgia could be for solar," said Rooks. "When we go to our cars in August, it's too hot to touch the damn steering wheel. Here in the South, we respect the sun."

Rooks had some early success. In 2008, he helped to persuade the Georgia Legislature to pass a state tax credit for the installation of residential and commercial solar power devices. Though the bill capped the available credit at $2.5 million annually (later raised to $5 million annually) and would expire in 2014, Rooks's effort was an important first step that gave him added credibility as a solar champion.[37]

The solar tax credit passed in part because Georgia Power and other utilities did not oppose the legislation. Rooks wanted to pass game-changing legislation that Georgia Power almost certainly would oppose—a bill to allow homeowners and businesses to lease solar power devices from third-party financing sources, so they would not be forced to pay for the infrastructure in cash. Though this initiative may sound innocuous, Georgia Power saw it as defiling the Holy Grail of the state's utility industry—the Territorial Act.

Passed in 1973, the Territorial Act divided Georgia into various energy districts assigned either to Georgia Power, ratepayer-owned electric membership corporations (EMCs), or small municipally owned utilities. Customers within each territory were required to use the assigned utility. In short, utilities were given monopolies over their respective territories.

Georgia Power took its rights under the Territorial Act very seriously. The company did not overlook any perceived incursions into its assigned territory, no matter how small. In 2010, when a small Presbyterian school in northeast Georgia wanted to generate power through rooftop panels installed and financed by a third party, Georgia Power wasted no time in firing off a cease and desist letter to Rabun Gap Nacoochee School alleging a violation of Georgia Power's exclusive rights under the Territorial Act.[38]

Many solar advocates were incensed. This was a school trying to save money through innovation and technology. The Georgia Legislature could clarify the Territorial Act to ensure third-party financing was allowed. But in order to overcome the likely opposition from Georgia Power and other utilities, Rooks needed a message that would appeal to conservative Republican elected officials.

---

[37] Melissa Stiers, "Solar Projects Could Get Boost," *GPB Media: NPR*, April 19, 2011, www.gpb .org/news/2011/04/19/solar-projects-could-get-boost

[38] AJC, "Solar Industry Challenges Georgia Power," *Atlanta Journal-Constitution*, October 11, 2010, www.ajc.com/news/business/solar-industry-challenges-georgia-power/nQgn9/

One evening, the message hit him. Like the eponymous hero of Cameron Crowe's 1996 film *Jerry Maguire*, Jason Rooks woke up in the middle of the night and came up with the mission statement to persuade legislators to accept solar energy. "I remember waking up and writing out a customer-centric view of solar advocacy," Rooks remembered. "We have to look at this from the customer's standpoint." Rooks then enlisted the help of Republican lobbyist friends at the Georgia Capitol to distill that message into three short sentences: "This is about the free market. This is about property rights. It is about technology and innovation."[39]

The message was perfectly tailored for his audience of decision makers. "We set out to come up with a message that Republican legislators would have a very hard time rejecting," Rooks explained. Though the mantra wasn't designed to attract the Tea Party to the solar energy cause, it was a happy development that Debbie Dooley and her allies recognized and adopted the same approach. "Every movement needs a Nancy Reagan," Rooks observed, remembering how effective the former First Lady had been in making the case for stem-cell research with conservatives. "For us, that was Debbie Dooley."

Dooley was a natural in arguing the populist case against the utility companies while also presenting a conservative case for solar. When she appeared before the Public Service Commission in May 2013 as it was considering the integrated resource plan, Dooley asserted that "[t]he sun is free, it's there. Understand Georgia Power is not being as aggressive on solar power and solar energy as they should be because they're trying to protect their monopoly."[40] As conservative publication *The Daily Beast* reported, Dooley was also expert at framing solar energy as a matter of liberty.

Ask most Americans to list the policy priorities they associate with the Tea Party, and promoting solar power or biofuels won't crack the top 50—or top 5,000. But as Dooley sees it, battling Big Energy and its government cronies who conspire to strangle competition, distort the market, and hold consumers hostage is *precisely* the sort of crusade that should fire up the movement. "This is about energy freedom. Energy choice!" explains Dooley. "We want to allow green energy companies to compete in the market. Let the market decide what's best. It's pro-consumer!"

As Dooley sees it, green energy is an issue tailor made for Tea Party types. "Conservatives need to be leading this effort!" she insists. For starters, she notes, Big Energy—especially utility monopolies like Georgia Power— have too much centralized power. Solar energy, by contrast, is highly decentralized. This not only puts more power in the hands of individuals who install their own solar cells, it opens up the possibility of allowing people to come off the power grid altogether.[41]

---

[39] Michael Kanellos, "Behind the Tea Party Push for Solar in Georgia," *Forbes*, July 16, 2013, www.forbes.com/sites/michaelkanellos/2013/07/16/behind-the-tea-party-push-for-solar-in-georgia/#1fc948bd33dc

[40] Ray Henry, "Solar Industry Pushes for More Use in Georgia," *Online Athens: Athens Banner-Herald*, May 21, 2013, onlineathens.com/breaking-news/2013-05-21/solar-industry-pushes-more-use-ga

[41] Michelle Cottle, "The Green Tea Party: Debbie Dooley Battles Big Energy," *The Daily Beast*, September 16, 2013, www.thedailybeast.com/articles/2013/09/16/the-green-tea-party-debbie-dooley-battles-big-energy.html

Jason Rooks was pleased to have Dooley's public support. Nearly 40 percent of Republican members of the Georgia Legislature identified with the Tea Party, and grassroots Tea Party activists had significant influence in statewide Republican primaries. Her embrace of the message would give political cover to key elected officials.

But Rooks and his team also knew the right message can flounder through the voice of the wrong messenger. Although Rooks appreciated the work of environmental and other progressive organizations in the pro-solar coalition, he knew that vocal advocacy on their part could scare off the very conservative Republican legislators they were trying to persuade on third-party financing. In order to enforce message discipline and prevent this possible messaging calamity, Rooks worked with outside organizations, such as the Georgia Property Rights Council and Georgians for Solar Freedom. People like Debbie Dooley would be encouraged to communicate. Advocates seen as left of center would not.

For the most part, solar advocates set aside egos and any discomfort with the right-leaning communications approach. As former Sierra Club Georgia chapter director Colleen Kiernan said, "It was not difficult getting environmentalists on board with the message. After all, this was Georgia."

The most important messaging came from outside the coalition. On a Friday night in February 2012, nationally syndicated consumer advocate Clark Howard joined equally well-known conservative commentator and blogger Erick Erickson on the latter's weekday evening WSB radio show. For an hour, the two popular hosts blasted Georgia Power for denying consumer rights and freedom on solar power.

The messaging was starting to have an effect on Georgia Power. According to Rooks, word of the Howard-Erickson broadcast reached company executives on the 24th floor of their headquarters in downtown Atlanta. Because Georgia Power was an active corporate citizen, "with employees who are in the Jaycees or deacons in their church, and a company sign at every little league baseball field," the battles over solar energy threatened to take a toll on the Georgia Power brand.

A LEGISLATIVE CHAMPION

Though solar power advocates now had a winning message, they still wanted legislation to turn third-party financing into reality. One of Rooks's mentors was former Georgia Governor Roy Barnes, who liked to repeat former U.S. House Speaker Sam Rayburn's famous mantra about legislating: "Any jackass can kick down a barn. It takes a carpenter to build one." Rooks and solar power advocates needed a legislative champion with the subject matter expertise and political skills to build support for clarification of the previously sacrosanct Territorial Act.

Finding the right legislator was no small task. In 2012, the coalition had managed to persuade the Senate president pro tem, the majority leader, and the appropriations chair to sponsor a third-party financing bill. Although Georgia Power took notice, the company enjoyed a strong relationship with the presiding officer of the Senate. The bill was sent to committee, never had a hearing, and died.

But two years is a long time in politics. By the time 2014 arrived, Georgia Power was no longer the impervious legislative juggernaut that it once was thanks to people like Debbie Dooley, Erick Erickson, Clark Howard, and Bubba McDonald. Just as the Georgia

PSC pushed back against Georgia Power, public service commissions in Mississippi and Alabama did the same with Southern Company subsidiaries in their states. Even Georgia's governor took up the cause. In May 2014, during a tough reelection campaign, Governor Nathan Deal was critical of Georgia Power's efforts to have ratepayers fund cost overruns on the Vogtle 3 and 4 facilities.

In short, Rooks and his team increasingly had the leverage they needed to bring Georgia Power to the table and pass a bill. The straw that broke the camel's back was a member of the Georgia House of Representatives named Mike Dudgeon.

Dudgeon had been elected to the House of Representatives in 2010, after serving for four years on the Forsyth County School Board. He represented a very conservative district, which gave Mitt Romney 85 percent of its vote in the November 2012 presidential election. Dudgeon was also known as a very strong conservative who was friendly to the libertarian, Tea Party base of the Republican legislative caucus.

Those were the political reasons that Dudgeon made sense as a third-party financing champion. The substantive reasons made even more sense. One sentence in his official biography said it all: "Representative Dudgeon has bachelors and masters degrees in Electrical Engineering from Georgia Tech, holds five U.S. patents, and has been in the technology business his entire career."[42] As an electrical engineer and a successful entrepreneur, Dudgeon had credibility on the subject.

"Mike Dudgeon is so smart," said Rooks. "When he speaks on an issue, every other legislator has confidence in what he is saying. When Mike Dudgeon sponsored that bill, the utilities had to scramble. He was the exact right choice."

Like Debbie Dooley, Dudgeon was a strong advocate of free markets and deeply suspicious of monopolies. But Dudgeon operated on a significantly lower key. "Energy executives and lobbyists respected me because I was measured," said Dudgeon. "They knew me to have a thoughtful, policy-oriented approach."

Under Georgia law, a homeowner who wanted to install solar panels on a property had to pay cash and buy the infrastructure from his or her own utility. In January 2014, Dudgeon introduced legislation—the Solar Power Free-Marketing Financing Act—to permit homeowners to contract with third parties that provide installation and financing. "We want to make it clear that you can use whatever financing is available to finance your solar panel," Dudgeon told the *Atlanta Business Chronicle*.[43]

Dudgeon knew that legislation rarely passed in the first year it was introduced, so he was not surprised when the bill did not move forward in 2014. The utilities were still resistant. But the introduction of third-party financing legislation had started the conversation, and the issue had enough momentum that Chairman Don Parsons of the House Energy, Utilities & Telecommunications Committee appointed a study committee on the issue chaired by Representative Harry Geisinger.[44]

---

[42] Georgia House of Representatives, "Rep. Mike Dudgeon (R-25): Biography," www.house.ga.gov/Documents/Biographies/dudgeonMike.pdf

[43] Dave Williams, "GA Republican Unveils Solar Bill," *Atlanta Business Chronicle*, January 28, 2014, www.bizjournals.com/atlanta/blog/capitol_vision/2014/01/ga-republican-unveils-solar-bill.html

[44] Tom Crawford, "Solar Energy Financing Bill Will Be Moved to Study Committee," Georgia Report, March 3, 2014, gareport.com/story/2014/03/03/solar-energy-financing-bill-will-be-moved-to-study-committee/

The 2014 Georgia legislative session ended on March 20. Dudgeon and Geisinger soon began a months-long process of negotiating with the various stakeholders to achieve a consensus bill in time for the January start of the 2015 session. It was an unwieldy task. Nearly 60 interests—from solar power advocates to third-party financing companies to Georgia Power to EMCs to municipally owned utilities—wanted a say.

Dudgeon again proved that he was the right person for the job. He knew that Georgia Power and the other utilities were incentivized to make a deal. They didn't want to be seen fighting solar energy at every turn. Third-party financing arrangements didn't have a big enough impact on the bottom line to justify risking more negative media—or to chance opening up the Territorial Act to even greater scrutiny that could really disrupt their business model. As Dudgeon explained, "Georgia Power was willing to give up a field goal to avoid giving up a touchdown."

Some matters were very technical, but as an electrical engineer, Dudgeon understood the issues well enough to resolve them. He was even-handed but forceful. As Jason Rooks explained, "Representative Dudgeon really pushed everyone to make a deal. He challenged us to examine our positions and see where we could give ground for the good of the process." Though Dudgeon preferred to be a mediator who coaxed the parties to settle disagreements amicably, he was willing, when necessary, to be an arbitrator who decided disputes unilaterally.

Due to Dudgeon's leadership, Georgia Power and the other utilities agreed to support third-party financing of solar energy infrastructure. Solar advocates agreed to ease the utilities' concerns about competition from large solar energy providers by keeping the application of the bill to "mom and pop" solar generating businesses. They also agreed that when a solar generating home or business had excess power to sell on the grid, the utility would pay only the "avoided cost"—the lowest rate of purchased power.

The end result was consensus. One week before the 2015 Georgia Legislature was schedule to convene, the stakeholders agreed on legislative language. The bill passed both the House of Representatives and Senate unanimously, without even a single word changing. When Governor Deal signed the legislation in May 2015, third-party solar power financing was now the law in Georgia.

For all of his skilled leadership, Mike Dudgeon continued to give much of the credit to grassroots advocates like Debbie Dooley. "The role of the Tea Party and its coalition partners was important. They worked for years to create the necessary public support that raised awareness among politicians and put pressure on utilities. The 2015 legislation would likely not have happened without them."

THE BRIGHT FUTURE

The enactment of third-party financing helped to unleash Georgia's potential as a solar energy state. On July 1, 2015—the same day the Solar Power Free-Marketing Financing Act took effect—Georgia Power launched its own solar rooftop generation and installation business, albeit without a financing component.[45] In November

---

[45] Julia Pyper and Eric Wesoff, "Georgia Power Is Launching Its Own Rooftop Solar Business, GTM: Green Tech Media, July 1, 2015, www.greentechmedia.com/articles/read/Georgia-Power-is-Launching-its-Own-Rooftop-Solar-Business

2015, Georgia Power and the United States Navy agreed to build a large solar genera-tion farm at the Kings Bay submarine base in southeast Georgia, with power generated for the overall electricity grid.[46]

In January 2016, the Public Service Commission launched the first IRP process since Bubba McDonald encouraged Georgia Power to incorporate more solar power into its energy mix. Three years before, Georgia Power's IRP proposal contained no solar energy. On January 29, 2016, Georgia Power submitted an IRP that called for an additional 525 megawatts of renewable energy—doubling the amount the PSC approved in July 2013.[47] To top it off, in April 2016, the Smart Electric Power Alliance named Georgia Power one of the top 10 solar providers in the nation for its installation of 218 solar systems in 2015, which could generate enough power for more than 75,000 homes.[48]

The work is far from done. Jason Rooks still wants to have the Georgia Legislature ensure equal property tax treatment for rooftop solar panels whether they are bought with cash or leased through third-party financing companies. Solar power advocates will have to remain engaged and vigilant.

But Debbie Dooley is optimistic. She sees the passage of third-party financing and subsequent developments as proof that "Solar in Georgia is going to explode. Georgia will challenge California—especially now that Republicans are leading the way and past opponents have become big supporters."

And Dooley will continue to believe that "the real power belongs to the people. People power will trump money from these big corporations any day. But you have to be smart and strategic, and have to be willing to walk across the aisle, respect your differences, and find a way to work together."

As for the other Dooley, the college football coach whose teams shone between the hedges at Sanford Stadium, his former employer has decided to join the solar energy playing field. On December 16, 2015, the University of Georgia announced a new partnership with Georgia Power to install panels on the university campus, generate power for utility customers, and research how to maximize the collection of energy from the sun.[49]

[46] News4JAX, "Georgia Power to Build Solar Farm at Kings Bay," News4JAX, September 21, 2015, www.news4jax.com/news/georgia/camden-county/georgia-power-to-build-solar-farm-at-kings-bay

[47] "Georgia Power Files Three-Year Electrical Generation Plan," Atlanta Business Chronicle, January 29, 2016, www.bizjournals.com/atlanta/blog/capitol_vision/2016/01/georgia-power-files-three-year-electrical.html

[48] Brennan Reh, "Georgia Power in Top 10 for Solar Providers," WRBL, April 13, 2016, wrbl.com/2016/04/13/georgia-power-in-top-10-for-solar-providers/

[49] Jim Thompson, "Solar Power Project Will Benefit UGA and Georgia Power," Online Athens: Athens Banner-Herald, December 16, 2015, onlineathens.com/breaking-news/2015-12-15/solar-power-project-will-benefit-uga-and-georgia-power

Introduction

In the Arena

"It is not the critic who counts; not the man who points out how the strong man stumbles or where the doer of deeds could have done better. The credit belongs to the man who is actually in the arena, whose face is marred by dust and sweat and blood; who strives valiantly; who errs, who comes up short again and again, because there is no effort without error or shortcoming; but who does actually strive to do the deeds; who knows great enthusiasms, the great devotions; who spends himself in a worthy cause; who at the best knows in the end the triumph of high achievement, and who at the worst, if he fails, at least fails while daring greatly, so that his place shall never be with those cold and timid souls who knew neither victory nor defeat."

—President Theodore Roosevelt[1]

Our tale starts with cold, greasy pizza.

In 1974, I was the chairman of the Florida Senate Education Committee. In preparation for the upcoming spring legislative session, the committee held a series of hearings in public schools throughout the state to hear suggestions for bills we might consider. One such hearing was at Samuel W. Wolfson High School in Jacksonville.

Our practice was to reserve a period of time during each hearing for student comments. In most endeavors, consumers of goods or services know how well their needs are being met—and students are the primary consumers of public education.

On this morning, a group of students came to the microphone to tell the committee of a serious school problem and ask for our help. The concern was bad food in the Wolfson cafeteria.

The complaint didn't shock me. As I recalled, the food at Miami Senior High School, from which I had graduated almost twenty years earlier, wasn't the most appetizing. But I was surprised that these students, so close to receiving their high school diplomas, thought the Florida Legislature was the place to seek redress.

So I asked if we were the first authority to whom they had taken their concerns. I was relieved to hear that we were the third. But I was distressed when I heard the answer to my next question: Which were the first and second?

---

[1] Theodore Roosevelt, "Citizenship in a Republic," speech given at the Sorbonne, Paris, April 23, 1910, www.theodoreroosevelt.org/site/c.elKSIdOWIiJ8H/b.8090921/apps/s/content.asp?ct=14605521

The students had first gone to the Jacksonville mayor, who agreed with the students as to the quality of the food but told them it was out of his jurisdiction. Their second request went to the Duval County sheriff, who also sympathized but said that although the food was bad it wasn't criminal. And as I had to inform the students, the Senate didn't control cafeteria menus either.

Less than a month later, a group of civics teachers invited me to speak to them in Miami. I related the Wolfson experience and expressed my dismay with the students' lack of knowledge about the roles and responsibilities of government. Perhaps not diplomatically enough, I told the teachers that the students' ignorance was a strong indictment of the quality of civics education in our state.

They reacted with controlled outrage. One teacher in the audience embodied this reaction when she upbraided me. "I am sick to death of you politicians telling us how to do our job better," she seethed. "You don't know what you're talking about, and the only place to learn is at school. You need to get in the classroom and see what it's really like—prepare the lesson plans that are intended to stimulate disinterested students, make outdated textbooks interesting, deal with all the hassle of paperwork and school bureaucracy, and try to implement politicians' nutty ideas." To deafening applause, she challenged me to come into the classroom and experience public education firsthand.

Figuring that I could afford to give up an afternoon—and reluctant to appear a coward in front of this important constituency—I accepted her challenge. She called three days later: "I have worked it out. You are to come to my school, Miami Carol City Senior High, on the day after Labor Day and report to room 207. I have arranged for you to teach a semester—eighteen weeks—of twelfth grade civics."

Eighteen weeks was far more than I had bargained for. But I felt that I had made a commitment, and I would keep it.

Looking back, the late summer and fall of 1974 transformed my life. Carol City High School assigned me to work with a young, talented, and enthusiastic civics teacher named Donnell Morris. Together we developed a curriculum aimed at students who might face the most formidable obstacles in solving neighborhood problems. The course would center on several questions. How do citizens make government work for them? Is it really possible to fight City Hall, the school board, or the employees who run the school cafeteria and win? How do we organize an effective grassroots campaign for change?

In addition to structuring a curriculum of required knowledge and skills, we taught through hands-on activities. The course exposed our 25 students to political practitioners—candidates, officeholders, journalists, civic activists, campaign professionals, and pollsters—so that they would hear firsthand how government could be made to respond to them.

On the first day of class, Mr. Morris and I asked the students to organize themselves into groups of three. The students in each group were to select a problem about which they were concerned—and which government at some level could play a role in fixing. They could select any topic. But we added an important caveat: At the end of the semester, one-third of each student's final grade would be based on their effectiveness in solving the problem their group had identified at the outset.

The results were startling. For example, one team tackled the long-standing suspicion that Miami Carol City High School received less funding per student than did a nearby Dade County public high school located in a higher-income neighborhood. After the high school's business faculty had given the students an introduction in reading and understanding budgets, the students pored over financial spreadsheets at the county school district headquarters. They proved that the disparity was more than a myth. Thanks to their work, the Miami–Dade County Schools superintendent recognized the inequity and vowed to correct it in the next budget cycle. That team of students received a very high grade.

I learned a lot during the course of the semester: how to teach citizenship; how to navigate the complex relationship among students, faculty, and parents; and how to understand the workings of a large urban high school. But my most important lesson was that learning by doing is very different from learning by listening. Active learning helps students understand the relevance of a subject to daily life. It provides a deep immersion into reality, not a theoretical laboratory. It contributes to a sense of self-confidence that can last a lifetime. At the end of our semester, Mr. Morris and I could almost hear the students thinking in this new way: "I can do this for myself and my family because I already have done it in the classroom and the community."

When I decided to run for governor in 1978, I needed something to grab the public's attention statewide—something that would help voters identify with me and my campaign, that would convey my concern for the average Floridian, and that would earn free media coverage. During discussions with family, friends, and advisers, I related the lessons I had learned and the joy I had felt in that classroom at Carol City Senior High School. That transformative experience became the catalyst for my campaign strategy of performing 100 "Workdays" around the state before Election Day in November 1978. During these Workdays, I worked full shifts next to real people in typical jobs throughout Florida— everything from construction worker to police officer to bellman. I declared that my job as a civics teacher at Carol City was Workday number one. For the next 26 years—through two terms as governor and three terms in the U.S. Senate—I worked a total of 408 Workdays, averaging more than one per month.

In late 2004, as my retirement from the Senate grew near, several Florida newspapers wrote articles looking back over my career. Many of those newspapers offered generous tributes. But the words of praise

Photo courtesy Senator Bob Graham

Senator Bob Graham during one of his 408 Workdays, as an iron worker in West Palm Beach, 1977.

that affected me most came from someone I had met three decades before. When the *Orlando Sentinel*'s valedictory focused on my Workdays, the story provoked an e-mail to the reporter from one of the Carol City students I had taught. Gary Cohen, then in his forties and a certified public accountant in Orlando, offered the best compliment I received in forty years of public service. He wrote:

> I remember getting a phone call from MCC's [Miami Carol City's] Guidance Department in the summer of 1974, inquiring if I would like to sign up for a class in Honors Contemporary Politics. The description sounded great, especially the involvement of our State Senator, Bob Graham. For the first 18-week semester, Bob came to our classroom on Mondays, Wednesdays and Fridays. We studied units on many topics, including the legislative process, public relations, and campaign advertising. His access to other politicians, staff and business professionals in Miami allowed him to also include other guest speakers in our class. A local television professional and a campaign manager spoke to us. Since it was an election year, he brought several politicians to our classroom. . . . It was a great experience. I have a keen interest in politics, especially at the local level, which touches the citizens most closely. . . . Bob Graham has been one of the 10 most influential persons in my life, though he probably doesn't even know this. The class at Miami Carol City was an amazing experience.[2]

After leaving the Senate in January 2005, I spent the 2005–2006 academic year as a senior fellow at Harvard University's Kennedy School of Government. During the fall semester, I led a group of undergraduates in a weekly seminar on the skills of effective citizenship. From those Harvard students, I learned that lessons in participatory democracy are needed also into adulthood. Even these highly motivated students had not been exposed to the basic skills of citizenship or given the opportunity to apply those skills. They wanted to be effective citizens who engaged government successfully. They just didn't know how.

Those experiences at the bookends of my career in public office reinforced my concern that we had a serious challenge in American democracy. If citizens do not master and use the basic skills of participatory citizenship to influence decision makers, our democratic institutions are in peril. As Robert Maynard Hutchins, former president of the University of Chicago, once observed, "The death of democracy is not likely to be an assassination from ambush. It will be a slow extinction from apathy, indifference, and undernourishment."[3]

Recent data suggest that the warned-of apathy, indifference, and undernourishment are at starvation levels. Between August 2015 and October 2015, the Pew Charitable Trusts, with support from The William and Flora Hewlett Foundation,

---

[2] Gary Cohen, e-mail to the *Orlando Sentinel*, December 23, 2004.

[3] Robert Maynard Hutchins, *Great Books, the Foundation of a Liberal Education* (New York: Simon and Schuster, 1954), 23.

surveyed 6,000 citizens to determine levels of confidence in public institutions.[4] The results were jarring.

- Seventy-six percent (76%) believed the federal government is "run by a few big interests," while only 19 percent said the government "is run for the benefit of all the people."
- Seventy-four percent (74%) said most elected officials "don't care what people like me think."
- Sixty-three percent (63%) had little faith in the public's ability to make political decisions.
- Nearly half of those surveyed believed there was little that everyday citizens could do to influence the government in Washington.
- Only 38 percent of those citizens under the age of 30 had much confidence in the nation's future.
- Only 19 percent said they trusted the federal government all or most of the time.

If these statistics don't convince you that we need to address the well-being of the social contract between the citizens of the United States and our government, nothing will. They suggest a toxic blend of cynicism, pessimism, self-doubt, and mistrust that could easily cause America to suffer the lethal perils about which Robert Maynard Hutchins warned. Our book is an effort to provide some of the missing enthusiasm and nutrition.

There are plenty of factors that have contributed to the poor health of citizenship: increasingly polarized political parties; the sense of gridlock and dysfunction in Washington and various state capitals; a media operating on a 24-hour news cycle that often prioritizes national news and drama over local news and substance; the increasing role of money in politics, a trend boosted by the United States Supreme Court's 2010 decision to allow virtually unlimited political expenditures in *Citizens United v. Federal Elections Commission*; and the actions of various special-interest groups. The democracy-rescuing cures for this ailment are education and participatory citizenship. In the upcoming pages, we try to provide immediate guidance so that any citizen from youth to retirement age can gain increased confidence through competence in his or her citizenship skills.

However, we also hope to provoke some desperately needed soul-searching in the American educational system. Our elementary schools, secondary schools, community colleges, and four-year colleges and universities must produce new generations of engaged citizens. President Thomas Jefferson said it best when he argued that one of the primary goals of our schools should be "[t]o give to every citizen the information he needs . . . [t]o understand his duties to his neighbors and country, and to discharge with competence the functions confided to him by either; [and] . . . [t]o instruct the mass of our citizens

---

[4]Pew Research Center, "Beyond Distrust: How Americans View Their Government," www.people-press.org/2015/11/23/beyond-distrust-how-americans-view-their-government/

in these, their rights, interests, and duties, as men and citizens."[5] To put it mildly, that goal is not being achieved at present.

While attainment of the Jeffersonian ideal can and should be a remedy to our citizenship ills, the instructional approach over the last few decades has instead been the academic equivalent of using a Band-Aid to treat a worsening wound. The failure to master the basic skills of participatory citizenship is not limited to students at Carol City or Harvard. Since the 1960s, citizenship education has withered in the vineyard of American education. Until that time, the average secondary student had taken three courses in civics. Today, a student is lucky to have taken one. The pace of decline has increased as high-stakes tests, such as those required by the controversial No Child Left Behind law, have pushed civics, as well as history, geography, economics, and the arts out of the curriculum.

This period of neglect has produced some unsurprising yet still discouraging outcomes. In 2014, the Annenberg Public Policy Center at the University of Pennsylvania, as part of the launch of the Civics Renewal Network (civicsrenewalnetwork.org), surveyed nearly 1,500 adults on their knowledge of American government. Barely one-third of those surveyed were able to name all three branches of the U.S. government, and another one-third could not name any of the branches. Not even 30 percent of those questioned knew that presidential vetoes can be overridden only by a two-thirds vote of both the U.S. Senate and the U.S. House of Representatives. More than 40 percent had no idea which political party controlled the Senate or House.[6] While our goal in this book is to help Americans do more than simply understand the institutions and processes of government—we want them to use citizenship skills to make government respond—it is troubling to see this lack of foundational knowledge.

In addition to the work being done by nonprofit organizations to boost citizenship education through initiatives such as the Civic Renewal Network, efforts are also being made in academia. For example, after I left the U.S. Senate in 2005, friends and University of Florida representatives approached me about establishing a center on citizenship. I was honored when the new venture was immodestly named the Bob Graham Center for Public Service. The center later formed a partnership with the University of Central Florida's Lou Frey Institute of Politics and Government and launched the Florida Joint Center for Citizenship, a collaboration to enhance citizenship, commencing in Florida's primary and secondary schools.

Some governments have even taken steps to mandate civics teaching and testing. In 2008, the Joint Center worked with former Congressman Frey, Florida State Senator Nancy Detert, and Florida State Representative Charles McBurney to persuade the Florida Legislature to pass the Justice Sandra Day O'Connor Civics Education Act. The law mandates that every Florida public school student

---

[5] Thomas Jefferson, James Madison, et al., *Report of the Commissioners Appointed to Fix the Site of the University of Virginia*, in *The Founders' Constitution*, vol. 1, chapter 18, document 33 (Chicago: University of Chicago Press), press-pubs.uchicago.edu/founders/documents/v1ch18s33.html

[6] Michael Rozansky, "Americans Know Surprisingly Little about Their Government, Survey Finds [news release]," The Annenberg Public Policy Center of the University of Pennsylvania, September 17, 2014, cdn.annenbergpublicpolicycenter.org/wp-content/uploads/Civics-survey-press-release-09-17-2014-for-PR-Newswire.pdf

successfully complete a middle school citizenship education course and pass a statewide civics assessment exam in order to advance beyond eighth grade. As of 2015, nine states—Arizona, Idaho, Louisiana, North Dakota, South Carolina, South Dakota, Tennessee, Utah, and Wisconsin—require high school students to pass a U.S. citizenship exam as a condition of graduation. In December 2015, Congress passed and President Obama signed the Every Child Succeeds Act, comprehensive legislation to reauthorize federal elementary and secondary education programs. That law includes provisions—sponsored by my daughter, U.S. Representative Gwen Graham of Florida—to create civics education academies for teachers and students and provide grants for nonprofit organizations to engage underserved students in history, civics, and geography.[7]

While all of these steps are positive, they are only part of the solution. Mandatory citizenship coursework and testing mainly helps up-and-coming citizens become better informed spectators—learning names, dates, the three branches of government, and the language of the Constitution and the Bill of Rights. While that knowledge is essential, it isn't enough. Our goal should be to graduate citizens who can pass the Jeffersonian test of discharging citizenship duties with understanding, competence, and confidence.

Perhaps an analogy better illustrates the overall educational mission. Anyone can attend a concert and appreciate the music. But there is a fundamental difference between listening from the audience and playing in the orchestra or band. Only those people who actually learn how to master an instrument or sing into the microphone will have the ability and power to change the tune. They don't give Grammys, Country Music Awards, MTV Video Music Awards, or International Classic Music Awards to onlookers.

Recent studies show that most Americans, particularly young people, are choosing to spectate rather than engage in the citizenship process. In reviewing census data on the 2014 midterm elections, the Center for Information and Research on Civic Learning and Engagement (CIRCLE) found that 19.9 percent of those aged 18 to 29 cast ballots in the 2014 elections. "This was the lowest rate of youth turnout recorded . . . in the past forty years, and the decline since 2010 was not trivial. The proportion of young people who said that they were registered to vote (46.7%) was also the lowest over the past forty years."[8] I strongly believe that young people have lower participation rates than the population as a whole in part because few have had favorable interactions with government. For example, some are stranded in a long line at a government agency only to be rewarded for their wait by a desultory clerk. Others watch elected federal officials hurl sound bites and insults but fail to address the serious challenges that will affect young people more than any others, such as the restrictions on life choices imposed by higher education debt, the prospect of post-graduation employment, or the future of Social Security. Other young people still see special interests pour unprecedented sums of money into elections and wonder how everyday citizens can possibly compete. If you are a young person,

[7] "Graham Civics Education Initiatives Pass House [press release]," Website of U.S. Representative Gwen Graham, Florida's Second District, December 3, 2015, graham.house.gov/media-center/press-releases/graham-civics-education-initiatives-pass-house

[8] CIRCLE, "2014 Youth Turnout and Youth Registration Rates Lowest Ever Recorded; Changes Essential in 2016," Website of the Center for Information & Research on Civic Learning and Engagement, www.civicyouth.org/2014-youth-turnout-and-youth-registration-rates-lowest-ever-recorded-changes-essential-in-2016/?cat_id=6

and these are your experiences, you and your peers are not likely to see government as an entity that affects your lives positively.

Even though adults participate in higher numbers than youth, their lack of active citizenship is equally troubling. During an August 2012 national survey of more than 2,500 adults about their political activity in the previous 12 months, the Pew Research Center found that only 39 percent of those surveyed had recently contacted a government official on a public issue of importance to them. Just 22 percent had "attended a political meeting on local, town, or school affairs," and only 13 percent had "been an active member of a group that tries to influence the public or government." A mere 7 percent had "worked or volunteered for a political party or candidate."[9]

Our goal here is not simply to curse the darkness. The entire point of this book is to light a candle and illuminate a path that will convince you that you *can* fight City Hall—and win. Despite some of those concerning numbers, there are signs of hope. For example, the definition of democratic participation may be changing. It used to be that statistics about voting and campaign involvement were a reliable barometer of overall civic engagement. In his seminal work *Bowling Alone*, Bob Putnam described declining electoral participation as "merely the most visible symptom of a broader disengagement from community life. Like a fever, electoral abstention is even more important as a sign of deeper trouble in the body politic than a malady in itself."[10] The appeal of a bombastic and authoritarian presidential candidate also speaks to the condition of the electorate.

While the above data about declining electoral participation, particularly among the so-called "Millennial" generation, are compelling, the benchmarks used to measure that participation may no longer be as applicable. In *The Good Citizen*, Russell Dalton suggests younger Americans appear to have bypassed influencing government through the election of representatives in favor of direct action to influence policy— contacting decision makers, working collectively, dissenting publicly, and interacting online.[11] One of our missions is to provide people who are looking for new ways to engage government with a sharper set of tools and some guidance on how to use them. We hope that a successful experience through hands-on involvement will reduce jaded feelings about democracy and increase electoral participation.

As you will see in the upcoming chapters, many of your fellow citizens have used the skills of effective citizenship to block unwanted road construction, protect historic structures, improve public schools, expand energy options, and take other actions to direct government to their will. It can be done. We hope that when you have finished reading, you will have the information and skills you need to do the following:

- Overcome the cynicism that says you can't affect government action and replace it with the confidence that says citizen participation is the lifeblood of democracy.

---

[9] Aaron Smith, *Civic Engagement in the Digital Age* (Washington, DC: Pew Research Center, 2013), 2, www.pewinternet.org/files/old-media//Files/Reports/2013/PIP_CivicEngagementintheDigitalAge.pdf

[10] Robert D. Putnam, *Bowling Alone: The Collapse and Renewal of American Community* (New York: Simon and Schuster, 2000), p. 35.

[11] Russell J. Dalton, *The Good Citizen: How a Younger Generation is Shaping American Politics* (Los Angeles: CQ Press, 2016), 60–87.

- Develop the sensitivity and awareness to recognize a civic issue susceptible to citizen solutions.
- Achieve a positive experience with your local, state, or federal government—one that breathes new life into the idea that governments work for you, not the other way around.
- Interact with government at the level where you are most likely to experience it—your college or university, city hall, county council, local school board, or planning and zoning commission.
- Understand the governmental map by becoming familiar with nuts-and-bolts concepts, such as determining which level of government—local, state, or federal—is responsible for an issue, and which specific agency or office at that level can address your concern.
- Develop the core personal skills necessary to influence democracy, including the critical thinking needed to analyze an issue and develop a strategy, the information gathering aptitude to determine the facts, the communication skills to shape public discussion and persuade the appropriate decision makers, and the organizational skills to cultivate allies and raise resources.
- Convince your local school, college, or university to shift civics teaching from a lecture-based approach that focuses on governmental structure and process to a dynamic experience that emphasizes personal engagement. Imagine if basketball coaches tried to teach the sport by teaching their players the history of hoops in the locker room rather than by taking them onto the court to dribble, pass, shoot, and play defense. Citizenship is often being taught in the locker room, and it is no surprise that many citizens can't play when they step onto the court of democracy.

This last point is one of the most significant for long-term change. Imagine if basketball coaches kept their teams in the locker room and taught players the history and rules of the sport, rather than taking them onto the court to dribble, pass, shoot, and play defense. Citizenship is often being taught in that locker-room style, and it is no surprise that many citizens can't play when they step onto the court of democracy.

The worst mistake we could make in writing this book would be to provide the "how to" of active democratic engagement—a lecture on paper—without showing you how citizens have succeeded in making government respond. That's why the book started with the story of a Georgia Tea Party founder who successfully partnered with solar power advocates and environmental activists to demand access to solar power, and why each of the next 10 chapters starts with a real-life case study of a citizen or citizens whose advocacy has influenced government. The chapters also include numerous other examples and what we call "Tips from the Pros"—direct advice provided exclusively for this book from experts in the skills of effective citizenship. These studies, examples, and tips should help you understand that citizenship is not a scientific experiment you can consistently replicate. Citizenship is exciting precisely because there is no set path to victory. Every citizen campaign is different from the last. As you will see, active citizen engagement requires flexibility and the ability to shift tactics quickly. That's the price of a democratic system in which human qualities and values—such as ambitions, capabilities, and emotions—affect both decision makers and those attempting to influence decision makers.

Each of the following 10 chapters will introduce a particular citizenship skill. First, you will learn how to identify and articulate the problem that you want to solve—not too narrowly, or too broadly, but just right. Second, you will discover how to gather the facts necessary both to solve the problem and to persuade decision makers to adopt your proposed solution. You are not a parent arguing with a child—"because I said so" will not convince anyone to support you. Third, you will identify the levels of government—local, state, or federal—and the particular agencies or entities within those levels that have the authority to act on your concerns and implement your proposed solutions.

Fourth, you will learn how to determine where members of the public who have an interest in your concern stand on your issue. Put another way, you will know how to put your toe in the water and determine whether and when it is prudent to jump into the pool. Fifth, you will learn how to influence the individual decision makers who have the power to propel your initiative to victory or doom it to defeat. Sixth, you will realize that the calendar or clock on your computer, tablet, or smart phone can be your salvation or your undoing. Government decisions come with deadlines, and those decisions are also affected by cycles and trends.

Seventh, you will appreciate that there is strength in numbers and learn how to find and unite with other individuals and groups who share your concerns. Eighth, you will see that the media can be a powerful ally in sharing your concerns and solutions with both decision makers and the general public to whom those officials are accountable. You will also see how the so-called "new media" and digital world give you opportunities to advance your message directly. Ninth, you will learn that civic engagement, like most things in life, has a price. You'll need at least a small amount of financial support to be successful. You will also need a credible answer when decision makers ask how to pay for your initiative. Tenth, you will recognize that politics is often a zero-sum game: You win or you lose. But winning or losing is not the end of your effort, and you will learn not to snatch defeat from the jaws of victory or surrender the entire season simply because you lose one contest.

While you are reading and absorbing the skills of participatory citizenship, we hope you will also be practicing those skills on a cause about which you are passionate—and in the process contributing to a better community, state, or nation. Nothing is more gratifying than seeing a problem and solving it by applying the talents you are mastering. Once you take those steps, you will have the satisfaction of success and the self-confidence that you can repeat that success throughout your lifetime. Remember that you hold the most exalted position in American democracy—citizen. Former Illinois governor, United States Ambassador to the United Nations, and presidential candidate Adlai Stevenson put it best: "As citizens of this democracy, you are the rulers and the ruled, the law-givers and the law-abiders—the beginning and the end."[12]

As you will see over the course of the next 10 chapters, active citizenship is flesh and blood, drama and comedy, triumph and tragedy, pleasure and pain. But what those highs and lows ultimately produce is the satisfying fulfillment of democracy's promise. We look forward to taking the journey with you.

---

[12] Adlai Ewing Stevenson, *The Papers of Adlai E. Stevenson: "Let's Talk Sense to the American People," 1952–1955* (Boston: Little, Brown, 1974), 129.

1 What's Your Problem?

Defining the Challenge That Active Citizenship Can Solve

"Let's work the problem, people."

—Gene Kranz (Ed Harris) in *Apollo 13*

Case in Point | **A Road through the Mountains***

Jerry Jaynes / BMUSA / Getty Images

Left: Road signs for NC 107 in Cashiers, North Carolina. The controversial Southern Loop, proposed as a bypass road for NC 107, would have threatened homes, businesses and the environment. Right: The bear-shaped shadow cast by Whiteside Mountain is one of many scenic views in the unique western North Carolina community that the Jackson County Smart Roads Alliance fought to preserve.

For the residents of Jackson County, North Carolina, the area's richest blessing has also turned out to be its worst curse. Wedged between the hills of South Carolina and the heart of the Appalachian mountain chain, Jackson County is one of the most picturesque locales in the United States. With its green mountains, brilliant autumns, and relatively mild summers, it is little wonder that Scotch-Irish Protestants used to life in the Scottish Highlands founded Jackson County in the 1850s.

---

*We are very grateful to Sarah Thompson, director of planning and development for the Southwestern Commission (regiona.org), for reviewing and suggesting updates to this case study. We also thank Roger Turner and Bob and Susan Leveille, members of the Jackson County Smart Roads Alliance, and Walter Kulash, the Smart Roads Alliance's consultant, for their contributions to the first edition.

During its first century, Jackson County was remote and isolated, its stunning beauty known only to residents and a few visitors. That all changed in the 1960s when Americans discovered the well-kept secret. Over the next five decades, Jackson County's population kept growing—more than doubling from 17,780 in 1960 to an estimated 40,981 in 2014. When Western Carolina College in the Jackson County community of Cullowhee became Western Carolina University in 1964, it had 2,659 students. By 2014, enrollment had skyrocketed to 9,800. But the surge in the number of permanent residents and students is only half the story. It does not account for the multitude of visitors who annually seek temporary refuge in the county because of the cool mountain air, its crystal clear lakes and streams, and the tranquility of mountain life. From April to October, towns such as Cashiers in Jackson County and Highlands in nearby Macon County are crawling with travelers from all 50 states.

Growth has brought change to Jackson County. Skeptics need look no further than NC 107, a north–south thoroughfare that mostly parallels the rippling, white-foamed Tuckasegee River. This strip is today lined with the telltale signs of urbanization: tourist motels, boat rental shops, gas stations, Walmarts, and fast-food franchises. The asphalt is sagging under the increased traffic, which frequently comes to a standstill when parts of the road are closed to accommodate maintenance crews or cleanups after accidents.

In the face of this growth and the resulting strain on the area's infrastructure, Jackson County leaders convened a series of public meetings in 2000 to determine the public's sentiments on possible responses to the population explosion. At these meetings, residents voiced overwhelming support for "smart" growth that would enhance their mountain communities and protect the heritage and beauty of the valleys and hilltops.

Some community leaders created a new initiative to give even louder voice to that sentiment. In 2001, the Tuckasegee Community Alliance began meeting to assess growth management in the county. The following year, that effort led to the formation of a new entity with a sharper focus: the Jackson County Smart Roads Alliance (smartroads.org/).

At its first meeting in September 2002, members of the Smart Roads Alliance advocated a comprehensive approach to Jackson County's traffic problems. Their recommendations included transportation planning, which would start with a feasibility study of NC 107; a possible redesign of roadside development; and other initiatives to maintain the community's character and preserve open spaces. This approach took official form in November 2002 when Jackson County and the towns of Sylva and Webster formally requested that the North Carolina Department of Transportation (NCDOT) conduct a comprehensive traffic management study of NC 107.

The department complied but only up to a point. In the summer of 2003, it released a less-than-comprehensive study on one option: a proposal to build two bypass roads around Sylva, Jackson County's largest town and county seat, to alleviate the congestion on NC 107. According to the plan, each segment would consist of a four-lane highway. One of the roads, commonly referred to as the Southern Loop, quickly became a source of great controversy. As designed, the bypass would cause the loss of 94 homes and 5 businesses, and it would have a significant impact on the county's farms, woodlands, and wetlands.

But the greater controversy was NCDOT's apparent determination to define the issue with a single choice—whether or not to build both the northern and the southern loops. The department's refusal to consider a more comprehensive set of options ignited the traditionally serene populace of Jackson County. In response, the alliance took steps that would ultimately force all participants to frame the debate in broader terms.

First, the Smart Roads Alliance, which was often viewed as a group of outsiders, had the good fortune to find two leaders with local credibility. Harold and Gwen Messer believed in the "cause." Their home, like those of hundreds of other Jackson County families, was in the path of the Southern Loop. The Messers, as respected general contractors and church members, led the way in getting the larger community involved. When others said the road was a done deal, Harold and Gwen refused to believe it. Both Messers were savvy in shaping the message and in raising money. Together with their friends and allies they raised money from prominent individuals and organized barbeque dinners with donated food from local restaurants. The money raised was spent in ways that broadened the debate—such as paying for crucial advertising and retaining a traffic expert and consultant whose opinions brought credibility to the alliance's arguments.

Second, the alliance identified other Jackson County residents who should have been involved earlier but were unaware of their stake in the outcome. A North Carolina law required county governments to advertise the names of all property owners delinquent in their taxes. Jackson County residents had long been so interested in these notices that the local newspaper printed extra copies to meet the demand. Knowing that many people who read the newspaper would be affected by the proposed corridors but were unaware of their significance, the Smart Roads Alliance paid for an advertisement that resembled the property tax notice—but it instead listed all of the residents who would be affected by the proposed highways. When the ad ran in the newspaper, local residents bombarded the transportation department with complaints against the proposal and joined the alliance en masse. Jackson County and the municipalities of Sylva, Webster, and Dillsboro passed resolutions of opposition to the Southern Loop.

Third, the Smart Roads Alliance rested on a broad base of support. Concerns about Jackson County road construction cut across political lines. In keeping with the old adage that politics makes for strange bedfellows, the alliance was a big tent under which conservatives, community activists, environmentalists, preservationists, and even some business leaders opposed the Southern Loop.

Fourth, the alliance targeted specific allies to help frame the debate. It sought advice from the Southern Environmental Law Center in Asheville, North Carolina, and reached out to young people. These new friends brought new skills, such as the best ways to obtain government records, organize and conduct meetings, and turn the alliance into an Internal Revenue Service–approved organization and raise tax-deductible contributions. Even more important, the inclusion of future Jackson County leaders helped to make the debate about more than just roads. Their presence helped the alliance to focus attention on the mountains, rivers, forests, and future generations of the community that the new highways would affect.

Fifth, the Smart Roads Alliance relied on experts whose opinions carried weight with decision makers. Some of the earliest opposition to the Southern Loop came from prominent citizens in Webster, the historical seat of Jackson County. Malcolm MacNeill, a local developer, was one of those leaders. MacNeill found Walter Kulash, a nationally known traffic engineer, to advise opponents of the road about possible alternatives to the new four-lane highway. Kulash voiced an expert's opinion to which North Carolina Department of Transportation officials would listen. Additionally, the alliance provided the public with information from experts on alternative transportation. Among them was Dan Burden, a national advocate for "walkable communities." In 2003, the town of Sylva officially incorporated the goal of becoming a walkable community into its long-term planning vision.

Sixth, the Smart Roads Alliance developed reasonable alternatives to the NCDOT's "build or no build" choice. In this task, the alliance was aided by an option proposed by Jim Aust, Sylva's town planner. In 2003, after carefully studying area traffic patterns, Aust proposed a network of new two-lane roads that would connect pre-existing roads to NC 107, thus funneling traffic away from that busy highway. The alliance also recommended the examination of all proposals related to 107 to determine secondary impacts, such as possible pollution of the Tuckasegee River. Though the Aust plan would ultimately prove to have challenges in terms of available funding, potential environmental impact, and neighborhood opposition, it helped the alliance switch from defense to offense. It could now challenge the department's position more effectively. Jackson County Smart Roads thus avoided the trap into which many citizen initiatives fall: expressing opposition to a proposal without offering a counter-proposal.

The alliance's years-long effort to expand the debate beyond a single construction proposal has made some notable achievements. Jackson County created a transportation task force to study the road issue and appointed two alliance members to the group. A headline in the *Sylva Herald* on December 11, 2008, spoke the loudest about how far the alliance had come: "DOT Officials Say They'll Explore All Options for 107."[1] The NCDOT planned to study alternatives, conduct environmental impact studies, and collect input from citizens at public hearings and workshops before choosing a course of action in late 2012. The alliance had succeeded in preventing the question from being only whether to build or not.

While the Jackson County Board of Commissioners voted on a narrow 3–2 majority to include a revised version of NCDOT's original connector project in the 2010 Jackson County Comprehensive Transportation Plan (CTP), the alliance's public outreach succeeded in convincing commissioners to make improving the existing road a higher priority than constructing a new one. The year 2012 came and went without a final decision on the Southern Loop.

Two years later, the local community and the Southwestern Rural Planning Organization conducted a NC 107 corridor study that recommended repairs to existing infrastructure over building a new one. When the study was released, it won the unanimous endorsement of the Jackson County Board of Commissioners and the Town of Sylva Board of Commissioners. As a result, the current road improvements were funded in the state transportation plan. The connector was on hold. As the NCDOT stated bluntly in its project timeline, "2014: Work on the N.C. 107 Connector is suspended. . . . Based on the results of the 2014 ranking cycle, the proposed N.C. 107 Connector is not funded at this time, and studies are concluded for the time being."[2]

---

[1] Stephanie Salmons and Lynn Hotaling, "DOT Officials Say They'll Explore All Options for 107," *Sylva Herald*, December 11, 2008.

[2] North Carolina Department of Transportation, "NC 107 Connector," www.ncdot.gov/projects/nc107connector/

By the time 2015 and a new round of prioritization arrived, the NC 107 connector was not even submitted for consideration. The project is at risk of being removed from the county's comprehensive transportation plan when Jackson County completes an update to that document in late 2016 or early 2017—an action that could be a final deathblow to ultimate project funding.[3] While North Carolina has initiated the improvements to the existing road, an August 2015 newspaper headline indicates just how far the alliance has come: "Controversial Connector Is Shelved for Good."[4]

HOW TO DEFINE THE PROBLEM

You know the feeling. You're listening to a speaker, watching television news, scrolling through your Facebook or Twitter feed, reading an Internet news site or smart phone app, or even talking to friends or family. You could be paying for electricity, taxes, insurance, or tuition. You might even be walking through a neighborhood park, canoeing down a river, or visiting a national park when it hits you. Something isn't right. You feel upset, even angry. Righteous indignation swells within you, and you find yourself saying something like, "There should be a law!" or "If only I were king or queen for a day!"

That feeling is the launching pad for active citizenship. When something you see, hear, read, or experience in your community, state, or nation causes you great anger or worry, and you realize that democratic institutions—the school board, city council, county commission, mayor, state legislature, governor, or even the U.S. Congress or president—have the power to address your concern, you are ready to embark on your journey as an effective citizen.

A Chinese proverb says that a journey of a thousand miles begins with a single step. Your first step in launching a citizen initiative is to understand and clearly state the problem you want to fix. Be specific and realistic. "I want my community to be a better place to live" is a nice sentiment with which almost everyone can agree, but it is far too broad and vague to be useful. More focused starting points might include the following:

- We don't feel safe because crime has increased in our neighborhood.
- Our drinking water looks, smells, and tastes nasty.
- In the past year, my property taxes have doubled.
- My small business is losing workers because I can't afford to set up a 401(k) plan for their retirement.
- Our daughter is one of 35 children in a single kindergarten class.
- The state wants to build a new expressway that would make it too noisy to think at my house.

---

[3] See Southwestern Commission Council of Government, "Jackson County," www.regiona.org/rpo/jackson-county/

[4] Quintin Ellison, "Controversial Connector Is Shelved for Good, Debnam Says," *Sylva Herald*, August 12, 2015, www.thesylvaherald.com/news/article_8ef88ecc-4113-11e5-ae6b-337c3799d9ed.html

Do you see the difference? The statement of the first problem is so nebulous that the democratic process would not be able to address it. On the other hand, the latter statements address particular concerns for which citizen action may produce results.

When you feel anger, concern, or a passionate desire for change rising up inside you, consider whether the source of that feeling could become a political issue. Many people miss the potential for citizen action when they ignore these gut reactions.

Take this example: At a university's foreign language studies conference, the program director announces that undergraduate foreign language course offerings are being cut. The students in the audience are dismayed. How can they continue their studies with fewer language courses? One faculty member observes that the issue is one of choices: The university has prioritized academic subjects, and languages didn't make the cut. The professor urges the students to organize a plan for citizen action to force a reexamination of the choices made. The students have been confronted with an issue that is vital to their academic and professional careers. This is their moment to exercise active citizenship. With the right definition of the problem, they could begin the process of convincing the university to see foreign language instruction as a vital tool in preparing students to compete in the accelerating global economy. But the students appear unable or unwilling to believe they have the power to reverse the university's decision, and their lack of faith makes the decision that much more final.

Once you have concluded that your concern can be addressed through citizen action, the following steps will help you define this concern in the manner most likely to produce a positive result.

1. Look with a Telescope, Not a Microscope

Place the problem you have identified in a larger context. If you do this, you may find that others have the same concern—and that the community faces a collective challenge that requires a democratic response. For example, if you notice that your child's elementary school classroom lacks the necessary technology for effective teaching and learning, other parents at your school or at other schools may have the same concern. Because your local school board is much more likely to address an across-the-board problem than one that affects only a single student, see whether you can define the problem as inadequate technology throughout the entire school system—not just in your child's particular class.

The telescope will work better if you use the lens of history. Remember the wisdom in Ecclesiastes 1:9: "What has been will be again, what has been done will be done again; there is nothing new under the sun."[5] While your citizen advocacy issue may seem new to you, chances are that it existed somewhere else in the past and produced insights and best practices that can be resuscitated.

Consider the example of prison reform, a goal that has gained bipartisan momentum at both the federal and state levels in recent years. As former National Rifle Association and American Conservative Union president David Keene

---

[5] Ecclesiastes 1:9 (New International Version).

explained the concern in a 2015 report from the Brennan Center for Justice at the New York University School of Law, "America locks up too many people for too long. We do little to prepare them for their release. Then we lock up more than half of them again and again."[6]

The support across ideological lines for prison reform has resulted in some old ideas becoming new again. Twenty years after Congress prohibited the use of federal dollars on prison college education programs, states are again prioritizing higher instruction as part of the rehabilitative process.[7] California, New York, Washington, and other states are directing more funding to inmate higher education, and almost every state has sought to participate in the U.S. Department of Education's 2015 initiative to make Pell Grants available for prisoners taking college courses.[8]

You don't have to reinvent the wheel. History will repeat itself. Adjust your telescope and look for opportunities to apply the lessons of past experience.

2. Focus the Telescope if Necessary

Politics is the art of the possible, and sometimes it is necessary to narrow the larger context if the wide-angle view presents an outsized target. Don't throw a Hail Mary pass when what you really need is a first down. For example, you may be a local store owner who is concerned that your state's taxation system does not treat small businesses fairly. However, you are even more concerned about the competitive advantage that Internet hardware suppliers enjoy. You are required to collect sales taxes when your customers buy hammers in your store. Because your Internet competitors can escape that requirement, they can sell hammers for less than you do. If you learn that the state is scheduled to explore the issue of sales tax fairness, and you want to present your side of the issue, you will increase your chances of addressing the most important part of the problem if you define and focus it as an Internet sales tax collection issue and leave other perceived tax inequities for future citizen action.[9] As we will discuss more in chapter 6, timing is everything when it comes to influencing policymakers.

---

[6] Times-Union Editorial, "Prison Reform Now Is Bipartisan Movement," *Florida Times-Union*, November 4, 2015, jacksonville.com/opinion/editorials/2015-11-04/story/prison-reform-now-bipartisan-movement; The reference cited here is David Keene, "A Real Mental Health System," in *Solutions: American Leaders Speak out on Criminal Justice*, ed. Inimai Chettiar and Michael Waldman, 49–54 (New York: Brennan Center for Justice at New York University School of Law, 2015), 49, www.brennancenter.org/sites/default/files/publications/Solutions_American_Leaders_Speak_Out.pdf

[7] Josh Mitchell and Joe Palazzolo, "Pell Grants to Be Restored for Prisoners," *Wall Street Journal*, July 27, 2015, www.wsj.com/articles/pell-grants-to-be-restored-for-prisoners-1438029241

[8] Donna Gordon Blankinship, "College Behind Bars: An Old Idea with Some New Energy," *The Big Story*, March 1, 2016, bigstory.ap.org/article/2d2d0b63ef054c5298a27da86a8bde95/college-behind-bars-old-idea-some-new-energy

[9] Brian Fung, "Why You're Paying Sales Tax on that Cyber Monday Deal, But Others Aren't," *Washington Post*, November 30, 2015, www.washingtonpost.com/news/the-switch/wp/2015/11/30/why-youre-paying-sales-tax-on-that-cyber-monday-deal-but-others-arent/

3. Begin with the End in Mind

In his famous self-help book *The Seven Habits of Highly Effective People*, Stephen Covey urges readers to "begin with the end in mind." As he explains, "To begin with the end in mind means to start with a clear understanding of your destination. It means to know where you're going so that you better understand where you are now and so that the steps you take are always in the right direction."[10] The same advice applies as you define your problem for citizen action. At the end of the process, elected or appointed decision makers at some level of government are going to give a thumbs-up or thumbs-down to your initiative. The chances of pointing those thumbs in the right direction increase if you think carefully about how to frame the problem so officials can relate to it. Fortunately, you have expert advice on how to hardwire yourself into an elected official's brain from a sitting member of the United States Congress.

TIPS FROM THE PROS

Anticipate the Decision Maker's Needs
CONGRESSMAN DEREK KILMER

The late great Native American leader Billy Frank Jr., when advising others regarding how to advocate effectively, gave a simple direction. "Tell the truth," he said, "and tell your story."

But how do you tell your story? There are a handful of questions an advocate can answer to make his or her case effectively.

1. What's the problem you're trying to solve or the opportunity you're trying to capture? Policymakers want to make a difference. That's easier when you can identify the difference you want to be made. What's wrong? What could be better?

2. Why is it a legitimate problem? Make a case for why you have a problem that needs solving. When possible, use statistics or stories to strengthen your argument. For example, it's one thing to identify a problem. Rising sea levels, for example, are a problem for coastal communities. But it creates a greater sense of urgency for a policymaker when he or she hears that the local childcare facility has persistently flooded, putting kids at risk. It's more compelling when one learns that the community has faced a "100-year flood" in four of the last seven years. Know the specifics of your story and have details to back it up.

3. What's your proposed solution? A public official needs to know how you plan to take this from a problem to a solution. If you were calling the shots, what would you do to fix the problem?

(Continued)

---

[10] Stephen R. Covey, *The Seven Habits of Highly Effective People* (New York, Free Press, 2004), 98.

(Continued)

4. Why is that a legitimate solution? You have to make sure that what you are pro-posing is realistic. If you want to solve a gridlock traffic problem don't say that we need flying cars on our roadways. Find out how—whether through construction projects or additional mass transit options—to solve the community's traffic con-gestion woes. If you have data or case studies or any backup sources to indicate that your solution is the right one, use them to strengthen your argument.

5. What are the consequences—intended or unintended—of the solution? Take a holistic approach to the problem you are trying to solve. Policymakers will often ask, "But if I do what you're asking me to do, won't 'x' happen?" Make sure you have thought through the outcomes your solution could produce.

6. Who are key stakeholders and what is their position on this issue? Policymakers will often want to know "who is for this?" and "who is against it?" You need to be able to say how your solution might affect others and what they might think. Elected officials will not want any surprises. And be honest. If you try to gloss over potential opposition, you might damage your relationship with the leader over the long haul.

7. What's "the ask?" Know what you want from the policymaker. Is it an endorse-ment of a plan? Or a letter to an agency? Do you want a bill introduced? Be specific and know what success looks like for your meeting.

Derek Kilmer was elected in 2012 to represent Washington State's 6th Congressional District in the United States House of Representatives. He serves on the House Appropriations Committee. Prior to his congressional service, Derek served in the Washington State House of Representatives from 2005 to 2007 and in the state Senate from 2007 until 2012. While in the Washington State Legislature, Derek was the principal writer of the state's capital budget.

4. Suggest Solutions as You Define the Problem

Whether you want to improve your neighborhood park or have the federal govern-ment change banking laws, your goal is to alter policy. Consistent with Congressman Kilmer's advice to be solution oriented, your definition of the problem should either implicitly or explicitly identify the desired outcome. In the Jackson County example that began this chapter, opponents of the proposed bypass shrewdly made the cam-paign about "smart roads" and "smart growth", setting up a litmus test the planned highway, which interfered with homes, businesses, agriculture, and the environment, could not pass.

5. Define the Problem in Public Terms

Political consultants correctly tell their candidates that voters will usually remember no more than a sentence or two about them. Depending on the size of the electorate and the office being sought, thousands or even millions of dollars are devoted to ensuring that voters remember the right sentence or two when they see a particular candidate's name on the ballot. Even though your "campaign" may be more about persuading policymakers than voters, you need to brand your issue in a succinct yet memorable way that drives home your central goal.

One group of motivated and creative citizens did exactly that in persuading voters to put new environmental protections in the Florida Constitution. This coalition was alarmed at the rate of development that was burying the state's coastal areas in condominiums, destroying forest lands, and paving over wetlands. Coalition members wanted to find ways to preserve more land for public use. They sought to persuade the state legislature to put two constitutional amendments on the next general election ballot—each to earmark a portion of the state real estate transfer tax for public land acquisition. The legislature agreed, even though many of those who voted to put the amendments on the ballot secretly believed they had no chance of passage in a state that prided itself on economic growth and individual property rights.

Early in the legislative session, the environmental advocates had secured the first and second general election ballot spots for constitutional amendments. They would be pushing Amendments 1 and 2, and they turned that favorable placement into a memorable slogan: 1 + 2 = Lands for You. When Election Day arrived, most voters knew that mantra by heart. The campaign imprinted all of its materials with the catchy label and unveiled two signature images: one, a lake with happy campers in canoes and, two, a pastoral wetlands landscape. A volunteer songwriter penned a 1 + 2 jingle, and the campaign gave donors its two signature images to distribute to other possible supporters. At every rally, press conference, and public appearance, the proponents of Amendments 1 and 2 drove home the point that the preserved lands "would be for you." Voters remembered that when they walked into polling places and overwhelmingly adopted the amendments.

6. Be Prepared to Refine the Problem

Take care not to think of defining the problem as a static step in the citizen engagement process. As you conduct research, determine which level of government is the appropriate place to address a problem, test public opinion, engage the media, and raise resources, you may need to refine your definition to make it as compelling as possible to decision makers and those people and public forces that influence them. While you will read more about this effort in chapter 7, you may already be aware that lesbian, gay, bisexual, and transgender (LGBT) advocates around the nation have worked for years to expand local human rights ordinances (HRO) to include sexual orientation and gender identity as characteristics protected from discrimination in housing and employment. Some of these initial efforts were unsuccessful. But then many HRO advocates correctly decided to focus on the economic impact of not offering this protection by showing that companies are less willing to invest in a community if they don't think all of their employees will be legally protected. That pivot reflected a wise refinement on their part to make the HRO a business development issue, one that could appeal to a broader range of the political spectrum.

7. Repeat, Repeat, Repeat

Over the next few chapters, you will learn many skills to help make your citizen initiative a success. Just remember that your definition of the challenge to be resolved is the North Star of your efforts. This statement of the problem is your inspiration, and to lose sight of it is to abandon the very concern that motivated you to act in the first place. Summarize your problem in a single sentence, and repeat it to yourself before and during each step in the process outlined in the pages ahead. You won't get lost if you hold tight to your compass.

CHECKLIST FOR ACTION

- ☐ Look with a telescope, not a microscope.
- ☐ Focus the telescope if necessary.
- ☐ Begin with the end in mind.
- ☐ Suggest solutions as you define the problem.
- ☐ Define the problem in public terms.
- ☐ Be prepared to refine the problem.
- ☐ Repeat, repeat, repeat.

2 Just the Facts, Ma'am

Gathering Information to Sway Decision Makers[1]

"Facts are stubborn things."

—President John Adams

Case in Point	A Penny Saved Is a Penny Earned
	By Nick Maynard, Brian Gilmore, and Mariele McGlazer*

Courtesy of One Detroit Credit Union

Melvin Oliver and Claudette G. Purdy pose with their winnings from Save to Win, a prize-linked savings program supported by credit unions including One Detroit (formerly Communicating Arts Credit Union).

---

[1] We are grateful to David Draine, a senior researcher at the Pew Charitable Trusts (pewtrusts.org/en/about/experts/david-draine), and Mike Rice, president of VR Research (vrresearch.com/who-we-are-mike-rice), for reviewing this chapter and providing expert advice on research strategies and tools for citizen success.

*Our thanks to Nick Maynard, Brian Gilmore, and Mariele McGlazer of the Doorways to Dreams (D2D) Fund (d2dfund.org) for writing this case study.

What are Prize-Linked Savings Accounts?

- Consumers earn entries into prize raffles for making savings deposits, often into traditional savings accounts or certificates of deposit.
- Typically, though not always, the accounts also earn interest at a rate that is comparable to similar products offered.
- Game rules (e.g., how to earn entries), prize structures (e.g., how often prizes are drawn and prize size), and business models vary to suit the needs of different financial institutions and their customers.
- Consumers are motivated to save through fun and excitement, rather than with a sense of sacrifice.
- Institutions benefit by attracting new—and newly excited—customers and earning media coverage whenever someone wins big.
- Prize-linked savings do not have to be linked directly to bank savings accounts. The core concept can be applied to a wide array of existing and new platforms, such as prepaid cards, mobile applications, or personal financial management systems.

Julia,* a single mother working two jobs while going to school and raising a daughter, dreams of owning a home. Her aspirations seem simple: "I want that American dream." But her fluctuating work hours, the changing day-to-day needs of her daughter, and the occasional unexpected expense make it difficult for Julia to build the savings she needs to manage her financial life. Without savings, Julia relies on credit cards to get by. Accumulating debt makes her financial dreams seem even further out of reach.

Julia's story is by no means unusual. Americans are struggling through a national savings crisis. In June 2015, the savings rate fell to 5 percent from a high of 17 percent in 1975.[2] While the top 20 percent of earners had emergency savings to cover about 52 days of expenses in 2013, the bottom 20 percent could cover their expenses for just 9 days.[3] Many families are not prepared for expected long-term expenses such as retirement or a child's education, let alone unexpected emergencies that can send a household budget into a tailspin. People overwhelmingly report that they want to save more, yet trends have moved in the wrong direction for decades. These facts led a nonprofit organization to ask what could be done to move the needle on household savings for Americans like Julia.

DISCOVERING PRIZE-LINKED SAVINGS

The financial system often fails vulnerable consumers, both in the products it offers and the policies that shape it. But the system can be changed. Doorways to Dreams (D2D) Fund (d2dfund.org) was founded in 2000 to drive the financial system to promote lasting social and economic prosperity for every American family. This Boston-based nonprofit pursues this work through a powerful model: discover ideas,

---

*Pseudonym

[2] Federal Reserve Bank of St. Louis, "Personal Saving Rate," *Economic Research*, research.stlouisfed.org/fred2/series/PSAVERT

[3] The Pew Charitable Trusts, *The Precarious State of Family Balance Sheets* (Washington, DC: The Pew Charitable Trusts, 2015), www.pewtrusts.org/~/media/assets/2015/01/fsm_balance_sheet_report.pdf

design and pilot test solutions, and drive tested innovations to scale. This is the story of how D2D and like-minded advocates applied this impact model to transform the act of saving money from staid self-denial to exciting reward by bringing prize-linked savings (PLS) accounts to millions of Americans. Internationally, the evidence suggested PLS, an initiative that offers consumers the chance to win prizes for saving money, could change behavior.

PLS transforms the savings experience into something both fun and rewarding. Each act of saving is a chance to win a game with real rewards, rules, suspense, and possibility.

D2D's initial research led it to the United Kingdom's Premium Bond program, which provided a powerful example of a large-scale PLS product that was both self-sustaining and highly impactful. Each £1 Premium Bond purchase earns a buyer an entry into monthly drawings to win one of two million monthly prizes, ranging from £25 to £1 million. Even if they don't win prizes, savers still have full access to their risk-free principal investment. They can't lose, and the chance that they may win encourages them to save. Premium Bonds have been available since 1956, and today about one in three Britons owns one.

The UK is one example among over 20 countries with PLS. But could D2D raise the profile of PLS enough—and overcome negative perceptions associated with "gambling"—to bring the innovation successfully to the United States?

PILOT TESTING PLS

The international success of PLS was a starting point, but D2D knew that it would also need to show the idea's viability in the United States. Data from the $70 billion/year lottery industry shows that games of chance appeal to many Americans: 57 percent report playing the lottery at least once in the past year.[4] Much of that money is coming from the pockets of the financially vulnerable, with as much as 80 percent of gambling revenue coming from households with annual incomes of $50,000 or less.[5] Many Americans even view the lottery as a form of financial planning. Over 20 percent of Americans, and over 38 percent of those with incomes under $25,000,[6] reported viewing lottery winning as the most practical way to amass several hundred thousand dollars. Julia, too, plays the lottery. When she comes up empty-handed, she thinks about what else she might have used those dollars for: "I go and buy a soda, and I can drink it. I go and buy a lottery ticket, and I can't guarantee that I'll get my dollar back."

But what if she could? What if D2D could design a savings innovation that used the lottery-like fun and excitement of winning to encourage saving, without the risk of consumers losing money?

---

[4] Mark Gillespie, "Lotteries Most Popular Form of Gambling for Americans," *Gallup News Service*, June 17, 1999, www.gallup.com/poll/3769/lotteries-most-popular-form-gambling-americans.aspx

[5] Peter Tufano, Nick Maynard, and Jan-Emmanuel De Neve, *Consumer Demand for Prize-Linked Savings: A Preliminary Analysis*, D2D Working Paper No. 08-061 (Roxbury, MA: Doorways to Dreams Fund, 2008), www.d2dfund.org/files/publications/consumer-demand-prize-linked-savings.pdf

[6] Consumer Federation of America and the Financial Planning Association, "How Americans View Personal Wealth vs. How Financial Planners View this Wealth," Monday, January 9, 2006, www.consumerfed.org/pdfs/Financial_Planners_Study011006.pdf

D2D knew that the biggest risk to adoption of PLS was its association with negative perceptions of the lottery and gambling. D2D needed a real-world example of PLS not as "gambling" but, in fact, as the very opposite—a product that promotes financially *responsible* behavior. To create this example in the United States, D2D partnered with Centra Credit Union in Indiana to design and pilot the Centra Super Savings account starting in the fall of 2006. Because Indiana—like most states—tightly restricts who can conduct raffles, this initial test was offered as a sweepstakes rather than a raffle. By law, sweepstakes must provide an alternate method of entry, creating a risk that a winner could be someone who didn't save or who is not even a member of that credit union at all. For this reason, raffles are usually the preferred model for PLS accounts. But the sweepstakes model used for the Centra Super Savings account pilot would be enough to provide proof of the PLS concept. And it did. The pilot showed that most consumers were interested in a PLS account, and that demand was strongest among non-savers and frequent lottery players, corroborating D2D's expectations. During the first three months of the pilot, customers opened 1,300 Super Savings accounts and saved over half a million dollars.[7]

With such promising early results, D2D was ready to test the concept at a larger scale. The lottery and financial institution laws in many states limited the ability to evaluate PLS models. Fortunately, Michigan law already had a carve-out allowing credit unions to conduct "savings promotion raffles." D2D had a venue for the next big trial.

EXPANDING THE PILOT AND GATHERING DATA

Leading a partnership that included the Filene Research Institute, the Michigan Credit Union League (MCUL), and the Center for Financial Services Innovation, D2D designed a PLS product called Save to Win™ to be piloted at eight credit unions across Michigan. Save to Win accounts were federally insured share certificates that saw each $25 increase in an account's month-over-month balance earning account holders an entry into raffles to win cash prizes.

In the 2009 pilot, over 11,600 Michigan credit union members saved more than $8.6 million in Save to Win accounts, with an average account balance of $734. Save to Win continued to grow over the next two years. By the end of 2011, 42 participating credit unions had over 25,000 unique accounts with savings of over $40 million.[8] In 2012, Nebraska launched the first Save to Win product outside Michigan at nine credit unions. As Save to Win expanded to new states and credit unions, it brought along its data collection machine, designed from the start to measure the demand for and impact of PLS. D2D compiled surveys, conducted interviews, and analyzed account data every step of the way.

Meanwhile, D2D continued to lead efforts to gather more information, and its staff became the leading experts in PLS. In 2011, they commissioned a five-state survey to get compelling, up-to-date data on Americans' demand for PLS and their

---

[7] Nick Maynard, "Prize-Based Savings: Product Innovation to Make Saving Fun," Doorways to Dreams Fund Publication, December 1, 2007, www.d2dfund.org/files/publications/prize-based-savings.pdf

[8] Sarika Abbi, Amanda Hahnel, Nick Maynard, and Joanna Smith-Ramani, *Playing the Savings Game: A Prize-Linked Savings Report* (Allston, MA: Doorways to Dreams Fund, 2012), www.d2dfund.org/files/publications/PlayingTSG_Report_2012_SinglePgs.pdf

preferences about product features. The same year, D2D convened a PLS conference attended by 80 representatives from government, nonprofits, academia, and the financial services industry. In 2012, D2D began a quarterly PLS newsletter to disseminate data and successes to a growing network of partners. D2D expanded this network and socialized PLS through conferences and presentations, producing more than 20 reports highlighting the impressive data and powerful human stories behind the concept. Through research, pilot testing, data collection, and network building, D2D had established itself as the authority on PLS.

The success of PLS—and the attendant positive media attention—motivated other states to pass legislation permitting "savings promotion raffles." Stakeholders often turned to D2D for support with advocating to state lawmakers, and technical assistance in writing bills and shepherding them through the legislative process. D2D provided targeted background information to policymakers, helped tailor the bills to meet the needs of each state, tracked progress, and marshaled support from key stakeholders. Rhode Island, Maryland, and Maine passed legislation in 2010, followed by Nebraska, Washington and North Carolina in 2011.

It was here, in North Carolina, that Julia crossed paths with prize-linked savings. She opened a prize-linked savings account at her local credit union (D2D's Save to Win design) in October 2013. At first, she deposited $25—the amount required to earn an entry—each week. After getting a new job a few months later, she was able to increase her deposit amount and set up automatic transfers into her PLS account. In her own words, "[Prize-linked savings] has really given me an opportunity to have somewhere to start. . . . It makes me really say 'there is a place for my money and there is somewhere I can save it and there is someplace I can do it on a consistent basis.' It really has given me a foundation."

Like many consumers, Julia had long had a traditional savings account—but it had never helped her to build meaningful savings. A prize-linked savings account assisted Julia in establishing and maintaining a regular savings habit—a practice that eludes so many of the financially struggling—through excitement and fun.

A DATA-DRIVEN APPROACH TO REMOVING FEDERAL BARRIERS

The success of Save to Win and the passage of state legislation were worth celebrating, but a significant federal roadblock stood in the way of activating those state law changes and bringing PLS to a national scale. The roadblock was rooted in the fears of corruption and illegality associated with early lotteries. This corruption led the United States to prohibit lotteries outright in 1895. Despite this prohibition, illegal lotteries thrived. As part of the effort to crack down on this criminal activity, Congress passed HR 10595 in 1967 to "prohibit certain banks and savings and loan associations from fostering or participating in gambling activities." This outdated legislation prohibited all banks and thrifts from offering PLS, as it was considered "gambling." Even if state law allowed banks and thrifts to offer PLS, they were still prohibited from doing so by federal law. D2D was not only battling the perception of PLS as gambling but also existing statutes that said this perception was reality.

Federal law would need to change in order to bring PLS to all Americans. To change the law, D2D needed to identify the relevant congressional committees with oversight of the banking law, draft legislation to carve out an exception to the law for

PLS accounts, find champions in the House and Senate to shepherd the bill, address the concerns of banking regulators, and generate support in the private and nonprofit sectors for PLS. Convincing all of these stakeholders would not have been possible without credible research and data from the PLS pilot demonstrating consumer demand for PLS and its proven effectiveness in reaching financially vulnerable consumers. Certain key data points were especially powerful in providing compelling evidence that PLS works for consumers and industry:

- PLS appealed to financially vulnerable consumers: an estimated 56 percent of Save to Win account holders were non-savers, 39 percent were asset poor, and 44 percent reported household incomes under $40,000.[9]
- Prizes attracted customers and encouraged them to try new products. Sixty-four percent (64%) of account holders had never had a certificate of deposit before.
- Winning even a small amount had a powerful impact on savings behavior. People who won prizes—regardless of the prize size—saved more consistently than non-winners and were more likely to continue their participation from one year to the next.

With this strong data, D2D began its policy efforts in the House. Both the Financial Services and Judiciary committees would need to move any federal legislation forward for a full vote. Representative Derek Kilmer (D-WA), who had sponsored PLS legislation as a lawmaker in Washington State, was a key ally on Capitol Hill. With Rep. Kilmer's help, D2D met with lawmakers in the House, particularly those on the Financial Services and Judiciary committees, to begin to make the case for PLS. Rep. Tom Cotton (R-AR), an early cosponsor and member of the Judiciary Committee, was another key ally in generating support from his colleagues.

To demonstrate the value of PLS, D2D presented reputable data from the Center for Enterprise Development regarding the low savings rate nationally and in each legislator's state. Not surprisingly given the negative association of lotteries and games of chance, the primary barrier D2D often needed to overcome was a general lack of awareness about PLS and the concern that it was gambling. Armed with deep knowledge about how the accounts operate, as well as extensive quantitative data from Save to Win showing that financially vulnerable consumers were demanding these accounts and were saving money, D2D could prove that PLS was an effective no-risk savings vehicle. The outdated lottery laws were not protecting consumers from gambling. They were creating an unnecessary barrier to offering a product that would help consumers save and imposing undue regulation on the banking industry.

These conversations were supported by another kind of data that added credibility to D2D's position. PLS was attracting media spotlight across the country, including pieces in the *New York Times*, *PBS News Hour*, *Wall Street Journal*, *Financial Times*, *Washington Post*, *USA Today*, and a feature on the popular *Freakonomics* podcast. The personal stories of grand prize winners were particularly effective in gaining the attention of media partners. This was no longer the story of a scrappy nonprofit trying to create change. It was the story of over 40,000 credit union members, more than $70 million saved, and public awareness about the value of these accounts.

---

[9] D2D Staff, *Save to Win: 2009 Final Project Results* (Allston, MA: Doorways to Dreams Fund, 2010), www.d2dfund.org/files/publications/save to win final_lores.pdf

Most important, it was the story of individual consumers like Julia, whose life had truly changed because of PLS. Julia's story, and the stories of others in similar financial situations, grounded the concept of PLS in the lived experience of the people who could benefit the most from a new way to save. Through a combination of compelling statistics, proximity to the consumer perspective, and experience guiding state legislation, D2D had become the national expert on PLS and was in an excellent position to lead the charge for federal policy change.

Following the meetings in the House, D2D expanded its advocacy efforts to the Senate. The Committee on Banking, Housing and Urban Affairs was the gatekeeper for legislation to move forward in the Senate. A member of that committee, Senator Jerry Moran (R-KS), led the way in partnership with D2D to raise awareness of PLS and generate support.

Congress heard the message clearly. Rep. Kilmer and Rep. Cotton (R-AR) introduced the American Savings Promotion Act (ASPA) in the House; companion Senate legislation was introduced by Senators Jerry Moran (R-KS), Sherrod Brown (D-OH), and Elizabeth Warren (D-MA). To support the movement of these bills, D2D held over 50 meetings on Capitol Hill to disseminate the research and findings generated from the pilot work. Making full use of its evaluation data and consumer stories, D2D also met with an array of federal regulators to understand and address any of their concerns. In addition, D2D held a high profile congressional briefing with leaders from the Congressional Savings and Ownership Caucus and the Financial and Economic Literacy Caucus to share data and research in support of PLS. Outside Capitol Hill, D2D continued to build a bipartisan coalition of allies to support the work. Finally, D2D commanded additional media attention by partnering with American Express to include PLS in a companion piece to the documentary *Spent*.

These efforts helped ASPA garner bipartisan support. It had ideological appeal on both sides of the aisle—Republicans saw deregulation, while Democrats saw a program to help working families—and it was a no-cost measure supported by a wealth of data demonstrating an effective savings solution with no risk to consumers. The American Savings Promotion Act passed unanimously in both houses of Congress, and President Obama signed the bill into law on December 18, 2014.

THE WORK CONTINUES

The unanimous passage of federal legislation was a major victory, but certainly not the end of the line. Following ASPA, and with additional credibility and publicity generated by the passage of federal legislation, D2D redoubled its state-level efforts. More state lawmakers were interested in PLS and reached out for support. In turn, D2D used the growing national network of PLS advocates to amplify the initiative's impact. For example, D2D connected lawmakers in states considering legislation to staffers in other states to help craft a bill or secure bipartisan sponsors. With the support of this network, 19 states—including populous New York and Illinois—have passed "savings promotion raffle" legislation as of June 2016, with more to come in the year ahead.

Today, PLS is flourishing in communities across the country. Save to Win is now available in 10 states at over 100 credit unions, making PLS accessible to 47 million consumers. Lucky Savers, a PLS product for New York credit unions, saw members save nearly a million dollars in its first month after launch.[10] And it's not just credit unions. In July 2015, Blue Ridge Bank in Luray, Virginia, became the first bank in the country to offer a PLS product when it launched its Jackpot Savings account.[11]

D2D continues to collect data to evaluate the impact of PLS, including intangible benefits such as increased financial confidence. True to its mission of impact at scale, D2D has set its sights on creating a market where every consumer has access to a PLS product that suits his or her needs. Beyond financial institutions, D2D has worked with tax preparers, prepaid debit card providers, children's savings account programs, fintech start-ups, and other financial services innovators to introduce PLS-inspired features across a range of platforms.

And what about Julia? Offered a new way to save, she was able to make great strides toward her dreams. She has paid down a significant amount of debt while accumulating a $500 cash reserve. After maintaining her PLS account for a full year, she used the money to cover an unexpected expense without taking on additional borrowing. Finally, she prequalified for a mortgage and saved enough to afford a down payment on a home for herself and her daughter.

THE INFORMATION-GATHERING PROCESS

In the previous chapter, we discussed the foundation of effective citizenship: You cannot solve a problem or successfully confront a challenge unless you have specifically, realistically, and clearly defined it. Once you have defined your problem, you are ready to find the facts that will persuade a decision maker to take on your cause—a process to be described in subsequent chapters.

English statesman and essayist Sir Francis Bacon declared that "knowledge is power." Citizens who have sufficient knowledge of their issue have credibility—and with credibility comes the power to influence other citizens, community leaders, members of the media, and, ultimately, decision makers. An informed citizen who makes persuasive use of facts, figures, and real-life examples is better positioned to sway the city council, county commission, or state legislature than is someone who speaks from ignorance or pure emotion, often claiming without substantiation to be the sole possessor of the truth.

Until about 20 years ago, collecting facts could be cumbersome and time consuming. Advocates who wanted to gather information in support of their cause spent hours in libraries poring over hardbound volumes or microfilm copies of old newspapers, magazines, government reports, and academic journals. Even on university campuses, materials were rarely centralized in a single location. Researchers who managed to discover reports or studies from foundations, advocacy organizations, and even some universities or governmental agencies had to request them by mail and then spend weeks awaiting their arrival.

---

[10]CUNA, "1st Lucky Savers in N.Y. Save $983K," *Credit Union National Association,* November 17, 2015, news.cuna.org/articles/108459-st-lucky-savers-in-ny-save-983k

[11]Mary Wisniewski, "Small Bank's Behavioral Experiment Spurs Saving with a Lottery," *American Banker,* August 13, 2015, www.americanbanker.com/news/bank-technology/small-banks-behavioral-experiment-spurs-saving-with-a-lottery-1076032-1.html

The Internet changed everything. Today the challenge is no longer finding enough information or locating it quickly. Now we have immediate access to nearly unlimited information on any subject, but we face a new but just as daunting challenge: How can we sort through countless resources and find reliable facts that will persuade decision makers? This chapter addresses that challenge.

WHY CONDUCT RESEARCH?

Many first-time advocates complain that gathering information is dry or academic. They regard it as not nearly as exciting as interacting with decision makers, building coalitions, or being interviewed on television—and thus give the research process short shrift. This attitude is a huge mistake that greatly imperils their chances of success. Although research may lack the glitz and glamour of the more public aspects of active citizenship, a cause that is not supported by credible data is in serious jeopardy. On the other hand, taking the time to research a subject thoroughly will pay many dividends. Here is what effective research can do for you.

Inform Every Citizenship Skill

In the coming chapters, you will learn citizenship skills such as building coalitions, engaging the media, raising resources, and persuading decision makers. Your research will have the vital purpose of improving your chances of mastering each of those skills. At each point in the advocacy process, you will be appealing to real human beings for assistance. Each of those stakeholders has a particular background, various policy interests, likes and dislikes. Your chances of enlisting their help will increase considerably if you have researched your subject thoroughly and cultivated multiple arguments that could be used to appeal to the specific individuals you are trying to convince or recruit. Some may be influenced by economic arguments. Others may prefer historical or comparative analysis. Others still may be more swayed by appeals to fairness or justice. Some may be sensitive to the political consequences of adopting or failing to adopt your position. Good research gives citizen advocates the versatility and flexibility they need to succeed.

Enhance Credibility

The more you know about a subject, the more those you are trying to persuade will respect your opinion. In the 1980s, a television commercial for a financial services company proclaimed simply, "When E. F. Hutton talks, people listen." Strive to be the E. F. Hutton of your issue. If you convince the ultimate decision maker that you know the facts backward and forward, you may get some benefit of the doubt as you advocate.

Do not underestimate the importance of being credible. When I was in the United States Senate, I had the privilege of being a member of the influential Finance Committee. One of our many responsibilities was Medicare. During one hearing in which the committee was considering legislation on an obscure issue affecting Medicare's payments to physicians, the representative of a health care organization misrepresented the impact of a bill provision on its members. Unfortunately for the speaker, I had previously helped a constituent with a problem involving that provision and knew the issue well. I also knew he was wrong, and I never again trusted information I received from his organization. Though politicians have their problems, short memories are not among them.

Doorways to Dreams (D2D) was successful in persuading financial institutions, state legislatures, and the United States Congress to authorize prize-linked savings largely because D2D employed data-based evidence and established itself as a reliable provider of information. Model your efforts after those of that organization. Credibility alone won't win every citizen advocacy effort, but it will give you a reputation for accuracy that helps to ensure long-term success.

Learn from the Past

We're not talking about *Star Trek* here. Chances are good that your goals are not taking you to a place where no one has gone before. In your research, you will likely discover other citizens in your area or elsewhere who have previously fought a similar battle. Were they successful? If so, how? If not, why not? What were the decisive moments of their effort that dictated either success or failure? If you have more information about previous efforts similar to yours, you can modify your strategic plan to enhance the chances of success.

Locate Precedent

Legal practitioners will tell you that every judge in the United States feels more comfortable making a ruling if he or she knows that another judge has made it first. Decision makers are no different. It will be harder for the person, panel, or organization you have identified as key to solving your problem to say "no" if others in similar situations have previously said "yes."

For example, let's say that you are concerned about your city's low ranking for bicycle and pedestrian safety.[12] You want the local government to enact measures to make streets friendlier to bicyclists and pedestrians. Because this is the kind of quality-of-life issue that could determine whether potential businesses and residents decide to make your city their home, it will benefit your cause if your research shows that similar cities have embraced those bike-friendly and pedestrian-friendly reforms—and how those reforms have enhanced the community's attractiveness.

Your effort will receive an even bigger boost if those other decision makers saw good results from their decision to support citizens with goals similar to yours. In this way, effective research helps to identify what many in the business world call "best practices" and allows you to propose specific solutions with positive track records. If you can show a decision maker that your solution has been previously adopted and successfully implemented, you are much likelier to win agreement than if you don't have this information.

Out-Prepare Your Opponents

One of the National Basketball Association's earliest stars, "Easy Ed" Macauley, is well known for his sage advice: "When you are not practicing, remember, someone somewhere is practicing, and when you meet him he will win."[13] While later in the

---

[12] See Alliance for Biking & Walking, *Bicycling and Walking in the United States: 2014 Benchmarking Report* (Washington, DC: Alliance for Biking & Walking, 2014), http://www.bikewalkalliance.org/storage/documents/reports/2014BenchmarkingReport.pdf

[13] Quoted in John McPhee, *A Sense of Where You Are: Bill Bradley at Princeton*, 3rd ed. (New York: Farrar, Straus and Giroux, 1999), 65.

book we will discuss in more detail the importance of identifying and outperforming your opponents, you must assume that whoever opposes your initiative is doing their homework. If you fail to do yours, that lack of diligence can doom a citizen cause to failure. Consider these two scenarios:

> You have formed a citizens' group to persuade the state legislature to impose limits on how much individual candidates can spend on their campaigns. After defining the problem—that the exploding costs of political campaigns are increasing the public's cynicism about the political process and denying many potential candidates the ability to run—you collect compelling data to support your argument. You present your proposal to the appropriate legislative committee and remain to watch the testimony of the leader of a citizens' group opposed to limits on campaign contributions. She presents several court decisions to demonstrate that your proposal would violate both your state constitution and the U.S. Constitution. Unfortunately, you have not read those decisions and cannot rebut them. Her credibility is enhanced and yours is diminished.

> The local government announces plans to widen a street through your neighborhood to accommodate four lanes instead of two. You are concerned that the widened road will increase noise and traffic. In studying the problem, you discover an article about a similar road project in another city that was halted when local parents highlighted the possible dangers to children playing or waiting for the school bus. This information leads you to contact the local parent-teacher association to involve it in the issue. Under the weight of opposition from neighbors, parents, teachers, and schoolchildren, the local government and road proponents withdraw their plans.

As you conduct your research, it's easy to become so focused on proving the merits of your cause that you forget the other ways that research can bolster your arguments. If you're not prepared to say why opponents are wrong, your chances of victory are slim.

If you think of research as a citizen advocacy tool beyond your grasp, think again. As everyday residents of the Florida Keys learned when they began receiving suspiciously high homeowners' insurance bills in their mailboxes, gathering the right information and presenting it to decision makers can build momentum for a cause.

Another Case in Point   Stormy Weather*

In 2004 and 2005, the nation watched as one hurricane after another battered Florida. But the driving rains, pounding waves, and destroyed homes and businesses were only the beginning of the problems for many of the state's residents. The storms unleashed an economic crisis that drove a group of Floridians in Monroe County, home to the Florida Keys, to organize and fight dramatic increases in homeowners' insurance premiums.

---

*This case study was written with the help of Cindy DeRocher, a leader of the successful initiatives for fair insurance rates in Monroe County, and Heather Carruthers, a Monroe County commissioner.

Richard Sheinwald/Bloomberg via Getty Images

A single palm tree stands beside the wreckage of a home destroyed by Hurricane Wilma in October 2005.

The Florida Keys are a string of low-lying islands as far south as you can go in the continental United States. Given their geographic position near the Gulf Stream and the entrance to the warm waters of the Gulf of Mexico, the Keys have seen their share of tropical weather. Yet the Keys were relatively unscathed in the 2004–05 barrage.

Florida property owners are encouraged or, in many cases, required to carry "windstorm" insurance to cover damages from high winds. Homeowners and businesses in hardest-hit Central, Northwest, and Southeast Florida could have predicted increases in their insurance premiums. But residents of Key West were perplexed in early 2006 when they started receiving renewals for their windstorm insurance and saw premiums that in some cases had tripled. Two Key West residents with huge premium increases—Cindy DeRocher and Donna Moody—learned they were not alone.

On the evening of February 8, 2006, Fair Insurance Rates in Monroe (firmkeys. org), or FIRM, was born when DeRocher, Moody, and 32 neighbors got together and compared notes on their insurance rates. The group called its first town hall meeting about a week later. Approximately 120 individuals convened in a local middle school cafeteria. From the outset, the leaders asked the group to refrain from anger and focus on constructive solutions to their problem—after all, decision makers were used to hearing residents complain about insurance premiums.

In order to influence key public officials, as well as to counter insurance company arguments in favor of the rate increases, FIRM determined that it would need more information on several central issues. The first was financial impact. FIRM asked county residents to provide their actual premium statements so that the group could calculate the real dollars associated with increasing rates. This approach to research yielded dramatic results. In one case, FIRM discovered that rate increases had produced a $5,000 annual premium on a 900-square-foot home. The owner of a historic property that had weathered storms for more than a century received a $31,000 bill. Even worse, the average homeowner in the Keys was paying $610 per month—more than $7,000 each year—solely for windstorm insurance.

Interviews with real estate companies and employers also revealed that the rate increases were devastating the local workforce. Monroe County was the only county in Florida with a declining population because its police officers, teachers, nurses, and service workers simply could not afford to pay the rising monthly costs of homeowners' insurance.

Second, FIRM investigated rates statewide and learned that Monroe County rates were significantly higher than those of other hurricane-prone counties. For instance, rates in the Keys were twice as high as those in Palm Beach County, which had seen the landfall of two hurricanes in 2004 and had suffered more damage in 2005. Rates were nearly three times higher than those of Charlotte County in Southwest Florida, which Hurricane Charley had devastated in August 2004. Finally, they were four times higher than those in Florida's Panhandle, where Hurricane Ivan wreaked havoc in September 2004 and Tropical Storm Arlene and Hurricane Dennis hit in 2005.

Third, FIRM consulted with experts at the National Weather Service to determine whether windstorm insurance rate increases could be justified by some particular vulnerability of the Keys to hurricane-force winds. The weather experts concluded that the Keys' greatest threat in a hurricane came from water, not wind. Though Monroe has the longest coastline of any county in Florida, meteorologists denied that it was two, three, or four times more likely to be struck by a hurricane than were other coastal areas—despite what the windstorm rate increases suggested.

Fourth, FIRM collected actual insurance claims data for different counties and different hurricanes. The statistics showed that insurance claim payments per policy for storms of equivalent strength were consistently lower in Monroe than in other counties. In other words, insurance companies paid property owners far less for wind damage claims in Monroe County than they did in other parts of the state—but Keys residents were paying significantly more for insurance than were most of their fellow Floridians.

During a meeting with their state representative and insurance company officials, FIRM members received a copy of a spreadsheet showing premiums collected and claims paid for windstorm coverage in Broward, Miami–Dade, and Monroe counties. Over the previous four years, Monroe County had produced nearly $250 million in net operating profits from the primary type of wind coverage alone—an 80 percent profit margin. In contrast, the Miami–Dade County profit margin was 46 percent. Broward County's profit margin was 1 percent.

Finally, FIRM investigated whether homes and other buildings in the Keys were structurally more likely to suffer wind damage than those in other areas of the state. In several ways, the answer was "no." Historically, many early Keys homes had been sturdily constructed by shipbuilders who understood the possible ravages of hurricanes. Architects explained that Monroe County had long utilized stricter building codes for wind resistance than had the state at large. Local building department officials confirmed that standard Keys home-strengthening techniques—such as hurricane straps and shutters—were not practiced in other high-wind coastal areas of the state. Similarly, construction experts and academics confirmed that the metal roofs predominant in the Keys withstood storms better than did the asphalt and shingle roofs that are standard in the Florida Building Code.

FIRM took the research it had gathered and shared it with other county residents, reporters, legislators, state insurance regulators, and the Florida Cabinet. The investment of time and effort in collecting data brought welcome results. In early 2007, the state government rejected the proposed Monroe County rate increases, ordered that rates for the county be rolled back to pre-2005 levels, and passed legislation to address the statewide hurricane insurance crisis.

EFFECTIVE RESEARCH: A STEP-BY-STEP GUIDE

1. Above All, Be Credible

From a research standpoint, the biggest danger of the Information Age is the proliferation of unreliable or biased data, particularly data found on the Internet. Remember this cardinal rule of effective citizen participation: If you present a decision maker with information in support of your cause that turns out to be false, misleading, inaccurate, knowingly incomplete, or irrelevant, he or she is unlikely to believe future presentations and just as unlikely to support your position. Be assured that your opponents will look at your research as soon as they see it. If they cannot verify it, or if they can discredit it, their next stop will be the media or the decision maker's office to destroy your credibility.

On the other hand, if you consistently provide reliable data, you will enhance your credibility and the chances that the decision maker will keep an open mind. A checklist to avoid bad information might include the following admonitions.

First, don't rely on outdated information. Work with the most recent data possible. A study from 2016 may in fact use 2010 census information that has been overtaken by more current numbers. If your opponents notice the stale data, they will not hesitate to question its relevance.

Second, don't confine your research to your local community. The whole world of ideas does not reside in your zip code. Knowing how other entities similar to yours do the same task puts your issue in perspective. Have other communities dealt with this problem in the past? If so, how did they resolve it? Concentrate on those places comparable to yours that have implemented solutions or that utilize practices similar to those you are proposing. If a decision maker particularly respects a particular institution, such as one from which she earned a degree, data drawn from that institution could be particularly persuasive.

Third, take care in your use of biased sources. Although many foundations, organizations, and academic institutions attempt to be balanced and unbiased, some groups and think tanks produce information that reflects a particular political agenda or ideological viewpoint. For example, data collected from a business advocacy group may not sway a decision maker with close ties to organized labor, and vice versa. Publications from the Center on Budget and Policy Priorities (cbpp.org) or the Center for American Progress (americanprogress.org) are likely to have a more progressive or liberal bent than those from the American Enterprise Institute (aei.org) or the Heritage Foundation (heritage.org). Use of biased sources may cause a decision maker to assume that there is no unbiased or balanced data to support your cause. If you use a source with a well-known point of view, be prepared to explain why the information is nonetheless valuable—and if possible reinforce that data with research from unimpeachable sources.

Fourth, don't fail to investigate the credentials of your data source. A layperson who posts an Internet article on the environment is less likely to sway policymakers than is the state president of the National Wildlife Federation (nwf.org) or a distinguished university professor who has multiple degrees and years of experience studying ecosystem management.

Fifth, don't limit your research to traditional, usually secondary, source information. Consider demonstrating support for your cause by presenting decision makers with a signed petition that has been carefully developed and inscribed. Don't let sloppiness thwart your effort. Make sure that every name on the petition is legible, legitimate, and accompanied by accurate contact information. If the organization or person to whom you are presenting the information finds even a single name that is bogus, your credibility could be undermined and the petition ignored.

After you learn more about public opinion research in chapter 4, integrate the results of your opinion gathering into the overall body of research for the advocacy cause. For example, you might want to survey a statistically selected portion of the affected population. If you decide to test public opinion without the help of a professional pollster, your methods must be airtight. Accurately identify the group whose opinions you want to gauge so that your responses are meaningful.

Sixth, don't try to bury information that is unfavorable to your cause or pretend that it doesn't exist. Since you found it, you can assume that your opponents have done so as well. Instead, proactively present the "bad facts" and show how the other information you have discovered undermines their significance. Your willingness to admit that your case is less than perfect will boost your credibility and prevent opponents from springing the negative information unexpectedly.

Seventh, keep up to date. In this era of rapid change, even the best-researched facts must be continuously monitored to ensure they are current and haven't been overtaken by events. In 2010, I cochaired the President's Commission on the BP Deepwater Horizon oil spill in the Gulf of Mexico. During our investigation, the oil industry was adamant that state-of-the-art safety procedures and supervision were in place on the doomed platform. But we discovered they were not. You can imagine what that discovery did to the industry's credibility with the commission members.

2. Stay on Target

Although it is easy to get lost in the vast expanse of the Internet and other online search tools, you can navigate these resources effectively if you stay focused on the problem you have defined and the specific questions you need to answer in order to clarify the problem and identify possible solutions. The best political campaigns do this well. In 1980, Ronald Reagan framed his contest with incumbent Jimmy Carter using this pointed question: "Are you better off than you were four years ago?" Twelve years later, when Bill Clinton was running for president, his campaign posted a sign in the campaign headquarters:

CHANGE VS. MORE OF THE SAME

THE ECONOMY, STUPID

DON'T FORGET HEALTH CARE[14]

In other words, if an issue wasn't directly connected to the previous 12 years of Republican rule, the ailing national economy, or the lack of affordable health care for many Americans, the campaign wasn't going to discuss it. In the midst of a challenged economy in 2010, Floridians elected a former hospital executive, Rick Scott, as governor. He ran on the slogan "Let's Get to Work" and focused relentlessly on a job-creation message. And in 2015, after nearly 10 years of Conservative rule that some believed had become cynical and negative, Canada chose a new Liberal prime minister who ran a persistently optimistic campaign and promised to return "Sunny Ways" to the national government. As you do your own research, if you can similarly resist the urge to be distracted, the information at your fingertips can greatly strengthen your chances of prevailing in your cause.

In the same way that good research hinges on a clear definition of the problem, you will find it much easier to tap into the huge reservoir of information available if you have a good sense of which level of government has jurisdiction over the issue you want to address. Chapter 3 will help you answer the following questions: Is it a local, state, or federal government concern? Is there a quasi-public entity that governs the matter, such as the NCAA on intercollegiate athletic issues? Or is this a matter to be decided exclusively by nongovernmental organizations? Your research will be much more focused if you have a clear sense of the problem and who has the power to solve it.

3. Use All Your Tools

Please note that, though the amount of information available today is vast, the tools with which to access that data are relatively finite. Whether your issue is one of local, state, or federal concern, the "hard" research you collect will likely come from one of four sources: official sources, such as public bodies or agencies; organizational sources, such as foundations, advocacy groups, and think tanks; media sources, such as newspapers, news magazines, and television and radio news; and primary sources, such as interviews and other firsthand accounts or government records like laws and regulations, reports, or legislative testimony and debate. All of these sources can be found on the Internet or in repositories like government agencies or libraries.

One of the best ways to persuade a decision maker is through information provided either by that decision maker's own governmental entity or by similar or related entities. The good news is that public data are readily available, either in open form or through the use of public records laws. Here are some suggestions for tapping into these resources:

1. Governments at various levels put their raw data up on the Internet at no charge for researchers to use. There are literally thousands of data sets from hundreds of jurisdictions available to citizens as they pursue change in their issue area of interest. This statistical information is accessible in raw form so that citizens can present it in whatever manner they desire in support of

---

[14]George Stephanopoulos, *All Too Human: A Political Education* (New York: Little, Brown, 1999), 88.

their position on the issues. The federal government has established Data. gov (data.gov) to host over 188,000 data sets from multiple federal agencies. Open data for other levels of government are available at data.gov/cities, data. gov/counties, and data.gov/states. As former Indianapolis Mayor Stephen Goldsmith explains in his tips (see Tips from the Pros: Data Engagement for Innovative Solutions), communities usually achieve the best results when public officials actively share data and collaborate with citizens on finding solutions to pressing challenges.

2. Visit the Internet site of the federal, state, or local department or agency with jurisdiction over the issue you wish to research. The site itself may provide information on the very issue you want to address. At the very least, it will probably tell you with whom you want to speak to gather more information on the subject. Please note that the Internet now has specialized search sites for government information. USA.gov is a one-stop search shop that links to any ".gov" site, unless a site specifically excludes it from doing so, and also to nongovernment sites that host government data. This site is especially useful in seeking comparative information on what other cities or states have done related to your issue.

3. If the documents you seek aren't readily available online, you may need to make public records requests to obtain them. Either through the Freedom of Information Act (FOIA) at the federal government level or through public records or "sunshine" laws at the state or local levels, governments are often required by law to produce certain records upon request. Just be aware that public agencies are often permitted to charge you for the reasonable employee time and records duplication costs necessary to fulfill a records inquiry. Determine the price before moving forward. If it is too expensive, your request may be overly broad. See if you can narrow the request to lower the price. Look for the very helpful tips from VR Research President Mike Rice later in this section explaining how to excel in finding public records (see Tips from the Pros: Finding Public Records).

4. If your citizen initiative requires legislative approval, determine which legislative bodies—such as Congress, the state legislature, county commission, and city council—publish legislation, bill analyses, and committee information online and in certain designated libraries. Your best first stop would be the webpage of the particular legislative body, which you may be able to find through USA.gov or a simple Internet search. For example, congressional information can be found at the Library of Congress's legislative database, known as Thomas, after Thomas Jefferson (thomas.loc.gov). Consult the National Conference of State Legislatures (ncsl.org) for links to your state legislature. The National Association of Counties (naco.org) and National League of Cities (nlc.org) will help you find county and city commissions or councils.

5. Locate and make use of the legislative history—in other words, prior testimony, statements, and voting records—of the governmental body you are trying to influence. Some governmental entities keep very detailed records of past proceedings and make them easily available through the Internet. Others will require that you find these documents at a designated library or make public records requests to retrieve them. This legislative history can provide invaluable information about how the decision makers in your case

have previously voted on your subject and on what they have previously said about their legislative intent on the issue.

6. Take advantage of your powers as a constituent. Contact your city council member, county commissioner, mayor, state legislator, member of Congress, or U.S. senator to determine whether they or their staff members know anything about the issue, can help you research it, or can connect you with other citizens who have similar concerns or have experienced problems in your area of interest. They may also be able to put you in touch with public agency officials or administrators with subject matter expertise.

7. Each level of government has entities that monitor the efficiency and productivity of individual agencies. The federal government relies on the Government Accountability Office (gao.gov). States and localities have similar watchdog agencies. For example, in Florida, the Office of Program Policy Analysis and Government Accountability (oppaga.state.fl.us) performs this function. When you find the local or state agency that performs this function in your area, visit its website or contact officials by telephone or e-mail to determine whether they have previously analyzed the problem you want to solve.

8. For problems at the state and local level, take advantage of the umbrella organizations of policymakers that focus on larger issues of universal state and local concern. For state-level governance, these include (among others) the Council of State Governments (csg.org), the National Governors Association (nga.org), and the previously mentioned National Conference of State Legislators. Uniquely local concerns are the province of the U.S. Conference of Mayors (usmayors.org), as well as the previously cited National Association of Counties and National League of Cities. These organizations provide a high-level, summary view of issues and potential solutions and direct you to research worth exploring in greater detail. Additionally, they may have staff members who specialize in various issue areas ranging from criminal justice to early childhood education to urban renewal. Finally, look for state affiliates or related bodies—e.g., Kentucky League of Cities (klc.org), Nevada Association of Counties (nvnaco.org), Texas Municipal League (tml.org)—that provide the same function as the national organizations but with a focus on your state.

9. National organizations also exist for specific policy issues at the federal, state, and local levels. Although there is no shortage of policy-oriented entities focused on Congress and the White House, make sure to determine which ones are most credible before you rely on research obtained from them. For state and local issues, take advantage of the fact that many governmental offices, elected or appointed, can be found in multiple jurisdictions, and lots of policy issues are of common interest across political boundaries. Just a few of the organizations that concentrate on shared state and local policy concerns include the Education Commission of the States (ecs.org), the National Association of Insurance Commissioners (naic.org), the National Association of State Budget Officers (nasbo.org), and the Environmental Council of the States (ecos.org). These organizations also have research arms and conference proceedings that can be valuable in finding information on specific state and local issues.

10. Some media outlets cover nothing but governmental policy and operations. Good examples of unbiased sources include *Governing* (governing.com) and *American City & County* (americancityandcounty.com). Keeping a close eye on these kinds of publications may help you discover new developments or innovations that would be useful to your own citizen advocacy.

11. Follow possible sources on social media, where they often post new data, research, or insights that could be vital to your cause. Most if not all of the governments, quasi-governmental agencies, and related advocacy or media organizations have active presences on various social media sites. For example, the City of Madison, Wisconsin (cityofmadison.com/outreach), is on Facebook, Flickr, Twitter, and YouTube. The California State Association of Counties (csac.counties.org) can be found on YouTube, Facebook, Twitter, LinkedIn, and Instagram. *Governing* (governing.com) is visible on Pinterest, Twitter, Facebook, YouTube, and LinkedIn. Stay connected online so you always have the freshest information to strengthen your case. Post, share, forward, tag, or re-tweet what you find to connect with others who may share your interest—and who can offer data of their own.

TIPS FROM THE PROS

Data Engagement Leads to Innovative Solutions
STEPHEN GOLDSMITH

True public value is created when citizens engage as partners with their governments, especially at the local level, to coproduce solutions and not simply to advocate for more public resources. How, then, should citizens and officials work together to achieve innovation and effectiveness in resolving challenges and translating engagement into effective service delivery?

Officials have a responsibility to provide well-visualized and transparent data that can be easily used by the public, whether community groups, civic hackers, data journalists, or app developers. The data should include detailed performance reports that are coded geographically and updated in real time. The raw data sets should also be downloadable so that interested citizens can draw their own insights from the data. Houston and Boston, for instance, have designed public-facing performance-analytics dashboards that allow interested citizens to gain insights on city operations, budgets and expenditures, 311 requests, and personnel metrics: see, respectively, performance.houstontx.gov/performanceinsight and cityofboston.gov/bar. Los Angeles is one of many cities that has

(Continued)

(Continued)

an open data portal, which provides up-to-date city information and analytics to the public (see data.lacity.org).

Voters and civic groups, in return, should help their elected representatives devise solutions to the problems they regularly identify. If a civic group advocates for a new program, it should be prepared to find evidence that the existing program is not effective in order to demonstrate why public investments should be repurposed. A group advocating for an increase in publicly funded pre-K programs, for instance, might help focus on issues of quality as well as quantity. Or a neighborhood group in a community suffering repetitive potholes might identify the underlying drainage issue that, if corrected, will prevent future problems and future spending.

Detroiters took up this role of tackling public problems with the Blight Removal Task Force (timetoendblight.com), which brought together public officials, private donors, and community volunteers to launch Motor City Mapping (motorcitymapping.org), a digitization effort inviting citizens to photograph and report information about blighted properties. The Task Force used the collected data to produce a report with recommendations to help the city understand urban blight and how to allocate resources more productively. Chicago resident Tom Kompare used open data about flu shot accessibility from the health department to create Chicago Flu Shots (chicagoflushots.org), a mapping tool hosted by civic organization Smart Chicago (smartchicagocollaborative.org) that helps city residents find free flu shot clinics in their neighborhood. In New York, Heat Seek NYC (heatseeknyc.com) accessed open 311 data, which showed that the Department of Housing Preservation and Development receives 200,000 heating-related complaints a year from tenants for which only a small percentage of landlords are held accountable. The team made a system of sensors that automatically collects heating data in apartments with unallowably low temperatures and records these measurements in an online log that is shared with city agencies to track patterns of landlord negligence.

Public officials need the public, and they need to respond to the public. Coproduction of governmental solutions to citizen challenges requires effective communication and depends on contributions from the public in the form of persuasive evidence or data, problem-solving insights, identification of programs that do not work, and suggestions for interventions that, if made, will prevent future expenses.

Stephen Goldsmith is the Daniel Paul Professor of the Practice of Government and the director of the Innovations in American Government Program at Harvard's Kennedy School of Government. He currently directs Data-Smart City Solutions, a project to highlight local government efforts to use new technologies that connect breakthroughs in the use of big data analytics with community input to reshape the relationship between government and citizen. He previously served as deputy mayor of New York and mayor of Indianapolis, where he earned a reputation as one of the country's leaders in public-private partnerships, competition, and privatization. Mayor Goldsmith was also the chief domestic policy advisor to the George W. Bush campaign in 2000, the chair of the Corporation for National and Community Service, and the district attorney for Marion County, Indiana, from 1979 to 1990.

 itizen researchers interested in effecting change should exercise their right to government records using the federal Freedom of Information Act (FOIA) and the various state equivalents known alternately as open records or sunshine laws. Here's how:

Know the law: As a starting point, familiarize yourself with the FOIA statute or your state open records law. The Reporters Committee for Freedom of the Press (rcfp.org) provides several online resources to help you draft and submit a request.

Advance your request: Like painting a house, obtaining government records is all about the preparation. Prior to drafting your request (and I do recommend submitting your request in writing), make sure you know where to send it. Identify a real person who can receive your request. At federal and state agencies, this person will be a government employee who spends his or her day working with requestors. In a city or county, it may be the city or county clerk or another official responsible for responding to records requests. These professionals have seen hundreds if not thousands of requests, so use them as a resource. Ask them how to frame your request and how others have done so in the past when asking for the same or similar information.

While knowing the law is a must, it is even more important to be nice when interacting with government employees. Remember, you own the information, but they control it. You are much more likely to get quick access to the data you are seeking if you don't walk around citing the law to everyone you speak with. You don't lose anything by being nice, nor do you give up your right to sue for information that you were wrongly denied.

One effective method when advancing your request is to first "FOIA the FOIAs." On the federal level, use FOIAonline (foiaonline.regulations.gov) to search for requests made by others with a similar interest. States, cities, and federal agencies that do not yet participate in FOIAonline keep their own log of past requests. Get the logs and you might find that you can save time and expense by simply asking (again) for a set of documents that have been prepared previously.

Follow up: Once your request is filed, a clock starts to tick and agencies must respond and provide responsive records within statutory time limits. However, requests that aren't properly followed up have a tendency to work their way to the bottom of the response pile, or worse, get lost. A good rule is to touch base with your agency contact no less than once a week. Doing so will have the dual benefit of letting the agency know that you care and that you are not going away.

Adjust: Think of open records requests as conversations between you and the caretaker agency. As people do in any conversation, you will need to adjust and respond. This often entails negotiating the order in which the records you have requested will be

(Continued)

(Continued)

released. There is no statutory requirement that agencies release the records you have requested all at once, and many agencies will attempt to slow down their overall response time, especially if you are requesting documents that could embarrass the agency. So request that the agency release records as they are prepared.

You may also learn in the course of your follow-up conversations that the information you originally requested is available more quickly in another form. For example, after you submit a request for an agency's expense reports, the agency might quote a lengthy response time to gather hundreds of individual expense documents. But, in conversation with the agency, you may learn that the same information you originally sought has already been summarized in an agency report or audit that can be provided to you immediately.

Happy FOIAing!

VR Research (vrresearch.com) President Mike Rice is a specialist in using the Freedom of Information Act and state public records laws. He works directly with clients to frame questions and design research methods. Mike has spent his entire career in public records and opposition research. Prior to co-founding VR Research in 1995, Mike worked as Research Director for the California Democratic Party and on political campaigns throughout the country. He heads VR Research's Oakland office.

Of course, public entities and their support organizations do not have a monopoly on helpful information. You should also explore nongovernmental sources in search of data that will be useful to your initiative. For example, consider these options:

1. Academic experts can be very helpful in your efforts to change public policy. As Scholars Strategy Institute (scholarsstrategynetwork.org) Executive Director Avi Green explains in his tips (see Tips From The Pros: Make the Most of University Researchers), professors are highly credible sources whose research and commentary can help you find solutions and bolster your cause with media, potential coalition partners, funders, and decision makers.

2. Many colleges and universities have public policy centers or special institutes. Examine universities and colleges in your state or locality to determine if any are studying your area of concern. If so, see what information they make available online, or contact the faculty member in charge of that field of research

3. Think tanks such as the Brookings Institution and the Cato Institute also produce extensive research on public policy issues, but as mentioned earlier, you should be mindful of potential biases. To find major think tanks, visit the Harvard Kennedy School's Think Tank Search page (guides.library.harvard.edu/hks/think_tank_search).

4. Check out various nonpartisan foundations that focus on public policy challenges, such as the Pew Research Center (pewresearch.org) or the Annie E. Casey (aecf.org), Bill & Melinda Gates (gatesfoundation.org), Ford (fordfoundation.org), Henry J. Kaiser Family (kff.org), MacArthur (macfound.org), or Robert Wood Johnson (rwjf.org) foundations to see if they have funded

research relevant to your problem. This information should be available on their respective websites, but you may need to call and speak to specific scholars directly.

5. Don't overlook advocacy organizations whose goals align with yours. If you are seeking a change in environmental policy, groups such as the National Recreation and Park Association (nrpa.org) and Sierra Club (sierraclub.org) might be able to share research that is useful to your efforts. If your aim is to expand energy production, the American Petroleum Institute (api.org) could be a helpful resource. At the local, state, and national levels, organizations focusing on subjects from agriculture to zoology exist and may be able to point you in the right direction.

6. Use the Internet to identify sources of information from newspapers and other credible online media sources. If you can't access articles through the Internet, a public or university library in your area may have full access to online news services and will have back issues of many publications. These articles will have their own news value and can also help point you to relevant studies, experts, and government data.

7. The same social media rule applies to these nongovernmental information sources: Follow them diligently so that you always have the most recent research, news, or studies on your citizen advocacy issue. Since credibility is king, your ability to provide reliable, up-to-the-minute data will give you an advantage over other advocates who are not as nimble. Tracking Pew Research Center (pewresearch.org/follow-us) at Twitter, Facebook, Tumblr, or LinkedIn; the Gerald R. Ford School of Public Policy at the University of Michigan (fordschool.umich.edu/about/contact-us) on those same outlets plus Pinterest, Flickr, or Google+; or another research source on social media puts you in the favorable position to be knowledgeable and current—a winning combination.

TIPS FROM THE PROS

Make the Most of University Researchers
AVI GREEN

America faces pressing challenges and needs sound policies to meet them. Yet from Washington to state capitals to city halls, public policy debates are rarely informed by the best research. All too often, they aren't even grounded in facts.

University professors can help. Among America's 1.5 million professors are researchers working on every issue. But with notable exceptions, the best scholars are seldom involved in public policy debates.

The Scholars Strategy Network was created to help. A voluntary, nationwide membership organization for professors and graduate students, the network seeks to improve

(Continued)

(Continued)

public policy and strengthen democracy by connecting scholars and their research to policymakers, citizens' associations, and the media. Professors can help citizens:

- **Understand complex problems.** In the wake of the death of Michael Brown and the unrest in Ferguson, Missouri, Todd Swanstrom, a professor at the University of Missouri-St. Louis, reached out to his colleagues to help citizens untangle the complex issues facing the region. In the St. Louis Post-Dispatch, Swanstrom and his colleagues published no fewer than five separate op-eds on issues ranging from disconnections between police officers and the community to low-turnout elections to municipal governments relying on fines.
- **Prioritize solutions.** When Massachusetts Senate President Stanley Rosenberg was looking for policies to help working families and reduce economic inequality, scholars considered dozens of ideas before identifying 15 promising options. Their top suggestion: raising the state's Earned Income Tax Credit. Rosenberg, a Democrat, reached out to Governor Charlie Baker, a Republican. As the debate moved forward in the legislature, scholars testified, briefed reporters, and provided expert support to Children's Healthwatch, the leading civic organization on the issue. Within a year, the state passed a law to increase the tax credit by 50 percent.
- **Send compelling messages.** College professors are ranked as highly trustworthy in polling. By speaking to the public, testifying at hearings, talking to reporters, or writing op-eds, they can make a difference in public debates. For example, when a bipartisan coalition in Oklahoma suggested that the state let citizens register to vote online, Oklahoma State University Professor Rebekah Herrick wrote an op-ed for the Daily Oklahoman explaining the merits of the idea. The reform became law soon after.

Although search engines such as Google can help you find professors, the Scholars Strategy Network is a better place to start because every researcher listed on the site wants to use her or his research to improve public policy. The network's website also features over 500 two-page briefs that use clear, everyday language to explain research findings without jargon. And SSN staff members, also listed on the website, are happy to help citizens find scholars whose expertise may be appropriate to address specific challenges.

Avi Green is the executive director of the Scholars Strategy Network (scholarsstrategynetwork. org) and hosts the network's podcast, No Jargon (www.scholarsstrategynetwork.org/no-jargon). Previously, Avi served as the executive director of MassVOTE (massvote.org), where he focused on searching for solutions to the problems that lead people not to vote.

4. Harness the Power of Real People

An old adage says, "A picture is worth a thousand words." Similarly, though information is important, a powerful human story is more compelling than a thousand statistics in persuading decision makers as to the rightness of a cause. Consider the following pieces of research:

Example A: Your town backs up to a forested area. On the other side of the woods is a small manufacturing plant that is rumored to have dumped toxic chemical wastes in the forest for many years. You find several complex scientific studies showing that your town's groundwater supply may have higher than normal rates of the chemicals used in or discharged from the plant.

Example B: Over the past five years the family whose house is closest to the wooded area has lost three children to a kind of leukemia often caused by the chemicals used by the plant. The parents had another child in hopes of finding a bone marrow match for the older children, but he has recently shown signs of leukemia.[15]

Both examples suggest that something is amiss with the local environmental conditions, but the latter is far more likely to draw media coverage and persuade regulators to investigate the plant than is the first example. It isn't hard to see why. Although collecting research studies, statistical data, and other facts on paper is critical to building a compelling case, human beings are creatures of both intellect and emotion. The best citizen initiatives take a two-pronged approach, using cold, hard facts to establish credibility and warm-blooded people to humanize an issue and build popular support. This does not mean that successful citizen advocacy requires a tragedy like the one described in "Example B." But it does require the involvement of everyday people because their opinions, comments, and stories are far more memorable than numbers on spreadsheets.

Finding the real people who can influence a public policy issue is not an easy task. It requires effective planning, persistence, and communication. But there are proven ways to gather information from real people in support of a cause:

First, revisit the problem you want to solve. Who else in the community might have a stake in your issue? Whether these stakeholders are neighbors, store owners, volunteer agencies, or organizations, get together with them in person, by phone, or by e-mail, and find out what they know and believe about the issue.

Second, use technology to your benefit. In the same way that social media has helped you reconnect with long-lost friends or participate in community conversations, tools like Facebook, Twitter, or Pinterest can help you track down real-life examples of people affected by the problem you are trying to solve. Some communities have online news analysis and discussion sites (such as metrojacksonville.com), which offer users the opportunity to post comments and exchange ideas. Visit YouTube or Vimeo to see if you can find anyone who has weighed in on your subject, or submit a video to solicit comments. Go live on Periscope or Facebook to generate responses. Provide compelling photographs on Instagram, Flickr, or Snapchat to see if your pictures are worth a thousand words or more of feedback. Launch a Reddit discussion by posting a link to the right subreddit.

Third, you can organize discussions, town meetings, and other gatherings to collect information and various viewpoints on your issue. These conversations may generate the personal anecdotes that are so powerful in persuading decision makers, or they could even produce possible solutions.

---

[15] The examples are inspired by Jonathan Harr, *A Civil Action* (New York: Random House, 1995).

Fourth, news reporters are likely consumers of any "real life" perspectives you can add to a public policy issue. But these media representatives can also *produce* this kind of information. If you build relationships with reporters and provide them with valuable research that informs their stories, you will encourage them to use their superior resources to dig deeper and uproot new sources and information that you could not find on your own. The deeper they dig, and the more they uncover, the more it will force a decision maker to pay attention.

KNOWLEDGE CAN BE POWER—IF YOU USE IT

Cynics claim that effective citizenship is more about who you know than what you know. In truth, what one knows is often the key to shaping debate and determining the final outcome of public policy controversies.

In this Information Age, anyone can use research effectively in a public policy debate. Elected officials—governors, mayors, city council members, county commissioners, state legislators, and members of Congress—rarely have the time or staff resources to research problems comprehensively on their own. A citizen who effectively informs them is much more likely to earn their support than one who does not.

Bacon's statement that "knowledge is power" is true—but only if those with the knowledge know how to use it effectively in advancing toward their goals. To lead a successful citizen action, you must use the knowledge you have gained to build a coalition of allies, rebut the arguments of those who may oppose you, enlist the media to help you win broad support for your aims, earn financial supporters, fashion techniques to help you gauge public opinion, and otherwise convince decision makers that your position should become theirs. The coming chapters will help you transform the raw knowledge you gain into a powerful tool for changing the way governmental decision makers handle your issue.

CHECKLIST FOR ACTION

☐ Above all, be credible.

- Work with the most recent data possible.
- Don't confine your research to your local community.
- Use unbiased resources.
- Investigate the credentials of your data source.
- Use more than secondary sources.
- Admit unfavorable information.
- Keep your data current.

☐ Stay on target.
☐ Use all of your research tools.
☐ Harness the power of real people.

- Find other community members who might have a stake in your issue.
- Use modern technology to locate examples.
- Gather people together to hear viewpoints and collect anecdotes.
- Build media relationships.

3 The Buck Stops Where?

Identifying Who in Government Can Fix Your Problem

"I'm the decider, and I decide what is best."

—President George W. Bush,
statement to the media, April 2006[1]

Putting the "Be" in South Beach*

Police officers escort design preservation activist Barbara Baer Capitman from her vigil protesting historic Art Deco building demolition on the porch of the Senator Hotel in Miami Beach.

---

[1] "Bush: 'I'm the Decider' on Rumsfeld," *CNN Politics*, April 18, 2006, www.cnn.com/2006/POLITICS/ 04/18/rumsfeld/

*Several distinguished South Floridians and three books provided the background for this case study. Arva Parks and Ruth Shack shared their extensive knowledge and memories of Miami–Dade County history. Historic Preservation Officer Daniel Ciraldo of the Miami–Dade Preservation League provided helpful information on current MDPL initiatives. The three books were Michael H. Roley,

Ask your friends and neighbors what they know about South Beach, and expect to receive a wide range of answers. Pop culture history buffs will recall undercover cops Sonny Crockett and Rico Tubbs speeding down Ocean Drive or across Biscayne Bay in *Miami Vice*, or they might think of more recent pop culture publicity, like the intelligence agents in *Burn Notice* or certain Kardashian children "taking" Miami. Celebrity watchers know it as the home away from home of Sean Combs, Rosie O'Donnell, and numerous other stars. Fashion mavens flock to South Beach to honor the late Gianni Versace, who died there in 1997 and whose home is now a luxury hotel and restaurant.[2] Partygoers celebrate the world-famous restaurants and nightclubs. Real estate experts think of multimillion-dollar condominiums. Movie fans laugh at memorable lines from *The Birdcage*. Seafood lovers flock to Joe's Stone Crabs. Architects marvel at the Art Deco structures. Sports fans remember LeBron James's announcement that he would "take . . . [his] talents to South Beach."[3] He has since taken them back to Cleveland, and helped both cities win NBA titles.

None of the people you ask are likely to know the name of the person most responsible for making South Beach what it is today. Barbara Capitman did not have Don Johnson's fame or Versace's following. But she did have a deep love and appreciation for South Miami Beach's unique architectural style, the determination to preserve that distinct look, and a keen understanding of those government agencies and programs that could help her safeguard this treasured piece of South Florida history and culture. Those qualities proved to be more than enough to overwhelm better-funded forces that would have consigned Miami Beach's Art Deco district to the dustbin of history.

For the fifty years after the end of World War I, Miami Beach was a haven for both millionaires and middle-class families, who used it as a vacation spot, winter retreat, or year-around home. Jackie Gleason taped his television show there in the 1960s. It became the center of the political universe in 1968, when Republicans held their presidential nominating convention there, and again in 1972, when both the Democrats and the Republicans met there. But by the mid-1970s South Beach had fallen on hard times. The economy was in recession, and tourism had slowed to a trickle. Many of the famous Art Deco hotels had become rundown apartments for fixed-income retirees. Others sat empty and deteriorated. Drug traffickers used the area as a base of operations.

In short, South Miami Beach was primed for a takeover—and local developers made the first move. In 1969, the Florida Legislature enacted the Community

---

Linda G. Polansky, and Aristides J. Millas, *Old Miami Beach, A Case Study in Historic Preservation, July 1976–July 1980* (Miami Beach: Miami Design Preservation League, 1994); M. Barron Stofik, *Saving South Beach* (Gainesville: University Press of Florida, 2005); and Bill Wisser, *South Beach: America's Riviera, Miami Beach, Florida* (New York: Arcade Publishing, 1995). All unattributed quotations are from these sources or individuals.

[2] Carol Driver, "Gianni Versace's Miami Mansion Reopens as Luxury Hotel," *Daily Mail Online*, March 17, 2014, www.dailymail.co.uk/travel/article-2582544/Gianni-Versaces-Miami-mansion-reopens-luxury-hotel-Villa-Barton-G.html and www.miami.com/gianni039s-villa-open-former-versace-mansion-south-beach-article

[3] "LeBron James Makes His Decision: Miami," Associated Press YouTube video, July 8, 2010.

Redevelopment Act, legislation that authorized the creation of special districts to encourage economic development in blighted areas. The Miami Beach Redevelopment Agency (RDA) was created in 1973. Three years later, on July 26, 1976, it proudly released its plans for a new Miami Beach. The RDA proposed to demolish all structures on the southernmost portion of the island and replace them with new luxury hotels, condominiums, restaurants, and shops. Conventional wisdom held that the RDA plan was actually the first step in a more ambitious redevelopment that would eventually encompass all of historic South Beach and wipe out its Art Deco heritage.

But the RDA had not counted on Barbara Capitman. Born Barbara Baer, Capitman was part of a family that had helped to pioneer the Art Deco boom of the 1930s and 1940s. She had grown up surrounded by the mixture of industrial design and regional architecture that was the essence of Art Deco.

Barbara married a man who was himself a pioneer in visual design and marketing. In 1976, at age 56 and recently widowed, she possessed the knowledge, passion, and skills to match the political and economic power of the Miami Beach establishment.

The same month that the RDA announced its plan, Capitman led the creation of the Miami Design Preservation League (MDPL). Not lacking in marketing savvy, Capitman realized that Vietnam and Watergate had taken a huge toll on the nation, and that Americans might respond favorably to cultural reminders of a time before the turmoil of the late 1960s and early 1970s. Powering memories of the celebrities and other "beautiful people" who had entertained and vacationed there, the Art Deco structures embodied a romance and sophistication that might be more valuable than the planned redevelopment. But even more important, Capitman discerned that a confusing labyrinth of governmental, quasi-governmental, and private entities would play a key role in deciding South Beach's future. She was determined to understand and successfully negotiate that maze—with the goal of designating South Beach as a historic district so as to frustrate the RDA's plans to turn the island into another garden-variety tourist destination.

Capitman's immediate goal was to persuade the U.S. Department of the Interior to include South Beach on its National Register of Historic Places. But she also knew that other government agencies would have to get involved first, so she engaged federal, state, and local entities in a variety of ways. Because no private developer would fund her admittedly risky plan, Capitman would need federal assistance to secure the required financing. After Congress passed the 1976 tax reform, the modernization of existing low-income housing was one of the few viable tax shelters. Working with her son, Andrew, a Yale University economics graduate with a master's degree from the University of Miami's Graduate School of Business, Capitman learned how the U.S. Department of Housing and Urban Development (HUD) and the National Trust for Historic Preservation administered those benefits. The mother-and-son team helped to demystify these arcane tax provisions for other investors. They also obtained funds from the federal Community Development Block Grant (CDBG) program to plan and design the restoration.

Although the federal government would decide South Beach's historical status, Capitman realized that she would probably not succeed in her goal if the City of Miami Beach opposed her efforts. In October 1977, the MDPL endorsed and campaigned for Dr. Leonard Haber, a Miami Beach mayoral candidate who was an Art

Deco restoration supporter. When Haber won the race, he carried into office a slate of like-minded city commission candidates.

Capitman's support of the Haber slate paid off immediately. Shortly after he was sworn in, Mayor Haber led the media on a walk through the Art Deco district and proclaimed that "there is a broad and deep national interest in this area and it looks like preservation and restoration can be the economic turning point for Miami Beach." Even more significantly, the city made MDPL a planning partner. In the early 1970s, the Florida Legislature and Governor Reubin Askew adopted sweeping new growth-management legislation—the Florida Environmental Land and Water Management Act of 1972, of which I was proud to be the primary sponsor. The plan required local governments to develop comprehensive land and water development plans with enforcement mechanisms. As the City of Miami Beach drafted its plan, it granted MDPL a contract to prepare the portion encompassing the historic areas of South Miami Beach.

In early 1978, with the city's support seemingly secured, the MDPL turned full time to the task of placing South Beach on the National Register of Historic Places. That spring, Capitman led a steady stream of federal and state officials—all of whose approval would be necessary to secure historic status—on tours of Miami Beach. Many were effusive in their praise of the Art Deco district. It seemed that restoration had the momentum it needed to succeed.

But a funny thing happened on the way to apparent success: The MDPL did its best to snatch defeat from the jaws of victory. Given the opportunity to shape Miami Beach's comprehensive plan, the MDPL submitted a historic district report that professional planners found confusing and unorganized and never took seriously. When the city updated its state-required comprehensive plan in June 1978, the proposal did not include historic preservation. Then, rather than attempting to work out their differences with the city, MDPL members sought to reverse the omission through publishing criticism in sympathetic local newspapers. Miami Beach leaders saw this media strategy as an end run designed to embarrass them, and they reacted angrily. This was a grave development. The MDPL would need the city's cooperation and support to implement historic preservation in South Beach. Less than six months before, that cooperation had seemed assured. Now it was in serious peril.

Into this breach stepped Barbara Capitman, aptly described as a leader "who is able to leap short and tall commissioners with a single bound, jumble city brass and red tape, never take no for an answer, leave the most poised and sophisticated politicians exasperated and scratching their heads in wonderment." Capitman refused to give up. In October 1978, she coordinated an "Art Deco Week in Old Miami Beach" in conjunction with the national convention of the National Recreation and Park Association. The two events combined to showcase the historic district idea to influential national visitors and unconvinced local residents.

Capitman's double whammy had the desired effect of bringing the city around and influencing key officials throughout government. During the Art Deco Week, the City of Miami Beach invited federal, state, and local officials to a workshop where they could learn more about the Art Deco district. The timing was perfect. Soon thereafter developers were blocked from razing historic motion picture houses, the post office, and certain hotels after Capitman and the MDPL staged dramatic demonstrations and challenged the reconstruction building permit.

In September 1978, the MDPL submitted its application for historic designation to Florida's state historic preservation officer, Robert Williams. Williams refused to accept the application after determining that it contained incorrect information and lacked a statement of significance. After two weeks of frenzied work, the MDPL eliminated those deficiencies, and Florida accepted the submission.

Barbara Capitman understood the critical importance of interacting with decision makers at every level of the process. Throughout the campaign, she had personally made contact with relevant officials from various levels of government, including two federal departments (Interior and Housing and Urban Development), the State of Florida, the City of Miami Beach, and Dade County. She wasn't about to let up now. Capitman made almost daily calls to Williams, his staff, and members of the review board to reiterate the importance of expediting a favorable review. She knew that Williams, a former North Florida state senator, had a passion for Florida history. Capitman emphasized that South Beach would be the first neighborhood established in the twentieth century to receive historic designation—a significant distinction for Florida. As one MDPL member put it, "It was her baby, and she intended to have a healthy, on-time delivery."

The Florida Historic Preservation Board met on February 8, 1979, at the University of Florida in Gainesville. Expecting fierce opposition to its plan, the MDPL assembled a team of fifteen experts and residents for the meeting. Following their presentations, the review board chairman admitted that he didn't "know a damn about Art Deco... but it does represent a distinct era of history." His colleagues agreed, and the board voted unanimously to approve the district.

The state forwarded its approval to the National Register of Historic Places in Washington, D.C. The agency gave affected Miami Beach property owners 30 days to comment. Federal officials made field visits. Finally, on May 14, 1979—two years, ten months, and nineteen days after the Miami Beach Redevelopment Agency announced plans to demolish the Art Deco area—the National Register officially designated a one-square-mile area of Miami Beach as a national historic district.

Over the next two decades, what we now think of as South Beach rose and flourished because Barbara Capitman and her allies clearly defined their challenge and then identified the governmental entities they needed to drive toward a solution. Their target wasn't cut and dried. Although only the National Register of Historic Places could ultimately grant an historical designation, the MDPL required approval and assistance from agencies and officials scattered throughout the local, state, and federal government before the National Register would even consider the proposal. Capitman's mastery of this spider's web of governmental involvement enabled her to recruit investors, block demolition permits, draft land use rules, defeat opponents with substantially greater financial resources—and rescue a neighborhood.

The MDPL won a critical triumph with the National Register designation. But, as is frequently the case with citizen initiatives, one victory was not all that was needed to protect historic South Beach. Although the National Register's designation gave South Beach recognition and tax benefits for its rehabilitation, the substance of preservation would be in local ordinances, codes, and enforcement. The continuing nature of the struggle was clear within months of the National Register's listing, when four landmarks—El Chico Restaurant, the Boulevard Hotel, the New Yorker Hotel, and the Senator Hotel—were reduced to rubble.

The battlefield shifted back to local government. Although Dade County had adopted a historic preservation ordinance by July 1981, the City of Miami Beach steadfastly resisted. When the Miami Beach City Commission finally passed its own ordinance—under threat of losing all authority in this area to the county government—preservationist attorneys described it as the weakest one in the nation.

Two years later, Barbara Capitman ran for a city commission seat in the 1983 city elections. Her confrontational style, which had been effective in securing the national designation, was equally ineffective in the election campaign. In a five-candidate field, she finished last. Two years later, Abe Resnick, a prominent Miami Beach developer who had tangled with Capitman over the demolition of the New Yorker Hotel, won a city commission seat. He quickly became the strongest and most assertive elected voice against South Beach preservation.

But these setbacks were temporary and against the tide of history. Continuing her work as a private citizen, Capitman expanded her coalition of allies, including sympathetic members of the city commission. It also helped that conditions on the ground were changing dramatically. South Beach was emerging as a new international destination for celebrities, show business personalities, supermodels and their photographers, arts and culture aficionados, and the LGBT community. South Beach's makeover was highlighted in *Miami Vice,* one of the most popular television series of the mid-1980s. The show introduced hundreds of millions of American and international television viewers to South Beach and depicted it as a neon paradise, filled with excitement, tinged with danger, and populated by beautiful people. *Travel and Leisure* magazine described South Beach as the "hippest hangout on earth."[4] This notoriety brought booming economic advantages, and many Miami Beach power brokers who previously had opposed preservation became supporters.

This new support produced tangible results. Between 1986 and 1990, Miami Beach created three preservation districts: Espanola Way, Collins Avenue, and Flamingo Park. These new safe havens combined to preserve 85 percent of the South Beach historic district. Unfortunately, these were the last triumphs in which Capitman would share. On the eve of her seventieth birthday, she fell ill, was hospitalized, and died on March 29, 1990. The city commission recognized her contribution by naming one block in the historic district after her: Barbara Capitman Way. Abe Resnick was the only commission member to vote no.

Capitman's death meant that she was not there to witness the climactic year—1992—in the preservation of South Beach. The year began with preservationists reaching a painful compromise with developers; they would allow a convention-scale hotel to be built in South Beach provided that historic oceanfront hotels in the northeastern sector of the district were incorporated into the design. In August, Hurricane Andrew ravaged Dade County but largely spared the historic buildings.

Finally, in October, the National Trust for Historic Preservation held its national conference in Miami. As Capitman had done fifteen years before, preservationists used the attention from this event to press the city commission for a final

---

[4] "Devine Deco-Dence: Miami's South Beach," *Travel and Leisure*, October 1992 quoted in *Saving South Beach*, by Mary Barron Stofik, xii.

vote that would extend a protective ordinance to the entire South Beach historic district. On October 24, with Resnick absent, the commission approved the extension unanimously. Seventeen years after the Miami Design Preservation League was founded, and thirteen years after national designation, historic South Beach was safe.

POSTSCRIPT: THE MISSION CONTINUES

Almost exactly forty years after Barbara Capitman launched the Miami Design Preservation League, the MDPL continues its advocacy with multiple levels of government—now with a focus on future threats to historic resources. Since Miami Beach is at risk of the effects of climate change and sea level rise, MDPL leaders are working to identify solutions that marry preservation and mitigation.

- Through local government, MDPL seeks new incentives to encourage property owners to make their buildings more resilient.
- Working with state officials, MDPL hopes to reform the Florida Building Code and facilitate the adaptation of historic properties.
- MDPL's efforts at the national level include pursuing Federal Emergency Management Agency (FEMA) grants to anticipate and blunt the effects of climate change and sea level rise.

Today's MDPL mission is the same as it was when the league faced down Miami Beach redevelopment plans: Protect historic structures through strategies that could become a model for other communities. More than 25 years after her death, Barbara Capitman's legacy is still preserving South Beach.

YOU KNOW THE PROBLEM—WHO HAS THE SOLUTION?

You should now have a better grasp on what it is to formulate a problem for which governmental action can provide a solution—and in the terms that will be most advantageous to your cause. But even a well-defined problem cannot be solved until you determine which government agency has the power to address your problem. Is it a local problem or a challenge that requires statewide or even national attention? Does your proposed solution require legislative, executive, or judicial approval, or some combination of all three? Which specific government agency has the power to make or break your initiative or, alternatively, has the most influence to determine its fate? The answers to these questions will light your path to the decision makers who can turn your vision into reality.

The identification of the appropriate decision makers is the source of some of the worst misconceptions in the entire citizen advocacy process. In the introduction to this book, I shared the story of my visit to Samuel W. Wolfson High School in Jacksonville, Florida, when I was a member of the Florida Legislature in the early 1970s. During that visit, students complained about the food in the school cafeteria, forcing me to explain that Tallahassee legislators had no say over local school district menus. When I asked who else they had consulted about their problem, they told me they had approached Jacksonville's mayor and sheriff, both to no avail because neither of those officeholders had any power to order changes in school cafeteria cuisine. The officials who could do something about it—the cafeteria manager, principal, school superintendent, and school board—had been let off the hook.

My purpose in sharing this story is not to criticize either Wolfson High School or those individual students. Wolfson has produced many outstanding graduates, and I'm sure that the students with whom I spoke are now productive members of their respective communities. But the story shows that even citizens with reasonable concerns and the best intentions can meet with failure if they don't take time to find out who can solve their problem and determine how that person or persons can be persuaded.

AIMING AT THE RIGHT TARGET

All of the time you spend formulating your problem into a cogent, specific challenge will be for nothing if you waste your research and advocacy time on the wrong decision makers. If your concern is neighborhood safety, you don't want to spend time trying to enlist the U.S. Army or call in the Federal Bureau of Investigation. Your local council member may feel great sympathy when you complain that public colleges and universities are underfunded, but he or she can't do anything about it. Your mayor would show understandable puzzlement if you ask him or her to stop a president from implementing a trade agreement with a foreign nation. Fortunately, the task of picking the right decision maker is intuitive if you follow several simple steps:

1. Determine Which Level of Government Is Involved

The American constitutional system provides for two sources of governmental power: state governments and the federal government. For the 10 years following the Declaration of Independence, in 1776, the United States was essentially a confederation of loosely affiliated independent states. Our first governing document, the Articles of Confederation, vested political authority in state governments and left the national government virtually unable to act without state consent. Because the new nation had many challenges that transcended individual state boundaries and required unified action, the states soon found the confederated arrangement to be unwieldy and ineffective.

When the Framers began drafting what would become the U.S. Constitution in the mid-1780s, they decided to take a different approach. Instead of subjecting central government actions to case-by-case state consent, the states would instead delegate certain powers to the national (federal) government so that it could act without prior approval. Articles I, II, and III of the Constitution, as well as the 27 amendments to the Constitution, define the federal government's powers and limitations. The Tenth Amendment specifies that "[t]he powers not delegated to the United States by the Constitution, nor prohibited by it to the states, are reserved to the states respectively, or to the people." In other words, states retain all constitutionally permitted powers not otherwise delegated to the federal government and are sovereign in their exercise of those powers. You can find the relevant sections of the Constitution at the end of this chapter.

We see this principle of reserved powers at work every day. Although jurisdictional lines can become blurred, as we discuss later in this chapter, states and the local governments they establish have exclusive jurisdiction over enforcing criminal laws within their borders. If your small business is robbed, your local police department, sheriff's office, and district or state attorney will apprehend and prosecute the thief unless he has fled to another state or somehow broken federal law as well. State law enforcement authorities will probably get involved if a crime is committed across county lines. But the Federal Bureau of Investigation rarely has the authority to intervene in cases of breaking and entering since it is almost always a state offense.

At both the state and federal levels, government is divided into three branches: the executive (U.S. president and state governors), legislative (U.S. Congress and state legislatures), and judicial (federal and state courts). States also have the authority to delegate their powers to local subunits, such as counties, cities, towns, and other municipal entities—which may have executives like mayors and legislatures such as city councils or county commissions. In addition, many states have created special-purpose districts with boundaries that may or may not coincide with units of general government. For example, depending on how your state organizes the administration of public education, one county may have multiple school districts or be limited to one. Many states have set up multicounty environmental districts to govern the use of water bodies, such as lakes, rivers, and aquifers, and those districts track watersheds rather than the boundaries of local governments. Others have established independent governmental agencies that oversee transportation matters such as highways and mass transit.

These levels and branches constitute "government" in the traditional sense. But plenty of institutions that have no connection to Washington, D.C., the state capital, or the county seat govern in other ways. If you are an intercollegiate athlete, the National Collegiate Athletic Association (NCAA) governs how you are recruited, the time of year you practice and play your games, and your relationships with university administrators, faculty members, coaches, alumni, and other athletes.

The key is determining which entity controls the particular problem you aim to solve. Although the answer to this question can be complicated, there are some hard and fast rules that can help you narrow the possibilities.

State or Local Government. Unlike now-defunct entities such as the Roman Empire and the Soviet Union, which centralized government to the point that officials in Rome or Moscow were involved in purely regional or even local matters, our states delegated some power to the federal government and retained the rest to manage their own particular affairs. But although state and local governmental actions have the most direct impact on our everyday lives, many—if not most—Americans know much more about what happens in the U.S. Capitol than in their own state house or county seat.

That lack of awareness is unfortunate. As a citizen advocate, you are far more likely to engage City Hall or your state legislature than the White House or the United States Congress. Think about the governmental challenges that usually inspire those feelings we discussed at the start of chapter 1. Garbage wasn't picked up for the third week in a row? County or city matter. Your child's school being assigned its fourth new principal in as many years? Only your local school district can help. The neighborhood park has become a nighttime hotspot for criminal behavior? They can't help you in Washington. Your favorite hiking trail in a state conservation area is again blocked with debris? Time to alert the proper state agency or your state legislator. Because you are more likely to test your citizenship mettle with local or state government, pay close attention to the advice provided by Miami Downtown Development Agency Executive Director Alyce Robertson on contacting local governments.

TIPS FROM THE PROS

Contacting Local Governments
ALYCE ROBERTSON

Local government actions (or inactions) have the biggest potential to affect citizens' everyday lives. If you need to flex your citizenship muscles at the city or county levels, here are some suggestions.

- Find information on the Internet. The quality of information and ease of navigating governmental websites varies by jurisdiction, but the Internet is a good starting point. Type your question in to your search engine to navigate in the right direction. Who are your elected representatives, what is the garbage pickup schedule, how much are my taxes, or what is the schedule for public meetings? These and other questions can be answered by looking them up on the city or county website.

- Some government websites organize information by department while others arrange content by the service you need performed. Many localities now provide web listings of services available over the Internet and also provide links to other government agencies. For example, you may be able to search property records, pay taxes and fines, or set a traffic court hearing online.

- If you don't have a computer, check the local library for free Internet services.

- In addition, government agencies have developed mobile apps for checking bus schedules, reporting problems you may encounter, parking availability, and many other helpful uses.

- Government agencies change names frequently—especially when newly elected officials want to put their own mark on local government or if a scandal prompts the rebranding of an affected entity. Keep your eyes on websites and local news outlets so that you don't lose track of renamed agencies.

- Many local governments take the alphabet soup approach and refer to agencies by acronyms (for example, FDOT for Florida Department of Transportation and BART for Bay Area Rapid Transit). If you're not sure what an acronym means, ask.

- Most governments have general-information telephone lines to direct you to the right agency. Check to see if your local government is using the easy-to-remember 311 prefix to provide citizens with information.

- E-mail is your friend. Governments increasingly publish e-mail addresses for elected officials and key appointed officials so that you can communicate your question or concern in writing and enhance accountability. Not only does this ensure a written record of your inquiry, but that e-mail is typically subject to public review from media and other citizens.

- Some governments have specific contact information to report problems with local services. For example, Jacksonville, Florida encourages citizens to contact (904) 630-CITY or 630city.coj.net to ask questions, register their concerns, or request public records.

- Both public television (your local PBS station) and public-access television (found on your local cable system) sometimes offer informational programming to educate citizens about the services that agencies provide. Consult your local television listings or the stations' websites.

- Government agencies also provide printed materials. For example, during Miami–Dade County's Adopt-a-Tree events, county officials teach people how to plant a tree and also give them a community forestry booklet in case they forget the details.

- Invite key government officials to your civic, homeowners, condominium, or apartment association meetings to explain what their agencies do and how you can report problems. Start with priority problems that are of interest to your neighborhood, such as police and fire services, traffic control, and park maintenance.

- Some communities have established programs to educate local residents about government services. Take advantage of these programs.

- Show resilience and persistence in seeking the right agency to address your problem. As Ralph Waldo Emerson said, "Patience and fortitude conquer all things."

- Remember the old maxim that you can catch more flies with honey than with vinegar. No matter how frustrating your search becomes, maintain a friendly and polite attitude. If you approach government officials with anger, you will discourage them from providing further assistance.

- You elected one or more city or county councilors or commissioners. They work for you. If a local government agency ignores you or declines to help, don't let that be the last word. Calling or e-mailing the local legislative official or board member who is responsible for funding that agency can do wonders for responsiveness to citizen concerns. While you don't want to make your city commissioner the first call always or play this card too often, keep it in mind for situations where the need is great and the response is unsatisfactory.

- Elected and appointed officials are increasingly sensitive to what appears on social media. For example, some mayors even pride themselves on personally responding to constituent services requests made in 140 characters or less. When he was mayor of Newark, now–U.S. Senator Cory Booker was nationally

(Continued)

(Continued)

known for engaging constituent concerns on social media.[5] Boston Mayor Martin J. Walsh made upgrading the city's digital responsiveness a priority when he took office in 2014.[6] If all else fails, a timely tweet or post from you might motivate official action.

The Pothole Scenario

You drive onto your street one morning and see one of the most common citizen complaints: a pothole. How do you get it fixed? Follow this step-by-step approach:

1. If there is an immediate life safety or health concern—for example, the pothole has exposed underground electrical cables—call 911 to report an emergency.

2. Otherwise, decide which level of government is responsible for fixing the pothole. If you live on a small, two-lane road, your town, city, or county is probably in charge. But if you live on a four-lane boulevard or expressway, the state department of transportation or county public works department may have the responsibility of fixing the pothole.

3. Assuming the pothole is a local responsibility, call 311 or another central government phone number to report the problem. Of course, the telephone is not the only tool at your disposal. As noted above in the Jacksonville example, some websites also accept citizen complaints. And you also have the option to e-mail your complaint either to a central citizens services e-mail address or to individual local officials.

4. Maintain a written record of your conversations and e-mails. This will be invaluable if later on you need to establish the timeline and substance of your efforts. If you are calling, ask the operator which department will handle the assignment. Ask for the operator's name, and note the date and time you reported the problem. Request an estimated time frame for fixing the problem and a return call or e-mail when the repair has been completed.

5. Don't get frustrated if the person who answers the phone or responds to your e-mail does not know every detail involved in solving the problem. Your goal is to find the agency that will know those details, and the public servant on the other end of the phone or electronic conversation can help you more readily if you are patient and respectful.

6. If the problem is not corrected within the specified time frame, call or e-mail back for a status update. If you don't get a satisfactory response, ask to speak with a supervisor, or e-mail your concerns to the person in charge.

[5] Krissah Thompson, "Newark Mayor Using Robust Twitter Presence to Reach Snowed-Under Residents, *Washington Post*, December 29, 2010, www.washingtonpost.com/wp-dyn/content/article/2010/12/29/AR2010122902206.html

[6] Jessica Van Sack, "New Boston Mayor Embraces Digital Technology, *Government Technology Magazine*, January 20, 2014, www.govtech.com/local/New-Boston-Mayor-Embraces-Digital-Technology.html

7. As the old adage goes, a picture is worth 1000 words. Take a photograph of the pothole and surrounding area with your camera or smart phone. E-mail it to the governmental representativeswith whom you have made contact, or highlight it via Twitter, Facebook, Instagram, or other social media site.

8. If all else fails, contact your town council member, city councilor, county commissioner, or other elected official. Provide details of the nature and location of the problem and when and to whom you reported it.

Alyce Robertson is executive director of the Miami Downtown Development Agency (MDDA). Prior to her current position, she was a 30-year veteran of Miami–Dade County, where she started as a management trainee in 1979 and served in increasingly responsible positions during her tenure.

Thanks to unprecedented advances in telecommunications technology, more and more Americans get their news on satellite and cable television, like Fox News, CNN, or MSNBC, rather than through local television news affiliates. They search the Internet or receive snippets of news on Twitter or Facebook rather than consult a city newspaper. Additionally, we live in an era of mass media consolidation, so ownership of newspapers, networks, and television and radio stations is becoming concentrated in the hands of a few large corporations. The combined effect of these phenomena is that media coverage of the White House, Congress, and other federal governmental entities often crowds out local stories. At the end of any given day, you may know that the president and Congress are locked in a legislative dispute, but you may not know that your local school board has decided to change graduation requirements or school boundaries. Guess which story will have the bigger impact on your everyday life? Here's a hint: not the one in Washington.

State governments are sovereign, and they typically delegate authority to local governments to regulate purely parochial matters, such as local road maintenance, parks and recreational facilities, trash collection, sports stadiums, zoning and planning changes, approval of new commercial or residential developments, fire and police service, and other matters that are confined within the city or county limits. When an issue goes beyond the city limits or county lines, however, states maintain and exercise authority. For example, states usually govern public colleges and universities, issue licenses to professionals and businesses, maintain prisons, regulate power companies, protect sensitive lands and waters, run the state lottery, oversee at-risk children through adoption and foster-parenting agencies, prepare for and respond to natural disasters, collect sales taxes, and mediate intercounty disputes.

Much to the dismay of county and city governments, states can also withdraw previously delegated authority or preempt local action on specific issues. The North Carolina legislature and governor highlighted this state power in March 2016 when they rushed to enact legislation blocking the enactment of local ordinances to ban discrimination against lesbian, gay, bisexual, and transgender (LGBT) citizens or raise the minimum wage.[7] Numerous other states have also passed legislation banning local minimum wage increases.[8] The *Indianapolis Star* chronicled the Indiana government's preemption of local action on issues ranging from banking regulation to livestock operations to employee benefits.[9] In 2014, Arizona prohibited localities from banning the use of plastic shopping bags.[10] Two years later, Florida banned local governments from restricting the use of Styrofoam containers.[11] While this power is not absolute and can be subject to judicial review, states are not hesitant to use it when they see fit.

As you can see, state governments have broad abilities to impact the fate of your citizen advocacy issue. But you have the power to shape their actions. In his tips (see Tips from the Pros: Success in Your State Capital), former Idaho Governor Dirk Kempthorne offers advice on how you can maximize your chances of moving state officials in your direction.

TIPS FROM THE PROS

Success in Your State Capital
DIRK KEMPTHORNE

In my 23 years of public service, with few exceptions, I have found all people working in government truly motivated to do good. Based on that, here are some suggestions on how to access those public servants so they can help you have a better world.

1. *Get to know elected officials.* Be an active citizen in all levels of government. Vote in local, state, and national elections. Attend local and state town hall meetings. Stay informed on issues and concerns important to you.

---

[7] Henry Gargan, "Triangle Governments Scramble to Decipher Law's Impact," *News & Observer*, March 24, 2016, www.newsobserver.com/news/politics-government/article68123457.html

[8] Mac Rivlin-Nadler, "Preemption Bills: A New Conservative Tool to Block Minimum Wage Increases," *New Republic*, February 29, 2016, newrepublic.com/article/130783/preemption-bills-new-conservative-tool-block-minimum-wage-increases

[9] Brian Eason, "State to Locals: You Can't Do That. Or That," *Indianapolis Star*, March 6, 2016, www.indystar.com/story/news/politics/2016/03/06/state-locals-you-cant-do/80607546/

[10] Patrick Gleason, "State and Local Bag Taxes and Bans Face Pushback," *Forbes*, May 27, 2015, www.forbes.com/sites/patrickgleason/2015/05/27/bag-ban-pushback/#798e5dad1868

[11] Mary Ellen Klas, "Legislature Poised to Pass Ban on Local Government Bans on Styrofoam Containers," *Tampa Bay Times*, March 8, 2016, www.tampabay.com/blogs/the-buzz-florida-politics/legislature-poised-to-pass-ban-on-local-government-bans-on-styrofoam/2268478

2. *Help them help you.* Elected officials are in public service and elected to serve the citizens they represent. They do want to hear the concerns of their constituents. Do your homework. Bring with you as much information as possible that defines the problem and possible solutions. They cannot help if they do not have the facts to look for a solution.

During a budgeting process, an agency chose to stop funding a particular program assisting special needs individuals. At a town hall meeting, a young man, with only the ability to speak through pointing to letters on a board attached to his wheelchair, came to me and communicated that the cuts would mean he could not remain at home. I saw the pleading in his eyes. I checked out his story. He was correct. We found budget changes elsewhere. His honest, straightforward call for help made the difference.

3. *Begin closest to home.* Often, beginning with your legislative or local representative in your city or home district is your best bet. That person can help you to identify the specifics of the problem and solutions at the government level. He or she can also be an effective ally with the administration should you need to go to that level.

4. *Do not sensationalize.* When presenting a legitimate problem to an elected official, stick to the facts of your case and don't sensationalize or embellish. Bring awareness to the problem and suggested solutions. This will help everyone to stay focused on the results needed and clarify the process required to find a solution.

5. *Go to the top if necessary.* Sometimes, the top official—mayor, county executive, or governor—is the only one with the authority to address your problem. Contact that official's office and ask for direction on how to pursue your concern. Come prepared for questions and legitimate challenges that may arise. Remember that the elected official does want to know your concerns and ran for office to find solutions for constituents.

One day I was informed that a woman had chained herself to the Liberty Bell in front of the Idaho State Capitol and demanded to talk to the governor. For several hours, she remained there with local news media set up waiting for the anticipated encounter. She left at night, vowing to return. At 7 a.m. the next morning, I brought two cups of coffee and sat down next to her before the media arrived. She wanted her husband released from prison. Having an inkling, I had done some research and found her husband was in prison for spousal abuse and had done nothing toward rehabilitation. I encouraged her to let the system work so he could avail himself of programs provided and she would be safe. When the media arrived there was no one at the bell. She could have avoided a lot of drama by setting up an appointment to meet with me in the office.

6. *Say thank you.* Let others know when the process works. This will remind all that an individual can make a difference and being responsive is the role of an

(Continued)

(Continued)

elected official. Concerns are often more complicated than they may seem at first. But believe in the process, and help to change it if it doesn't work. Show appreciation when it does.

The Honorable Dirk Kempthorne began his commitment to public service in 1985, when he was elected mayor of the City of Boise, Idaho. After serving seven years as mayor, he was elected to the United States Senate in 1992. He was elected governor of Idaho in 1998, and was reelected for a second term in 2002. While serving as governor, Kempthorne made improving education, especially early childhood education, a priority. In 2006, President George W. Bush appointed Governor Kempthorne as the 49th secretary of the interior. In this role, Governor Kempthorne managed 20 percent of U.S. lands with an annual budget of $18 billion. He currently serves as president and CEO of the American Council of Life Insurers (ACLI).

Federal Government. For the most part, problems that affect individual localities or states exclusively do not rise to the level of federal concern. In determining whether your issue is a matter of federal concern, ask yourself whether the problem exists with a federal asset, crosses state boundaries, or has an effect on citizens throughout the nation. For example, the federal government exerts exclusive or primary jurisdiction over the U.S. military, international relations and trade, immigration, foreign intelligence gathering, Social Security, Medicare, national parks and monuments, interstate commerce, the national economy and the Federal Reserve (banking) system, and other matters that affect Americans whether they live in Seattle, St. Louis, or St. Petersburg. The federal government is also involved through specialized agencies such as the Federal Bureau of Investigation (FBI), Drug Enforcement Agency (DEA), Food and Drug Administration (FDA), and Bureau of Alcohol, Tobacco, Firearms and Explosives (ATF), which enforce federal laws and partner with state and local entities.

Given some of the media tendencies we mentioned earlier in this chapter, citizens often mistakenly assume that the solution to their problem must be found in Washington—a demoralizing assumption given the intense partisanship and gridlock seen recently in the nation's capital. Take heart. Many of your challenges will find solutions in your state or local governments. If transportation or infrastructure is your major concern, an issue involving airlines, interstate highways, or rail lines will likely have a federal solution. But many other transportation issues—disrepair of state or county roads, city water taxi service, bicycle paths, or pedestrian-friendly streets—are resolved in state capitals, city halls, and special districts.

Blurred Lines of Authority. Despite those clearly labeled descriptions of the levels of government, here's the rub: Issues sometimes do not fit neatly into just one category. Your initiative may cross jurisdictional lines. An example is the same law enforcement we discussed earlier in this chapter. Although colleges provide training for police officers and local governments largely fund and administer their police forces, state governments determine the criminal laws that police are charged with enforcing. They also regulate training, licensure, and pension and other retirement issues for law enforcement officers. The federal government has the smallest role in police protection, but it retains influence through grants that have assisted local law enforcement agencies in hiring new officers, training police, conducting joint operations, and making equipment purchases. As noted above, it also has special purpose law enforcement agencies such as the ATF, DEA, and FBI, which become involved when a crime has national ramifications, such as a bank robbery or certain drug, alcohol, and weapons offenses. Additionally, the U.S. Department of Justice has the authority to intervene if local law enforcement officials are alleged to have violated the constitutional rights of affected citizens.

Environmental matters are another example. Local governments usually control their own land use decisions. States determine water-quality standards under state law, offer the first line of defense for environmentally sensitive lands and waters, and become involved with development issues that affect multiple jurisdictions across county lines. The federal government identifies and protects threatened or endangered species and regulates interstate environmental issues, such as the use and protection of navigable waters. Additionally, through enactments such as the Clean Air and Clean Water Acts, federal policymakers establish national standards in air, soil, and water quality and then give states the right to enhance, administer, and enforce the standards. Conflict often arises when a state wants to set more stringent standards than those of the federal government. It took a presidential election to resolve California's effort to set automobile-emission limitations greater than those established in Washington. President George W. Bush had repeatedly denied California's request. One of Barack Obama's first actions as president was to grant it. The pendulum could swing again when a new president takes office in January 2017.

In the area of public education, state governments retain the ultimate control of schools and often directly set curriculum standards, approve textbooks, certify teachers, and provide significant funding. States delegate other responsibilities to local school districts, which manage the schools through such tasks as hiring principals, teachers, and other personnel and providing funding for school operations and facilities by levying property taxes or other funding sources.

The federal government has almost no formal authority over education. Education is one of the powers reserved to the states. States administer public education through school districts, college or university boards of trustees, and other agencies. However, particularly since the passage of the Land Grant College Act of 1862 and the G.I. Bill in 1944 for returning World War II veterans, Washington has played a role in public education. At the collegiate level, this primarily consists of providing universities with financial support through student grants and loans, assistance with construction of facilities, and scientific research. The federal government also protects civil rights at all levels of education through laws like Title IX of the Education Amendments of 1972, which "protects people from discrimination based on sex in education programs or activities that receive federal financial assistance."[12]

---

[12] "Office for Civil Rights: Title IX and Sex Discrimination," U.S. Department of Education, www2 .ed.gov/about/offices/list/ocr/docs/tix_dis.html

In elementary and secondary schools, the federal government provides help to economically disadvantaged students and children with disabilities or special needs, and maintains data and funds research on educational issues. These tools give Washington some power to influence how states and school districts manage public education. Passage of the so-called No Child Left Behind Act was a hallmark of President George W. Bush's first term in office. The legislation conditioned states' receipt of federal education funding on the implementation of new testing and accountability measures to improve student performance. After criticism that No Child Left Behind overly infringed on powers reserved to the states, President Obama signed a revamped version—called the Every Student Succeeds Act—to give states more flexibility.[13]

In addition to situations such as those noted, in which different levels of government exercise discrete forms of authority on broad policy issues, the federal and state governments sometimes share responsibility for particular initiatives. Perhaps the best example is Medicaid, which helps to provide a national health care system for low-income Americans. Medicaid is "federal" in the sense that Congress established the program, and the federal government sets general guidelines and appropriates about 60 percent of the cost. But Medicaid is also a "state" program in that state health care agencies help to determine eligibility for individuals who need care, administer the delivery of health care, enhance benefits consistent with federal guidelines, and provide the nonfederal balance of funding.

The passage of the Affordable Care Act, also known as "Obamacare," has heightened this shared federal-state relationship. Medicaid used to cover individuals and families who lived below the federal poverty level. Obamacare expanded Medicaid to insure all Americans whose household income is below 138 percent of the federal poverty level.[14] As of this writing in early 2016, the federal poverty level is $11,880 for an individual, $16,020 for a family of two, and $24,300 for a family of four.[15] The U.S. Supreme Court ruled that the federal government could not require states to expand Medicaid but could incentivize them to do so. According to the Kaiser Family Foundation, as of February 2016, 32 states have agreed to expand Medicaid and another 2 are actively considering expansion.[16]

Joint federal-state initiatives to address region-specific challenges also exist. For example, the federal government and affected states have agreed to share the costs and responsibilities involved in restoring the health of America's Everglades, the Chesapeake Bay, and other threatened environmental treasures. The same is often true for major infrastructure projects like seaport deepening or highway construction. Though the federal government may have to authorize the initiative and will

---

[13] Gregory Korte, "The Every Student Succeeds Act vs. No Child Left Behind: What's Changed?" *USA Today*, December 11, 2015, www.usatoday.com/story/news/politics/2015/12/10/every-student-succeeds-act-vs-no-child-left-behind-whats-changed/77088780/

[14] "Medicaid Expansion and What It Means for You," U.S. Centers for Medicare & Medicaid Services, www.healthcare.gov/medicaid-chip/medicaid-expansion-and-you/

[15] "Federal Poverty Level (FPL)," U.S. Centers for Medicare and Medicaid Services, www.healthcare .gov/glossary/federal-poverty-level-FPL/

[16] "Status of State Action on the Medicaid Expansion Decision," *State Health Facts*, kff.org/health-reform/ state-indicator/state-activity-around-expanding-medicaid-under-the-affordable-care-act/

provide part of the funding, state and/or local governments often share the expense and manage the construction.

Your job is to determine the authority that each level of government exercises over your issue—and then to address each level to achieve your goal. Start at the level of government closest to you and work upward. Let's say that your goal is to expand the State Children's Health Insurance Program (SCHIP), a joint program much like Medicaid, so that more children will have access to health insurance. Check with the state health care administration agency. Are all eligible children in your state currently covered? If not, there is work to do in your own backyard. But if all eligible children are covered, and if you believe that even more children should have access to the program, you will have to persuade the federal government to expand eligibility, and then persuade officials in Washington *and* your state capital to increase funding so that the newly eligible kids can be included.

Nobody ever said that federalism was simple or for the weak of heart. Our uniquely American multilayered system of government is complex—a condition befitting a nation of our large size, political history, varied geography, and rich diversity. Don't be frightened by this complexity, but master it. Those citizens who recognize and understand the nuances of our federal system are the ones most likely to transform their initiative into action.

2. Pinpoint Your Specific Targets within the Proper Level of Government

Determining whether a problem is local, state, federal, or nongovernmental in nature is only the first step. You must also determine which entities at different levels have the power to solve your problem. Note the use of the plural. In our system of government, sole decision-making authority is an increasingly rare occurrence.

The Almanac of American Politics once described my friend and former Senate colleague, the late Daniel Patrick Moynihan of New York, as "the nation's best thinker among politicians since Lincoln and its best politician among thinkers since Jefferson."[17] Senator Moynihan observed that our form of government was the first one created with the deliberate goal of having it not work. Having rebelled against the monarchical rule of King George III, the Framers did not want a government that could easily deprive citizens of life, liberty, or property. They addressed this concern through the U.S. Constitution's intricate system of checks and balances and the subsequent adoption of the Bill of Rights. For the most part, individual states have used the same model. The practical consequence of the Framers' design is that our democracy has established multiple checkpoints on the road of governmental decision making.

Let's look at an example of how you can use those checkpoints to your advantage. Imagine you learn that a 10-acre park in your neighborhood has been identified as a potential site for a new county government complex that would include a new county hall, police and fire stations, and a regional courthouse. The project will increase traffic congestion and eliminate the largest swath of green space in your part of town.

---

[17] *The Almanac of American Politics 1998*, ed. Michael Barone (Washington, DC: National Journal, 1997), 962–63.

First, congratulations on finding this information now. Had you waited until the site was selected, you would have faced the task of reversing a decision already made, which is much more difficult than influencing one to be made in the future. While you still face a challenge, your chances of success are better than they could have been.

You are determined to stop this government construction project, which you see as a fundamental change in the quality and character of your neighborhood. But where do you begin? The first step is to determine who has the power to halt the new complex. Think carefully about the governmental or administrative bodies that affect your life. Assume for the sake of this scenario that the new government center will not be limited to your local community but will serve several counties due to the regional courthouse and county agreements to cooperate in police and fire services. Through the process of elimination, you determine that your concerns will likely be addressed at either or both the local and state levels of government. But how do you determine which entities have any say over the problem? Here are the steps:

- At the local level, consult your county's main website. You can find it through a simple Internet search, through the National Association of Counties at explorer.naco.org or at usa.gov/local-governments. Study the information on each of the county agencies to determine which ones can help you. The goal should be to find the *enabling* departments or agencies that will plan and execute the proposed project and the *regulating* departments or agencies that will ensure the project is planned, constructed, used, and maintained consistent with other public priorities, such as environmental protection, safety, and growth management. With the information gathered from the website, you should be able to determine the department or agency that is responsible for planning and constructing the new complex, as well as the departments or agencies with jurisdiction over parks and other natural resources, building inspection, and land use planning.
- Once you have the proper local agencies identified, make sure you have also pinpointed all necessary county elected officials. This will almost certainly include a county commission or council, and may include a county executive. In many counties, the commissioners appoint a professional county manager who runs the day-to-day business of the county. Because these officials will have the final say over whether the project moves forward, you will need to know who they are and how you stay in contact with them.
- Determine the same information for the other counties that will share in the new government center. Their appointed officials may be involved in planning and developing the project, and the county commissioners may have to approve the center and will probably help to finance it. Later in the citizen engagement process, you may need to cultivate allies in those other counties to prevail on their elected representatives to oppose the project.

- Don't forget about state government. Especially because this is a multi-county initiative, it may require approval from various state agencies. Visit the website of your state's department of environmental protection (consult epa.gov/epahome/state.htm). In most states, the agency that regulates environmental matters is required to study proposed projects that could threaten natural resources and issue permits before work can begin. You will derail the proposed center if you can convince state regulators to deny or delay permitting.

- Follow the same process to locate your state's growth management or planning agency. Multiple states regulate so-called developments of regional impact (DRI), which are "defined as a land use project which, due to its character, magnitude and/or location could have substantial effect on the health, safety, or welfare of citizens in a given region, often affecting more than one governmental jurisdiction."[18] If your state utilizes the DRI model or one like it, that process may be another way to slow down or stop the proposed government center.

- Last but not least, the federal government may have jurisdiction. Was your local park built using any federal funds? If so, the county may be prohibited from changing its use without repaying those funds or obtaining permission from the U.S. Interior Department (doi.gov) or National Park Service (nationalparkservice.org). Will any sensitive lands or waters be affected or wildlife disturbed? At the federal level, the Environmental Protection Agency (epa.gov), Forest Service (fs.fed.us), Fish and Wildlife Service (fws.gov), or Army Corps of Engineers (usace.army.mil) may well have the authority to examine the environmental impacts of the proposed government complex and halt construction if the project falls short of federal standards for the protection of air, water, wildlife, vegetation, and wetlands.

- Finally, be sure to keep one eye on the clock at all times. As you will read in chapter 6, timing is everything. All of the processes, reviews, and decisions described here occur in specific time frames and are subject to strict deadlines. You may have a winning defense, but if you don't get it on the field in time, you will lose.

As we will discuss more in chapter 5, once you have identified the appropriate agencies and officials at each level of government, you will need to frame the most effective arguments for your position. For example, if you can show that there is not a demonstrated need for the complex, but its construction is politically or personally motivated, you may be able to persuade local governments to deny authorization. If the project passes the need test but the proposed site is problematic, move the conversation to finding a new location that does not threaten precious green spaces or cause unacceptable traffic congestion. Consult chapter 7

---

[18] MDT, "Growth Management—Development of Regional Impact (DRI) Review," *Montana Transportation and Land Use*, www.mdt.mt.gov/research/toolkit/m1/pptools/gm/dria.shtml

to determine how to seek out others who share your opinion, so they can also share the workload of convincing decision makers at every level.

3. Use Representative Democracy to Your Advantage

In writing the Declaration of Independence, Thomas Jefferson penned these famous words: "We hold these truths to be self-evident, that all men are created equal, that they are endowed by their Creator with certain unalienable Rights, that among these are Life, Liberty and the pursuit of Happiness. — That to secure these rights, Governments are instituted among Men, deriving their just powers from the **consent of the governed.**"[19] As citizens in a republic, we find in those final four words our greatest source of power to influence public decisions. Elected officials at every level govern because we hire them to represent us. We grant them the power to approve the initiatives we want and deny those we oppose. As you will learn in later chapters, our job as citizens is to remind elected officials of this relationship and persuade them to adopt our position.

Most levels of government have an elected executive—president, governor, county executive, or mayor. Even more representatives require consent of the governed on the legislative side. You have one or more city councilors or commissioners and, unless you live in a consolidated city-county government, more of the same at the county level. Also, unless you live in Nebraska, the only state to have a one-house, or unicameral, legislature, you have at least one state senator and one lower house member who were elected to represent your interests in state government. Two U.S. senators and a congressperson serve you in the federal government. Find out who your elected representatives are and contact their offices to make known your concerns.

Remember that legislative staff members play a critical role in shaping policy. Most state and many local legislators have at least some staff. U.S. representatives and senators typically will have staff assigned to specific areas of governmental authority, such as transportation or the environment. Determine the appropriate staff members and work with them to leverage your influence with the legislator.

It is possible that the legislator may exercise direct oversight of the proposed government center or play a role in approving and appropriating funds for the proposed project. Furthermore, because other legislators are likely to defer to the elected representative whose district will host the proposed new complex, you will go a long way toward killing a project if you can convince your legislators and their staff it is a bad idea.

However, elected officials can give you more than their votes and voices. They can also be powerful allies. The United States is rare in that its elected legislative representatives provide constituent services that range from assisting you in replacing a lost passport to helping you communicate with government agencies. This service does not exist in most parliamentary democracies outside the United States. In her tips (see Tips from the Pros: Maximizing Customer Service), former congressional chief of staff Karen Feather explains that you don't need to take no for an

---

[19] Italics are added. A transcript of The Declaration if Independence is available from the Independence Hall Association (IHA) site: www.ushistory.org/declaration/document/

answer from government agencies when you are seeking change. She describes how you can productively engage your member of Congress, state legislator, or local councilperson through the casework process.

TIPS FROM THE PROS

Maximizing Customer Service
KAREN FEATHER

Think of your elected officials as customer service representatives to whom you can appeal if your interaction with a government agency was unsatisfactory. Congressional offices routinely serve as a liaison to every branch of the federal government, including the Social Security Administration, the Veterans Affairs Department, and the IRS, and most state legislators have staff to work with state agencies. An experienced caseworker can make sure that your case is reviewed by a decision maker in a timely manner.

- Always try to work through an agency's standard application and appeal process before contacting an elected official.
- Remember that an elected official cannot tell an agency how to decide a case, but that official can make sure your matter is given serious consideration.
- Contact your own representative, even if you don't belong to the same party. Constituent casework is strictly nonpartisan.
- If you meet your elected official at a public event, don't hesitate to mention your problem to get the name of a staff person who can help you. But don't expect that the official will remember enough of the details of your case to resolve it.
- Think through your problem and be prepared to explain it as concisely as possible when speaking to a caseworker. It can be helpful to create a timeline to indicate when you filed an application, received a phone call or letter, or took any other steps toward resolution.
- Never send an initial e-mail seeking help to an office's main mailbox; it is likely to be lost amid hundreds of e-mails about legislative issues that are less time sensitive than your case.
- Try to speak personally with a caseworker before you send something in writing, so you know exactly what documents should be included in a follow-up letter or e-mail. If a caseworker is not available when you call, get an e-mail address so you can communicate directly. You will be asked to sign a privacy release form allowing staff to communicate with an agency about your personal information.

(Continued)

(Continued)

- Always make copies of any documents before sharing with anyone. If you are seeking compensation for an injury or illness, you will need documentation from a doctor.
- The person with the dispute, not a friend or relative, should make at least the initial inquiry. Once an inquiry has begun, permission can be given to someone who may have more time or ability to handle follow-up questions.
- Never lie to a caseworker or hide relevant facts. If she senses you are being dishonest, she will stop helping, even if she doesn't say so directly.
- Always be polite, no matter how frustrated you are.
- Military service members should always work through their chain of command before contacting an elected representative.
- Don't ask a member of Congress for a civil service job recommendation.
- Keep in touch with a caseworker, but not too often. Most caseworkers seek to resolve cases within 30–60 days, so it is appropriate to check in if you have not heard back after a month.
- Don't forget to say thank you! Even if you were disappointed in the result, be sure to thank both the staff and the elected representative who made an effort on your behalf. If you were especially pleased with the service you received, let others know by writing a letter to the editor of the local newspaper, posting a message on social media, or attending a public meeting with the official. A few words of gratitude can make a staff member's day and inspire new enthusiasm to help others.

Karen Feather worked for Congressman Paul E. Kanjorski (D-PA) from 1985 to 2011, the last 18 years as chief of staff. She learned a great deal about casework from Becky Eshenbaugh, who handled congressional casework for more than 40 years, including 26 with Congressman Kanjorski. She is currently serving as director of the Center for Municipal and Corporate Sustainability at Lebanon Valley College (lvc.edu) in Annville, Pennsylvania.

Think of your elected officials as governmental traffic cops who can point you in the right direction. Newly elected officials at all levels of government should learn enough about the public issues affecting their constituents so they can offer helpful guidance. When a constituent asks a city council member for help on a Social Security challenge or asks a congressperson to intervene in a local zoning dispute, the wrong answer for the elected official to give is "None of my business. Sorry." The right answer is for the elected official to express empathy and direct the constituent to the proper level of government and provide names and contact information on officials at that level who can help. For tips on how to engage those who represent you, please see the good advice of the 2016–2017 National Association of Counties President Bryan Desloge offers advice (see Tips from the Pros: I'm Your Elected Representative—and Also Your Neighbor) on how to engage those who represent you.

I'm Your Elected Representative—and Also Your Neighbor

BRYAN DESLOGE

I've always believed serving as an elected official is the highest calling. There is no other position in which you are closer to the residents of a community, more aware of their concerns, or is better positioned to directly affect positive change for your constituents.

To be elected to office, candidates must live in the area they serve. That means they may be related to you, work at the same company, be a member of your church or possibly your neighbor. They live where you live. I naïvely came into office thinking I could work three or four days a week on county issues—little did I know being an elected official is a 24/7 responsibility. When constituents of mine have problems, they want to talk to me wherever they find me. And that shouldn't be a problem—after all, citizens elect an official to serve, and help is what the elected official should provide.

How to Get Things Done

There are thousands of programs offered through all forms of government, and at times problems arise. If you have been unable to get an issue resolved and you need help, call your elected official. Your first contact will more than likely be with an aide to the elected official. Don't discount the power of an aide to get things done—at times, the aide can get the issue resolved more quickly than the official, especially when that official's calendar is already packed with meetings. The aide will also readily recognize if your concern requires the direct intervention of the official or of other government staff, and will schedule it expeditiously. Be sure to come prepared with documents or any other pertinent material to help better define the problem. One man who was concerned about the condition of his lake brought jars of the lake water to his first meeting, which helped define his issue in a very real way.

If a resolution is identified, it may take time to implement. You've heard the expression "the wheels of government grind slowly." It doesn't necessarily run slowly, although it may appear that way from the outside. Most agencies are running at maximum capacity and are trying to balance the needs of the entire community. Some issues may take time to resolve or may require a number of actions to come together to correct the problem.

As much as an elected official would like to be able to address all concerns brought to his or her attention, it's not always possible. Some requests are simple, and just a few phone calls can remedy the problem. However, some problems can't be

(Continued)

(Continued)

solved by government, whether it's because the resolution to the problem lies outside a particular jurisdiction, the expense exceeds available funds, or local, state, or federal statutes preclude help. There could be other viable options, and your elected official may be able to help identify them.

Let's Work Together

It can be very frustrating when things aren't working correctly and the fix is slow to come. However, please know that government employees and elected officials are like everyone else. They are working within the confines of their schedule, their budget, their staffing levels, and a multitude of other restrictions. Government agencies are far from perfect, but they have employees who are there to help. Like your elected official, the employees are also your neighbors, your friends, or your family. But mistakes will happen, the wrong switches will get flicked, buses will run late, trash pickups will get missed, and potholes will open up. The best way to get a problem solved is to understand that there are people in government who will help if they can, and if they can't, they will try to help connect you with someone who can. Elected officials welcome your input and appreciate all who act as their eyes in the community. Many of the improvements, programs, or services implemented by governments come from citizen suggestions or observations, so don't hesitate to ask for help or provide feedback. After all, it's your government and your elected official!

Bryan Desloge is the 2016–2017 president of the National Association of Counties (naco.org) and a past president of the Florida Association of Counties (fl-counties.com). He has served as a Leon County (FL) commissioner since 2006. Read more about him at cms.leoncountyfl.gov/Home/County-Commission/Bryan-Desloge.

CHECKLIST FOR ACTION

☐ Determine which level of government is involved.

- Is it a local matter involving city or county government or a special services district of some kind?
- Is it a matter of state concern about which state agencies or legislators have final say?
- Is it a federal matter about which final decisions are made by executive agencies or Congress?
- Is it a matter of blurred jurisdiction involving multiple levels of governmental decisions?

☐ Pinpoint your specific targets within the proper level of government.

- Consult the primary jurisdiction's main website to identify key agencies.
- Pinpoint the names and contact numbers of appointed and elected officials and contact them.

- Determine if other levels of government play roles in your issue. Engage them if necessary.
- Keep an eye on the clock.

☐ Use representative democracy to your advantage.

Constitutional Sources of State and Federal Authority

I. Article I (Legislative Power)

. . .

Section 8. The Congress shall have power to lay and collect taxes, duties, imposts and excises, to pay the debts and provide for the common defense and general welfare of the United States; but all duties, imposts and excises shall be uniform throughout the United States;

To borrow money on the credit of the United States;

To regulate commerce with foreign nations, and among the several states, and with the Indian tribes;

To establish a uniform rule of naturalization, and uniform laws on the subject of bankruptcies throughout the United States;

To coin money, regulate the value thereof, and of foreign coin, and fix the standard of weights and measures;

To provide for the punishment of counterfeiting the securities and current coin of the United States;

To establish post offices and post roads;

To promote the progress of science and useful arts, by securing for limited times to authors and inventors the exclusive right to their respective writings and discoveries;

To constitute tribunals inferior to the Supreme Court;

To define and punish piracies and felonies committed on the high seas, and offenses against the law of nations;

To declare war, grant letters of marque and reprisal, and make rules concerning captures on land and water;

To raise and support armies, but no appropriation of money to that use shall be for a longer term than two years;

To provide and maintain a navy;

To make rules for the government and regulation of the land and naval forces;

To provide for calling forth the militia to execute the laws of the union, suppress insurrections and repel invasions;

To provide for organizing, arming, and disciplining, the militia, and for governing such part of them as may be employed in the service of the United States, reserving to the states respectively, the appointment of the officers, and the authority of training the militia according to the discipline prescribed by Congress;

(Continued)

(Continued)

To exercise exclusive legislation in all cases whatsoever, over such District (not exceeding ten miles square) as may, by cession of particular states, and the acceptance of Congress, become the seat of the government of the United States, and to exercise like authority over all places purchased by the consent of the legislature of the state in which the same shall be, for the erection of forts, magazines, arsenals, dockyards, and other needful buildings;—And

To make all laws which shall be necessary and proper for carrying into execution the foregoing powers, and all other powers vested by this Constitution in the government of the United States, or in any department or officer thereof.

Section 9. The migration or importation of such persons as any of the states now existing shall think proper to admit, shall not be prohibited by the Congress prior to the year one thousand eight hundred and eight, but a tax or duty may be imposed on such importation, not exceeding ten dollars for each person.

The privilege of the writ of habeas corpus shall not be suspended, unless when in cases of rebellion or invasion the public safety may require it.

No bill of attainder or ex post facto Law shall be passed.

No capitation, or other direct, tax shall be laid, unless in proportion to the census or enumeration herein before directed to be taken *(amendedby Sixteenth Amendment)*.

No tax or duty shall be laid on articles exported from any state.

No preference shall be given by any regulation of commerce or revenue to the ports of one state over those of another: nor shall vessels bound to, or from, one state, be obliged to enter, clear or pay duties in another.

No money shall be drawn from the treasury, but in consequence of appropriations made by law; and a regular statement and account of receipts and expenditures of all public money shall be published from time to time.

No title of nobility shall be granted by the United States: and no person holding any office of profit or trust under them, shall, without the consent of the Congress, accept of any present, emolument, office, or title, of any kind whatever, from any king, prince, or foreign state.

Section 10. No state shall enter into any treaty, alliance, or confederation; grant letters of marque and reprisal; coin money; emit bills of credit; make anything but gold and silver coin a tender in payment of debts; pass any bill of attainder, ex post facto law, or law impairing the obligation of contracts, or grant any title of nobility.

No state shall, without the consent of the Congress, lay any imposts or duties on imports or exports, except what may be absolutely necessary for executing it's [sic] inspection laws: and the net produce of all duties and imposts, laid by any state on imports or exports, shall be for the use of the treasury of the United States; and all such laws shall be subject to the revision and control of the Congress.

No state shall, without the consent of Congress, lay any duty of tonnage, keep troops, or ships of war in time of peace, enter into any agreement or compact with another state, or with a foreign power, or engage in war, unless actually invaded, or in such imminent danger as will not admit of delay.

II. Article II (Executive Power)

. . .

Section 2. The President shall be commander in chief of the Army and Navy of the United States, and of the militia of the several states, when called into the actual service of the United States; he may require the opinion, in writing, of the principal officer in each of the executive departments, upon any subject relating to the duties of their respective offices, and he shall have power to grant reprieves and pardons for offenses against the United States, except in cases of impeachment.

He shall have power, by and with the advice and consent of the Senate, to make treaties, provided two thirds of the Senators present concur; and he shall nominate, and by and with the advice and consent of the Senate, shall appoint ambassadors, other public ministers and consuls, judges of the Supreme Court, and all other officers of the United States, whose appointments are not herein otherwise provided for, and which shall be established by law: but the Congress may by law vest the appointment of such inferior officers, as they think proper, in the President alone, in the courts of law, or in the heads of departments.

The President shall have power to fill up all vacancies that may happen during the recess of the Senate, by granting commissions which shall expire at the end of their next session.

Section 3. He shall from time to time give to the Congress information of the state of the union, and recommend to their consideration such measures as he shall judge necessary and expedient; he may, on extraordinary occasions, convene both Houses, or either of them, and in case of disagreement between them, with respect to the time of adjournment, he may adjourn them to such time as he shall think proper; he shall receive ambassadors and other public ministers; he shall take care that the laws be faithfully executed, and shall commission all the officers of the United States.

Section 4. The President, Vice President and all civil officers of the United States, shall be removed from office on impeachment for, and conviction of, treason, bribery, or other high crimes and misdemeanors.

III. Article III (Judicial Power)

Section 1. The judicial power of the United States shall be vested in one Supreme Court, and in such inferior courts as the Congress may from time to time ordain and establish. The judges, both of the supreme and inferior courts, shall hold their offices during good behaviour, and shall, at stated times, receive for their services, a compensation, which shall not be diminished during their continuance in office.

Section 2. The judicial power shall extend to all cases, in law and equity, arising under this Constitution, the laws of the United States, and treaties made, or which shall be made, under their authority;—to all cases affecting ambassadors, other public ministers

(Continued)

(Continued)

and consuls;—to all cases of admiralty and maritime jurisdiction;—to controversies to which the United States shall be a party;—to controversies between two or more states;—between a state and citizens of another state (amended by Eleventh Amendment);—between citizens of different states;—between citizens of the same state claiming lands under grants of different states, and between a state, or the citizens thereof, and foreign states, citizens or subjects.

In all cases affecting ambassadors, other public ministers and consuls, and those in which a state shall be party, the Supreme Court shall have original jurisdiction. In all the other cases before mentioned, the Supreme Court shall have appellate jurisdiction, both as to law and fact, with such exceptions, and under such regulations as the Congress shall make.

The trial of all crimes, except in cases of impeachment, shall be by jury; and such trial shall be held in the state where the said crimes shall have been committed; but when not committed within any state, the trial shall be at such place or places as the Congress may by law have directed.

Section 3. Treason against the United States, shall consist only in levying war against them, or in adhering to their enemies, giving them aid and comfort. No person shall be convicted of treason unless on the testimony of two witnesses to the same overt act, or on confession in open court.

The Congress shall have power to declare the punishment of treason, but no attainder of treason shall work corruption of blood, or forfeiture except during the life of the person attainted.

. . . .

United States Bill of Rights

Amendment I

Congress shall make no law respecting an establishment of religion, or prohibiting the free exercise thereof; or abridging the freedom of speech, or of the press; or the right of the people peaceably to assemble, and to petition the government for a redress of grievances.

Amendment II

A well regulated militia, being necessary to the security of a free state, the right of the people to keep and bear arms, shall not be infringed.

Amendment III

No soldier shall, in time of peace be quartered in any house, without the consent of the owner, nor in time of war, but in a manner to be prescribed by law.

Amendment IV

The right of the people to be secure in their persons, houses, papers, and effects, against unreasonable searches and seizures, shall not be violated, and no warrants shall issue, but upon probable cause, supported by oath or affirmation, and particularly describing the place to be searched, and the persons or things to be seized.

Amendment V

No person shall be held to answer for a capital, or otherwise infamous crime, unless on a presentment or indictment of a grand jury, except in cases arising in the land or naval forces, or in the militia, when in actual service in time of war or public danger; nor shall any person be subject for the same offence to be twice put in jeopardy of life or limb; nor shall be compelled in any criminal case to be a witness against himself, nor be deprived of life, liberty, or property, without due process of law; nor shall private property be taken for public use, without just compensation.

Amendment VI

In all criminal prosecutions, the accused shall enjoy the right to a speedy and public trial, by an impartial jury of the state and district wherein the crime shall have been committed, which district shall have been previously ascertained by law, and to be informed of the nature and cause of the accusation; to be confronted with the witnesses against him; to have compulsory process for obtaining witnesses in his favor, and to have the assistance of counsel for his defence.

Amendment VII

In suits at common law, where the value in controversy shall exceed twenty dollars, the right of trial by jury shall be preserved, and no fact tried by a jury, shall be otherwise reexamined in any court of the United States, than according to the rules of the common law.

Amendment VIII

Excessive bail shall not be required, nor excessive fines imposed, nor cruel and unusual punishments inflicted.

Amendment IX

The enumeration in the Constitution, of certain rights, shall not be construed to deny or disparage others retained by the people.

Amendment X

The powers not delegated to the United States by the Constitution, nor prohibited by it to the states, are reserved to the states respectively, or to the people.

. . .

Amendment XIV

Section 1.

All persons born or naturalized in the United States, and subject to the jurisdiction thereof, are citizens of the United States and of the state wherein they reside. No state

(Continued)

(Continued)

shall make or enforce any law which shall abridge the privileges or immunities of citizens of the United States; nor shall any state deprive any person of life, liberty, or property, without due process of law; nor deny to any person within its jurisdiction the equal protection of the laws.

Section 2.

Representatives shall be apportioned among the several states according to their respective numbers, counting the whole number of persons in each state, excluding Indians not taxed. But when the right to vote at any election for the choice of electors for President and Vice President of the United States, Representatives in Congress, the executive and judicial officers of a state, or the members of the legislature thereof, is denied to any of the male inhabitants of such state, being twenty-one years of age, and citizens of the United States, or in any way abridged, except for participation in rebellion, or other crime, the basis of representation therein shall be reduced in the proportion which the number of such male citizens shall bear to the whole number of male citizens twenty-one years of age in such state.

Section 3.

No person shall be a Senator or Representative in Congress, or elector of President and Vice President, or hold any office, civil or military, under the United States, or under any state, who, having previously taken an oath, as a member of Congress, or as an officer of the United States, or as a member of any state legislature, or as an executive or judicial officer of any state, to support the Constitution of the United States, shall have engaged in insurrection or rebellion against the same, or given aid or comfort to the enemies thereof. But Congress may by a vote of two-thirds of each House, remove such disability.

Section 4.

The validity of the public debt of the United States, authorized by law, including debts incurred for payment of pensions and bounties for services in suppressing insurrection or rebellion, shall not be questioned. But neither the United States nor any state shall assume or pay any debt or obligation incurred in aid of insurrection or rebellion against the United States, or any claim for the loss or emancipation of any slave; but all such debts, obligations and claims shall be held illegal and void.

Section 5.

The Congress shall have power to enforce, by appropriate legislation, the provisions of this article.

Source: U.S. Constitution[20]

---

[20] For the U.S. Constitution, see the Cornell University Law Center website, www.law.cornell.edu/constitution/overview

4 Testing the Waters

Gauging and Building Public Support for Your Cause[1]

"In this age, in this country, public sentiment is everything. With it, nothing can fail; against it, nothing can succeed. Whoever molds public sentiment goes deeper than he who enacts statutes, or pronounces judicial decisions."

—Abraham Lincoln

Case in Point | **Reversal of Fortune in Steamboat Springs***

John F. Russell

School buses leave from Strawberry Park Elementary School and Steamboat Springs Middle School in Steamboat Springs, CO, December 2011. In 1996–97, Steamboat Springs community leaders reversed a previous bond issue defeat when their10 Plus 2 campaign led to the approval of a remodeled and expanded high school. Following another school construction bond issue defeat in 2015, the community launched a new effort based on 10 Plus 2.

[1] We are very grateful to pollsters David Beattie of EMC Research (emcresearch.com/emcstaff .html#daveb) and Michael Bocian of GBA Strategies (gbastrategies.com/michael-bocian/) for their thorough reviews of and insightful feedback on this chapter.

*We are grateful to Dr. Cyndy Simms, Bob Maddox, and Dr. David Hill, three of the principal figures in the educational reform initiative in Steamboat Springs, for their explanations and insights.

High in the mountains west of Denver is the majestic valley and beautiful ski resort of Steamboat Springs, Colorado. A Rocky Mountain community blessed with magnificent vistas, Steamboat Springs surged in population in the 1970s and 1980s as the Colorado skiing industry boomed. In 1970, Steamboat Springs had 2,340 residents. Ten years later, that number had more than doubled to 5,098. By 1990, the population was 6,695.

This huge growth greatly affected the community's public schools. In 1970, voters had approved a $5 million bond issue for new school construction. But two decades later, with student enrollment growing at the rate of 4 percent annually, elementary and secondary schools were bulging at the seams. Steamboat Springs High School, built in 1964 to hold 434 students, had 528 pupils to accommodate. In the short term, school officials managed the overflow through unpopular split sessions and portable classrooms. But that was triage at a time when the town really needed a cure.

Responding to community pressures, the school board placed a $41.8 million school bond issue on the November 7, 1995, ballot. An advisory question also asked citizens where they wanted the new high school to be located: in town, out of town, or no preference. It was not until October 25 that citizens learned that the question about location was rhetorical—the school board had already tentatively selected a site just south of town in a known flood plain.

On Election Day, voters spoke loudly against the bond issue, defeating it by the surprisingly wide margin of 70 percent to 30 percent. The morning after the election, one of the principal opponents of the bond issue—Bob Maddox, a highly regarded business and civic leader—sent a two-page letter to the superintendent of schools, Dr. Cyndy Simms. Stunned at the results of the election, Simms didn't open the letter for two days. When she did read it, she saw that Maddox had provided a detailed analysis of the reasons the bond issue failed.

Simms called Maddox on the Friday after Election Day. They met for lunch and had a three-hour conversation about their different views of the failed school bond issue. Simms stressed the strong results on standardized tests and the success rate of graduates in their subsequent college and university educations. Maddox recounted the concerns of many citizens and parents about the high school and what he felt was the school district's tone deafness to those concerns.

During the lunch, Maddox and Simms agreed to organize a citizen committee for which he would select five bond issue opponents while she selected five proponents. With the two of them also participating, the group would be known by its number: the 10 Plus 2.

The 12 participants represented a cross section of the Steamboat Springs community, including a local hotel manager, a contractor, a third-generation civic activist, and the new principal of the high school. All were considered to be people "of good heart" and genuinely interested in what was best for the town and its future.

The initial meeting of the 12 was limited to a discussion of concerns—such as why bond issue proponents felt a new high school was necessary and why opponents disagreed. The meeting went well enough that the dozen decided to open the process to the entire Steamboat community. They organized a forum to be held in the ballroom of the Sheraton Hotel and selected other community leaders to serve as facilitators to keep the meeting moving in a productive direction.

Two hundred citizens attended the forum, gathering around dining room tables in the conference center to discuss their concerns. During the course of the evening, it became clear that voters rejected the new high school for reasons having little to do with the pros and cons of school construction. Instead, they were angry because they felt that the school district was not open to citizen input and feedback on educational matters. Parents of the brightest students had urged the high school to provide gifted programs, such as advanced placement. Parents of struggling students felt their children were not receiving appropriate supplemental services. Others were concerned that the cohesion of the town would be threatened if the school district relocated the high school from its downtown site to a place outside town. Many bond opponents saw the advisory committee that had supported the new high school as nothing but a rubber stamp for the school district and felt it did not represent a variety of community perspectives.

The level of skepticism toward the school district led the 10 Plus 2 to take detailed minutes of each table discussion and send copies to all 200 participants. This transcription and mass distribution ensured that every participant would receive the same factual information about the concerns expressed. The school board stood back, recognizing that it was perceived as part of the problem by many Steamboat residents.

After this successful community forum, the 10 Plus 2 followed up with a second forum, inviting every resident who had attended the first. Two hundred new citizen participants attended as well. The third and fourth community forums transitioned from expressing concerns to discussing and compiling possible solutions.

It was now the fall of 1996, almost a year before the 1997 election during which the 10 Plus 2 wanted to place a school construction bond issue on the ballot. In November, the group received some positive foreshadowing. In 1993, voters in Steamboat Springs had approved a half-cent sales tax for schools. Three years later, they renewed the sales tax by a wide margin, 60 percent to 40 percent. Community leaders saw passage of the extension as a reaffirmation of the town's essential support for public education.

The 10 Plus 2 reviewed and organized the recommendations from the final community forums, grouping the suggestions under six categories: curriculum, finance, facilities, communication, innovative concepts, and accountability. The 10 Plus 2 then established action task forces comprising 12 to 18 persons for each of the six categories. Each action task force was led by cochairs—one who had supported the bond issue, the other who had opposed it. The membership of each task force was equally divided between "yes" and "no" voters on the failed 1995 bond issue.

For two months, these task forces met, with cochairs holding monthly meetings with the 10 Plus 2 to facilitate information flow among the six groups. By the spring of 1997, the 10 Plus 2 had received the task force reports. After refining and integrating the reports, the 10 Plus 2 was prepared to submit a series of recommendations to the school board for its consideration and submission to the voters.

The 10 Plus 2 was not the only entity promoting a spirit of change. The school board had previously dismissed the architect who designed the proposed 1995 high school and the bond underwriter who would have procured the financing. The new bond underwriters agreed to provide the funding for a professional pollster to assess public opinion before the bond issue was finalized. They recommended a Texas academic and long-time Republican pollster, Dr. David Hill.

Hill arrived in Steamboat Springs in early June 1997. Through a series of face-to-face meetings and conference-call discussions, Hill gained perspective on the schools from a diverse set of community members. Aware that the school board had the final say as to whether and how a bond issue would appear on the 1997 ballot, Hill was especially attentive to board members' questions.

By late August 1997, Hill was ready to go into the field. He and his survey research team conducted 304 telephone interviews with local voters who had been selected to represent the diversity of the community (see excerpt of the poll in the appendix at the end of this chapter). Hill described the effort as one of assessment rather than persuasion. His goal was to determine voter attitudes on the bond issue and use that information to refine the campaign message. The results were illuminating and encouraging:

- Overall, voters were inclined to support the bond issue by a margin of 62 percent to 26 percent.
- The two groups that most influenced community opinions on the bond issue were local schoolteachers (39 percent of those surveyed listed them as most influential) and students currently enrolled in Steamboat schools (30 percent rated them as most persuasive).
- Of the 47 percent of Steamboat voters who were familiar with the work of 10 Plus 2, two-thirds evaluated its work as open, fair, and complete.
- Fifty-seven percent (57%) thought the level of local and school taxes was "about right."
- Steamboat Springs schools received a grade of A or B from 53 percent of the respondents; only 6 percent rated them D or F.
- Sixty-six percent (66%) thought most local public schools in Steamboat were overcrowded, and 47 percent thought school maintenance was insufficient.
- Two-thirds believed that the school board had been more responsive to parents and taxpayers following the 1995 bond issue defeat.
- A massive majority—85 percent—stated that striving for educational excellence was a high priority. Two-thirds ranked giving teachers the tools and space to be effective instructors as a critical goal.
- Of those surveyed, 78 percent gave as a reason to support the bond issue the new architect's provision of facilities for the visual arts and music.

Armed with these data, the 10 Plus 2 worked feverishly to turn public opinion into actual votes. On November 4, 1997, Steamboat Springs saw a record turnout of voters. When the votes were counted, the bond issue had passed, 77 percent to 23 percent. Looking back at the events that led to victory, Jim Gill, one of the school board members, summed them up as follows: "The defeat of the 1995 bond issue was a train wreck. But it took a train wreck to help us get back on the right track. The train wreck was a blessing in disguise."

POSTSCRIPT: BACK TO THE FUTURE

History has a funny way of repeating itself. Two decades after the 10 Plus 2 effort turned initial defeat into ultimate victory and with the town's population having grown to 12,100, the Steamboat Springs Board of Education voted unanimously to put a $96 million school construction and renovation bond issue on the November 2015 ballot.[2] When the results were announced on Election Day, voters had defeated

[2] Teresa Ristow, "$92 Million Steamboat Springs School Construction Bond Will be on November Ballot," *Steamboat Today*, August 25, 2015, www.steamboattoday.com/news/2015/aug/25/92-million-steamboat-springs-school-construction-b/

the measure even more soundly than they had the 1995 version—by a margin of 79 percent to 21 percent.[3]

In a post-election editorial, *Steamboat Today* urged school leaders not to give up, but to reflect on history and use the lessons of 10 Plus 2 to rebuild their effort.

> The school district and school board must now find a way to bring together people from both sides of the issue and seek common ground. . . .
>
> Exactly 20 years ago, the school district stood at the very same crossroads after a $41.8 million bond issue to build a new high school outside of downtown failed by a more than two-to-one margin. School leaders then were able to chart a new course that two years later resulted in overwhelming support for a $24.75 million bond issue that financed remodeling and expansion of the existing high school on Maple Street.
>
> This effort, known as the "10-plus-two" campaign, became a model for other school districts across the state. . . .This effort . . . attracted hundreds of community members, and the discussions eventually produced a solid solution to the district's need for more space.
>
> Through this community-minded approach real buy-in was achieved, and on Nov. 4, 1997, Steamboat Springs voters approved the new bond issue proposal for a new high school downtown by an impressive 77 percent to 23 percent.
>
> It's a smart strategy that worked well then, and we believe it can work now.[4]

Local leaders took that advice and appointed a diverse 18-member Community Committee for Education (cc4e.org) to prepare for the next possible bond issue in 2017. Like 10 Plus 2, the group included people who had voted for and against the November 2015 ballot proposition. Like 10 Plus 2, the committee scheduled multiple public forums in March 2016 to "spark a community dialogue on how to provide the best education for Steamboat Springs students."[5] Like 10 Plus 2, the group collected and published public comments from the meetings. And like 10 Plus 2, the effort may succeed in reversing the previous electoral outcome. Stay tuned.

WHY DOES PUBLIC OPINION MATTER?

As you have no doubt noticed, none of the skills presented in these chapters is sufficient, on its own, to turn your well-intentioned initiative into governmental reality. Instead, you will have to use these skills in combination with others if you want to persuade decision makers to embrace your cause. The court of public opinion is the place where your efforts find synergy. If you have your finger on the pulse of popular

---

[3] Teresa Ristow, "Steamboat Says "No" to $92 Million School Bond, 79 Percent Opposed," *Steamboat Today*, November 3, 2015, www.steamboattoday.com/news/2015/nov/03/steamboat-says-no-92-million-school-bond-77-percen//

[4] "Our View: A History Lesson for School Leaders," *Steamboat Today*, November 3, 2015, www.steamboattoday.com/news/2015/nov/03/our-view-history-lesson-school-leaders/

[5] "Our View: Get involved, get informed," *Steamboat Today*, March 29, 2016, www.steamboattoday.com/news/2016/mar/29/our-view-get-involved-get-informed/

thinking, you can more effectively define your problem, focus your research, determine your optimal coalition partners, engage reporters, raise money, and apply all of the other tools presented in this book.

This is not to say that you should simply determine public opinion and design your initiative to follow it blindly. The act of telling people just what they want to hear is not leadership. But if you know where people stand at the start of your citizen advocacy, and keep a close watch on their ever-shifting feelings and impressions, you will have a strong sense of what arguments will persuade them to adopt your position. Once you have key stakeholders and the public on your side, your chances of convincing the officials accountable to them will increase immeasurably.

Put another way, you will know how to connect with the decision makers (e.g., government officials) or with the people who heavily influence them (e.g., voters, citizens, coalition partners, media). In order to connect, you need to know where your targets stand now—and what data or arguments will move them to a position of support.

In addition to gaining these strategic benefits, you will also enjoy tactical advantages if you stay abreast of public opinion. Your initiative is no place to fly blind or utilize a one-size-fits-all approach. If you analyze relevant public opinion thoroughly from the outset, and continue to update the analysis throughout your campaign, you will be able to take the following steps that will help you reach your ultimate goal.

1. Determine the Level of Support

The first step is to determine whether you have strong public support at the beginning or whether you will need to convince people to support you. This is a vital action that you should not take lightly. More than one advocacy effort has foundered because its advocates were convinced of the righteousness of their cause, and they assumed that decision makers would do the right thing and support them without question. Barack Obama learned this lesson during his first two years as president. Though he was elected in 2008 by a relatively large margin and enjoyed sizeable Democratic majorities in both houses of Congress, his administration struggled to pass key priorities like economic stimulus legislation and health care reform. The president's favorability ratings plummeted. Interviewed by the *New York Times Magazine* in 2010, President Obama candidly admitted he and his team had focused on being right at the expense of being successful:

> "Given how much stuff was coming at us," Obama told me, "we probably spent much more time trying to get the policy right than trying to get the politics action right. There is probably a perverse pride in my administration—and I take responsibility for this; this was blowing from the top—that we were going to do the right thing, even if short-term it was unpopular. And I think anybody who's occupied this office has to remember that success is determined by an intersection in policy and politics and that you can't be neglecting of marketing and P.R. and public opinion."[6]

Former Senate Majority Leader Tom Daschle, a close Obama ally, echoed the president's sentiment when he observed in the same article that "If anybody thought

---

[6] Peter Baker, "Education of a President," *New York Times Magazine*, October 12, 2010, www.nytimes.com/2010/10/17/magazine/17obama-t.html?_r=0

the Republicans were just going to roll over, we were just terribly mistaken. . . I'm not sure anybody really thought that, but I think we kind of hoped the Republicans would go away. And obviously they didn't do that."

The merits of your citizen advocacy plan are never enough to win public support and decision-maker backing. Even if your goal is as seemingly noncontroversial as curing cancer, cleaning up a local lake, or creating more after-school activities for kids, don't assume that you have an automatic reservoir of support with the decision maker or with the stakeholders—not the least of which is the citizenry—that influence the decision maker. Make the effort to know for sure.

2. Identify the Arguments
Most Likely to Resonate with the Public

You almost certainly have your own reasons for wanting the relevant decision makers to embrace your cause, but others may have different reasons, even if they support the same goal. When you test public opinion, you can identify which arguments are appealing and which are not so effective. For example, assume that you want your local town council to install a traffic light at a busy intersection near your home. Your motivation is simple: A light will better regulate traffic flow, ease congestion, and make it easier for you to drive in your own neighborhood. But your neighbors and others positioned to sway the council may have other concerns. Residents who have children or pets may be concerned about safety. Others may see the traffic light as an improvement that increases neighborhood property values. If you take the time to learn all of the reasons that other people might have for supporting your idea, you will discover multiple arguments that can be used to persuade the decision maker.

3. Anticipate and Rebut the Opposition's Arguments

As President Obama learned in 2009 and 2010, it isn't enough to have strong points on your side. In order to be successful, you must anticipate, evaluate and rebut contentions that your opponents will make. Public opinion research gives you the ability to test the opposition's arguments and determine which ones are most likely to resonate with both decision makers and those stakeholders who can influence decision makers. If you have that information, you can be ready with responses when the inevitable pushback comes. Rest assured that it is coming.

4. "Microtarget" Specific
Groups of Persuadable Officials or Citizens

Whether you are running a candidate for office, supporting an issue initiative for voters' approval, or working to persuade elected or appointed officials to adopt your position on a governmental matter, the same argument won't necessarily appeal to every member of the electorate. In any advocacy effort, different groups of voters may have different interests and be open to different methods of persuasion. This is why public surveys always ask a wide range of demographic questions (age, race, gender, occupation, geographical location, income, and political party membership and identification). Once armed with that information, you can tailor your message for a particular group.

But although demographic distinctions are extremely helpful in targeting segments of the public, other distinctions also matter. If you are trying to change policy through your local school board, you may determine that one method will best persuade parents, another will influence faculty and administrators, yet another will appeal to business and community leaders, and still another will attract students' interest. The point is to know various segments of the public so well that you can communicate effectively with all of them, regardless of their differences.

My home state of Florida provided an early yet telling example of effective microtargeting in the 1974 race for the U.S. Senate. At that time, Florida still employed a system in which no candidate could receive the party's nomination for office unless he or she received an electoral majority (50 percent plus one vote). If no candidate received a majority during the first primary election, the top two vote getters advanced to a second primary election. The candidate who won this runoff would become the party's nominee and compete in the November general election.

In 1974, 11 Democrats ran for the U.S. Senate nomination. Two emerged from the pack: front runner and U.S. Representative Bill Gunter, a Central Floridian, and Florida's secretary of state, Dick Stone, a Miami resident who would become the first directly elected Jewish senator from a southern state if he won in November. Gunter had won a convincing victory in the first primary, but he did not achieve an electoral majority. On the other hand, Stone finished a distant second and barely edged out the third-place candidate. While it was assumed that Stone would run well in South Florida, most political observers believed that Gunter would capture large margins in Central and North Florida, where his southern accent and folksy manner would be decisive factors in winning votes.

But Stone had refused to concede any territory. He showed a folksy side of his own by playing the harmonica and spoons on campaign stops in North Florida, and he criticized what he saw as excessive federal government spending. His parochial appeals and conservative message paid off. On the day of the runoff, Stone won strong support at home in South Florida and added enough votes in North Florida to win statewide by a narrow margin, 51 percent to 49 percent. One month later Stone won the general election and became a U.S. senator.[7]

More than four decades later, microtargeting is far more sophisticated and technological than it was in 1974.[8] Public opinion researchers have long mined publicly available data such as voter registration lists and corresponding election activity to attain as much precision as possible in surveying members of the public. The evolution of so-called voter data files in the past decade means even more information that can be used to thin-slice the electorate or citizenry. As pollster Mike Bocian explains, "Statistical modeling has dramatically improved microtargeting. We apply

---

[7] Jack Bass and Walter De Vries, *The Transformation of Southern Politics* (Athens: University of Georgia Press, 1995), 125; Alan Abramowitz and Jeffrey Alan Segal, *Senate Elections* (Ann Arbor: University of Michigan Press, 1992), 79; Michael Barone, Grant Ujifusa, and Douglas Matthews, *The Almanac of American Politics 1976* (New York: Dutton, 1975), 161–62. Please note that Stone and Gunter had a rematch in the 1980 Democratic primary, and this time Gunter won.

[8] Gwen Ifill, "How 'Microtargeting' Works in Political Advertising [Interview with Ken Goldstein and Eitan Hersh]," *PBS*, February 18, 2014, www.pbs.org/newshour/bb/how-microtargeting-works-political-advertising/

a score to every person on the voter file. The score could be the likelihood of them voting, how liberal or conservative they are, whether they are likely to support a tax increase for education or senior services. These types of models have moved us from blunt targeting to much more precise targeting that massively improves our ability to conduct targeted persuasion and get out the vote communications."[9]

Now political campaigns and citizen efforts can use nonpolitical information such as charitable giving, online purchases, Internet music selection, and vehicular ownership to develop household profiles and target advertising and messages directly to individuals.[10] This tool has become very valuable to campaigns, which explains the furor in December 2015 when some Democratic political operatives improperly accessed voter file information from another candidate's database.[11]

In their respective submissions to Tips from the Pros, Michael Meyers of TargetPoint Consulting and Dylan Sumner of Mack Sumner explain how modern microtargeting works.

TIPS FROM THE PROS

Microtargeting 101
MICHAEL MEYERS

Microtargeting is a tool for candidates, campaigns, and advocacy causes that answers the most fundamental questions: Who supports my candidate or cause? Where do I find them? How do I motivate them to provide support? How do I persuade others to support us?

The process works at the crossroads of three related disciplines: customer relationship management technologies, advanced marketing techniques, and traditional political targeting. By merging together the best practices of the fields, microtargeting can sequence each individual voter's unique political DNA to identify that person's likely political attitudes and behaviors.

Microtargeting informs, sharpens, and increases the efficiency of a campaign's or cause's direct citizen contact plans, allowing politicians or advocacy groups to send individually targeted messages delivered by the proper messengers. For example, even

(Continued)

---

[9] Electronic mail from Mike Bocian to Chris Hand, November 18, 2015.

[10] Tanzina Vega, "Online Data Helping Campaigns Customize Ads," *New York Times*, February 20, 2012, www.nytimes.com/2012/02/21/us/politics/campaigns-use-microtargeting-to-attract-supporters .html?_r=0

[11] Evan Halper, "Fallout from Data Breach Threatens Bernie Sanders' Campaign," *Los Angeles Times*, December 18, 2015, www.latimes.com/nation/politics/la-na-sanders-campaign-data-breach-20151218-story.html

(Continued)

if they lived right next door to each other, a "Faith and Family Republican" might receive literature from prominent religious leaders on efforts to promote adoptions, while a "Tax and Terrorism Moderate" could get an automated call from Rudy Giuliani talking about the "War on Terror."

Microtargeting begins with this basic assumption: no single data point can tell you the whole story. Survey research that focuses on crosstabs such as income, gender, race, and other demographics only provides a fraction of the story. Looking at the interaction between the various data provides a far more detailed look at your voters. By using hundreds of data points, comprised of voter information, life cycle information, lifestyle information, financial data, consumer behavior, geographic data, and political attitudes and preferences, microtargeting can be used to assign each of your voters or advocacy targets into one of a number of custom-designed message groups, each defined by a unique combination of a host of data points.

Yes, the car you drive and the coffee you drink may have something to do with how you vote or what motivates your support, but what if that SUV you drive is a hybrid? What if the driver is a married man living in Sioux Falls? What if that Starbucks drinker is sipping in an evangelical coffee house? What if this Bible reader also belongs to Greenpeace? How does the aggregate effect of each data point increase or decrease the likelihood a voter will support your side?

For decades, campaigns have relied on different types of targeting, mainly based on geography, party registration, and vote history. Increasingly, however, this level of targeting was leaving some of the campaign's best voters stranded and untouched.

Think of that blue-collar "independent" who sat out the last election and lives in an overwhelmingly Democratic precinct. Microtargeting allows you to look at that voter and see that he also drives a truck, owns a gun, has three kids, and is very angry about illegal immigration. It not only adds him and others just like him to your pool of potential voters, but it also allows you to communicate with them more effectively. In that way, microtargeting is the difference between shouting to a group and speaking intimately with each individual voter.

Microtargeting becomes the search and rescue mission for a campaign or cause, connecting with supporters who would have remained untouched under traditional targeting programs.

Perhaps no example better illustrates the value of microtargeting than that of former Governor Linda Lingle's 2006 reelection campaign in Hawaii. Governor Lingle knew she faced steep odds of being reelected—Hawaii, never an especially hospitable state for Republicans, was turning further blue as the Republican Party's overall image declined heading into the midterm elections. She needed to put together perhaps the most diverse coalition in America in order to be successful in her reelection efforts.

Governor Lingle needed to go far beyond the traditional Republican "customer" and expand her voter base into independents and traditional Democrats. First, microtargeting helped her to find dispirited Republicans on whom she focused her GOTV efforts. Second, she finely honed her message to the diverse groups spread across Hawaii, talking about the issues that mattered most to them—focusing on the Republican message of crime and punishment but also including nontraditional messaging on the environment, affordable housing, and education.

By carefully selecting her messages and pairing them with the audiences most likely to care about those messages, Governor Lingle not only survived a year that saw many Republicans turned out of office but also received the highest vote margin in the history of the state, winning 63 percent to 35 percent.

Microtargeting has undoubtedly changed the face of political campaigning and issue advocacy. But avoid the temptation to see it as a computer-generated, turnkey solution for the challenges of a modern political campaign or advocacy effort. It isn't a silver bullet—it's a tool. And like any tool, its use is part of the collaborative, strategic decision-making process between the microtargeting team and the campaign.

At the end of the day, microtargeting becomes another arrow in the advocacy quiver—an arrow your opponent likely already has. On its own, microtargeting will never win any campaign. But used appropriately in a tight election or challenging citizen cause, it can provide the competitive edge you need to win.

As president of TargetPoint Consulting (targetpointconsulting.com), Michael Meyers helps guide the company and maintains a broad range of political and corporate clients. Michael's past political clients include presidential, senatorial, gubernatorial, and congressional candidates, such as Mitt Romney; Senators Rob Portman, Richard Burr, and Pat Toomey; and Governors Nathan Deal and Chris Christie. He has represented ballot campaigns such as Michigan's Clean Affordable Renewable Energy initiative. While at TargetPoint, Michael has also worked with a number of corporate and association clients including Walmart, AT&T, Magnolia Pictures/2929 Entertainment, and a number of energy related clients such as the American Petroleum Institute. He also serves as an adjunct professor at The George Washington University.

TIPS FROM THE PROS

Targeting (aka Microtargeting)
DYLAN SUMNER

Every campaign or grassroots effort has limited resources. The relative lack of money and time are significant challenges to achieving any "victory" in public relations, policy, ballot initiative, or campaign efforts. Targeting maximizes efficiency for these efforts by simply and specifically choosing which voters/citizens to contact and which ones to leave alone.

Hundreds of books have been written about the complex and intricate targeting methods used by national and high-profile campaigns. At its core, good targeting is simply about using target-specific data to ensure that you are delivering the right message to the right people. And, it's remarkably simple to do.

(Continued)

(Continued)

Four Steps to Better Targeting

1. Understand Your Mission

What are you trying to accomplish? Maybe you're trying to mobilize married women to contact their legislator to urge them to increase funding for your local schools. Maybe you're working to persuade undecided voters to support your ballot initiative. Or perhaps you're concerned that people who support your cause won't show up on Election Day.

No matter your program, you can't begin the process of targeting voters without a clear understanding of the goals for your voter contact program.

Targeting for Persuasion. If you're trying to convince voters to support your candidate or cause, don't spend money talking to people who are registered but consistently do not vote in elections—they're a waste of your time and money. Target voters who are likely to be undecided but are almost certain to show up at the polls.

Targeting for Turnout. When mobilizing voters specifically to turn out, keep in mind that some people never vote. Others vote every time they can. Neither of these groups should be the focus of your turnout communications. Concentrate on people who are likely to support your cause but have a spotty voting history.

Targeting for Signatures and Volunteers. "Birds of a feather flock together" is as true in politics as anywhere else; faith communities, social clubs, and even neighborhoods can be somewhat predictive of a person's attitudes on political issues. Using polling research (see below) or even simple observation, you can identify parts of your district that are more likely to be home to supporters than others. Anyone can volunteer, but if you're looking for signatures, make sure you understand who is eligible to sign your petition.

2. Start with Research

The foundation for everything in a grassroots effort is research; targeting is no different. Do everything you can to understand your district, your campaign, your messaging, and your targets.

Election and Voter Data. How many people voted in this election last time it was held? Who were they? Who's eligible to vote this time around? It may sound simple, but basic research into past data is a key component to understanding the race you are running.

Polling Research. What arguments are effective, and with whom? Who is already supportive of your initiative? Who opposes you, no matter what? Polling is the only reliable way to get answers to these questions.

You'll often find different subgroups of people respond to your message in different ways. Sometimes, different groups find different aspects of your campaign or issue appealing. Other times, you're best off not communicating with a specific group of citizens at all. You should ask your pollster to provide crosstab data for targetable attributes (age, race, gender, party affiliation), so you can make sure the right citizens/voters are hearing the right thing from your campaign.

3. Learn What Tools Are Available to You—and How to Use Them

Unless you're running for class president of a small high school, you can't run an effective targeting operation out of a spreadsheet. Fortunately, over the past several years, powerful, state-of-the-art voter file systems have moved online and are more accessible than ever.

Online Voter File Systems. Talk to your state party or an allied organization about gaining access to an online voter file. There may be a small fee (usually based on the size of the campaign you're running), but you will more than recoup the cost from the efficiency that comes with using a state-of-the-art targeting program—and you will benefit from the advice and training that comes from the party's staff.

Voter files will contain lists of registered voters, along with their voting history, party registration, what precinct they live in, and at least some contact information. All of this is critical for targeted communications.

Predictive Modeling. Many, if not most, voter file systems come with generic predictive models. By looking at voters who share characteristics, models seek to quantify the likelihood a voter has a certain characteristic (such as support of a candidate, issue, or party) or the likelihood an individual will take a certain action (such as voting in an upcoming election).

In the right hands, these can be great tools to simply and accurately target key voters in your race. But beware: the incorrect use of a model can have disastrous consequences. Always confirm the model is up to date and accurate before using it for your campaign.

If you have the resources, your pollster may be able to create custom predictive models for your race and provide instructions on how to use them.

4. Remember That Targeting Is Not a Silver Bullet

Targeting helps your operation save resources by increasing the efficiency of individual contact programs. It does not replace or reduce the need for a robust contact program.

Communication Still Matters Most. Identifying the perfect targets won't do you any good if you can't communicate to those targets effectively and turn them into votes. It's always best to invest in high-quality, effective communications.

Target to Win. Targeting makes everything you do more efficient. But don't make the mistake of maximizing efficiency at the expense of not moving enough bodies or voters. If you need to persuade 10,000 voters to win, targeting 5,000 voters doesn't do you any good. If you need 2,500 petitions sent to a specific policymaker, you need to target at least twice as many.

Dylan Sumner is a senior partner at Mack Sumner (macksumner.com). He previously served as district manager and press secretary for Congressman Pete Peterson and as a senior field director and political director for the Academy of Florida Trial Lawyers (now the Florida Justice Association, floridajusticeassociation.org). For nearly a decade, he has worked as lead mail strategist for major organizations and for dozens of U.S. Representatives, U.S. Senators, state legislators, and parties.

Once you have identified the distinct segments of the public and have determined which arguments are most likely to persuade each of them, you will find that each of the citizen advocacy tasks identified in the other chapters will come into better focus. To use a slightly modified example of the problem mentioned earlier, let's assume that you are concerned about increasing traffic on a street in your neighborhood, and your goal is to have the local government install new safety devices (lights, stop signs, or traffic calming circles). In an effort to find coalition partners, you determine there are three groups that will have the most interest in the traffic devices: families with children who must cross the street to reach the neighborhood elementary school; store owners at a nearby strip mall, who depend on street traffic for most of their customers; and students and faculty at a commuter community college branch located near the strip mall.

Effective public opinion analysis may show which of these groups is more likely to persuade elected officials (city commissioners or council members), key appointed officials (police and traffic planners), and different types of citizens who influence both groups. Once you have recruited the elementary school parent-teacher organization, merchants' association, and community college faculty senate and student government to join the cause, you can ask them to take responsibility for individual groups of decision makers or segments of the general public with whom they can have the most impact. As your advocacy progresses, keep a close eye on social media to see if one or more coalition partner is having more of an impact on public opinion than the others, and should be moved to the forefront of your persuasion campaign. Regardless of whether your advocacy effort is at the local, state, or federal level, you can still build public support across the spectrum of the citizenry. Although diversity is one of the strengths of our democracy, it also complicates the tasks of gauging and shaping overall public opinion. Microtargeting helps to organize the members of the public into persuadable parts.

5. Get the Most Bang for Your Buck

Any campaign or citizen initiative that fails to allocate its main resources efficiently is probably doomed to failure. Public opinion research is critical to ensure that time, money, and energy are spent wisely. Successful advocacy efforts don't waste significant resources trying to persuade either true believers or lost causes. If your analysis demonstrates that people in Group A strongly support your cause, make sure that they register their opinion with the decision maker—don't waste time trying to convince them. If those in Group B strongly oppose your initiative, don't waste energy trying to convert them. Instead, focus your persuasion efforts on Group C, whose members are predominantly undecided and may break your way if you communicate with them frequently and effectively.

HOW DO I DETERMINE WHAT PUBLIC OPINION IS?

In many respects, politics is an art rather than a science. Although the goal of this book is to provide you with the basic skills and insights you need to be an effective citizen advocate, you'll find that political success involves lots of improvisation, learning by experience, and good fortune. However, the accurate determination of public opinion is one aspect of the political process that often relies on scientific principles. This analysis can take many forms.

Polling

Polling is one of the most effective ways to gauge public opinion accurately. In American politics today, nearly all candidates—from citizens running for city council and state legislative seats to those seeking to win the presidential nomination—utilize polling as part of their road map to victory. Political candidates, issue campaigns subject to voter approval, and many citizen advocacy initiatives often use it for diverse reasons: to measure support for their candidacies or issues, to gauge support for the opposition, and to determine where voters stand on a variety of issues. Polling is useful in determining how prospective voters or decision makers will react to potential policy proposals, to positive or negative information about a candidate or an issue, and to opponents of the candidate or issue—and to opponents of the candidate or issue. Polling has become popular because it maximizes limited resources. In any kind of campaign, it is virtually impossible to contact every potential voter or every individual who might be affected by the outcome of an initiative to determine where each stands on the candidates or the issues. In statewide, county-wide, or even citywide efforts, this could mean making contact with thousands or even millions of individuals. The cost of such an effort, in terms of both time and money spent, would be prohibitive.

Pollsters employ a shortcut. They analyze the group in which you are interested to determine certain key demographic statistics (such as age, sex, party affiliation, ethnic background, and geographic location). Using that data, they poll not the entire target population but instead a representative sample that mimics the demographic characteristics of the whole population. Let's say your goal is to pass an amendment to the county charter that would sharply restrict the construction of billboards along local roadways. Because voters must approve the measure, and a poll would be worthless without a representative sample that accurately mimics the electorate, your pollster will need to know that your county's registered voters are 43 percent Republican, 43 percent Democratic, and 14 percent third party or unaffiliated. The pollster will need to know that 52 percent of the county citizens registered to vote are female and 48 percent are male. Similar statistics about age, race, and other demographic categories will ensure that the polling sample is a microcosm of the entire voting-eligible population.

Once a pollster has set the sample characteristics, he or she conducts telephone interviews with anywhere from 200 to more than 1,000 people to determine how these individuals feel about candidates, issues, and other subjects. The number of interviews conducted is significant because it affects the poll's margin of error. Simply put, the margin of error is the numerical amount by which the poll results could be off in either direction. For example, a countywide poll that completes 200 interviews likely has a margin of error of plus or minus 7 percent. In other words, if the poll results show that Issue Position A has 43 percent support and Issue Position B has 36 percent, Position A's lead could be as much as 14 percent or there could be no lead at all. Position A's advantage is said to be "within the margin of error," meaning the contest is too close to predict a result with any certainty.

Most pollsters contend that 200–300 interviews are the minimum number needed to generate meaningful public opinion data. Each additional interview beyond 200–300 reduces the error rate but also adds to the expense of the poll. If you have sufficient funds, you may want to consider conducting as many as 600 to 1,000 interviews as that large sample size will help distinguish differences between diverse groups.

An increased poll size is especially important if you want to test attitudes both generally and among a discrete group of the overall population. Assume your goal is to convince a majority of the seven-member county commission to oppose a proposal to build a new solid waste landfill near environmentally sensitive lands. Three commissioners have announced support for the project. Three are opposed. The remaining member—the "swing" vote on the commission—is undecided. In your poll of the entire county, you would need to include enough people from that commissioner's district so you can reliably gauge how his or her constituents feel about the proposal. Your chances of persuading that member to side with you increase if you have credible information about both countywide and district-specific responses to the landfill.

This polling method generally produces accurate results indicating what the target population is thinking about a candidate or an issue. Rather than having to spend the enormous energy and time necessary to communicate individually with, say, 100,000 people, you can obtain virtually the same data after talking to less than 1 percent of that population. Just know that polling can be very expensive. Depending on the sample size and complexity of the questionnaire, pollsters charge tens of thousands of dollars to design the poll, hire call centers where professionals conduct telephone interviews with voters, and compile and analyze the results.

TIPS FROM THE PROS

The Dos and Don'ts of Public Opinion Surveys
MICHAEL BOCIAN

Surveys remain the best way to measure public opinion in a scientific, statistically representative way. Here are some key steps to follow when conducting a poll:

1. Identify what sample size makes sense for your campaign's goals and budget. A bigger sample size is always better—it provides a greater degree of confidence with more subgroups of your target population. But you need to weigh the benefits of a large sample size with the cost of conducting the survey.

2. Determine the target universe for your survey. If it's an election survey, look at similar previous elections, population changes, and project what the electorate is likely to be. Understand that you are fallible and should consider a range of possibilities, depending on how the campaign progresses.

3. Ensure that the sample of people who take your survey resembles the target universe. Younger people, low-income people, and communities of color are

typically more difficult to reach, so you need to ensure you are reaching them. Prepare to do some post-survey weighting to account for people who were harder to reach, but try to deal with the issue at the front end by ensuring you interview a sufficient number of hard-to-read populations.[12]

4. Start by outlining your goals. What are you trying to learn? How will it be actionable?

5. Draft a survey instrument that starts by measuring public opinion as it exists today through asking unbiased questions. Have several people, including those with little knowledge of the topic, read the questionnaire to ensure there are no confusing or ambiguously worded questions.

6. Give careful consideration to question order, ensuring that the placement of a question does not produce a biased result because respondents are influenced by a previous question.

7. If you want to test messages, do so from both sides. Imagine you are on the other side and write messages from that perspective. This will also help you prepare for the campaign. Retest public opinion on the issue after respondents hear your arguments and after they hear your opposition's arguments. Rotate which sides arguments are heard first.

8. Consider A/B experiments during which some voters hear one message and some voters hear another. Then retest the issue afterwards. This enables you to measure not just conscious opinions but unconscious ones.

9. Monitor the survey to ensure the questions are being asked correctly and that you can make any adjustments needed before it's too late.

10. Conduct a full analysis of the results. Don't rely on any one question, but look for the story line that runs through the data. Pay attention to both breadth of support and intensity of support. Breadth of support is most important when you are trying to pass a ballot initiative or bond measure. Intensity of support is most important when you are trying to motivate people to take action or when we are trying to help a candidate stand out in a race with many candidates.

Michael Bocian, founding partner at GBA Strategies (gbastrategies.com), serves as pollster and strategist for gubernatorial, senate, congressional, state legislative, mayoral, and ballot initiative campaigns. With 15 years of experience, he has worked for political organizations, issue advocacy groups, and membership associations.

---

[12] Weighting data is the process of compensating for known differences between the sample of people you survey and the full universe from which you are sampling. For instance, let's assume your universe is all residents of a given city. We know from census data that 15% of residents are African American, but the composition of your sample is 13% African American. In order to make the sample consistent with the actual population, you would weight the 13% up to 15%. Weighting is more challenging in situations where you are projecting a universe that is not totally set, such as who will vote in a given election. As noted in the tips, it is best to use rigorous calling procedures to ensure you are reaching your target populations in the right percentages. Calling procedures that require excessive weighting introduce greater sampling error.

OTHER METHODS OF MEASURING PUBLIC OPINION

Traditional telephone polling of the citizenry has its challenges and its detractors. For example, the nature of polling is changing as home telephone lines have become an endangered species. More and more people use cell phones exclusively or predominantly. In December 2015, the Centers for Disease Control released survey results showing that nearly half of United States homes only used cell phones.[13] For those adults renting their homes, or between the ages of 25 and 34, more than two-thirds lived in households without landlines.

With this rapidly changing dynamic, it is little wonder that a June 2015 study from two Oklahoma State University professors concluded that overuse of home telephone numbers likely affects the accuracy of polling results.[14] As Professor Mark Payton told *Campaigns & Elections*, "The cellphone-only households don't poll the same as the landlines, in general. If [pollsters] continue to do business like they did in 2012, I expect they'll have some bias [this cycle]."[15] As a result, pollsters are routinely conducting a significant share of their interviews via mobile phone. But since cell phones must by law be hand dialed rather than using so-called "auto-dialers," incorporating them into a polling sample adds time and expense.

Other factors also seem to be affecting pollsters' abilities to obtain a truly representative polling sample. For example, fewer people are responding to telephone surveys.[16] According to the Pew Research Center,

> It has become increasingly difficult to contact potential respondents and to persuade them to participate. The percentage of households in a sample that are successfully interviewed—the response rate—has fallen dramatically. At Pew Research, the response rate of a typical telephone survey was 36% in 1997 and is just 9% today.[17]

These factors may explain why polling has recently suffered some high-profile embarrassments. As Kentucky's Election Day approached in November 2015, Democratic gubernatorial candidate Jack Conway had a small but consistent lead in the polls. It was widely believed that he would win and serve as the next Kentucky governor. But when the votes were counted, Republican Matt

---

[13] Stephen J. Blumberg and Julian V. Luke, "Wireless Substitution: Early Release of Estimates from the National Health Interview Survey, January–June 2015," *National Health Interview Survey Early Release Program*, December 2015, www.cdc.gov/nchs/data/nhis/earlyrelease/wireless201512.pdf

[14] See Ole J. Forsberg and Mark E. Payton, "Analysis of Battleground State Presidential Polling Performances, 2004–2012," *Statistics and Public Policy* 2, no. 1 (2015): 1–10, dx.doi.org/10.1080/2330443X.2015.1034389

[15] Sean J. Miller, "Study Tells Pollsters: Call More Cellphones," *Campaigns & Elections*, June 16, 2015, campaignsandelections.com/campaign-insider/2472/study-tells-pollsters-call-more-cellphones

[16] Nate Silver, "Polling Is Getting Harder, But It's a Vital Check on Power," *FiveThirtyEight*, June 3, 2015, fivethirtyeight.com/features/polling-is-getting-harder-but-its-a-vital-check-on-power/

[17] Pew Research Center, *Assessing the Representativeness of Public Opinion Surveys* (Washington, DC: Pew Research Center, May 15, 2012), 1, www.people-press.org/2012/05/15/assessing-the-representativeness-of-public-opinion-surveys/

Bevin had won by nearly 10 percentage points—practically a landslide.[18] One year earlier, polls had underestimated the ultimate success of Republican candidates in the midterm congressional and U.S. Senate elections by overestimating Democratic electoral performance.[19] In the 2012 presidential election, the final Gallup Poll showed former Massachusetts Governor Mitt Romney narrowly defeating President Barack Obama. When the president actually won by four points, Gallup had some explaining to do.[20] Each case reinforced the key point that the most accurate polls use the most representative samples—and those can be difficult and expensive to obtain.

Keep in mind that telephone polling is not always the appropriate or most accessible public opinion research method. If this type of polling does not satisfy your goals, or is not compatible with the scale of the population you need to sample or the size of your budget, other methods exist to take the public's temperature on a candidate or an issue.

Different Types of Survey Research

Interactive voice response (IVR) surveys. If you have ever received a "robo-call" touting a political candidate, selling a product, reminding you about a medical appointment, or providing information from the police department or school system, IVR polling—also known as "robo-polling"— won't be a mystery to you. Public opinion researchers who use this survey method program computers with lists of citizens to call and questions to ask those citizens.[21] People on the receiving end of IVR polling enter responses using their telephone keypads. This survey method can be less expensive than live telephone interviewing, but some question its methodology and accuracy. IVR surveying also benefits from an exemption in federal law. As of this writing in the spring of 2016, the Do Not Call Registry does not prohibit political robo-calls to landlines.

Internet polling. During the time you have read this chapter, chances are good that you have checked the Internet. That's not a guess. The World Bank found that nearly 90 percent of Americans had used the Internet at least once in 2014.[22] A Pew Charitable Trust survey released in June 2015 found that 84 percent of U.S. adults

---

[18] Alan Greenblatt, "The End of Political Polling," *Governing the States and Localities*, November 11, 2015, www.governing.com/topics/elections/gov-polling-problems-kentucky-presidential-elections.html

[19] Nate Silver, "The Polls Were Skewed toward Democrats," *FiveTirtyEight*, November 5, 2014, fivethirtyeight.com/features/the-polls-were-skewed-toward-democrats/

[20] Scott Clement, "Gallup Explains What Went Wrong in 2012," *Washington Post*, June 4, 2013, www.washingtonpost.com/news/the-fix/wp/2013/06/04/gallup-explains-what-went-wrong-in-2012/

[21] Éric Grenier, "How Robo-Calls Work: The Cheap and Easy Way to Poll," *Globe and Mail*, August 8, 2013, www.theglobeandmail.com/news/politics/how-robo-calls-work-the-cheap-and-easy-way-to-poll/article13656102/

[22] "Internet Users (per 100 people), 2011–2015," *World Bank*, data.worldbank.org/indicator/IT.NET.USER.P2

used the Internet.[23] Online polling has grown along with Internet usage. For example, as of late 2015, the Republican presidential nominating process had seen nearly as many Internet polls (90) as live telephone surveys.[24]

Participants can be invited to participate online by phone, via e-mail, on a website, or in other ways. As the *New York Times* reported in November 2015,

> The online pollsters may get clumped together because they use the Internet, but there's far greater diversity of methods among these polls than among telephone polls. The diversity is a reflection of the still-developing science of Internet polling. No one is sure of the right way to do it.
>
> Reuters has the most traditional approach: It recruited its panel from a traditional telephone and mail survey. YouGov and Morning Consult use panels recruited from a variety of sources on the Internet. Google entices people to take a poll. SurveyMonkey has the most novel approach: It turns to the millions of people who participate in any number of SurveyMonkey's unscientific polls on other subjects—the kind you can make yourself—and adds questions about politics.[25]

Internet polling has enough traction that major news organizations, such as CBS News, NBC News, and the *New York Times*, now work with online survey companies in their political coverage. But while online surveys may be increasing in usage and popularity, many pollsters question the reliability of Internet polling.[26] Part of this doubt reflects the fact that online polls, unlike live telephone surveys, do not at the time of this writing have tried-and-true methods of ensuring accurate samples of the population they are trying to measure. As Rutgers University professor of public policy and political science Cliff Zukin, a past president of the American Association for Public Opinion Research, opined in 2015, "we simply have not yet figured out how to draw a representative sample of Internet users."[27] But as Zukin also noted, the relatively low cost of these surveys has made them attractive even though they are "largely unproven methodologically."

Leadership polling. When a certain level of knowledge is needed, it is sometimes more effective to survey a distinct group of opinion leaders rather than the citizenry at large. In his tips (see Tips from the Pros: Leadership Polling), Jeffrey Boeyink explains a polling innovation focused on the most informed members of the citizenry.

---

[23] Andrew Perrin and Maeve Duggan, "Americans' Internet Access: 2000–2015," *Pew Research Center*, June 26, 2015, www.pewinternet.org/2015/06/26/americans-internet-access-2000-2015/

[24] Nate Cohn, "Online Polls Are Rising: So Are Concerns about Their Results," *New York Times*, November 27, 2015, www.nytimes.com/2015/11/28/upshot/online-polls-are-rising-so-are-concerns-about-their-results.html?_r=0

[25] Cohn, "Online Polls Are Rising," para. 8–9.

[26] Chris Cillizza, "The New York Times Rocked the Polling World over the Weekend. Here's Why," *Washington Post*, July 31, 2014, www.washingtonpost.com/news/the-fix/wp/2014/07/31/the-new-york-times-rocked-the-polling-world-over-the-weekend-heres-why/

[27] Cliff Zukin, "What's the Matter with Polling?" *New York Times*, June 20, 2015, www.nytimes.com/2015/06/21/opinion/sunday/whats-the-matter-with-polling.html

Leadership Polling
JEFFREY BOEYINK

While it might sound blasphemous, there are times when the opinions of the general public are simply of no value in a public policy debate. That's not to say the public doesn't matter, it just recognizes that often the public doesn't have enough knowledge of an issue to have an opinion that is truly instructive.

Does that mean there is no place for opinion surveys when the issues being tested are complex and require a level of engagement that isn't widely held by the general public? Absolutely not, and that is where leadership polling comes front and center as a method to gather opinion, but from a more narrowly selected sample that contains individuals with enough knowledge of the subject to matter.

When it comes to complex problems and even more complex proposed solutions, policymakers can benefit from a finely tuned leadership poll that targets the very populations with enough knowledge of the issue to have opinions relevant to the solutions at hand.

The key to a leadership poll is sample selection. Such a sample will often include

- Elected and appointed political officials;
- Neighborhood, civic educational, and religious leaders;
- Business owners or operators;
- Advocates, activists, and political and philanthropic donors; and
- Individuals with a particular knowledge base necessary for participation.

By the very nature of sample selection, the sample is likely to be skewed toward older, better educated, and more partisan individuals than a traditional sample of the general public. But it is a sample that will render results that are relevant to policymakers and the broad policy discussion on important, complex issues.

This very process was recently used by the Partnership to Fight Chronic Disease in a survey to garner views on how the new health care exchange was working in Iowa and to determine the level of support for potential state-based reforms.

Using a sample of 404 opinion leaders (selected as suggested above), policymakers learned there was support for three major state-based reforms regarding the health insurance exchange:

1. Requiring insurance companies to be completely open and transparent when Iowans are comparing coverage and benefits offered by competing insurance companies through the exchange. (92% support)
2. Mandating full and open access to information about appeals and denial procedures of insurers. (81% support)

(Continued)

(Continued)

   3. Eliminating discrimination against patients with preexisting or chronic conditions. (76% support)

Based on this leadership poll, legislation was developed and introduced in the Iowa General Assembly. Eventually, two of these three policy recommendations survived the legislative process and made it to the governor's desk.

Had the survey been conducted using traditional means, the vast majority of the respondents would likely have been individuals with no individual experience using the exchange, let alone specific knowledge of how the exchange was working in Iowa. The use of a leadership poll brought together a sample that rendered opinions based on knowledge and experience that made the policy recommendations that much more useful to policymakers.

Simply put, opinion polling is not just for the masses. It is also an appropriate tool to engage with smaller subsets of thought leaders to bring clarity and instruction to policymakers on solutions to complex issues. Leadership polling provides just such a tool and policymakers will benefit from its expanded use.

Jeff Boeyink is a partner at LS2group (ls2group.com) and specializes in government affairs. Before joining LS2group, Jeff was named Governor-Elect Terry Branstad's chief of staff and cochairman of Branstad's transition team on November 3, 2010. After spearheading the transition, Jeff served as chief of staff until September 6, 2013. He currently serves as a trusted policy and campaign advisor to many of Iowa's top political and business leaders.

Focus Groups

While telephone surveys, IVR techniques, and leadership polling are more quantitative in nature, professional pollsters and corporate market researchers often use the more qualitative method of convening focus groups to test candidate, issue, or product profiles; concepts; and arguments on potential voters or consumers. A focus group usually consists of a small gathering of individuals who represent the audience targeted by a campaign or advocacy effort. Focus group leaders engage the participants in conversation, show them advertisements, or use other interactive techniques to assess how a particular candidate, issue, or product should be presented to the public at large. Although focus groups are not designed to determine how the public at large feels about your cause, they do give insights into how people think and talk about the campaign or issue in their own words.

If it's beyond your means to hire a firm to conduct a focus group, you can organize your own. Geoff Garin of Hart Research Associates explains how in his Tips from the Pros.

TIPS FROM THE PROS

The Dos and Don'ts of Focus Groups
GEOFF GARIN

Focus groups are a good way to elicit opinions about your candidate or issue and help you shape your campaign message. If you want to organize an effective focus group, here are 10 steps to follow.

1. Invite 10 to 12 people you don't know who are representative of the people you will have to win over in your campaign or other initiative. As much as possible, make sure the group represents a cross section of the targeted community—not just the people who are likely to agree with you.

2. Give participants some incentive to show up at the focus group. Common inducements are checks or gift certificates—but sometimes a free meal will do the trick. Use your best judgment depending on whom you hope to recruit to the focus group.

3. Hold the focus group in a relaxed environment. Your goal is to engage the participants in conversation and encourage them to voice opinions and answer questions candidly. People are much less likely to cooperate if the room feels like Antarctica in winter or the Sahara in summer or if the chairs are so uncomfortable that they want to stand up every few minutes.

4. If it is economically feasible, hold the focus group in a room with a one-way window. This will allow you and other advocates—such as the campaign manager or communications director in a political race or various coalition leaders in an issue campaign—to listen to the participants without distracting them or intruding on their thoughts. You must tell participants they are being observed, but assure them that their names and responses will be kept confidential—and keep that promise.

5. Carefully select your focus group moderator. The best facilitators are even-tempered but have warm, engaging personalities well suited to drawing out reluctant or shy participants. They must also be able to politely control any participant who tries to dominate the group. Moderators must avoid steering responses to a particular outcome. Your goal is to learn from the participants, and leading questions will interfere with your achieving that goal.

6. Don't dive straight into your topic. The focus group guide should move from the general to the specific. Include some warm-up questions, and try to understand the broader context before you get into the details.

(Continued)

(Continued)

7. Use handouts and other visual aids to stimulate the discussion and give participants ideas to which they can react. For example, a newspaper article that discusses your issue may be a useful way to present the kind of information that might be heard during a campaign. You might ask people to react to a page with arguments in favor of your position so that you can identify the most persuasive ones. Don't forget to have participants react to arguments from the other side as well.

8. Include the moderator in your preparation of questions for the focus group. If the moderator fully understands the questions in advance, he or she is more likely to ask them in an informal way that elicits honest answers from the participants and will know when to ask probing follow-up questions.

9. Engage the participants in conversation for no more than 90 minutes about the subjects on which you are trying to measure public opinion.

10. Record the session so that you can go back and review what people said and the words they used to express their ideas—but make sure to let participants know you are recording the session for this purpose.

Geoff Garin has been president of Hart Research Associates (hartresearch.com) since 1984. For more than three decades, he has brought his skill, insight, and innovative approaches as a researcher and strategist to a wide variety of fields—including social and economic policy, consumer marketing, and politics. His clients have included the Bill and Melinda Gates Foundation, ESPN, Planned Parenthood, the League of Conservation Voters, and many leading Democratic members of the U.S. Senate.

Cost-Effective Public Opinion Research

Explore pro bono polling. Although it won't be easy to convince a pollster to offer services for free, it doesn't hurt for you to ask. If a pollster believes in your cause, he or she may be willing to provide you with some resources at no or little cost.

Use social media. It is all but certain that you have used Twitter, Facebook, Instagram, Google+, Pinterest, Periscope, Snapchat, LinkedIn, Flickr, Tumblr, YouTube or some other social networking app or site multiple times today. In October 2015, Pew announced that more than 65 percent of adults in the United States use social media— a massive increase from7 percent since 2005. This includes 90 percent of young adults between the ages of 18 to 29, and 77 percent of adults between 30 and 49. Even 35 percent of adults over the age of 65 utilize social media. And social networking usage is fairly diverse, with relatively comparable usage rates between men and women; whites, Hispanics, and African Americans; and rural, urban, and suburban dwellers.[28]

---

[28] Andrew Perrin, "Social Media Usage: 2005–2015," *Pew Research Center*, October 8, 2015, www.pewinternet.org/2015/10/08/social-networking-usage-2005-2015/

In later chapters, we will discuss how social media and other digital communications can be powerful tools in persuading decision makers, building coalitions, engaging the media, and raising funds for your citizen advocacy effort. But they also have their uses in testing your citizen advocacy initiative. Host a Facebook Live or Periscope chat and collect the real-time responses. Record a video, post it on YouTube or Vimeo, and encourage comments on multiple social media channels. Share your concerns, solutions, and best arguments on Facebook or tweet them on Twitter, or create a Facebook or Twitter poll. Pin a note about them on Pinterest. Post a link on Reddit and start the conversation. Knowing that a picture is worth a thousand words, capture one that shows the problem you want government to solve and share it on Instagram or Flickr. Although the responses you receive will not be a scientifically accurate sample of public opinion, they will nonetheless represent genuine feedback that helps you shape the course of your effort to alter public policy.

Conduct a town hall meeting. In the past, many elected officials have held town meetings to gather constituent feedback. Though town halls are less common today than a decade ago, they can also help you test public opinion. These meetings provide a less controlled environment than focus groups, but they can generate even more reactions. However, be mindful that town halls are notoriously unrepresentative. Unless you have taken great care to ensure a relatively balanced audience of the type of citizens whose opinions you are attempting to test, you may end up with a skewed sample.

The process is straightforward. Set a public meeting in a central and easily accessible location and invite any people who are interested in your issue to attend. It should be a neutral site. For example, the school board conference room would probably not be the best location to discuss a controversial matter related to local education.

As is the case with focus groups, you will boost attendance if you can give members of the public an added incentive—such as free food—to attend. Present your initiative and invite legitimate questions and feedback from the audience. Many elected office-holders and political candidates who have held town hall meetings have made the mistake of screening questions in advance or planting friendly questions with supporters in the audience. Those tactics cheapen the meeting and insult citizens who took time out of their busy schedules to attend. A better methodology is the one that Sen. John McCain of Arizona used in his 2000 and 2008 presidential campaigns, which he described in his memoir: "We didn't pick or screen the audience. We didn't plant questions. We took them as they came. Nor would I use every question to nod my head in agreement and compliment the questioner's intelligence. When I disagreed with someone I said so."[29] Because town hall meetings allow for give-and-take exchanges, see if you can engage audience members in a way that elicits all of their reactions to your issue.

Invite media representatives to your town hall meeting and publicly thank them for attending. Their presence gives you an opportunity to generate coverage of your issue, and your greeting informs other attendees that their remarks could end up in a news story. At the end of the meeting, hold a "press availability" where you and other citizen leaders involved in your cause provide information, answer questions, and clarify any statements made at the gathering.

---

[29] John McCain with Mark Salter, *Worth the Fighting For: A Memoir* (New York: Random House, 2002), 370–71.

Try the old-fashioned way. Before there were scientific techniques to measure public thinking, politicians and citizens simply walked around and asked questions. Their experience told them which people in their school, local community, state, or even nation were reliable barometers of more general opinion.

As you begin your citizen advocacy effort, try the throwback approach. If the problem you defined is a neighborhood issue, attend your homeowners or tenants association meeting and ask a few of your peers what they think. E-mail or text your neighbors. Go door to door to solicit opinions. Post your idea on social media and seek feedback. Write an op-ed piece for the weekly neighborhood newspaper—make sure to include your phone number or e-mail address in the byline—and see if readers respond. Your efforts will not only help you determine where your neighbors stand on your issue but also lay the foundation for a supportive coalition.

TIPS FROM THE PROS

Affordable Public Opinion Research
DAVID HILL

For several decades, the mainstay of accurate public opinion polling has been the telephone-based survey. But that option is becoming less viable from an accuracy perspective. Even the famed Gallup organization announced that it is opting out of the presidential election polling business beginning with the 2016 election cycle. The transition of many (or most, depending on the state) households from landline phones to cell phones, along with the refusal of many Americans to take calls from pollsters, has made it all but impossible to collect a true random sampling of opinions from a representative cross section of adults or voters.

Furthermore, the public opinion polls still being attempted by telephone are based on a random sampling of a particular public, such as all adults or all voters or likely voters in a city, state, or the nation. These polls are becoming prohibitively expensive, beyond the financial means of many entities that would benefit from knowing what the public thinks about issues, programs, and social or demographic change. A single interview can cost $100 or $150 or more, and normally hundreds of such calls, or even a thousand, would need to be completed.

What sort of affordable alternatives would allow you to discover public opinion?

Going forward, the next best option to traditional live interviewer telephone polls might be the so-called robo-polls or online surveys. Both are cheaper than live interviewer polling, though the best are not that much cheaper, and both alternatives suffer when it comes to accuracy.

Robo-polls rely on a computer server that places calls to hundreds or even thousands of telephones in a few hours, conducting the "interviews" with interactive voice response (IVR) technology. A recorded voice—not a live interviewer—asks the questions and then expects the respondent to push telephone keys to respond, giving directions such as "Press 1 for YES and press 2 for NO." By current federal law, robo-poll calls can only be made to landline phones. This restriction makes it very hard to reach a representative sampling of some voters, such as younger voters, who have access only to a cell phone. One advantage of robo-polls is that an affordable sample is readily available from various vendors, either by randomly dialing numbers known to live in a target geography or by purchasing voter lists that have been previously matched to landline phone numbers.

Online interviewing can be also affordable because it also uses computer technology, which companies such as Survey Monkey (surveymonkey.com) or Qualtrics (qualtrics.com) have made available to almost anyone with a computer and Internet access. But here's the problem: If you don't have a list of e-mail addresses to invite to take your survey, you must purchase a sample from a "panel" provider. Panel providers gather e-mail addresses from individuals and have obtained permission from these individuals to send them surveys. The panel providers often charge a high fee because they must spend a lot of money to acquire a broadly representative cross section of panel participants, and they also pay the participants for every survey completed. Additionally, the composition of the panel and those that agree to take a particular survey may not be truly representative of the population you want to poll. The best option may be to develop your own in-house panel, harvesting e-mail addresses from the population that you want to study.

All of these means of polling—traditional live interviewer polls, robo-polls, and online polls—can be inaccurate because they depend on the cooperation of those asked to participate. The resulting sample is potentially biased by the exclusion of opinions of those who refuse to participate. This problem of noncooperation by upwards of one-half of those asked to give their opinions makes any given poll suspect today. There really are almost no truly random samples any more.

So what do we do? We can broaden the ways we think about assessing public opinion, perhaps gathering information from multiple sources. And we can focus more on examining change in opinions over time rather than expecting any one survey at a single point in time to reveal what the public is thinking.

Some organizations could benefit from greater use of the old-fashioned "suggestion box," placed where people congregate, either in person or online. Encourage members of the public, employees, stakeholders, or voters to tell us what they are thinking. Track the trends over time. Similarly, analysts can systematically track letters to the editor and comments written on Internet discussion boards to assess changes in sentiment over time.

The rage in research today is multimode data collection. Use a variety of tools, including some of these low cost options, to get a broad and multifaceted view of what people out there are thinking. No single tool alone will ever suffice.

David B. Hill, the director of Hill Research Consultants (hillresearch.com), is a leading pollster and research-based strategist. For the past 25 years, in addition to serving top Republican candidates across the nation, Hill has polled for more than 100 successful ballot measures, from Alaska to Florida.

CONCLUSION: PUTTING
PUBLIC OPINION DATA TO GOOD USE

As you now understand all too well, the process of gathering information on where the public stands on your candidate, issue, or cause is laborious and time consuming. But the road map that results from your efforts will make your hard work worthwhile. Now that you have a better idea as to which arguments will persuade undecided citizens to support your advocacy effort, and how best to respond to opposition attacks, you can craft your plan to convince decision makers to take on your cause (see chapter 5), attract coalition partners (chapter 7), engage the media's attention (chapter 8), and locate financial support (chapter 9).Your success in earning media coverage will disseminate those strong arguments to decision makers as well as to a wide range of potential supporters. Decision makers will be impressed with both statistical and anecdotal data showing support for your position.

The data you have collected on specific groups gives you a unique opportunity to engage them, through their representative organizations, as coalition partners. Conversely, you now have a better idea of how to convince groups that are undecided to join you or to persuade those who oppose you to change their minds. Asking questions has given new momentum to your cause, but public opinion is an ever-shifting phenomenon that requires regular testing. As Albert Einstein observed, "The important thing is not to stop questioning."

CHECKLIST FOR ACTION

☐ Set public opinion research goals.

- Determine your level of support.
- Identify your strongest arguments.
- Anticipate and rebut opposition arguments.
- Microtarget specific groups.
- Use resources wisely.

☐ Select strategies to gauge public opinion.

- Polling
- Different Types of Survey Research
  - Interactive Voice Response (IVR) Surveys
  - Internet Polling
  - Leadership Polling
- Focus Groups
- Cost-Effective Public Opinion Research
  - Pro Bono Polling
  - Social Media
  - Town Hall Meetings
  - The Old-Fashioned Way

APPENDIX

Steamboat Springs Schools Survey

Steamboat Springs Schools Survey

HILL RESEARCH CONSULTANTS
25025 I-45 North, Suite 380
The Woodlands, Texas 77380
281-363-3840

VER A: Final draft; #CODB0871; n=300LV; Field 8/25-27/97

Hello, this is _____ calling for Hill Research Consultants, a public opinion polling firm. We are calling people like yourself throughout Steamboat Springs seeking the opinions of registered voters about important issues facing your community and its public schools today.

May I speak with_____.

1.__ Is anyone in your household an elected state or local government officeholder, or an employee of a news organization?

YES ....THANK & TERMINATE
NO .... CONTINUE

2.__ <u>VERSION A:</u> The Steamboat Springs School District Board of Education may recommend a bond issue of $24.2 million. With principal and interest over the next 20 years, the bond program will cost taxpayers $48.4 million dollars. Annual taxes on the typical $200,000 home would be increased about $146. Over the next 3 years, the bonds would pay for renovation and expansion of the existing High School, the Strawberry Park Campus and the Soda Creek Elementary Campus If the election were held today, and you had to decide, would you vote for or against this $24.2 million school bond proposal?

VOTE FOR THE BOND PROPOSAL 1
VOTE AGAINST THE BOND PROPOSAL 2
UNSURE 8
REFUSED 9

IF DECIDED (FOR OR AGAINST) ABOVE, ASK THIS Q; OTHERWISE, SKIP THIS Q

2.1. And would you describe your feelings about this issue as strong nor not-so-strong?

STRONG 1
NOT-SO-STRONG...2
UNSURE 8
REFUSED 9

ASK EVERYONE

Now, I'll read you the names of several individuals, organizations, and publications that are sometimes active in Steamboat Springs political or civic affairs. Please tell me how influential each might be in helping you make up

your mind about a school bond proposal. Will
they be very influential, somewhat influential,
only a little, or not at all influential on you?
ROTATE ORDER

	VERY	SOME WHAT	ONLY LITTLE	NOT AT ALL	UNS	RF
3. __ Local school teachers (PROMPT: Will they be very influential, somewhat influential, only a little, or not at all influential on your views?)	1	2	3	4	8	9
4. __ Members of the Steamboat Springs School District Board of Education	1	2	3	4	8	9
5. __ The Steamboat Springs Chamber Resort Association	1	2	3	4	8	9
6. __ The P.I.C. or Principal's Information Committee	1	2	3	4	8	9
7. __ S.A.C., The Schools Accountability Committee	1	2	3	4	8	9
8. __ The Steamboat Pilot	1	2	3	4	8	9
9. __ Students currently enrolled in Steamboat Springs schools	1	2	3	4	8	9
10._ School Superintendent Cyndy Simms	1	2	3	4	8	9
11._ Your own friends and neighbors	1	2	3	4	8	9

END ROTATION

12._ Members of the 10 Plus 2 Committee   1......... 2.......... 3.......... 4 ....8 9

13._ As you may recall, the 10 Plus 2 Committee
is a group of concerned local citizens, some
who favored the last school bond proposal
and some who opposed it, who have
organized and lead a community-wide
exploration of attitudes and opinions toward
facility needs as well as other issues facing
Steamboat Schools. Would you say that you
are very familiar, somewhat familiar, or not
very familiar with actions of the 10 Plus 2
Committee?

VERY FAMILIAR 1
SOMEWHAT FAMILIAR..2
NOT VERY FAMILIAR/NOT AT ALL FAMILIAR 3
UNSURE 8
REFUSED 9

**IF NOT VERY FAMILIAR/UNSURE/REFUSED,
SKIP NEXT TWO QUESTIONS**

(Continued)

13.1. And would you say that you participated directly in any of the activities or meetings organized by the 10 Plus 2 Committee, or did you not?

PARTICIPATED DIRECTLY 1
[DO NOT READ] UNSURE 2
DID NOT PARTICIPATE DIRECTLY 3
REFUSED 9

13.2. From all that you may have read, heard, seen, or experienced directly, would you say that 10 Plus 2 Committee has generally been open, fair, and complete in its hearing of issues and positions on school facilities and policies, or would you not say that?

WOULD SAY OPEN, FAIR 1
[DO NOT READ] UNSURE 2
WOULD NOT SAY THAT 3
REFUSED 9

13.3. Besides studying school facility needs, the 10 Plus 2 Committee and its task forces have studied other matters including curricula, school accountability, communications, and other important topics. Would you say that you generally approve or disapprove of the way in which the committee has handled these matters?

APPROVE 1
UNSURE 2
DISAPPROVE 3
REFUSED 9

14._ Before now, how much have you read or heard about the possible $24.2 million bond proposal to finance Steamboat School's facilities renovation and expansion? Have you read or heard a lot, some, just a little, or absolutely nothing about this matter?

A LOT 1
SOME 2
JUST A LITTLE 3
ABSOLUTELY NOTHING 4
UNSURE 8
REFUSED 9

15._ In 1995, Steamboat Springs voters resoundingly rejected a $41.8 million school bond proposal by a vote of 61% to 39%. Do you happen to recall whether you voted for or against that bond proposal in 1995?

DON'T RECALL/DIDN'T VOTE/WASN'T HERE 0
VOTED FOR BOND PROPOSAL [SKIP NEXT Q] 1
VOTED AGAINST BOND PROPOSAL 2
UNSURE 8
REFUSED 9

IF 'VOTED FOR' THEN SKIP THIS Q

15.1. Given that the 10 Plus 2 committee and the school board may agree to a new bond proposal of only $24.2 million, much less than the bond proposal that was rejected two years ago, and for different projects, are you much more likely to vote for the new proposal, somewhat more likely to vote for it, or are you no more likely to vote for this proposal?

MUCH MORE LIKELY...1
SOMEWHAT MORE LIKELY 2
NO MORE LIKELY 3
UNSURE 8
REFUSED 9

16.___ Overall, how satisfied are you with the level of communication you receive from or about the Steamboat Springs school district? Are you very satisfied, somewhat satisfied, or not very satisfied?

VERY SATISFIED 1
SOMEWHAT SATISFIED..2
NOT VERY SATISFIED 3
UNSURE 8
REFUSED 9

17.___ Do you feel that your combined local and school taxes today are much too high, a little too high, about right, a little too low, or much too low?

MUCH TOO HIGH..1
LITTLE TOO HIGH...2
ABOUT RIGHT 3
LITTLE TOO LOW...4
MUCH TOO LOW..5
UNSURE 8
REFUSED 9

18.___ How concerned are you about the impact of the proposed school bond issue on your own home or residential property taxes? Are you extremely concerned, very concerned, somewhat concerned, not very concerned, or not at all concerned?

EXTREMELY...1
VERY...2
SOMEWHAT 3
NOT VERY 4
NOT AT ALL 5
UNSURE 8
REFUSED 9

19.___ And how concerned are you about the impact of the proposed school bond issue on business or commercial property taxes? Are you extremely concerned, very concerned, somewhat concerned, not very concerned, or not at all concerned?

EXTREMELY...1
VERY...2
SOMEWHAT 3
NOT VERY 4
NOT AT ALL 5
UNSURE 8
REFUSED 9

Thinking about local Steamboat Springs public schools...

20.___ Students are often given the grades A,B,C,D, and FAIL to rate the quality of their work at school. Suppose the public schools themselves were graded in the same way. What grade would you give the public schools as a whole in the Steamboat Springs School District?

A...1
B...2
C...3
D...4
FAIL..5
UNSURE 8
REFUSED 9

21.___ Regarding the facilities of your local public schools, which one of the following do you believe is the most pressing need today?
READ LIST AND ROTATE OPTIONS

USING SPLIT-SESSIONS OR YEAR-ROUND SCHOOL
   TO RELIEVE OVERCROWDING...1
RENOVATING OR UPDATING OLDER SCHOOL FACILITIES................2
EXPANDING EXISTING SCHOOLS TO RELIEVE OVERCROWDING....3
BUILDING NEW SCHOOLS TO RELIEVE OVERCROWDING.................3

(Continued)

[DO NOT READ]
NONE PRESSING 6
ALL PRESSING 7
UNSURE 8
REFUSED 9

Now I am going to read you some opinions that other Steamboat residents have expressed about your local schools. Obviously, some of these are opinions and may not be true in your view. Please tell me if you agree strongly, agree somewhat, disagree somewhat or disagree strongly with each statement.
ROTATE ORDER

	STRG	STRG AGREE	STRG AGREE	STRG DIS	STRG DIS	STRG
22._ The use of more split sessions and a year-round calendar could comfortably delay the need for expanding local school facilities.	1	2	3	4	8	9
23._ My local school district spends its money wisely.	1	2	3	4	8	9
24._ School officials need to reconsider the configuration of grades assigned to each school. Some grades should be sent to different schools.	1	2	3	4	8	9
25._ Most public schools in Steamboat Springs are overcrowded.	1	2	3	4	8	9
26._ Most public schools in Steamboat Springs are in good repair with few pressing maintenance needs.	1	2	3	4	8	9

5 Winning Friends and Influencing People

How to Persuade the Decision Maker

"If you would persuade, speak of interest, not reason."

—Benjamin Franklin

Candy Lightner, founder of Mothers Against Drunk Drivers (MADD), speaks at a 1983 rally on Capitol Hill alongside (L to R) Senator Frank Lautenberg (D-NJ), Serena Lightner, Senator Richard Lugar (R-IN), and U.S. Transportation Secretary Elizabeth Dole. President Ronald Reagan later signed legislation that required states to raise the minimum drinking age to 21 years or lose federal transportation aid.

---

*Three sources were particularly critical to the development of the MADD case study. Karolyn Nunnallee, who served as MADD president from 1998–1999, generously shared her insights when we wrote the previous edition of this book. Current MADD Executive Director Debbie Weir provided invaluable assistance as we updated the MADD story for this edition. We also relied on Laurie Davies's piece, "Twenty-Five Years of Saving Lives," *Driven* (Fall 2005): 8–17, www.madd.org/about-us/history/madd25thhistory.pdf. We are very grateful to all three sources.

Cari Lightner should have spent her fourteenth birthday celebrating with family and friends and looking forward to future successes—starting high school, attending the prom, walking across the stage at commencement, going to college, pursuing a career, getting married, and raising a family. But in May 1980, four months short of that birthday, a repeat drunk driver with a blood alcohol level twice the legal limit killed Cari as she walked on the sidewalk in her suburban Sacramento neighborhood on the way to a church carnival. She left behind her parents, a brother, and a sister—her twin.

It would have been easy for Cari to become just another statistic. After all, more than 27,000 Americans died in 1980 because of alcohol-related traffic crashes. But Cari's mother, Candy Lightner, wanted her daughter's death to be more than another senseless tragedy. So on the day that Cari should have been celebrating her birthday, Candy channeled her grief into what would soon become a national movement to change attitudes and laws on drunk driving.

On September 5, 1980, Lightner, along with a group of women sitting around a table, founded Mothers Against Drunk Driving (MADD). The gender designation was purposeful. Their initiative was a statement of feminine and maternal anger against a primarily male-perpetrated offense, one that largely male police officers, prosecutors, and judges sometimes trivialized. Popular culture mimicked these attitudes, with movies frequently depicting drunk drivers as comical figures rather than public safety threats. MADD aimed to persuade policymakers that driving while intoxicated was no laughing matter but rather an action fraught with potentially devastating consequences for families.

MADD started as a neighborhood organization on the same street where Cari died. Within five years, hundreds of local MADD chapters had been located nationwide. Knowing that policy change would alter society's view of drunk driving, these advocates persuaded decision makers in Washington, D.C., all 50 state capitals, and countless municipalities to raise the drinking age from 18 to 21, establish breath and blood alcohol standards, require mandatory sentences for violations of those standards, and improve police procedures for targeting motorists suspected of driving under the influence of alcohol. How did MADD act so fast and so effectively? The answer is that MADD's organizers understood the skills and techniques needed to influence officials at every level of government.

These insights took several forms. First, MADD never lost sight of the critical need to put a human face on its cause. It consistently made sure that decision makers and those people and organizations that influenced decision makers thought of drink driving victims not as statistics but as real people whose deaths and injuries forever changed the families affected. While MADD certainly directed data and well-reasoned arguments at officials' heads, it particularly excelled in appealing to their hearts.

Second, MADD understood the "follow the leader" effect. In other words, MADD leaders realized that certain elected officials are powerful not only in their authority to make decisions but also in their ability to galvanize the public and generate action. If MADD could persuade that special breed of political leader, then, with that support, the organization could start an avalanche of publicity that would attract more allies in other communities across the state and nation.

Fortunately for MADD, one of the nation's most visible and influential public officials also lived in Sacramento: California Governor Jerry Brown. Within weeks of founding MADD, Lightner convinced Brown to establish a state task force on drunk driving. Brown appointed MADD leaders to the task force. In fewer than two years, California became the first state to increase its legal drinking age from 18 to 21—a policy change that has saved hundreds of thousands of lives across the nation.

After persuading Brown to support the cause, MADD set its sights on Brown's gubernatorial predecessor: Ronald Reagan, who was then serving as president of the United States and had more influence on public opinion and power to set the domestic agenda than any governmental official at any level. Reagan was not a natural ally. He won the presidency on a platform deeply suspicious of the federal government's role in anything other than national defense, and he professed a strong belief in states' rights on policy matters. In his first inaugural address, on January 20, 1981, Reagan famously observed that "government is not the solution to our problems; government is the problem." When MADD began clamoring for the federal government to persuade all states to increase the drinking age, Reagan seemed the least likely president to impose a top-down solution from Washington.

But MADD's third skill was its ability to read and understand individual decision makers. As much as Reagan resisted large-scale government action, he was by his own admission very sympathetic to hard-luck stories. In his chronicle of the Reagan presidency, *President Reagan: The Role of a Lifetime,* Lou Cannon writes that Reagan's aides "tried to limit the number of letters he received from people undergoing hardships, to which the president would often respond with advice and a small personal check."[1] By this time, MADD had collected many heartbreaking stories of families who had lost loved ones to crashes caused by drunk drivers but were determined to find triumph in tragedy—exactly the kind of emotional evidence that could override Reagan's antigovernment instincts.

For Reagan, the issue had come down to a simple question he posed to Elizabeth Dole, then transportation secretary, in an Oval Office meeting: "Doesn't this help save kids' lives?" Dole replied in the affirmative. In 1984, at Reagan's urging, Congress voted to condition the granting of federal highway funds to state governments on an increase in the drinking age from 18 to 21. Any state that did not comply would lose tens or even hundreds of millions of dollars in federal bridge and road funds. All 50 states eventually met the age 21 standard.

Fourth, MADD was effective because it employed an organized and streamlined system of member advocacy. The organization provided helpful instructional manuals and trained its members in classroom-like settings, giving MADD the ability to screen for unpredictable individuals who might hurt the cause. When MADD spokeswomen appeared before executive or legislative bodies, they were armed with research supporting their positions.

Fifth, MADD avoided a one-size-fits-all approach to advocacy. Although Lightner's grief inspired her to found MADD, the organization's advocates did not rely solely on emotional arguments. Instead, MADD struck a balance between facts and emotions—explaining the large number of traffic fatalities, but speaking of them as daughters, sons, husbands, wives, and friends who had been killed by a preventable crime. MADD also put a price tag on the problem. In addition to emphasizing how drunk driving took innocent lives, MADD also cited the economic consequences— lost wages, declining productivity, and increased health care costs.

---

[1] Lou Cannon, *President Reagan: The Role of a Lifetime* (New York: Simon and Schuster, 1991), 118.

Sixth, MADD chose its battles carefully. It concentrated on four goals: raising public awareness about drunk driving, supporting victims of drunk driving, increasing the legal drinking age from 18 to 21, and establishing .08 (80 milligrams of alcohol in 100 milliliters of blood) as the blood alcohol threshold across the nation. MADD resisted entreaties to be involved in other anti-alcohol crusades that might have undermined its core mission. If MADD was not certain that a proposed policy idea had clear factual support, it did not risk its credibility.

Seventh, MADD used its feminine origins to shape public opinion. The compelling facts and figures against drunk driving may have been enough to sway the public, but the marriage of that data to the emotions of motherhood gave MADD almost unparalleled credibility. Even if numbers don't lie, it was much easier for policymakers to ignore statistics than grieving mothers who had lost children or other loved ones to drunk driving. This powerful combination also helped to draw coalition partners, such as General Motors, Chrysler, Allstate, Nationwide, State Farm, Coca-Cola, and Avis.

Eighth, MADD understood how powerful the media could be in influencing policymakers. On October 1, 1980, Lightner and Cindy Lamb, a Maryland woman whose five-year-old daughter became the nation's youngest paraplegic because of a drunk driver, held a dramatic press conference on Capitol Hill to announce MADD's formation. Their story appeared on television screens and in newspapers across the country. In 1983, the NBC television network produced and aired a made-for-TV movie, *MADD: Mothers Against Drunk Drivers*, starring well-known character actor Mariette Hartley as Lightner. Other celebrities, including Connie Sellecca, Stevie Wonder, and Aretha Franklin, made public-service spots and personal appearances on MADD's behalf.

Five years later, MADD was once again in the national spotlight. On May 18, 1988, in the nation's deadliest drunk-driving incident, a repeat drunk driver with a high blood alcohol level killed 27 people, most of them children, and injured 34 more in a bus crash in Carrollton, Kentucky. In recent years, performers such as country music star Brad Paisley and television host Kelly Ripa have helped to sustain public awareness by serving as MADD celebrity spokespersons.

Finally, MADD never stopped trying to persuade decision makers. Even after it had won monumental national victories on raising the legal drinking age in the 1980s and setting the .08 blood alcohol standard in the early 2000s, MADD focused on law-enforcement officials charged with enforcing the new standards. The organization worked with police and prosecutors to prepare officers to testify against drunk drivers in court. It held special-recognition ceremonies for those who distinguished themselves in enforcing DUI charges.

In 2006, MADD renewed the fight against drunk driving by launching its Campaign to Eliminate Drunk Driving based on three goals: continuing to support high visibility law enforcement, requiring all convicted drunk drivers to use an ignition interlock device, and developing new advanced automotive technologies to stop a drunk driver from starting his or her vehicle—research that has the potential to eliminate drunk driving. By the end of 2015, the campaign has resulted in 26 states passing all-offender ignition interlock legislation and has reduced drunk-driving deaths by 25 percent.

The combined effects of MADD's persuasive skills have been nothing short of amazing. Over nearly three decades the organization can claim the following accomplishments from its grassroots efforts:

- Starting with one member in September 1980, MADD had 650,000 members in 47 states by 1985, and it had inspired the founding of a Canadian organization, which eventually became MADD Canada in 1989.
- In 1984, Congress induced states to increase their drinking age from 18 to 21. By 1988, all states had complied.
- By 1986, MADD coined the phrase "designated driver."
- The *Chronicle of Philanthropy* declared in 1994 that MADD was the most popular charitable organization in America.
- In 1995, Congress persuaded states to make it illegal for anyone younger than 21 to drive with any alcohol in their system.
- By 1998, MADD had chapters in all 50 states.
- In 1999, MADD added the prevention of underage drinking to its mission statement and created new policies and programs to address the problem and its consequences.
- In 2000, when MADD celebrated its twentieth anniversary, 97 percent of the public recognized its name.
- By 2005, under threat of losing federal highway funding, all 50 states had set .08 as the legally intoxicated blood alcohol content (BAC) for drivers 21 and older.
- In 2015, MADD added a related substance-impaired driving issue as a stand-alone prong to its mission statement—efforts to "help fight drugged driving."
- Annual alcohol-related deaths in the United States have dropped more than 55 percent since MADD's founding—from 30,000 in 1980 to fewer than 10,000 in 2014.

That record of success is not the product of good fortune or happenstance. Before MADD's emergence, drunk driving had long been a serious problem without a serious effort to solve it. But the grassroots movement that was MADD understood how to motivate policymakers and produce solutions. The lesson is that no matter how intractable a problem may appear, you can find ways to make it a priority on a decision maker's agenda.

INFLUENCING AND PERSUADING THE DECISION MAKER

If you have correctly identified the person or persons who have the power to solve your problem, the next step is to persuade the decision maker to support—and, if possible, advocate for—your position. MADD's organizers were masterful in that task. If you learn from their example and follow the steps outlined below, you will increase your chances of turning a policymaker into an ally.

If you see this long list of steps and start to panic, rest assured that you aren't expected to handle all of these tasks on your own. Look for opportunities to divide labor among your colleagues, allies, and volunteers such as students looking for internships or service experience. As we will discuss more in chapter 7, success depends in part on the ability to build a broad coalition of support. Look for those coalition partners who are well suited to help in decision-maker communications and those who are better suited to assist with the background research critical to the relationship-building process.

1. Educate Decision Makers
before They Become Decision Makers

Many of the governmental officials you will be working to persuade are elected. Before they took office, those officials were candidates for office, and before that they were probably community leaders of some kind. If you are wisely looking to build long-term relationships with decision makers, the best time to start is before they take office— when they are learning about and formulating their positions on issues like yours.

You need not wait until someone has filed to be a candidate. Look for key community organizations that tend to produce candidates for elected office or high-level appointments—and educate those organizations on your issue and advocacy efforts. These groups could include your regional chamber of commerce, local bar association, political party committees, or leadership organizations that seek to train future community trustees such as Leadership Greater Chicago (lgcchicago. org), Leadership Florida (leadershipflorida.org), Leadership Houston (leadershiphouston.org), Greater Tucson Leadership (greatertucsonleadership.org) or whichever version exists in your area. If you can join or build allies within these organizations, or secure the opportunity to educate them on your initiative, you will have a head start when one of their members decides to run for office or is selected for a significant appointed office.

Once a candidate has announced her or his intention to run for office, you have even more opportunities to shape that person's thinking for years to come. Let's say your goal is to increase the amount of money that your state allocates for purchasing and preserving environmentally sensitive conservation lands. While taking care to abide by all election laws—especially if you are advocating for a nonprofit entity, which has restrictions on how it can engage in political campaigns[2]—identify the candidates for your state legislative district. Provide information and answer any questions on the importance of land acquisition and preservation. Invite the candidate to tour some of the natural treasures in what could be his or her district. Help him or her understand how additional state funds could benefit lands like those you have toured. These efforts will make your issue tangible to the aspiring lawmaker, who will enter the legislature with a positive frame of reference that will benefit you when land preservation funding is debated and decided.

2. Define the Relationship with
the Decision Maker before You Create It

The type of relationship you need to build with a decision maker will dictate how you first approach him or her. If your interaction with an official is likely to be short

---

[2]For a succinct primer on how nonprofits can and cannot engage in political campaigns, please see www.nonprofitvote.org/nonprofits-voting-elections-online/

term—that is, you want help on a single problem—your "relationship" will consist of educating the decision maker on the specific challenge and how it might be solved. On the other hand, if your goals have a long-term focus, you will need to build an actual relationship through frequent contacts over time. Consider the following situations and determine which kind of relationship is most applicable to the problem you want to solve:

A specific, singular situation that requires relatively immediate attention. In some cases, you may need to apply your political skills to public officials only once. For instance, if your local school board is considering a boundary change to balance shifting student populations, you may want to intervene if you believe the changes being considered would be disadvantageous to your child. Your goal would be to persuade your specific school board member and his or her colleagues on this single boundary change.

A policy issue that requires continuing interest and activism. Sometimes your goal can't be achieved in one fell swoop. You may need to win many small battles before you can claim ultimate victory. For example, the effort to restore the health of America's Everglades or, on a smaller scale, an attempt to clean up a polluted lake or river, requires policymakers to make multiple decisions incrementally over the years. These types of challenges require you to build long-term relationships of trust and confidence with a few elected legislators and some elected but mostly appointed executive officials who are responsible for your specific area of concern.

During my career, I found Florida's chiropractors to be very effective at building these lasting political-policy relationships. Chiropractors are highly motivated because government decisions substantially influence the success of their practice, including such matters as whether health insurance carriers are required to recognize chiropractic services for reimbursement. When I was in the Florida Legislature, the chiropractors' association assigned a member to each state legislator to keep the legislator well informed on chiropractic issues. The association designed this effort to foster personal friendships between chiropractors and legislators.

It worked. The Miami-area chiropractor assigned to me, Dr. Hubert Ross, asked for a meeting at my local office where we could meet in person. He then called me on the first Monday of each quarter for a 10- to 15-minute chat. The calls during times when the next legislative session was distant were focused on topics such as baseball, the Miami Dolphins and Florida Gators, our respective businesses and families, and other everyday matters. He would end with a brief mention of the chiropractors' upcoming legislative priorities. But as session grew closer in time, his calls were all about the legislative agenda. Between calls, we would occasionally have lunch. During the busy days of session, when I had to decide which telephone calls to return first, Dr. Ross was generally at or near the top of the list. While I didn't always vote with the chiropractors, I took their views seriously because of the strong relationship Dr. Ross had built.

A continuing concern that never changes with specific issues that often change. Some groups have broad interests that remain constant over time, but those interests are advanced through a constantly shifting series of issues. For example, although a state chamber of commerce's general interest is the protection and advancement of the business community, that interest may be asserted in tax policy one year, government regulation the next, and education the next. In this or a similar case, you will want to be close to officials who can influence a broad array of matters—such as the House Speaker, Senate president, and governor. That means you will need not only to cultivate relationships with the current officeholders but also to start early in building ties with officials who could rise to those positions.

Once you have decided which type of relationship you need to form, determine whether the decision maker is singular—for example, a strong mayor—or plural, such as a city council. If you are trying to persuade a collegial group, such as a school board, determine which of the members has the greatest commitment to your position and is best able to persuade his or her colleagues. Ask that individual to be your advocate in chief.

3. Follow the Chain of Command

Your initial contact should be with the individual closest to the problem for which you are seeking a solution. If a neighborhood park is poorly maintained, start with the superintendent of that park. The condition of the park is the superintendent's responsibility, and you must give him or her a chance to discharge the obligation. If you don't get results, you can then go to the director of the city or county parks system. When you start with the person closest to the problem, you maximize the chance of an expedited resolution. And if you give people a chance to do their jobs, and they are unable or unwilling to help because they have different priorities, they are less likely to become an obstacle if you have to go over their heads—and their boss orders a solution.

In her tips (see Tips from the Pros: Back to School), Maine school board member Caitlin Hills explains the importance of utilizing the chain of command to benefit your goals. Citizens who understand where to address their concerns have an advantage over those who are less focused.

TIPS FROM THE PROS

Back to School
CAITLIN HILLS

Your local school board is arguably the most directly impactful of all elected bodies when it comes to your family and wallet. It makes decisions about public education in your district and directly affects the quality and administration of your children's education. It also sets a budget and school tax rate, which comprises a significant portion of your property tax bill. Though you should closely monitor every level of government, pay special attention to school boards—which affect you and all other district residents whether you have school-age kids or not.

School boards are generally responsible for

- Holding open meetings where the public can attend and speak
- Providing and overseeing implementation of the school district vision
- Developing school policy and educational standards
- Establishing school boundaries
- Managing schools, including approval of curriculum
- Hiring and oversight of superintendents and other key district staff
- Dismissing administrators and/or teachers and expelling students
- Approving the annual school budget
- Seeking voter approval of the annual budget in states where that is required
- Setting the tax rate for the property tax portion of school district revenue

Many parents and other stakeholders have a difficult time grasping how school boards work. One key insight is common in organizations: Most issues concerning students, sports, buildings, or policy must be brought up through the proper chain of command.

The relationship between citizens, school board members, and a superintendent can be very complicated. The best way to ensure that your voice is heard is to follow the established protocols and communicate your needs to the proper person. Those protocols and responsible officials will vary based on the laws of the state in which the school is located, the local processes established by the school board, and the history, culture, size, and complexity of the district. Check with the school administration for the specifics applicable to your situation.

In RSU71 (rsu71.org), the Maine school district where I serve as a board member, we have nine schools and just over 1600 students. My advice to constituents with concerns is twofold:

- If you have a concern with a specific student (for example, your child), first contact your child's teacher. If the issue is not addressed to your satisfaction, you then must contact the school principal. If the issue remains unresolved, you should then bring your concern to the superintendent of schools.
- If you have a concern with a budget matter or a policy issue, bring the matter to a board member's attention. Ask that he or she bring it to the superintendent. If the issue is unresolved, ask the board member to request that the issue be placed on the agenda for the next board meeting.

Another important way to stay educated about school district issues is to attend board meetings. If you are unable to attend, most school districts have websites where you can view upcoming agendas, board meeting minutes, and other helpful information. For example, RSU 71 board information can be found at rsu71.org/home/board-of-directors.

With the exception of closed executive sessions to discuss personnel and student discipline issues, school board meetings are open to the public and typically have a public participation segment on the agenda. This is a time when any member of the

(Continued)

(Continued)

public can speak to the board about issues of concern. Some states require public participation by law.

Remember that school board members are elected representatives who work for you. In order to ensure that your school board is running as effectively as possible, you must accept your responsibility as a constituent to demand transparency and accountability. Stay educated and active on school issues so you can do your part.

Caitlin Hills is a business school lecturer and vice chair of the Maine RSU 71 School District, which includes the towns of Belfast, Belmont, Morrill, Searsmont, and Swanville. She previously served on the staff of U.S. Senator Bob Graham in Washington, D.C., as a senior policy advisor on environmental and agricultural issues.

4. Respect Professional Staff

Remember that behind most decision makers is a staff person or persons who also need to be persuaded. Given the sheer number and complexity of policy issues that both executive and legislative officials must address as part of their duties, staff members play a vital role in helping to set and manage schedules, prioritize and research issues, and counsel decision makers on the relative merits or demerits of policy options. When you approach a mayor, county commissioner, state legislator, or another decision maker, make sure you take the time to engage and educate staff members. Give them your respect and gratitude. They can help you gain access to the decision maker and likely will provide input into the deliberations on your issue. Ignore them at your peril. Elected officials come and go. Staff members remain and remember.

5. Know the Decision Maker before You Advocate

You wouldn't build a home without examining the record of the prospective contractor. You wouldn't send a child to a day care center without thoroughly investigating that facility's administration and teachers. For similar reasons, you shouldn't approach decision makers without knowing who they are, what they believe, and why they believe it.

First of all, know the decision maker's name and be able to pick him or her out of a lineup. Many citizen advocates do not take the time to put a name and face together. When I joined the U.S. Senate in 1987, one of my classmates was John Breaux from Louisiana. He had come to the Senate after 14 years in the House of Representatives, which he joined at the age of 28. In a January 24, 2007 op-ed, Breaux told readers of *The Hill* this story from his early days in the House:

A senior chairman of a major maritime company came down with several lawyers in tow to lobby me on an issue of great concern to him. After several minutes of looking directly at me and explaining his problem, he asked, to the gasps of his lobbyist lawyers, "When do you think the congressman can come in?" It was certain he was paying his legal team a lot of money to explain how he should present his case to members of Congress, and they hadn't even bothered to tell him who the congressman was![3]

Second, unless you are in the category of a specific, singular situation that requires relatively immediate attention, strive to establish a relationship with the decision maker before focusing on your issue—as Dr. Hubert Ross did. Success in this task requires knowing the personal as well as the political side of the man or woman you want to persuade. It is always helpful if you are a constituent of the decision maker, as the "all politics is local" adage we discuss later in this chapter also applies to interpersonal relationships with appointed or elected officials. Look for common interests that have nothing to do with politics or government, e.g., place of birth and upbringing, education, age of children, sports, or hobbies. Establishing a friendship eases the transition to the serious and sometimes contentious requests you will make of that decision maker.

Third, stay abreast of what that decision maker is saying and doing on a regular basis. If he or she has an e-mail list that you can join to receive newsletters, press releases, public statements, or other updates, join it immediately. Follow him or her on Facebook, Twitter, Instagram, and any other relevant social media sites. All of these sources will give you real-time information on what the official is saying or doing on public issues.

Fourth, know what interests or values motivate the decision maker. If you are lobbying an elected officeholder, you can be sure that a key interest is the desire to advance policy initiatives that benefit constituents and ensure voters' goodwill in the next election. Your job is to show the decision maker that adopting your position is both good policy and good politics. Be able to provide specific instances of the benefits to be gained if your proposal is adopted. Provide letters of support from constituents and statistics on its positive impact.

But don't stop at that superficial level. All citizen advocates worth their salt know to portray their issue as a challenge that, if solved, will confer great economic, social, or other benefits on the elected official's constituency and thus electoral benefits on the official. You can distinguish yourself by digging deeper into the decision maker's biography and public record and finding other ways to show the merits of your position.

Use the Internet, social media, past newspaper stories, previous television reports, and any of the other research tools we discussed in chapter 2 to discover the following information about your decision makers:

- Places of birth and upbringing
- Undergraduate and graduate alma maters
- Marital status and number of children and grandchildren
- Professional history before entering politics

---

[3] John Breaux, "K Street Insiders: When They No Longer Call You 'Senator,'" *The Hill*, January 24, 2007, thehill.com/20827-k-street-insiders-when-they-no-longer-call-you-senator

- Other appointed or elected offices held
- Priority issues in current or former offices
- Past public service awards or honors received
- Previous bills introduced (particularly in your area of interest)
- Prior positions or votes on similar issues
- Relevant press releases or public statements
- Related posts on social media such as Facebook and Twitter
- Campaign donors and supporters
- Prospects for next campaign or future political office
- Hobbies or sports interests

Although this list is not exhaustive, you'll be surprised how far this kind of information can go in helping you to persuade an elected decision maker. For example, if you have studied her past positions as a candidate and elected official, you may be able to show that support for your initiative is consistent with her previous stances. That kind of consistency will make it easier for her to support your position. Even more important, you need to know if you are asking the decision maker to deviate from past positions so that you can be ready with a suggested rationale for change.

Fifth, realize that many decision makers are not elected. Most have been appointed to their jobs by elected officials or higher-level appointees. In the introduction, you learned about my visit to Wolfson High School in the early 1970s. At Wolfson, the decision maker on food quality could have been the school cafeteria manager, the principal who appointed the cafeteria manager, or the county superintendent of schools or school board who appointed the principal. But the analysis you need to do is the same as it is with elected officials. If you know how the person came to his position of responsibility, understand what personal values and professional interests influence his behavior, and establish a personal relationship, you will have a much easier time persuading him to take up your cause.

If your decision maker is the local public health officer, and she was given the job because of his professional competence, you will likely influence her through well-researched and effectively presented data. If she won his job through political connections, you will need to understand those relationships and determine how to use them to your advantage. If she has a chip on his shoulder, don't hesitate to make use of it. For example, pretend that your community's highly respected school superintendent has retired after many years of service. The school board selects a new leader who is intimidated by the reputation of her predecessor and reluctant to take new initiatives. If you want to persuade the new superintendent to support your cause, convince her that the previous one would have handled it as you suggest.

6. Determine Who Influences
the Decision Maker—and Influence Them

Poet John Donne famously wrote that "no man is an island." Every official, appointed or elected, receives advice and counsel from someone else. As a citizen advocate, your job is to try to learn the identities of these influencers and, if appropriate, persuade them to support your cause.

It's fairly straightforward to know who influences an appointed governmental decision maker—whoever appointed that individual to office. Though appointed officials still bring their own ideas, interests, and relationships to their roles, these are subordinate to those of the elected official or higher appointed official who gave them their job and overall marching orders. As a result, they will view your request through their employer's lens. If an appointed official is the final decision maker in your advocacy effort, make sure you are also familiar with who holds that person accountable.

Determining who influences elected officials is much more complicated. Every city council member, county commissioner, mayor, state legislator, governor, congressperson, and senator is different, each having her or his own network of family, friends, supporters, and occupational or professional colleagues who likely give advice. Although these advisors are not always readily apparent, you have tools at your disposal to find at least some of them. Consider these questions:

- Does the decision maker have a well-known group of friends or key advisers? Ask his or her colleagues, your coalition partners, financial backers, and anyone else who regularly pays attention to the elected official.
- If the elected official serves in a typically part-time office, such as city council or a state legislature, determine that person's primary employment. Is he an attorney who has partners you could approach? Does she work at a local corporation or business where you could persuade owners, executives, or colleagues?
- Who supported the elected official in his or her last campaign? You can find this information through an Internet search on political endorsements in that election, or check your city, county, state, or federal elections websites to look up his or her campaign contributors. Don't limit yourself to just the actual campaign. In recent years, many candidates have exercised the option to raise money into political committees that can accept unlimited contributions. Find out if your elected official had or benefited from such a committee, and the names of its major donors.
- Does the official belong to any professional or civic organizations with which you could interact?

Although this list of options is not exhaustive, they will give you a sense of the questions you should be asking to determine who could help you persuade the decision maker as to the righteousness of your cause.

7. Understand Internal Politics and Dynamics

Like any organization, governmental bodies have their own internal politics. Especially in a collegial setting—such as your town commission, school board, or state legislature—it is not enough to know the decision maker's résumé and relevant personal characteristics. You need to know the interplay among the members. Do certain officials band together on every issue and form a bloc? If so, you may be able to secure multiple votes for your position if you can win over just one or two policymakers in the bloc. Conversely, you will go down to defeat if one or two members of the bloc are persuaded to vote against you and bring their allies along for the ride.

Unrelated internal animosities within many groups can inflict serious collateral damage on your goals. For example, has the member you selected to sponsor your bill recently voted against or offended the legislative leadership or a key committee chair? In that event, you may need to find a new advocate.

The better you understand these intangible factors, the better your chances of maneuvering around them in support of your initiative. But how can a citizen advocate not serving in government become aware of these dynamics? Two ways. First, pay close attention to media coverage of the elected body you are trying to persuade. News reporting on that body will often include information on important interpersonal relationships. Follow key legislators, staffers, and reporters on Twitter, Facebook, and other social media outlets where finding nuggets of insider information is common. Second, talk to your allies and coalition partners to find out what they know. Let's say that you are advocating for your local parent-teacher-student association (PTSA) to reduce the amount of standardized testing in public schools. Ask supportive legislators or like-minded groups such as the statewide PTSA, state teachers' union, school board associations, and other organizations that regularly lobby in the state capital to help you navigate the institutional complexities of the state legislature. Though people understandably pay little attention to the "inside baseball" of politics and government, citizen advocates who want to succeed should know who's on first and what's on second.

8. Do Your Homework—Always Be Credible

It is essential to know your decision maker, but all the knowledge in the world about that individual won't make much difference if you can't provide critical information on the issue for which you seek help. There is no substitute for adequate preparation. At the very least, you should know the topic better than the decision maker. Ideally, you will know it better than anyone else.

But don't let your superior knowledge get the best of you. Never overstate or misstate. When confronted with other people's assertions, my father applied the "China standard." Dad was a mining engineer by training, but he spent most of his adult life in the dairy business. If a person was speaking on a subject Dad knew little about— such as China—he gave the speaker the presumption of accuracy. But if the speaker wandered into a discussion of mining or cows and misrepresented what Dad knew to be the facts, the speaker was summarily dismissed on the subjects of mines, cows, *and* China. The late Senator Daniel Patrick Moynihan attributed this line to former Federal Reserve chair Alan Greenspan: "Everyone is entitled to their own opinions, but no one is entitled to their own facts." Remember that bit of wisdom as you argue your case.

Since the decision maker will likely press you to explain why you are right and your policy opponents are wrong, you should know your adversaries and their arguments. The research you conducted in chapter 2 and the public opinion you gathered in chapter 4 should help you prepare convincing answers to a decision maker's questions. Show respect when you discuss the opposition, but know how to counter your opponents' assertions on the issue you are advocating.

9. All Politics Is Local

Never forget that most governmental decision makers, especially those who are elected, examine every issue through the lens of how it affects the constituency they represent. You simply must respect former U.S. House Speaker Tip O'Neill's warning that "all politics is local." There is no alternative. If your goal is to convince your legislator to support a corporate income tax break on manufacturing, you had better be able to explain how that bill will create jobs or provide other benefits in his or her district. Be prepared to suggest ways that the legislator can portray the vote to constituents as a win, especially if the loss in revenue from the tax break means that other priorities of importance to constituents cannot be fully funded. Help your legislator anticipate criticisms she or he may receive for the vote, and suggest persuasive responses.

Ridesharing network Lyft (lyft.com) successfully applied this lesson in its efforts to access the Portland, Oregon, market. In their tips (see Tips from the Pros: Ridesharing Gets a Lyft in Portland), Annabel R. Chang, Laura Bisesto, and Felipe Pereira of the Lyft Government Relations team explain how they presented Lyft as a service that would both help Portlanders and advance Portland's civic goals.

TIPS FROM THE PROS

Ridesharing Gets a Lyft in Portland[4]
ANNABEL R. CHANG, LAURA BISESTO, FELIPE PEREIRA

Crowned as the city with the most microbreweries in the world and home to an epic food truck scene, Portland, Oregon, is unsurprisingly one of the top U.S. cities for Millennials. This younger generation of Americans is ditching car ownership at an unprecedented rate and increasingly relying on a combination of walking, cycling, public transit, and ridesharing to move around communities.

Yet even as recently as 2014, Portland was one of the few major American cities that lacked access to app-based ridesharing options for its residents. Though antiquated rules prevented Lyft (lyft.com) from launching, we believed that Portlanders would embrace ridesharing if allowed the option. So we embarked on a four-step journey to persuade key Portland decision makers to expand the city's transportation options.

Doing the Research

Our very first step was to develop a deep understanding of Portland's political and regulatory landscape. The for-hire

(Continued)

---

[4] We are grateful to attorney Steve Diebenow of the Jacksonville, Florida, law firm of Driver, McAfee, Peek & Hawthorne (northfloridalaw.com/professionals/attorneys/steven-diebenow & linkedin.com/in/stevediebenow) for making a connection with the Lyft Government Relations team.

(Continued)

vehicle regulations in Portland were outdated and complicated. Our research of the transportation landscape demonstrated the clear need for alternatives. We learned that typical wait times for passengers in Portland needing a ride could be up to 35 minutes. The need for additional options had only grown more urgent since Portland was attracting more tourists and convention attendees. Simply put, if you used Lyft at home and on other travel, you came to expect the same choice when you visited Portland—especially after a day of sampling the city's ample microbrew selection.

Sharing the Story

Sharing our story with governmental decision makers was a top priority. Because we were pioneering a completely novel policy area, we started by familiarizing legislators and regulators with the technology itself. We not only walked through the functions and features of our mobile app but also shared Lyft's long-term vision for drivers and riders. As the City of Portland convened citizen task force meetings, we also spent time explaining the benefits of ridesharing for the community. Like the City of Portland, Lyft shares a vision of a green future with residents tapping into different modes of getting around town. We also emphasized that Lyft shared Portland's goals of increasing equity and access across all existing and new transportation modes.

Plugging into the Network

We knew that our voice could not be the only one to call for app-based ridesharing in Portland. Success hinged on our building a broad coalition of support. Before launching in Portland, our team spent months engaging with local community organizations, nonprofits, and thought leaders to better understand the transportation landscape and explore partnerships with the individuals and groups that were most impactful in the area. From the beginning, our goal has been to identify how increased access to transportation could help different cross sections of the community and better connect long-isolated geographic regions. What developed from this initial series of meetings was an unlikely coalition that included natural allies, such as economic development organizations, visitors' bureaus, and transportation policy experts, as well as new supporters like environmental advocates, Portland brewery and culinary industry members, and disability community advocates. Our months-long effort to convince city officials of the benefits of ridesharing was reinforced by a growing chorus of community leaders who shared our vision and helped make the case at City Hall.

Show and Tell

We believe that drivers and passengers using the Lyft platform are uniquely fun and creative individuals. Lyft not only fills a transportation need but, more importantly, it also helps create memorable experiences that stem from the personalities of our community members. This dual benefit is even more true in a town like Portland. As Lyft's Government Relations team, one of our central roles was to help lawmakers understand who would be most affected by the regulations that they were drafting. So we tapped into our vibrant driver community and relied on the power of storytelling to make the process more personal. From the shaman, to the professional roller derby player, to the pastry chef, our driver community shared with councilors why the opportunity to drive and make a few extra dollars with Lyft was so important. In the weeks leading up to the votes to approve and finalize ridesharing, the Lyft community met with council members personally, made phone calls, and sent e-mails to share their stories. During a critical vote, supporters of Lyft and of ridesharing in general packed the two-story Portland City Council Chambers. The energy in the room was electric.

By the end of 2015, Lyft and ridesharing were finally in Portland for good. The relationships we had built not only created the support we needed to pass the regulations but also showed our dedication to the citizens of Portland. Portlanders—whether taking a rose-covered Lyft to get to the annual Portland Rose Festival or a ride home late at night from an Eastside restaurant or bar—can now experience a safe and affordable ride.

As Director of Public Policy for the West, Annabel R. Chang develops and oversees political and policy strategy impacting state and local legislation and regulation for Lyft's western markets, including major markets such as California, Illinois, Arizona, and Washington. Public Policy Manager Laura Bisesto oversees political and policy strategy in the Pacific Northwest, Arizona, and California by advocating for Lyft's interests with legislators and regulators on state and local bills relating to ridesharing. Community Affairs Manager Felipe Pereira works with community partners as well as Lyft drivers and passengers to develop Lyft's grassroots campaigns and coalition-based advocacy across the country.

10. Maximize Your Face-to-Face Opportunities with the Decision Maker

It has finally arrived: the big day when you will meet the decision maker in person and try to convince him or her to help solve your problem. Since the course of that meeting may well determine whether you succeed in your initiative, it is important that you choose the right venue and prepare a concise, effective presentation that will leave the decision maker inclined to support you. In addition to the detailed expert advice provided from a former elected member of Congress and a former congressional staffer in the following submission to Tips from the Pros, remember three key principles in your quest for a successful meeting.

First, as to location, many citizen activists wrongly assume that the best place to meet is in the decision maker's office in the courthouse, city hall, state house, or U.S. Capitol. Often the office is not the best place. In an official setting the decision maker is on a tight schedule with frequent appointments and interruptions, especially if he or she is a legislator and needs to respond to the bell announcing a floor vote is underway. A priority for many legislators—at least those not running for president—is to maintain as close to a 100 percent voting record as possible.

In any event, your meeting may be affected by stressful time constraints. The decision maker has probably already had several meetings that day with several more to follow. Actions generated from those earlier meetings or mental preparations for the later ones will distract, diverting attention from your presentation. Staff will be in and out of the meeting to manage the day's busy schedule. If the decision maker is a legislator, I recommend that you have the meeting in the person's home district, either at an office or at a more informal off-campus site. If the person you are trying to persuade is an appointed official, ask people who know the official and the area to recommend a location that would facilitate a successful meeting. Think strategically and creatively. As media analyst Marshall McLuhan famously said, "The medium is the message." For example, if your mission is more financial support to protect a local river, consider having the meeting in a location that emphasizes the river's beauty or highlights its challenges.

As a former congressional staffer whose job responsibilities included facilitating dialogue between a U.S. senator and various constituents, Mark Block has considerable know-how when it comes to connecting with elected officials. In his tips (see Tips from the Pros: Getting in the Door), he explains how you can maximize your chances of scheduling face-to-face meetings with key decision makers.

TIPS FROM THE PROS

Getting in the Door
MARK BLOCK

Persuading the decision maker often requires direct communication. How do you get in the door to make your case? Here are four keys to the door.

1. **Do your research**

   - Know the names and correct spellings and pronunciations of the official and the staff members with whom you will be meeting.
   - Recognize the potential impact that this decision maker might have on your issue. For example, does he or she chair a committee that will consider your proposal? Does the official represent constituents or interests that will be affected by your proposal? Don't waste the decision maker's time asking for an action beyond his or her authority to deliver.
   - Identify individuals who are close to the official and ask them to identify any personal or political idiosyncrasies that might affect the official's receptivity to your efforts.

2. *Initiate your scheduling request with candor and specificity*

- Bring to the meeting only those participants necessary to the discussion, and don't add to your contingent at the last moment. Staff members responsible for managing an official's time don't like surprises, and no decision maker wants to meet with a cast of thousands in his office. Provide to the staff member who is facilitating the meeting each participant's name and concise biography.
- Request only the least amount of time that you need to present the problem you want to solve, possible solutions, and reasons the official should support your proposal. Strictly enforce that time limit during the meeting. If you fail to respect the time limitations for the meeting, the decision maker and his staff may take a dim view of your issue and any future meeting requests.
- Stay focused on the agenda. With limited time, the last thing you want to do is distract from the purpose of the meeting. Stick to your points and do not raise extraneous and unexpected items. Additionally, avoid time-consuming personal requests such as photographs with the official unless you have previously arranged them with staff members.
- Don't bring gifts. You may have the best of intentions in delivering a tangible gesture of thanks and respect, but your gift will put the official in an awkward position and could leave the inappropriate impression that you are attempting to buy his support.

3. *Be flexible, versatile, and concise*

- Manage expectations of your group in advance of the meeting time. It is not uncommon for the meeting to be delayed or even cancelled because of last-minute demands on the official. As a result, the formal meeting that was scheduled in her office may become a brief courtesy meeting followed by a more detailed discussion with staff. In some cases, a meeting may become a "walk and talk" as you and your associates join the official in moving to her next commitment. Do not interpret these changes as snubs—they simply reflect the realities of a busy official's uncertain schedule.
- As close as possible to the meeting, determine if there have been any late-breaking developments affecting your issue. The official will expect you to have the most current information. If you haven't scanned relevant newspapers, scrolled through your news feeds on social media or conducted a last-minute Internet search on your issue prior to the meeting, you are not ready.
- Minimize the use of handouts and other materials. You can give them to staff, but don't add to the clutter on the official's desk.
- Before the meeting, determine which members of your group will cover which points and establish strict time limits.

(Continued)

(Continued)

4. Stay in touch

- Send handwritten thank you notes—one to the official and others to any staff members who attended or assisted with the meeting. Your notes to the staff should include an additional typewritten page that summarizes your arguments, provides your contact information, and supplies the names and points of contact for anyone who accompanied you to the meeting.
- Respond quickly if the official or members of the staff request additional information during or subsequent to the meeting. If you don't answer their questions in a timely fashion, they may receive answers from other citizens or groups who don't share your interests or values.
- Keep staff members regularly updated on your issue with brief, factual communications. When the official takes an action that indicates receptivity to your cause, call, write, e-mail, or give kudos on social media with recognition and appreciation.

Mark Block lives in New York City. He is the founder and chairman of Block By Block Productions, LLC, specializing in event development and public relations. For nearly 15 years, he worked for Sen. Bob Graham in Florida and Washington, D.C., where his staff positions included scheduler, campaign scheduler, and deputy chief of staff.

Second, when you are presenting your case, focus on the bottom line: know precisely and state clearly what you want the decision maker to do: authorize rideshare companies like Lyft to operate in your city, deny a permit application to construct a cement plant near a pristine spring, or vote for a precise amount of money to put a certain number of additional police officers on the streets. Be specific as to your purpose, and be prepared to present a specific amount or at least a range of costs if your initiative will require public expenditure.

Third, don't lose sight of the need for sustained communications. Don't view that meeting as a one-time contact. Use it as a springboard to a long-term relationship. As Miami chiropractor Hubert Ross did with me, be strategic in regularly refreshing your contacts with the official and his or her team. Share important updates on your cause, but don't overdo it. Congratulate the decision maker on key accomplishments. Reinforce your impression as someone who is a credible source of information and assistance.

Nobody is better positioned than a current or former elected official to teach you how to succeed in a meeting with the decision maker you are trying to persuade. Fortunately, we have expert advice from former U.S. Congressman Jason Altmire. In his tips (see Tips from the Pros: Make a Lasting Impression on a Decision Maker), Congressman Altmire provides a six-step plan for making the most of your time.

TIPS FROM THE PROS

Make a Lasting Impression on a Decision Maker
JASON ALTMIRE

1. Prepare

Once you have determined which government official is the appropriate person to visit to advocate for your cause, it is important that you do the necessary preparation work in order to maximize the effectiveness of your upcoming meeting. This includes researching the interests, background, and policy positions of the official, especially as they relate to the issue you plan to discuss. Be sure you know your subject in depth and are clear about what action you want the official to take. Stay aware of new developments. Political issues can change daily. Keep tabs on the latest news, and make sure your information is timely and relevant. Know the process and don't ask the official to do something that he or she is unable to do.

2. Engage staff

Staff members are a key to your access to the official and are often the people to whom the official first turns to seek more information about a pending issue or request. The scheduler, legislative assistant, and even the front desk receptionist can negatively impact your advocacy efforts if you offend them, so always treat them with respect. Establish an ongoing dialogue with the key aides in the decision-maker's office. Make sure to get their names and the correct pronunciations of their names. Know their phone numbers and e-mail addresses. In most cases, these staff members will be your primary points of contact.

3. Be memorable and credible

One of your top priorities during your meeting with a government official should be to make a lasting positive impression. The official with whom you will be meeting will most likely be in the midst of a busy day, especially if you are meeting with that person at the office, where many potential distractions can unexpectedly present themselves. Your meeting could be just one of many constituent meetings the official has that day, covering a wide variety of subjects and requests for assistance. This is especially true for elected officials, who are often pulled in so many different directions during a business day that they may have difficulty remembering all the different people they met with and discussions they had during the day. In this environment, how can you ensure that yours is not one of the meetings the elected official forgets? How can you be certain that the information you convey hits home with the official

(Continued)

(Continued)

and is both memorable and persuasive? They key is to use examples of how the issues that are important to you will affect real people, especially the constituents the official represents.

Because policymaking affects every interest group and often occurs in an environment where multiple different issues are being discussed, officials will hear from many constituencies during the decision-making process. Each concerned citizen will advocate for the issues he or she finds important, but not every meeting will be effective in influencing the official.

Being able to stand out from the crowd—by conveying a positive and memorable message—is often the key to success.

4. Have a compelling story and focus on the positive

Nothing is more memorable to an elected official than a constituent with a compelling story. A common mistake made in meetings with elected officials is for the individual to focus too much on the negative business or economic consequences of the policy decision being discussed. You should avoid leading the discussion with comments suggesting that your business or personal finances will be negatively impacted if the policymaker fails to take your advice. Similarly, never allude to political consequences for the official if the position for which you advocate fails to gain support. Intentional or not, this approach may come across to the official as politically threatening and will ensure that the meeting gets off on the wrong foot. Focus instead on the positive. Discuss how the community or an affected population is benefiting from the policy at hand, or show how various people could benefit if changes were made.

Use your own personal experience to your advantage. The most impactful and memorable constituent meetings a government official will have are those featuring constituents who are able tell their own stories about how they are benefiting from the program being discussed. Examples include a veteran who benefits from a veterans' student loan program, a teenager who benefits from an after-school program, an Alzheimer's patient who benefits from medical research, a recreational boater who benefits from local water resources, just to name a few. Whatever your cause or issue, it is always better to focus on the positive and tell your own story. Even if the official is unable to support your cause to the degree you would like, with this approach you can be assured that your voice will be heard in the most effective way possible.

5. Succeed at the meeting

Your meeting is likely one of several the official will have that day and your time may be limited. It is important that you convey your message in a clear and concise manner to maximize its effectiveness. Here are some tips:

- Avoid unnecessary distractions, and be sure to bring the official back to topic respectfully should he or she direct the conversation away from the issue you want to discuss.

- Always stay positive, and never hint of political consequences for the official if your issue or request fails to advance.
- Use your personal experience to your advantage. The most memorable and effective meetings are those during which the official hears directly from a constituent personally affected by the issue under discussion.
- Be aware of the signals you are sending through your actions. For example, advocates of a small nonprofit organization seeking more funding should think twice before handing out an expensive-looking glossy pamphlet that might cause the official to question whether the organization is using appropriately the funds it is already receiving.
- Offer to serve as a resource for the official or appropriate staff on matters pertaining to the issues you are discussing. This opens the door for further discussion with the official and increases the possibility that your opinion will be considered when the issue is debated.
- Be sure to leave the official with a clear request for the action you would like taken. If appropriate under the circumstances, ask the official to be an advocate for your issue, rather than just a supporter.

6. Follow up effectively

It is surprising how often people forget the common courtesy of a thank you note, preferably a handwritten note. Take the opportunity to follow up with the official to thank him or her for the meeting and briefly reiterate the issues discussed and your request for action. Also send a note to thank the staffer assigned to oversee your issue, using the opportunity to send follow-up information, if necessary.

Taking these steps will not guarantee that you will be successful in your advocacy efforts. But it will ensure that you are in the best position to be as successful as possible given the many competing interests and factors that will impact the outcome.

Jason Altmire is the former U.S. representative from Pennsylvania's fourth district. He is currently senior vice president for public policy and community engagement at Florida Blue (floridablue. com), the largest health insurer in Florida.

11. Don't Assume that the Final Decision Maker Is the Right Target

It sounds strange, but sometimes the decision maker you need to persuade is not the one who will ultimately decide. At times, citizens have to persuade third governmental parties to use their influence with policymakers to produce positive results. Although this can be cumbersome and time consuming, it is sometimes the only way to motivate a decision maker who has proven unwilling or unable to act.

States and localities often engage federal action or inaction both directly and indirectly. For example, a groundswell of opposition has erupted since the Obama administration proposed in 2014 to allow so-called "seismic testing" off the Atlantic coast so energy producers could explore possible oil and natural gas reserves. Citing potential economic impacts on coastal communities and possible disruption to marine life, more than 80 state or local governments have either passed resolutions or written letters opposing seismic testing.[5] The effort produced results. In March 2016, the U.S. Interior Department announced it was abandoning plans to lease drilling rights along the Atlantic coast between Florida and Delaware.[6]

But third-party intervention can also be effective indirectly. In the 1980s, nearly 150 state and local governments protested South Africa's apartheid (government-sponsored racial segregation) by voting to divest themselves of South African companies or of companies doing business in South Africa, or to give preference in government purchasing to companies that did not engage in business with South Africa. Similarly, states and localities used their economic power to persuade companies to adopt the MacBride Principles, a corporate code of conduct created in 1984 to prevent anti-Catholic workplace practices in Northern Ireland. That action helped force the United Kingdom to adopt new antidiscrimination measures. At present, some colleges and universities, states, and local governments are considering the same approach toward fossil fuel companies to raise concerns about climate change and global warming.

Once you have defined the problem you want to solve, consider all of the other public entities that could be positioned to help you address the problem. Usually, your target will be the decision maker, but be prepared to enlist governmental intermediaries that might be more effective in achieving results.

12. Don't Let the Perfect Be the Enemy of the Good

Some citizen activists define success as achieving 100 percent of their agenda—and they almost always end up disappointed. Don't make that mistake. The ideal result is rarely the actual result. Be prepared with fallback options if the decision maker can't or won't give you all of what you want. The official may be constrained by time, fiscal limitations, or other parochial, political, or policy considerations. Your effort to persuade the decision maker is a negotiation of sorts. Keep an open mind and consider alternatives as you work to secure your vital interests. Stay positive if you don't hit a grand slam in your first at bat. Learn to embrace the 80 percent or even 50 percent solution for now, and then rethink your strategy so you can make even more progress in the future.

CHECKLIST FOR ACTION

- ☐ Educate decision makers before they become decision makers.
- ☐ Define the relationship with the decision maker before you create it.
- ☐ Follow the chain of command.
- ☐ Respect professional staff.

---

[5] "Grassroots Opposition to Atlantic Drilling," *Oceana*, usa.oceana.org/seismic-airgun-testing/grassroots-opposition-atlantic-drilling

[6] Jennifer A. Dlouhy, "Obama Bars Atlantic Offshore Oil Drilling in Policy Reversal," *Bloomberg*, March 15, 2016, www.bloomberg.com/news/articles/2016-03-15/obama-said-to-bar-atlantic-coast-oil-drilling-in-policy-reversal

- ☐ Know the decision maker before you begin to lobby.
- ☐ Determine who influences the decision maker.
- ☐ Understand internal politics and dynamics.
- ☐ Do your homework—always be credible.
- ☐ Remember that all politics is local.
- ☐ Maximize your face-to-face opportunities with the decision maker.
- ☐ Don't assume that the final decision maker is the right target.
- ☐ Don't let the perfect be the enemy of the good.

6 Timing Is Everything

Using the Calendar to Achieve Your Goals[1]

"For everything there is a season, and a time for every matter under heaven."

—Ecclesiastes 3:1

Case in Point Why the Mizzou Football Protests Are a Watershed Moment in Sports Activism*

November 10, 2015

By Maxwell Strachan, Senior Editor, The Huffington Post

Chris Lee/St. Louis Post-Dispatch via AP, File

University of Missouri head football coach Gary Pinkel (center) celebrates with his team after they defeated Brigham Young University on November 14, 2015. Earlier that week, Pinkel had publicly supported his players when they protested the university president's handling of racial tensions on campus.

[1] We are very grateful to highly regarded Florida political and legislative strategist Steve Schale (steveschale. com) for his thorough review of and insightful feedback on this chapter.

On October 17, 1969, fourteen football players at the University of Wyoming walked into their head coach's office with a request. The players, all black, were upset that the Mormon church continued to prohibit black men from entering its priesthood, and so hoped to wear black armbands during their game against BYU the next day in quiet protest.

Instead of receiving permission, they received dismissal. Head coach Lloyd Eaton kicked all 14 players off the team that day, a firm pronouncement that dissent was not allowed anywhere within the Wyoming football program. "We do not build winning teams by debate," Eaton was later quoted as saying in The New York Times.

The dismissal of the 14 students, who collectively came to be known as "The Black 14," became a national story, but the news that a football team was at odds with its coach was hardly surprising. Throughout the civil rights era, protests by football players often pitted players against coach. Less than one year after the Black 14, nine black football players at Syracuse University — later known, incorrectly, as the "Syracuse 8" — boycotted the team's opening game to bring attention to institutionalized racism within the program.

There were dozens, if not hundreds, of disturbances within college football in the late 1960s and early 1970s, according to David Wiggins, co-director for George Mason's Center of Study of Sport and Leisure in Society. All too often, the players at schools, including Oregon State and the University of Washington, ended up pitted against coaches.

"[In] many of the disturbances in the late 1960s and early 1970s, the black athletes were going head to toe with white coaches, disturbed by what they thought was ill-treatment, the disciplinary nature of white coaches, the fact that white coaches weren't really sensitive to their needs," Wiggins told The Huffington Post.

But when more than 30 black football players at the University of Missouri joined protests in November 2015 over how the school's president, Tim Wolfe, had handled a series of racially charged incidents, their coach didn't discipline them. Instead, Gary Pinkel, the highest-paid public employee in the state of Missouri, lent his support.

"My players—they're my kids," Pinkel said Monday after Wolfe resigned. "They had tears in their eyes and asked if I would support them and I said I would—it's about supporting my players when they needed me."

Pinkel's support should not be seen as the most important moment in the events that have transpired in Missouri—that would be an injustice to the members of the football team who put their scholarships on the line; to Michael Sam, who came out quickly and fervently in support of the team; to the many passionate black students at the university who raised the issue; to the protesters who came before them in nearby Ferguson and elsewhere; and most of all to Jonathan Butler, the graduate student who went on a hunger strike for the cause.

But Pinkel's support should be seen as proof that the relationship between a coach and his football players has changed since the 1970s. At least in one case, the coach's loyalty was to his players first and to the administration second. Pinkel is not the hero here, but his willingness to stand behind his players is a sign that football players have new and tangible power.

"You have [in Missouri] a white coach who is sensitive to [black athletes'] desires," Wiggins said. "It's kind of fascinating to me how different it is from what we saw in the late 1960s and early 1970s."

"I can't tell you how surprised I was to see coaches participating in something like this," agreed Chuck Korr, professor emeritus of history at the University of Missouri-St. Louis.

That Pinkel supported his players is a result of many factors. It could be argued the situation had reached a head even before the team jumped in, and very few people want to be on the wrong side of a racial controversy in 2015. But Pinkel's support, and the inarguable power of a united Division I football team, is also a result of the shifting economic realities of college sports. If money talks, Pinkel is the most powerful man at the school, the athletic department its most powerful institution, and football its most powerful sport. The department had an operating revenue of $83.7 million during the 2014 fiscal year, a 10 percent jump from the previous year, and the department sent $2.2 million of its $3.5 million profit back to the university for nonathletic expenses. That's what real influence looks like.

The players might not make money, but they do have the ability to make sure the school doesn't either, should they refuse to play any given Saturday. "So much is invested in [the athletes'] labor, we're talking millions of dollars," said Louis Moore, an associate professor of history at Grand Valley State University. "They have power."

More and more, it's clear they know they do. On the Monday after Wolfe announced his resignation, the Tigers' defensive end Charles Harris said, "Let this be a testament to all of the athletes across the country that you do have power." In early 2015, members of the Oklahoma football team released a statement asking for "severe discipline" of the Sigma Alpha Epsilon fraternity's senior leadership after a video was released of members chanting "there will never be a n****r in SAE." (In that case, head coach Bob Stoops supported his players as well.) Student athletes took similar stands in 2013 at schools including UCLA, where players criticized a lack of diversity, and Georgia Tech, Georgia and Northwestern, where players at each school wrote "APU"—All Players United—on their wrist tape in response to a range of issues.

Northwestern's quarterback at the time, Kain Colter, was among those who wrote the letters onto his wrist tape. He told HuffPost he believes situations like the one in Missouri help athletes realize their influence. "The more athletes stand up and use that power, the more they'll realize how much value they have. And college presidents and administrators, athletic directors, they have to listen," Colter said.

Jeffrey Sammons, a professor of history at NYU, said he believes college athletes not just in Missouri but around the country are experiencing something of a political awakening. "I think we're seeing a kind of radicalization—I hate to use that term, but maybe a much more socially conscious and aware student-athlete," Sammons said.

As in the 1960s, the recent rise of social consciousness in sports, pro or not, didn't appear in a vacuum. Then, the civil rights movement contributed to its growth; now, it's Black Lives Matter. The Miami Heat wore hoodies in the aftermath of Trayvon Martin's death. The Los Angeles Clippers staged a silent protest against Donald Sterling. St. Louis Rams players put their hands up in solidarity with protesters in Ferguson. Football players at Northwestern fought for unionization, much to the chagrin of head coach Pat Fitzgerald. Each of these moments paved the way for Missouri.

"[These protests] started to open the door for athletes to think that this is an appropriate outlet to use their status as athletes to show their convictions," said Richard Lapchick, director of The Institute for Diversity and Ethics in Sport at the University of Central Florida.

In some ways, signs of social progress, while small, have allowed athletes to stand up more easily. Back in the 1960s, all but the biggest athletes risked their livelihoods by taking political stands. "Tommie Smith and John Carlos were unemployable for six years after Mexico City," Lapchick said, referring to the pair's famous Black Power salute at the 1968 Olympics. Today, few would think an athlete unemployable for taking a public stand against racism or mistreatment.

But even in an environment more amenable to black men taking political stands, the football players at Missouri still took an unambiguous risk. Many college football players in the U.S. are still on one-year scholarships, making them easily expendable should conflict arise. Often, if their coach won't back them, few others will. Outside of the football and basketball teams, black men on college campuses are often few and far between. Eleven percent of Missouri identified as black in 2010. Yet as of 2014, only 6 percent of the school's male students were black. Among the leadership ranks at major colleges, the athletic scene is still dominated by white males, especially compared to professional sports, according to Lapchick. A climate was created outside the University of Missouri that allowed the football team to take a successful stand, but it still took bravery within the school to make it happen.

"I've been involved in [college sports-related political actions] since the 1970s, and I've never seen anything of the magnitude or the impact that the football players had [in Missouri] since they jumped in," Lapchick said.

Sammons agreed. "It's the biggest thing that I can remember at least at the collegiate level since the '60s or '70s," he said. "I'm really quite proud of them."

MANAGE THE CLOCK

Before the University of Missouri Tigers football team took a stand in the middle of the 2015 college football season, it was unclear how the situation on the Columbia, Missouri, campus would be resolved. But the team used the leverage of timing to force change. Faced with the prospect of football players and coaches from the two-time defending SEC East champions refusing to take the field in a game against Brigham Young University, and the massive loss in revenue that could follow their boycott, the university president who was seen as indifferent to racism on campus had no choice but to resign.

Another football-related scenario helps to illustrate why timing has similar importance in your citizen advocacy initiative. All college and professional football fans know the pain of watching their teams try to come from behind as time is running out. Anxiety builds every time the quarterback seems to take too long behind center. Spectators hurl curses at every play that fails to gain significant yards or at least stop the clock. Anger rains down on any player who loses time. And when the clock expires before your team can make the winning touchdown or field goal, the resulting feeling is one of emptiness and demoralization.

It is no less painful to watch your citizen initiative go down to defeat because you didn't manage the clock correctly. The good news is that you can dramatically increase your ability to make time an ally rather than an enemy by following a few guidelines.

1. Be Aware of Fixed Deadlines—and Start Long in Advance

There is almost always an optimum time for citizens to intervene in government decisions. But some government time lines are set in stone, and failure to honor them can spell death to your initiative. Probably the best examples come from the legislative process. If you have identified a problem that requires the passage of legislation, be aware that every bill has a built-in expiration date: the end of the legislative session.

In Washington, D.C., congressional sessions run for two years, from January of one odd-numbered year to January of the next odd-numbered year. Thus the 114th Congress, which began January 3, 2015, will end January 3, 2017. Any bill introduced in a Congress that is not passed before the Congress ends automatically dies—meaning that any work that has been done on that bill must be started from scratch during the next two-year Congress. When you consider the extensive work that is required to pass legislation—finding a sponsor or sponsors in both the Senate and the House who will champion the bill, helping them build support among their colleagues, heading off opponents' efforts to kill the bill, convincing the relevant congressional committees to endorse the bill, securing initial passage, reconciling any Senate and House differences in a conference committee, passing the resulting compromise bill in each chamber, and then securing the signature of the president or finding enough votes to override a presidential veto—it is obvious that a late start will increase the chances of your bill dying at the hands of the two-year clock.

Other legislative bodies have similar rules. The two-year congressional deadline seems generous compared to the time limits imposed in many state legislatures, where bills do not carry over from one year to the next. If you cannot secure passage of your initiative in 2017, you will have to start anew in 2018. In some states, legislators are limited in the number of bills they can introduce during each legislative session. If you want a state senator or representative to sponsor your bill, you're out of luck if the officeholder has already reached the limit for that session. But you can increase your luck by being first in line when your legislator begins to consider what should be on his or her legislative agenda. County and municipal legislators (council members and commissioners) may have even tighter restrictions than do their state and federal counterparts. Depending on which level of government controls your issue, check to see which rules apply so that you can plan appropriately.

In addition to these automatic end-of-Congress or end-of-session deadlines, legislators sometimes impose other time limitations that can affect your advocacy efforts. For example, legislative bodies sometimes authorize programs for a finite period of time—a process commonly known as "sunsetting." If Congress, a state legislature, a county commission, or a city council fails to reauthorize that program by its expiration date, it ceases to exist. We saw this scenario unfold in the summer of 2015 with the U.S. Export-Import Bank, a federal agency that helps American businesses finance export activity so they can compete in the global marketplace.

The Export-Import Bank describes its mission as helping to "level . . . the playing field for U.S. goods and services going up against foreign competition in overseas markets, so that American companies can create more good-paying American jobs."[2] This isn't just happy talk. Major U.S. manufacturers and small businesses alike depend on the bank to extend financing to foreign purchasers so those American firms can sell their products around the world.[3] As a result, the bank had long enjoyed support from Republicans and Democrats as well as from the business community and organized labor. But the Export-Import Bank had a problem: Its authorization was set to expire on June 30, 2015. Some leading House members and outside advocacy groups

---

[2] EXIM, "About Us," *Export-Import Bank of the United States*, exim.gov/about.

[3] Simone Pathe, "Stop Pretending You Know What the Export-Import Bank Is," *PBS Newshour*, September 15, 2014, www.pbs.org/newshour/making-sense/stop-pretending-know-export-import-bank/

saw the bank as "a prime example of corporate welfare and so-called crony capitalism."[4] When they were able to block efforts to reauthorize the bank, its authority to operate expired, and the Export-Import Bank stopped accepting new business on July 1, 2015. For five months, the bank was in governmental purgatory. It was saved when a big push from the business community led by the U.S. Chamber of Commerce convinced enough members of Congress to vote for reauthorization in December 2015. The lesson is clear: in our democracy, legislative deadlines give a huge advantage to those playing defense. They simply have to stall long enough to run out the clock on your citizen initiative. If you are to overcome this built-in advantage, you must plan well in advance, do your homework, find the right coalition partners, and tell your story through the media. Look for more on the latter skills in the next few chapters.

Of course, do-or-die deadlines exist even in situations where a citizen initiative doesn't depend on the passage of legislation. Let's assume that your goal is to win a government contract that is bid through a competitive procurement process. Most jurisdictions have the clear, bright-line rule not subject to appeal that your bid is automatically disqualified if you miss the submission deadline and file it late. Because contracts can be worth anywhere from thousands to millions of dollars, a lack of timeliness can be financially devastating to your company. Imagine having to explain to your supervisor or shareholders why your bid was denied.

If you believe your local property appraiser has overvalued your home, leading to an increase in your ad valorem (property) taxes, you should quickly determine the required deadlines for challenging that assessment. Overlooking that date likely means you're stuck paying a bigger tax bill. Deadlines even affect the most fundamental aspects of the democratic process. Consider this unsettling scenario: Your advocacy organization is conducting an ambitious voter registration drive. You carefully follow all state and local election laws with one exception—you miss the deadline for submitting registration applications. None of those new voters you recruited will be casting ballots in the next election.

Though we are not trying to scare you, we do want to leave no doubt that missing governmental deadlines can have serious consequences for your citizenship goals. Pay close attention to key dates in whatever process you are pursuing. Don't squander the opportunity for success through tardiness.

2. Know the Official Time

Governmental bodies have hard deadlines, as shown in the examples we provided in the last section, and they also have soft deadlines that will also stymie your efforts if you do not account for them. When I was in the United States Senate, we had an annual budget deadline of October 1 to pass either a budget or a continuing resolution that would fund the federal government by extending the previous year's appropriations legislation until we could pass a budget.[5] I distinctly remember one of those

---

[4]Jackie Calmes, "Ex-Im Bank Is Reopened, but Big Loans Are Stalled," *New York Times*, December 7, 2015, www.nytimes.com/2015/12/08/business/ex-im-bank-is-reopened-but-big-loans-are-stalled.html

[5]In Congress, the regular order is for the House and Senate to pass individual appropriations bills for the 12 major components of the federal government—such as agriculture, commerce, defense, energy, financial services, homeland security, health, interior, labor, transportation, and others—in time for them to take effect on October 1. But thanks to the general dysfunction of the legislative

budget years. It was September 19. With only 11 days left in the federal government's fiscal year, we faced a major crunch time in the congressional calendar. The budget and appropriations process that had started a year earlier was rapidly coming to a close, and I had a problem: A Floridian I knew and respected needed funding for a worthy cause, but he was out of time.

The federal government's fiscal year officially begins on October 1 of each year, but it is labeled by the year in which the budget will conclude. Thus the budget year that begins on October 1, 2016, will be known as fiscal year (FY) 2017. The federal budget is actually the compilation of individual appropriations bills for the 13 major components of the federal government, such as defense, transportation, environment, and health. My staff and I were closely monitoring scores of spending priorities we had advocated throughout the year to make sure they would be included in the final budget negotiation.

These efforts were critical to Floridians and required my year-round attention and vigilance. Some were titanic struggles with national implications, such as the battle for federal funds to restore the environmental health of America's Everglades. With a 25-year window to complete this large and complex project, Congress had to ensure that it appropriated funds to keep the restoration on schedule. Other initiatives had statewide significance, such as road construction grants to the Florida Department of Transportation. Others still were community-specific projects, including beach restoration, cancer research at a state university, and the expansion of a national wildlife refuge. All spending items, regardless of size, are politically important to members of Congress. Appropriations usually create economic activity, which typically means profits and jobs. Members of Congress who don't care about creating jobs at home probably won't keep their own jobs in Washington for very long.

In the midst of this annual budget pandemonium, a venerable Florida university professor asked to meet with me. During this period of the year, I tried to keep office meetings to a minimum so that I could focus on the inevitable appropriations emergencies. But the professor was an exception—and proof that relationships matter.[6] I had been his student four decades earlier. I had great respect for his contributions to urban planning and land use, and I enjoyed his company. To the consternation of the harried staff members responsible for my schedule and our appropriations agenda, I told them to make room in that day's schedule for the professor.

The professor was describing an urban housing program he had initiated at a Florida university—a program for which he was seeking federal funding. Though the hour was late, I was willing to listen when the initiative was worthwhile and the advocate was credible. The professor's project passed both tests. Every element was in place for congressional support but one: the clock. As I explained to him, "The federal fiscal year begins on October 1. Congress is in the eleventh hour of its budget negotiations. If I were a senior member of the Senate Appropriations Committee, I might have a slim chance of getting your idea in the budget, but I am not. You are a year too late."

---

process in recent years, these individual appropriations measures have often been rolled into one mammoth spending bill and passed in time for New Year celebrations.

[6] Had the professor not known me, he would have been well advised to find someone who could make an introduction. If you need to connect with a decision maker but don't have a personal relationship, ask friends, colleagues, and allies if they know the official and can help you make contact.

He was obviously deflated, but I continued to explain. "My advice is to identify the federal agency with the greatest interest in your initiative—probably HUD, the Department of Housing and Urban Development. With your reputation and that of the university, you might persuade HUD to include your proposal in the departmental budget. HUD will submit its budget to the White House Office of Management and Budget in December. The president will then submit a proposed federal budget to Congress, which will start its annual appropriations process. With the support of the HUD secretary, your idea may well be included in the president's budget. You will be riding with the budget tide rather than swimming upstream. That is your best path to get the program in the budget for the fiscal year that starts 376 days from now."

Still disappointed, but chastened and informed of the realities of the governmental hourglass, the professor left with a promise to give it a try. He quickly contacted HUD and was greeted with interest in his proposal—well in advance of the department's deadline for submitting the next year's budget.

As my former professor learned, citizen advocates are far more likely to be successful if they understand the basic timing of whatever process they are seeking to influence. For example, many city councils and county commissions have a relatively short period of time—anywhere from four to eight weeks—from the date legislation is introduced until the final vote on that legislation. Since legislative committees routinely defer legislation, the process can take even longer. Set your strategic clock to provide a safety margin. If you persuade a legislator to file a bill on your behalf, make sure that act of filing happens well in advance of the internal deadline you have set for passage. If you don't, you may find yourself depending on a legislative body to do something that doesn't come naturally: act without delay. Even worse, you could end up asking legislators to consider the bill on an expedited or emergency basis, a step they almost universally disfavor and one that usually requires more than just a simple majority to pass.

Citizens who learn the internal timing rhythms of the governmental bodies will have a huge advantage over those who do not. Put yourself in the first category. Understand how long it takes public decision makers to act, and you'll be able to plan for success.

3. Study the Budget

As my professor friend learned on his visit to Washington, no area of governmental policymaking is more fraught with time constraints than is the budgetary process. The work of enacting the annual budget typically has three main parts:

1. Agencies and departments submit their individual budget requests to the budget and planning office of the chief executive (president, governor, county chairperson, or mayor).
2. After reviewing the individual requests and merging them into a single, integrated budget, the chief executive presents a proposed budget to the legislative branch (Congress, state legislature, county commission, or city council).
3. The legislative branch reviews, revises, and approves the budget and sends it to the chief executive for his or her final signature.

Time is short at each stage in this process. The agencies and departments have a deadline to submit their budget requests to the chief executive's office of budget and planning. The chief executive usually has a statutory deadline to submit a proposed budget to the legislative branch. And legislators are required to pass a budget that the chief executive will sign before the end of the fiscal year (usually June 30, September 30, or December 31 depending on the calendar used). If your citizen initiative requires public spending and you miss any of these deadlines, your chances of success will be severely diminished.

Several guidelines will help you negotiate the key first step of the tricky budgetary process.

First, give the person closest to the problem the chance to provide the solution to the problem. Whether you are dealing with a rural village with an annual budget of $10,000 or the Pentagon with its hundreds of billions in annual appropriations, determine the person responsible for your issue of concern. If you are well prepared and make a good presentation, you stand a reasonable chance of convincing that decision maker to favor your proposal for inclusion in the annual budget.

Second, as the saying goes, if at first you don't succeed, try, try again. Government agencies are often and accurately accused of being bureaucratic. Bureaucracy, however, gives you multiple chances to sell your idea. The people who occupy the lowest rungs of the ladder are usually long-serving, steady, and reliable people, but they are not always visionary or receptive to new ideas. You might well find someone further up the chain of command who will take a more open view on your proposal and say "yes" to it.

Third, look for someone who can help you demystify the often-baffling budget process. At the local level, this could be someone in the chief executive's finance department or budget office. But it could also include other citizens who have dealt successfully with your target agency in the past. Legislative aides—staffers who assist members of Congress, state legislators, county commissioners, or city councilors on budget matters—can also help to shine the light of understanding on the often dark and murky appropriations process.

Depending on your issue, you may be able to seek advice from a like-minded advocacy organization. If your goal is to increase funding for grants that support new business ventures, for example, consult with the legislative affairs staff at an entity like the National Federation of Independent Business (NFIB). If your aim is to create a new veterans health care clinic in your community, the American Legion, AMVETS, or another veterans association may have experts who can help. Finally, if you have sufficient financial resources, you can hire a governmental affairs consultant or lobbyist with expertise in the budget process.

Fourth, aspire to become an expert in the unique role that legislators play in the budget process. Just as our Constitution gives Congress the power of the purse in our federal government, most states give that same power to their legislatures. Congress and many state legislatures—and frequently local legislative commissions or councils— employ a two-step process for budget approval. Once the president, governor, or mayor has presented a proposed budget, these legislative bodies must authorize the proposed spending. For example, let's say the president has proposed $100 million to fund a new federal highway bridge over the Missouri River in North Dakota. Both the House and the Senate are required to give permission for the funds to be spent in that manner—to approve the president's policy goal. But that is only half the battle. If Congress merely authorizes the bridge, the bridge won't be built. Before construction can begin, the House and the Senate must also appropriate the necessary funds. That is, they must open up the national wallet and provide the $100 million to the U.S. Department of Transportation—or, more likely, to the state of North Dakota.

Fifth, present your ideas in strategic terms. In well-run budget offices, the annual allocation of public funds is a means of implementing goals that will guide the government over a five- or ten-year cycle. Convince budget planners that your proposal is consistent with their long-term priorities, and they are more likely to accept it.

The importance of mastering the budget process has grown in recent years. In 2011, Congress eliminated the controversial practice of "earmarks"—specific projects inserted in the appropriations legislation, without advance executive branch review, which generally benefitted a local community, constituent, or supporter. Earmarks became the subject of great controversy in the first decade of this century. For example, the Democratic Party's 2006 recapture of the House of Representatives is attributed in part to furor over the "Bridge to Nowhere," a nearly $400 million project linking the Alaskan city of Ketchikan to a small island with an airport and fewer than 100 residents. Two years later, Sen. John McCain made earmarks a centerpiece of his presidential campaign. When Republicans took control of the United States House of Representatives in 2010, they voted unanimously to ban earmarks.[7]

Although many state and local legislators continue the practice, budget watchdog organizations (e.g., see Florida Tax Watch and its annual "Turkey Watch" at floridataxwatch.org/ResearchAreas/turkeys) and governors or mayors with line-item veto authority often resist individual spending items that appear late in the spending process. With the side door of earmarks closed at the federal level and harder to open at the state and local levels, you must understand how to enter the budgeting process through the front door of the executive branch.

Just don't forget the legislative branch, which has the ultimate power of the purse at every level of government and still provides opportunities for citizen input even in the post-earmark era. For example, the federal government spends around $4 trillion annually. Three-fourths of that amount automatically goes to entitlement programs like Medicare, Medicaid, and Social Security. Congress invests the other $1 trillion among other programs administered by the federal government.

As winter turns to spring, the chairs of the U.S. House and Senate appropriations committees ask members to outline priorities they would like to see funded in each of 12 discretionary appropriations bills which allocate the $1 trillion. Additionally, members of Congress who are not on the committees submit letters requesting funds.

Whether or not they are on an appropriations committee, members of Congress establish priorities based on requests they have received from their constituents. If you want to make a funding request, contact the offices of your elected U.S. Representative and two U.S. Senators to determine which staff members are responsible for appropriations matters. Many offices provide this information on their official websites, or you can call and ask for the name and email address of the appropriations staff members.

Find out from the staff member when your congressperson must submit an appropriations request. At soon as possible—but at least several weeks in advance of the deadline—email your request to the elected officials and staff members. Follow up with a call to explain the proposal to the staff members and answer any questions they might have. After the deadline passes, contact the staff again, ask whether the

---

[7] Patrick O'Connor, "House GOP Bans Earmarks," *Wall Street Journal*, November 18, 2010, blogs.wsj.com/washwire/2010/11/18/house-gop-bans-earmarks/

proposed investment was included, and if it was, offer to be of assistance in securing its passage. If it wasn't included, ask for guidance on how you can improve your proposal to increase its chances in the next fiscal year.[8]

4. Think in Terms of "Best Time" to Achieve Your Goal

Although the governmental decision-making process has plenty of time constraints that require you to start early in order to achieve success, you must also pay attention to the optimal time to convince the decision maker to take on your initiative. For deadline-dependent issues, such as the budget, you will have little discretionary time: The legislature will appropriate money when it is legally required to do so. But for other initiatives, you must think about how the timing of the ultimate decision may affect the decision maker and thus your prospects for success.

Examples of this need to pay attention to timing abound at every level of governmental decision making, especially for issues tinged with any controversy. For example, in local, state, and federal governments, elected officials are much more likely to make tough decisions in years that don't end with an election or in lame duck sessions that take place after an election has passed but before the legislative session expires. Conversely, they love to deliver good news—such as appropriations for their districts—in election years when such actions could increase their standing among the voting public.

Your dealings with agency and departmental officials will be more successful if you apply the same insights. If a state or local government is experiencing a budget crunch and looking for ways to reduce spending, don't ask an official to take action that may draw negative attention. She may soon find herself out of a job. On the other hand, many ambitious government officials are looking for opportunities to make a name for themselves. If presented at the right time, your initiative may be the star to which they will hitch their wagon.

5. Play the Long Game

Unless you have an issue that must be resolved in the short term, consider running a citizenship offense that favors steady downfield movement over throwing a Hail Mary pass. Working in stages can be more effective. We learned this lesson as part of an effort with former Republican Congressman Lou Frey to persuade the Florida Legislature that every middle school student should take at least one semester of civics. Our effort took several years. In the first year, our coalition gathered data that showed Florida miserably near the bottom of national civic health statistics. We used the second year to craft the legislation, inform stakeholders, recruit bipartisan allies, find House and Senate sponsors, generate favorable media coverage of the issue, and recruit a high-profile celebrity supporter. When the bill was introduced, it carried the name of a former Republican state legislator who later became the first female justice on the United States Supreme Court. In our third year, the Justice Sandra Day

---

[8] We are grateful to Russ Sullivan (mcguirewoods.com/People/S/Russell-W-Sullivan) for providing this guidance on legislative funding opportunities. Mr. Sullivan began working on Capitol Hill in 1995 and joined the Senate Finance Committee staff in 1999. He served as the staff director to the committee from 2004 until his retirement from the Senate in 2013. Sullivan is now a partner at the McGuire Woods law firm, where he provides strategic counsel to the firm's clients, offering comprehensive solutions from an administrative, regulatory and legislative perspective.

O'Connor Civics Education Act passed the Florida Legislature unanimously because we used the first two years to build a foundation for success.

As former county manager Randall Reid reinforces in his tips on local government timing (see Tips from the Pros: Time After Time), questions of time infuse every aspect of the citizen advocacy process.

TIPS FROM THE PROS

Time after Time
RANDALL REID

It is within local communities that citizens will most directly seek to influence political decisions, experience civic life, and engage with the policymaking cycles of their democratic institutions. Here are 10 critical timing tips for citizens seeking to influence government actions locally.

1. *Every issue has its own time horizon and scale.* A community zoning issue may be a single legislative action regarding a single property that requires attendance at several governmental meetings over the course of weeks. In contrast, the development of a comprehensive growth management plan affecting all properties in a local jurisdiction may continue over decades, involving scores of meetings and repeated orientation of new residents.
2. *Elections results matter over time.* Elections results matter over time. Elected officials make critical decisions. Take the time to attend candidate forums and ask questions of potential officeholders about their positions on issues of concern before they are elected.
3. *Determine the timeliness of your goals.* Annual 'State of the City' presentations or strategic goal-setting retreats are used by chief executives to identify policy issues to be addressed in the upcoming year and shape the policy calendar that drives agendas. These public meetings may allow you to learn your local official's priorities and potential actions being considered to advance those priorities in time to influence them through public comments or preemptive communications (e.g., social media) campaigns.
4. *Understand the issue and the time frames for response or appeal.* Citizens learning of a community issue through traditional media may enter late into the decision-making process. Call your governmental officials and ask that they assist you in determining the status of any proposed action. Request that you be provided with all relevant public records and that they outline for you the mandated or planned legislative time frames.
5. *The earlier the involvement, the better.* Regardless of how many citizens pack the council chambers, waiting until the last public hearings on an issue is usually unwise if your goal is to be a meaningful participant. Don't neglect the traditional, legally required meetings, but take advantage of early

(Continued)

(Continued)

   opportunities for input into civic decisions. These include town hall meetings, community design charrettes, social media platforms, and focus groups.

6. *Take time to meet with elected officials.* Local elected officials are easily accessible, so call, e-mail, or meet personally with them to provide information and suggest reasonable compromises. You can even invite them to events, such as community or neighborhood meetings, so they can begin to understand issues from your perspective and learn more about your ideas.

7. *Use informal workshops and formal meeting agendas for timely participation.* Issues are rarely resolved immediately. Most city/county councils and commissions use an agenda process that keeps legislation pending for at least several weeks before a final vote. But that same process gives citizens multiple points of influence at commission workshops, regular governing body meetings, and budget adoption hearings. Keep your eye on local government websites, which often post minutes of prior meetings and future meeting agendas complete with back-up documents and staff recommendations online. Use these resources to monitor legislation, organize your advocacy efforts, and arm yourself with the most recent staff analysis or relevant performance metrics.

8. *Time the length of public presentations.* Since councils or commissions typically permit only a few minutes of public comment for each individual speaker, you must plan your public comments in advance. Be succinct. Complex issues may require you to assign various aspects of an issue to different coalition members. If so, coordinate presentations to cover all points within the limited speaking time afforded in public hearings.

9. *It is never a good time for making threats.* You need positive relationships to gain a favorable outcome. Though emotions often run high in public meetings, you must avoid outbursts of anger or character assassinations that waste time, alienate others, and reduce your group's likelihood of swaying opinion and gaining an acceptable compromise later.

10. *It is not over till the work is done.* Mobilized citizens often achieve temporary victories, such as approval of a proposed road or park project, but forget that implementation of these triumphs takes place over a longer-term time frame involving multiple budget appropriations and numerous business decisions. The incremental nature of policy change usually requires that a core group of citizens remain vigilant for years.

Randall Reid is the southeast regional director of the International City/County Management Association (icma.org). He served nearly 35 years as a county and city manager in Florida, Ohio, and Wyoming.

TAKE ADVANTAGE OF TRENDS AND CYCLES

If you think timing matters only in the short term, think again. When you are interested in influencing decisions over a long period of time or in achieving permanent change at the local, state, or federal level, you will have to monitor the tide of history, which is governed by the ebbs and flows of trends and cycles.

Trends

Trends are a function of historical momentum—events evolving over time to form a pattern that influences the fate of various policy matters. Trends may involve population growth or decline, demographic changes, economic growth or stagnation, partisan realignment, subtle shifts in public perceptions about issues, or other factors.

To give some examples, the post–World War II migration of African Americans from rural southern states to industrial midwestern cities was a trend. Nicholas Lemann describes how the Great Migration changed the political character of cities such as Detroit, Chicago, and Cleveland to the point that each of these elected African American mayors in the 1970s and 1980s.[9] One relatively recent demographic trend has been the growth in the nation's Hispanic population. According to the Pew Charitable Trusts, the U.S. Hispanic population has grown from 9.6 million in 1970 to 55.4 million in 2014.[10] The 2014 number includes 15 million in California, 10 million in Texas, and nearly 5 million in Florida. Not coincidentally, Hispanics have elected numerous officials in all three states and have had a major impact on culture, politics, business, and government.

Another trend is the overall shift in population from northeastern states to the Sun Belt. This trend has had monumental effects on both policy and politics. Presidential politics changed as southern and western states picked up electoral votes at the expense of the Northeast and the Midwest. The same was true of the U.S. House of Representatives, where the allocation of seats is based on the populations of states. In 1950, New York had 43 House members; Texas had 22. Today, the numbers are starkly different—the 2010 Census left New York with 27 members, while Texas now has 38. State and local governments in the Sun Belt have gained residents that generate tax income, but increases in population have also placed more demands on their budgets. As Americans have moved from one part of the country to another, the federal government has had to change the formulas it uses to distribute veterans' benefits, highway funding, and other types of spending.

Because of our home state of Florida's explosive growth in the 60 years after World War II, it offers many examples of how trends can powerfully reshape the political and policy landscape. Here's one: Before the 1960s, Floridians strongly resisted state interference in their private rights over land and water. In 1939, when Florida gave municipalities the authority to enact zoning ordinances, it was the 48th state to extend that power to cities and towns. Thirty years later, it was the last state in the nation to give counties general zoning power. This reluctance to let government play a role in determining how lands and waters were used affected a number of policy areas, but none more so than efforts to safeguard and preserve Florida's environmental treasures.

During the 1960s, a combination of events resulted in the fastest reversal of state environmental policy in U.S. history. Florida's population was expanding at a massive rate, largely fueled by new residents moving from other states. The mild climate and environmental quality were major draws for these newcomers. These new Floridians

---

[9] Nicholas Lemann, *The Promised Land: The Great Black Migration and How It Changed America* (New York: Vintage Books, 1991).

[10] Jens Manuel Krogstad and Mark Hugo Lopez, "Hispanic Population Reaches Record 55 Million, but Growth Has Cooled," Pew Research Center, June 25, 2015, www.pewresearch.org/fact-tank/2015/06/25/u-s-hispanic-population-growth-surge-cools/

shared a deep desire to preserve Florida as it was when they crossed the state line for the first time. A small but influential group of these new residents consisted of affluent citizens who had been national environmental movement leaders. Additionally, the new population and the resulting reapportionment of the Florida Legislature transformed the state's political scene. Although rural interests and Democrats had once dominated the agenda, urban areas and Republicans now had a much greater say. Finally, Florida was in what would prove to be a 30-year period of lessened rainfall.

This critical mass generated a new trend: greater state participation in matters affecting the natural environment. Environmental leaders saw and understood Florida's demographic and meteorological trends and had the political skills to make those developments work in their favor. Starting at the local level, they enacted some of the most aggressive environmental legislation and policies in the nation.

Many of the environmental leaders' initial successes were defensive. Their insight that Florida was changing helped them reverse or prevent government actions that could have severely damaged certain natural habitats. These triumphs included saving the brown pelican and manatee from near-certain extinction, blocking the construction of a large commercial airport in America's Everglades, and halting construction of the controversial Cross Florida Barge Canal.

Those defensive stands gave environmental advocates the energy and momentum to play offense and push for systematic policy changes that have provided long-term benefits for the state as a whole. The successful transition from defense to offense led Florida policymakers to embrace a number of monumental reforms, including

- Establishing state control over areas of critical concern, such as the Florida Keys;
- Building a statewide network of regional water-management agencies;
- Persuading the state to purchase extensive amounts of sensitive lands; and
- Initiating an ongoing effort to save America's Everglades.

But the Sunshine State is also an example of how circumstances—in this case, a massive economic downturn—can halt or even reverse other previous trends, namely, environmental preservation. When the Great Recession afflicted the U.S. economy in 2008, Florida was especially stricken. A 2012 study sponsored by the Rockefeller Foundation showed that Florida was the one of the six least economically secure states from 2008 to 2010, and that it had more households experience a 25 percent or greater economic loss than all but three other states.[11] In the last quarter of 2010, nearly 25 percent of Florida homes were being foreclosed or in some form of delinquency—the worst record in the nation.[12]

Not surprisingly, the 2010 Florida gubernatorial race largely focused on the economy. The winning candidate ran on a slogan—"Let's Get to Work"—that promised job creation through reductions in taxation, litigation, and regulation. Elections always have consequences; this one was no different. On a single day in May 2011,

[11] Jacob S. Hacker, Gregory A. Huber, Austin Nichols, Philipp Rehm, and Stuart Craig, *Economic Insecurity Across the American States* (New Have, CT: Economic Security Index, June 2012), www .economicsecurityindex.org/assets/state_reports/ESI_cross_state.pdf

[12] MBA, "Short-Term Delinquencies Fall to Pre-Recession Levels," *Mortgage Bankers Association* [Press Release], February 17, 2011, www.mba.org/x73907

the Florida Legislature dismantled several decades of growth management policy. It abolished the state's planning agency, repealed a 30-year-old law that required developers to consider the environmental impacts of their projects, and imposed new burdens on citizens looking to challenge water permits for developments.[13] The new governor also launched an effort to centralize state water policy decisions in Tallahassee as opposed to leaving authority in the five water management districts, a move that some critics said effectively politicized those agencies.[14]

College campuses have also been significantly affected by trends. Sixty years ago, a significant number of colleges and universities still restricted their enrollment to men. Some of your grandfathers or even fathers likely did not attend class with women. But the positive national trend in favor of granting women equal access and prohibiting gender-based discrimination has reshaped campuses across the United States. Today, men and women apply to college, live in university housing, attend classes, earn degrees, win scholarships and fellowships, and take advantage of other academic offerings on relatively equal terms. The trend in favor of equal gender opportunity also led Congress to pass legislation in 1972 (Title IX) that requires universities to provide women with equal opportunities for athletic participation. These collegiate trends mirror those in the political and governmental arenas. Shortly after being elected, Canadian Prime Minister Justin Trudeau appointed a cabinet that had 15 men and 15 women. When asked why, he responded simply, "Because it's 2015."[15]

Cycles

Trends represent long-term, or even permanent, changes, while cycles are recurring phenomena that influence the timing and impact of trends. Republican control of the White House for all but four years from 1969 to 1993 was a cycle that was not broken until Bill Clinton won the presidency in 1992. In the 24 years since he took office, the parties have alternated 8-year periods of presidential control. Conversely, Republicans ended a 40-year cycle of Democratic control of the House of Representatives with their November 1994 sweep of congressional elections. Except for the brief period from 2007 to 2011 when Democrats regained control of the House, Republicans have led the body for the better part of two decades.

Cycles take different forms, each offering challenges and opportunities to the participating citizen. For example, when you consider policy cycles, it is important to remember that most government policy decisions are based on a yearly cycle, but others operate in different time frames. Because of processes put in place through legislation such as the National Environmental Policy Act, the federal government's

---

[13] Mary Ellen Klas, "Florida Lawmakers Wipe Out 30 Years of Growth Management Law," *Tampa Bay Times*, May 7, 2011, www.tampabay.com/news/environment/florida-lawmakers-wipe-out-30-years-of-growth-management-law/1168328

[14] Craig Pittman, "State Environmental Chief, Gov. Rick Scott Shaking Up Water Management Districts," *Tampa Bay Times*, September 3, 2011, www.tampabay.com/news/environment/water/state-environmental-chief-gov-rick-scott-shaking-up-water-management/1189732 and Christopher Curry, "Critics Say Budget Cuts, Hand-Picked Leaders Have Hurt Water Districts," *Gainesville Sun*, October 10, 2015, www.gainesville.com/article/20151010/ARTICLES/151019996?p=4&tc=pg

[15] Jessica Murphy, "Trudeau Gives Canada First Cabinet with Equal Number of Men and Women," *Guardian*, November 4, 2015, www.theguardian.com/world/2015/nov/04/canada-cabinet-gender-diversity-justin-trudeau

environmental decisions are intended to be on a two-year cycle.[16] Local government comprehensive plans, which set the overall guidelines for how a county or municipality will grow and develop, are often five years in the making. A college or university often has a 10- or even 20-year strategic plan to govern its institutional priorities.

Citizen activists who pay attention to these policy cycles can take advantage. As you may recall from the Green Tea Coalition case study, Public Service Commissioner Bubba McDonald leveraged the fact that Georgia Power was required to seek approval of its long-term utility energy plan every three years. Knowing that cycle, he used the next approval process to make solar energy a meaningful part of Georgia Power's plan.

You can also make cycles work for you. Each year, your state legislature, county commission, city council, or school board must enact an annual budget. In the aftermath of the Great Recession, when state economies were recovering and generating additional revenue, many took advantage of the cycle to advocate for tax cuts or new or expanded state programs. Every decade or two, your state or county may have a mandated constitutional or charter reform commission or task force. Look for those built-in, cyclical opportunities to advance your citizenship advocacy goals.

Those who do not pay homage to cycles often find themselves on the outside looking in. I am familiar with a group of citizens concerned about the quality of civics textbooks in their state who wanted to reform the criteria for their selection. They received a harsh dose of reality when they learned that the state textbook selection was on a six-year cycle and that the cycle had started just one year before.

Political cycles are crucial for three admittedly cynical reasons. First, as elections approach, politicians are interested in advocating policies that make their constituents feel good and thus make them look good. The month of October in an even-numbered year is not the time to go to your state legislator or member of Congress and ask him to visit pain—such as tax increases or spending cuts to a popular program—on constituents. Second, if an elected official either cannot or does not run for reelection, she may feel liberated to take risks if she doesn't have to face the voters again. On the other hand, a lame duck politician generally has less power than one who may still be around at the start of the next legislative session. Third, the longer an elected official's term, the more power she has to help you. In the nineteenth century, many state governors served for a term of only one year. Today, the usual term is four years with the chance for reelection—a change that has made governors the primary factor in state politics.

However, be wary of any one-size-fits-all approach to political cycles. In some nations, such as the United Kingdom, voters can endorse or reject the status quo by keeping or changing the entire government in a single election. Our divided system often produces muddled results. When voters in 2006 returned the Democrats to power in both the House of Representatives and the Senate, many were expecting a sharp turn in policy, especially on the war in Iraq. They were disappointed. Because the elections did not produce a new president or give Democrats a governing 60-seat majority in the Senate, policy changes were slow at best. Similarly, when Republicans regained control of the House of Representatives in 2010 and the United States Senate in 2014, those voters who thought that federal spending would immediately drop were left with unmet expectations.

---

[16] Please be aware that in recent years, congressional gridlock has resulted in longer and less dependable cycles for major federal programs such as transportation and water resources development.

Political cycles can be internal as well as external. The national GOP, with its mix of economic, social and Tea Party conservatives, looks a lot different today than it did in the 1960s and 1970s when relatively liberal "Rockefeller Republicanism" was in sway. Just 20 years ago, during Bill Clinton's two terms in the White House, the national Democratic Party spoke with a moderate, business-friendly voice that echoed the president's centrist ideology. Today, with the rise of influential leaders such as Vermont U.S. Senator Bernie Sanders and Massachusetts U.S. Senator Elizabeth Warren, more Democrats speak in progressive tones. As you are working to persuade elected decision makers, put your finger on the pulse of their political party.

As was the case with Florida's growth management policy, economic cycles inevitably affect policy matters. If you're not convinced of this relationship, try asking your city commission for additional spending in a year when local government is fighting a budget deficit. Politics regulates the economy and, at the same time, is captive to its consequences. This is why the British define the study of government as political economics.

Here is one example of how an understanding of economic cycles powers political success. In the 1980s, a group of parents and educators across the nation enthusiastically noted a trend toward commencing children's education before the kindergarten year. They were supported by convincing scientific studies of the brain's development that offered a possible antidote to the low student achievement pervasive in secondary schools. But the movement's leaders had the wisdom of patience and waited until the booming prosperity of the 1990s to press their case before school boards, governors, legislatures, and the public. The result in many states was publicly-funded education for three- and four-year-olds in voluntarily participating families.

Finally, never forget the importance of individual politicians and the cycles in which they played a role. The passion, energy, and inspirational qualities of the individual at the helm can sway the day, whether it is a national leader, such as Winston Churchill, Britain's prime minister in the 1940s, or a visionary mayor in an American city today. But look beyond the question of who's in charge now to who might be in charge down the road. A newly elected official without seniority, but also without the time commitments that come with longevity, might be the leader to whom you can entrust your cause. Twenty years ago, U.S. House Speaker Paul Ryan was on the verge of running for Congress from Wisconsin. Oregon Governor Kate Brown had just risen from the Oregon House of Representatives to the Oregon State Senate. South Carolina U.S. Senator Tim Scott was a new member of the Charleston County Council. San Francisco Mayor Edwin Lee was the head of the city's purchasing department. Their political descendants are out there today and might be available to champion your cause.

CHECKLIST FOR ACTION

☐ Manage the clock.

- Know deadlines and start long in advance.
- Keep the official time.
- Study the budget.
- Select the best time to achieve your goal.
- Play the long game.

☐ Take advantage of cycles and trends.

7 All for One, and One for All

Coalitions for Citizen Success[1]

"[I]f you don't have a coalition with you, you will have a coalition against you."

—Former Israeli Prime Minister Shimon Peres

Case in Point	Equality Means Business
	By Nadine Smith*

From left: Mark Creek, Jane Keys, John Huls, and Linda Smith applaud the Hillsborough County Commission's unanimous vote to repeal the county's ban of gay pride recognition, a reversal that followed nearly eight years of advocacy by citizen groups such as Equality Florida.

[1] We are very grateful to Ryan Smart, president of 1000 Friends of Florida (1000fof.org) and former manager of the Florida Conservation Coalition (floridaconserva tioncoalition.org) for his insightful feedback on this chapter.

*Our thanks to Nadine Smith for writing this Case in Point. She is the co-founder and CEO of Equality Florida (eqfl.org), the state's largest organization dedicated to ending discrimination based on sexual orientation and gender identity. A former award-winning journalist turned organizer, Nadine is a Florida Chamber Foundation trustee. In 2013, she was named one of the state's "Most Powerful and Influential Women" by the Florida Diversity Council. She currently serves on the U.S. Commission on Civil Rights Florida Advisory Committee. Nadine lives in St. Petersburg with her wife Andrea and son Logan.

In January 2015, Indiana Governor Mike Pence was considered a strong contender for the Republican presidential nomination. Touting two balanced budgets, 100,000 new jobs, and an overall record that he called the envy of "49 other governors," Pence had joined the field of prospects in Las Vegas to meet top GOP campaign financiers. But within three months, Governor Pence's presidential hopes were dashed and his political future in jeopardy.

The reversal of political fortunes began on March 26, when Pence signed Senate Bill 101, the so-called Religious Freedom Restoration Act, over the sustained objections of civil rights advocates and business leaders across his state. At least 30 law professors had warned that the Indiana bill was part of an antigay backlash and would permit businesses to turn away lesbian, gay, bisexual, and transgender (LGBT) customers.

The Indiana Chamber of Commerce and other local employers spoke out against the new law, calling it bad for business. CEOs from nine major employers—Angie's List, Salesforce Marketing Cloud, Anthem Inc., Eli Lilly and Company, Cummins, Emmis Communications, Roche Diagnostics, Indiana University Health, and Dow AgroSciences—called for an immediate repeal of the law and urged Republican leadership to ban discrimination based upon sexual orientation or gender identity.

Max Levchin, who co-founded PayPal and now serves as chairman of Yelp and CEO of Affirm, tweeted to his followers: "What is happening in Indiana is pretty unbelievable. However it's dressed up, it's a signal that discrimination is welcome in this state."

Salesforce's CEO Marc Benioff announced his company would reduce any investment in Indiana and tweeted "Today we are canceling all programs that require our customers/employees to travel to Indiana to face discrimination."

Tourism officials were panicked. At least 10 national conventions threatened to pull out of Indiana. Entertainers canceled tour dates, and nearly a dozen state governors and big-city mayors banned taxpayer-funded travel to events in Indiana by government employees. NASCAR publicly criticized the move, and the NCAA began discussing moving its headquarters away from Indianapolis.

Governor Pence and legislators scrambled to reverse the bill, but the damage lingers. The call for a clear nondiscrimination law has intensified, and polls show Pence in a political toss-up for reelection. A survey taken in November 2015 showed that the governor's approval rating had dropped to 47 percent—a 15 percent decline from its 62 percent level in 2014.[2] As of March 2016, the *Washington Post*'s political blog —*The Fix*— noted that Pence, "once a safe bet for reelection, is now considered vulnerable after his approval ratings plummeted in the religious freedom debate."[3]

---

[2] Tony Cook, "Poll: Pence Approval Still Sags," *IndyStar*, November 5, 2015, www.indystar.com/story/news/politics/2015/11/04/poll-pence-approval-still-sags/75178220/

[3] Amber Phillips, "How North Carolina's Controversial 'Bathroom Bill' Could Backfire on Republicans," *Washington Post*, March 24, 2016, www.washingtonpost.com/news/the-fix/wp/2016/03/24/like-indiana-north-carolinas-controversial-lgbt-law-could-be-a-blessing-in-disguise-for-democrats/

The Fix ranked Pence as one of the five incumbent governors most likely to lose their reelection bids in November 2016.[4]

Although the Indiana controversy grabbed headlines around the world, it was not the first time that major companies had weighed in on the topic of LGBT rights. In February 2014, then-Arizona Governor Jan Brewer waited until the 11th hour to veto a similar bill that had drawn strong opposition from major corporations and sports organizations, including Apple, American Airlines, AT&T, Intel, Delta Air Lines, the Super Bowl host committee, and Major League Baseball.

Beyond speaking out against anti-LGBT legislation, companies have coalesced to support LGBT-inclusive laws. Hundreds of top-brand businesses signed onto a friend-of-the-court brief as the U.S. Supreme Court considered the cases that made marriage equality for same-sex couples the law of the land.

So why would major corporations, which aim to maximize profits and often eschew controversy, wade right into the middle of the contentious battle for LGBT rights? Though individual leaders may be moved by the message of equal rights and social justice, they have also come to the clear understanding that economic viability is affected by diversity. As a result, LGBT advocates around the nation are actively making common cause with business leaders to form pro-equality coalitions that transcend any other partisan or ideological differences.

LGBT rights are a proxy through which top talent evaluates which companies, municipalities, and states are modernizing for a vibrant future. Millennials, who already make up the largest generational cohort in the workforce, will be 75 percent of all employees by 2030, according to the Bureau of Labor Statistics.[5] For this generation diversity and inclusion are nonnegotiable, according to a Deloitte study on the impact of millennials on the workplace. "Millennials value inclusion as a critical tool that enables business competitiveness and growth, and as millennials flood leadership ranks, their perspectives will demand a shift in traditional diversity and inclusion models," the authors state. "Millennials are refusing to check their identities at the doors of organizations today, and they strongly believe these characteristics bring value to the business outcomes and impact."[6]

Today, companies are using their diversity ratings across a spectrum of issues as a competitive edge. They know that the action or inaction of cities, counties, and state government on these matters directly affects their ability to draw and retain top talent.

---

[4] Amber Phillips, "Republicans Have a Shot at a Record Number of Governors' Seats in 2016," *Washington Post*, March 11, 2016, www.washingtonpost.com/news/the-fix/wp/2016/03/11/republicans-have-a-shot-at-a-record-number-of-governors-seats-in-2016/?tid=a_inl

[5] Alastair Mitchell, "The Rise of the Millennial Workforce," *Wired*, August 2013, www.wired.com/insights/2013/08/the-rise-of-the-millennial-workforce/

[6] Christie Smith and Stephanie Turner, *The Radical Transformation of Diversity and Inclusion: The Millennial Influence* (New York: Deloitte University Leadership Center for Inclusion, 2015), 15; See for the first quotation the introduction to this publication, at www2.deloitte.com/us/en/pages/about-deloitte/articles/radical-transformation-of-diversity-and-inclusion.html

And business has been playing a role at the local and state level for years on LGBT issues, including in Florida where 56 percent of the state's 20 million residents are protected from discrimination based on sexual orientation and gender identity.[7]

The case of Hillsborough County—best known for its county seat, Tampa—represents an excellent example of the impact of business leadership on equality issues even in the face of legislative hostility. The path to victory included rallying public support while businesses articulated a strong economic case. This combined approach provided entrenched opponents a face-saving path to support LGBT equal rights and basic protections.

HILLSBOROUGH'S NOTORIOUS GAY PRIDE BAN

In May 1995, Hillsborough County Commissioners voted 4–3 to repeal a county non-discrimination ordinance that banned discrimination based on sexual orientation. The measure had passed four years earlier, prompting LGBT rights opponents to launch an effort to rescind the protections. They managed to undo the county's law by a one-vote margin.

Ten years later, in 2005, the county commission had shifted more dramatically to the right. In a 5–1 vote, the commission banned the county from "recognizing gay pride." An overzealous manager in the county library system ordered a gay author's display removed, but the ban appeared to have no actual legal impact. County attorneys could not identify one activity that was permitted before the ban passed that was no longer permitted afterward. Still the measure did achieve its primary goal: to single out and denigrate gay residents in the county. The backlash began immediately.

Convention planners announced Hillsborough County was being taken off the list for future consideration. The Florida Library Association passed a resolution refusing to hold conferences in Hillsborough until the antigay law was rescinded. At least one convention, organized by the Mississippi-based Sardis Mini Systems, cancelled plans to bring 2,000 people and an estimated $1 million to the county.[8]

In response, Key West hosted a "Pride in Exile" event, letting Hillsborough know that LGBT people and their economic clout were welcomed further south.

For nearly two decades, Hillsborough held the reputation as a hostile place for LGBT people. The City of Tampa tried to distance itself from the economic fallout, but Tampa Pride, one of the largest events in the city, faded away. St. Petersburg capitalized, launching what became one of the largest gay pride events in the country.

The Hillsborough pride ban vote provoked sustained protests, and it also inspired a former police officer to make an historic run for office. In 2008, Kevin Beckner became the first out gay person on the Hillsborough County Commission.

His first few years of service saw little progress, but Beckner's presence reignited the community's engagement, especially as LGBT equality initiatives met with continued opposition from county officials. In 2009, the Republican majority struck

---

[7] Florida Business for a Competitive Workforce, "Fast Facts," flcompetitiveworkforce.com/fast-facts-update/

[8] Fidel Ortega, "Tampa's Pride Ban Hits City in Pocketbook," *LNEWS*, August 9, 2005, lnews.blogspot.ca/2005/08/tampas-pride-ban-hits-city-in.html

down Beckner's proposal of domestic partnership benefits for county employees. The next year, they blocked an effort to pass a Hillsborough County employee non-discrimination policy. And during Beckner's first five years, the majority of commissioners refused to sign a proclamation to recognize the GaYBOR District Coalition, the alliance of LGBT-owned or -supportive businesses in Tampa's Historic Ybor City neighborhood, or to welcome the weeklong celebration "GaYBOR Days."

By 2013, the tide began to turn. Beckner was reelected handily, and he convinced the board to adopt an economic development strategy endorsing the principle that inclusion and diversity would help the county attract jobs. Major metropolitan areas around the state, like Orlando and Miami, had adopted strong LGBT-inclusive nondiscrimination laws, and Hillsborough's refusal to do so was a continuing thorn in the Tampa Bay region's reputation.

When the GaYBOR Days proposal came forward this time, it reflected the goals of the adopted job creation strategy. Commissioner Ken Hagan became the fourth to sign the GaYBOR Days proclamation in support of gay tourism and business, and the rest of the commission quickly followed suit. For the first time since 1991, a majority of county commissioners took a pro-LGBT stance. The economic argument was providing long-time opponents a place to stand; one foot planted in the past comforting their political base, the other navigating the rapidly growing public and corporate support for LGBT equality.

This first win created momentum in Hillsborough County. Commissioners next turned to the pride ban, which they repealed unanimously despite the fact that the majority of board members had previously voted to pass it or uphold it. The winds had shifted, and it was time for equality advocates to pursue protections that had been stripped away or denied.

Commissioners at first refused to take up the issue of a domestic partnership registry. But community leaders were already moving swiftly to garner support for a countywide nondiscrimination ordinance that included sexual orientation and gender identity.

Working with Equality Florida and key supporters, Commissioner Kevin Beckner began to reach out to the local business community. Some key leaders were already part of Equality Means Business, a program Equality Florida had launched in 2008 to improve Florida's national and international reputation as a welcoming and inclusive place to live and play. The advisory council roster for the program boasts 50 major corporations including Disney, Florida Blue, Wells Fargo, CSX, Morgan Stanley and a host of top law firms including Carlton Fields Jorden Burt, a firm that became a leading advocate in Hillsborough County. Large and small employers began adding their names to a letter calling for an LGBT-inclusive nondiscrimination law:

> We are area business people who believe that updating our County's Human Rights Ordinance to include sexual orientation and gender identity is critically important to our future. There are specific reasons this effort has attracted our support.
>
> First, it would be very good for our businesses. Studies have shown that businesses of all sizes simply cannot discriminate and at the same time maximize profits and outperform the competition. We know that discrimination is hurtful, divisive, and artificially excludes highly talented employees from our businesses, and this ordinance will help eliminate it.

Second, enacting this ordinance is critical to our County's overall economic development. In order to grow, prosper, and provide the kinds of jobs and economic opportunities our citizens rightly expect, Hillsborough County must attract the best and the brightest. Currently 91% of Fortune 500 companies have sexual orientation protections and 61% have now added gender identity. Those are values shared by us and many local companies in addition to ours—Raymond James, Tech Data, Wells Fargo, Home Shopping Network, CSX, Florida Blue, C1 Bank, to name a few. Taking this important step will not only help all persons who want to live and work in Hillsborough County feel welcome regardless of their sexual orientation or gender identity, but it will attract employers and workers who choose to live and work in communities that are diverse and inclusive. These companies and individuals turn away from areas that fail to provide protections for diverse populations; 25 other Florida cities and counties know this and have already passed similar ordinances.

Third, Floridians believe this is the right thing to do. A recent survey by the Bob Graham Center for Public Service shows that 73% of respondents in Florida support this type of ordinance, and a recent national poll shows that 70% of American small businesses already prohibit discrimination on the basis of sexual orientation.

As local business people, we need your help and support. We'd like very much to discuss this matter further at your convenience.

The passage of this important Equal Rights Ordinance will help us grow and prosper along with hundreds of other businesses throughout the County.

The time has come—and it's the right thing to do.[9]

On Oct 2, 2014, the Equal Rights Ordinance passed unanimously.

That letter from business leaders wasn't the only correspondence commissioners received that week. Three major hospitals in Hillsborough wrote letters calling for the passage of a domestic partnership registry as a tool to help them serve the community better. Domestic partnership registries give unmarried people who live together the right to have health care visitation and make decisions on matters like medical care and funeral arrangements. The measure that had been killed twice before sailed through fewer than two weeks after the Equal Rights Ordinance was passed. Hillsborough had gone from one of the worst counties on equality to a leader on LGBT-inclusive protections. The voice of the business community had been crucial.

And the connection to economic impact was more than a talking point. Business executives agree that LGBT discrimination has a substantial impact on the workplace. Research shows that, conservatively, Florida businesses are losing more than $362 million annually in productivity and turnover costs alone."[10]

---

[9] BOCC Meeting Agenda Supplement, Hillsborough County Florida, October 1, 2014, Agenda Item No. D-1, "As Local Businesses, We Seek Your Support for an Equal Rights Ordinance," agenda .hillsboroughcounty.org/cache/00003/533/D-1.PDF

[10] Thinkspot Inc., *The Link between Economic Competitiveness & Workplace Equal Opportunity in Florida* (St. Petersburg, FL: Equality Means Business Advisory Board, 2015), eqfl.org/emb/economic_impact_study

A December 2015 column in the *Times* of London—"Corporate America Has No Choice But to Join the March to Equality"—succinctly explained why corporations understand that equality means business:

> As Bob Witeck, an LGBT business strategist in Washington, says, many big American companies feel they have no choice but to embrace inclusive advertising: "A lot of the companies that are doing this are legacy brands. They have been around for more than a century. They have a constant challenge to remain relevant. That means being expansive and inclusive."
>
> So if American companies are taking this route, it is not only to reach gay audiences, and their collective buying power estimated at $884 billion, but to connect with younger generations who expect inclusion as a reflection of their outlook. More than 45 per cent of consumers under 34 years old say that they are more likely to do repeat business with an LGBT-friendly company, according to a Google consumer survey. Of these, more than 54 per cent say that they would choose an equality-focused brand over a competitor. Overall levels of support in America for same-sex marriage are running at 58 per cent, rising to 76 per cent among 18 to 29-year-olds and 62 per cent for those aged 30 to 49.
>
> Corporate America is only too aware of these numbers.[11]

POSTSCRIPT: THE ALLIANCE CONTINUES

Business leaders soon validated in North Carolina the premise of that December 2015 *Times* column.

In February 2016, the Charlotte City Council voted 7–4 to extend antidiscrimination measures to LGBT residents—reversing a failed vote from the previous year.[12] But Charlotte's new law did not last long. In late March 2016, the North Carolina Legislature convened a surprise session to pass legislation banning local governments from enacting their own antidiscrimination policies—and prohibiting transgender citizens from using bathrooms that do not match the gender of their birth.[13] North Carolina Governor Pat McCrory signed the bill on the same day it was passed.

The new state law created a strong reaction from the North Carolina and national business communities. Companies with major North Carolina operations, such as American Airlines and Bank of America, condemned the legislation.[14] Organizers of

---

[11] Alexandra, Frean, "Corporate America Has No Option but to Join the March to Equality," *Times*, December 22, 2015, www.thetimes.co.uk/tto/business/columnists/alexandrafrean/article4646768 .ece?shareToken=a8b3640aa8ad19bc48ae45ed55644749

[12] Steve Harrison, "Charlotte City Council Approves LGBT Protections in 7–4 Vote," *Charlotte Observer*, February 22, 2016, www.charlotteobserver.com/news/politics-government/article61786967 .html

[13] "Dave Philipps, "North Carolina Bans Local Anti-Discrimination Policies," *New York Times*, March 23, 2016, www.nytimes.com/2016/03/24/us/north-carolina-to-limit-bathroom-use-by-birth-gender .html

[14] Emery P. Dalesio, "N.C. Law Angers Businesses," *U.S. News & World Report*, April 1, 2016, www .usnews.com/news/us/articles/2016-04-01/companies-reconsidering-north-carolina-over-lgbt-rights

the High Point Market—a biannual furniture expo with an estimated $5 billion annual economic impact to the state—expressed concern over the effect of the new law on their trade shows.[15] More than 130 major business executives from around the nation asked the governor and legislature to repeal the law.[16] The National Basketball Association (NBA) hinted that it might relocate its 2017 All-Star game away from Charlotte without a change in the law.[17]

While many businesses expressed concern about the legislative and gubernatorial actions, at least one started the shift to real economic consequences. In April 2016, PayPal reversed plans it had announced just two weeks earlier to place a global operations center in Charlotte—thus depriving North Carolina of 400 well-paying jobs and nearly $4 million in capital investment.[18] As PayPal President/CEO Dan Schulman said in his announcement, "This decision reflects PayPal's deepest values and our strong belief that every person has the right to be treated equally, and with dignity and respect. These principles of fairness, inclusion and equality are at the heart of everything we seek to achieve and stand for as a company. . . . As a company that is committed to the principle that everyone deserves to live without fear of discrimination simply for being who they are, becoming an employer in North Carolina, where members of our teams will not have equal rights under the law, is simply untenable."[19]

BUILDING YOUR OWN COALITION: A STEP-BY-STEP GUIDE TO FORGING AN EFFECTIVE ALLIANCE

Whether you are a utility ratepayer concerned about new federal air quality regulations, a developer frustrated with the local zoning process, a farmer who wants the state to invest more in research to prevent agriculture disease, or a small businessperson worried about the impacts of a nearby proposed mega shopping center, you are much more likely to succeed if you have the active support of a broad base of citizens and interests. The following guidelines will help you create and sustain the coalition that you will need to turn your goal into reality.

---

[15] Jackie Wattles, "North Carolina's $5 Billion Trade Show Says LGBT Bathroom Law Is Bad for Business," *CNN Money*, March 28, 2016, money.cnn.com/2016/03/28/news/economy/north-carolina-bathroom-bill-high-point/

[16] Letter addressed to Governor McCrory, from Human Rights Campaign and Equality North Carolina, rc-assets.s3-website-us-east-1.amazonaws.com//files/assets/resources/NC_CEO_Letter_(3).pdf

[17] Si Wire, "NBA: North Carolina anti-LGBT Law Could Impact Charlotte All-Star Game," *Sports Illustrated*, March 24, 2016, www.si.com/nba/2016/03/24/north-carolina-anti-lgbt-law-all-star-game-charlotte

[18] Michael Hiltzik, "As PayPal Cancels Expansion, the Consequences of N.C.'s anti-LGBT Law Get Real," *Los Angeles Times*, April 5, 2016, www.latimes.com/business/hiltzik/la-fi-hiltzik-paypal-nc-20160405-snap-htmlstory.html

[19] Dan Schulman, "PayPal Withdraws Plan for Charlotte Expansion," PayPal news release, www.paypal.com/stories/us/paypal-withdraws-plan-for-charlotte-expansion

1. Define the Problem to
Attract the Widest Possible Coalition

As noted in previous chapters, effective citizenship—including coalition building—hinges on the formulation of a concise, fact-based, and compelling statement of the problem you aim to fix. A well-stated problem helps to recruit and motivate potential coalition members, particularly if the timing and circumstances create a sense of urgency.

If you are concerned about crime in your neighborhood, define that concern in a way that speaks to fellow neighbors, local businesses, nonprofits focused on fighting the causes of crime, and law enforcement officials. Few if any of those potential coalition partners will be motivated to act if you simply declare that "crime is a problem." But if the facts support your statement that "twenty homes and ten stores have been robbed in the past six months," you are more likely to inspire others to help you fix a problem that you all share.

Remember that coalitions form only if multiple parties believe the alliance will benefit their particular interests. Define the problem in a way that appeals to those varied interests. Recall the case of the Green Tea coalition. Had solar power advocates insisted on making this an issue of alternative energy, the efforts to bring more solar power to Georgia might have flopped. But they were savvy. Knowing that the Georgia Public Service Commission and the Georgia Legislature were conservative organizations, they wisely took a libertarian approach and made the issue one about personal freedom and liberty. That argument found a sympathetic audience in not only the Georgia Tea Party founder but influential public officials who ultimately produced regulatory and legislative victories. You are much more likely to capture the support of those disparate groups if you formulate the problem in a way that broadly yet succinctly targets all these various concerns.

Schedule a brainstorming session to determine potential coalition partners. Look for individuals and organizations that share your values or who have economic, political, or personal interests in addressing the problem you have identified or the solution you have proposed. With careful consideration, the meeting should produce a list of individuals and groups you need to contact.

Many potential coalitions lose steam at this stage because nobody takes responsibility for turning a great idea into an even greater alliance. Don't make that mistake. Pick up your cell phone or turn on your laptop or tablet and start calling or e-mailing your potential partners. Use social media to identify prospective teammates who might be communicating about the overall subject online, or launch a Facebook group, Twitter poll, or Periscope chat to see who responds. Ask those interested to get together for lunch or coffee at a location convenient to them so that you can discuss your idea in person.

Though time and circumstances do not always allow it, recruiting prospective allies in person is very important. Please do not underestimate the power of personal contact. Nothing communicates respect like going to a potential partner and asking for input and support for your cause. Your mere act of showing up at a prospective ally's house, so to speak, and seeking her or his assistance sends a strong message that you take that person seriously.

In his tips (See Tips from the Pros: Ingenuity and Innovation Are Keys to Effective Coalitions), former Chattanooga, Tennessee, mayor Ron Littlefield draws from his municipal experience and explains the benefits of thinking outside the box when looking for your coalition partners.

TIPS FROM THE PROS

Ingenuity and Innovation Are Keys to Effective Coalitions
RON LITTLEFIELD

While certain universal principles tend to guide the building of coalitions, several episodes from my time in city government have convinced me that the most effective ones are often a product of creative thinking.

When I was starting my first term as mayor of Chattanooga in 2005, I almost immediately encountered a common story, repeated in communities all over the country: a quiet neighborhood is disrupted when a bold outlaw group decides to set up shop selling illegal drugs on a well-traveled street corner.

Eastdale is a middle-class "inner ring" suburb just outside downtown Chattanooga. Neighborhood leaders came to me complaining about the detrimental effects of a newly established drug market in their previously safe and stable neighborhood. They were frightened and wanted the police to solve the problem. The police (like police everywhere) were stretched thin and really couldn't provide the sort of full-time coverage that might be required over an extended period.

So we thought innovatively, brainstormed with a coalition of the neighborhood, and collectively found a low-cost tool to support neighbors in their efforts to overcome drug dealers. Relying on the available resources of our police department, we borrowed a reserve police cruiser from the department's vehicle pool. The windows were heavily tinted to obscure the interior, and a large camera was installed in the passenger seat. Just to be fair to the criminal element, the cruiser was fully marked and fitted out with all the lights, bells, and whistles of a frontline cruiser. It even bore the special identification "Surveillance Unit" in large, very readable letters on both front fenders. Then, it was parked in a prominent location near the troublesome corner. Soon, to no one's surprise, the drug market moved—and so did the "Surveillance Unit." Our police officers dubbed this new tool "the unwelcome wagon"—and it continues to work even today.

Novel ideas can also help you follow the authors' good advice to "attract the widest possible coalition." That goal might seem almost totally out of reach in some rapidly changing communities. Urban neighborhoods of today—made up of such

(Continued)

(Continued)

a wide diversity of races, cultures, religions, and income levels and often further complicated by the effects of gentrification and immigration—are hard to pull together toward a common goal.

Like most cities, Chattanooga has such neighborhoods. People in one of these neighborhoods had the idea to have a gathering in a community center with a focus on desserts from all over the world. They called it "The Taste of Diversity," and invitations went out using conventional mail, e-mail, and social media. People were encouraged to come with trappings of their native cultures and bring the foods that they most loved to share.

Frankly, I really didn't expect it to work very well. When the evening came, I drove out to the center and noticed that the parking lot was full. I assumed that there must be a basketball game in addition to the diversity event. But when I walked in my eyes were greeted with a swarm of people of every culture and color, all decked out in the bright clothing of their native lands and moving from table to table sharing dishes and smiles and hospitality. I quickly became a believer in the power of food to bring people together.

I also discovered that coalition partners can be found in the unlikeliest of places if you are willing to keep an open mind. Political campaigns produce long lists of both friends and rivals, but I have learned those lists don't have to be the last word—particularly the "enemies" list. The simple act of asking for a favor or for advice can turn an enemy into a friend. One of my most effective appointed boards was intentionally made up of political opponents. The board of directors managed a local utility, so the issue went beyond politics. After a few months and more than a few notable successes, the "enemies" in question all thanked me for enabling them to work together on a shared interest and for the good of the community.

Finally, digital tools make it easier than ever to build coalitions. Technology is so much better now than just ten or even five years ago. Today, it is much easier to sort and select individuals, to keep track of special characteristics, to connect with neighborhoods and address their needs, and to communicate with diverse populations. The rapidly advancing world of social media and enhanced digital tools (smaller, faster, cheaper) provide new ways for people to stay in touch and work together.

So, what are you waiting for? Cast a wide net, apply your imagination, and build the coalition that will help you achieve your citizenship goals.

A city planner by profession, Ron Littlefield was public works commissioner, city council chair, and mayor of Chattanooga. He is presently a senior fellow with the Governing Institute and its lead analyst on the City Accelerator initiative. He also provides consulting services to governments through Littlefield Associates.

2. Build the Coalition around a Solution

What comes first, the chicken or the egg? The answer is that it depends on your point of view and circumstances. Some coalitions form around a problem and use their membership to generate solutions. Others will emerge in support of a solution and work on transforming that solution into policy.

Just as a clear definition of a problem can attract coalition members who share your frustration about conditions that need to be changed, your identification of well-received possible solutions to that challenge can both motivate new recruits and give them the hope of an outcome around which to rally. The use of proposed solutions to find allies takes place every day right in our own backyards. If a local street or highway is gridlocked from traffic, or unsafe from poor construction or years of wear and tear, a proposal to build a new road or improve public transportation will likely draw the support of motorists, businesses, developers, homeowners, and consumer safety advocates.

The recent explosion of ridesharing services such as Lyft and Uber and accommodation-sharing services such as Airbnb also shows how solutions can drive the formation of coalitions. For example, as these app-based innovations have increased in popularity, more traditional transportation providers, such as taxicab companies, have battled back at the local and state government levels to try to limit the ability of ridesharing services to do business. Housing providers like hotels have joined forces with landlords, affordable housing advocates, and organized labor to wage similar battles against accommodation sharing. This coalition has persuaded at least some elected officials. New York City Council members proposed to levy large fines against homeowners who rent out their homes through sharing services, and the New York Attorney General launched an investigation.[20]

But the sharing companies have fought back by forming coalitions of their own. For example, ridesharing services have recruited key elected officials, business advocates, restaurant owners, and anti–drunk driving advocates. They have also built support across demographic and ideological lines. Some of their most enthusiastic supporters are Millennials who lean to the left and free-market conservatives who lean to the right. They have won praise from Republican presidential candidates and hired senior Democrats such as long-time Democratic strategist Chris Lehane, who now serves as Airbnb Director of Global Policy and Public Affairs. This coalition building has produced results, with perhaps the most high-profile triumph being Airbnb's November 2015 defeat of a San Francisco ballot initiative that would have restricted short-term rentals.[21] In his tips (see Tips from the Pros: Home Defense in San Francisco), Lehane describes how Airbnb continues to build coalitions for citizen success.

[20] Jennifer Fermino, "Airbnb Fights 'Freddy Krueger of Bills' That Would Hit NY Homeowners Who Rent out Their Pads with Up to $50G in Fines," *New York Daily News*, October 22, 2015, www.nydailynews.com/new-york/exclusive-airbnb-fights-bill-hit-n-y-homeowners-article-1.2406451

[21] Mollie Reilly, "San Francisco Votes Down Tough Airbnb Regulations," *Huffington Post*, November 4, 2015, www.huffingtonpost.com/entry/airbnb-san-francisco-vote_5637d49ae4b027f9b969ac7c

Home Defense in San Francisco
CHRIS LEHANE

Winning local political victories—or any political victory for that matter—almost always comes down to one key factor: people. The case of the Airbnb community's November 2015 defeat of an anti–home sharing ballot measure in San Francisco is illustrative of this principle.

Airbnb (airbnb.com), founded in 2008, is a people-to-people platform that makes it possible to rent out your couch or a spare room, or even your entire place while you're gone, to guests from around the world. Currently, Airbnb has more than 2 million spare bedrooms, apartments, homes, castles, and even tree houses in 191 countries and 34,000 cities around the globe. To date, more than 70 million people have stayed in Airbnbs around the globe.

When anti–home sharing forces put an extreme, restrictive measure on the November 2015 ballot, an attempt to essentially ban home sharing in San Francisco, the Airbnb community quickly organized. Hosts and guests, together with the small business owners who benefit from the patronage of visitors staying in their neighborhoods, joined together to defeat the measure.

Across San Francisco, more than 5,000 people are opening up their homes to domestic and international visitors via the Airbnb platform, often doing so in order to make ends meet and stay in the city they love. Joining these 5,000 Airbnb hosts are more than 140,000 San Franciscans who have used the Airbnb platform to stay somewhere around the globe in the past year. This large collection of San Francisco Airbnb advocates was vital in the November 2015 election, demonstrating the power of a people-to-people platform—in this case, Airbnb—to network a large group of people for political engagement. Thanks to their advocacy, home sharing won the support of 55 percent of the 133,000 San Francisco voters who cast ballots—and the proposed measure was decisively defeated.

The lessons we learned could be applied to a whole host of other issues in any number of communities. By answering a few important questions, you'll be on your way to building a winning community coalition.

1. **What is the specific issue we're concerned about? And who are the relevant stakeholders?**

   - Identify the issue your community faces. Whether the issue you're advocating for is old hat or brand new, clearly defining the problem is an important first step and will keep everyone on the same page.
   - Create a list of potential stakeholders. A stakeholder is anyone that will have a vested interest in the issue. For example, community members, businesses organizations, and elected officials can all have a shared interest in the same issue.

2. **How can I unite people around this issue? Who else can I bring to the table?**

   - Establish the goals and values of your cause and identify leaders who embody them. This is a critical step in creating a strong and successful coalition.
   - Once the framework of your coalition takes shape, drafting and sharing a clear set of messages that explain the group stance on an issue, what you stand for, and why you are fighting will ensure everyone is singing the same tune.

3. **Who else can I bring to the table? How can I use my existing network to win?**

   - Sometimes the answers to these questions are not immediately obvious, but getting it right can go a long way towards landing a victory. For Airbnb hosts in San Francisco, it was the thousands of small business owners who benefited from having new visitors to their neighborhoods.
   - Maybe you are a member of the Sierra Club or a merchants' association. Perhaps another member of your coalition has joined the local Chamber of Commerce or any other number of local civic organizations. Seeking the support and endorsement of these groups can go a long way to growing your coalition while also putting additional pressure on elected officials.

4. **Now that I've brought together a coalition, how do I engage decision makers in government? What about voters?**

   Advocacy can be intimidating, but it doesn't have to be. Explaining which local officials do and do not have authority on this issue, how to schedule meetings with elected officials, and how to participate in public meetings will all go a long way in making participation easier. The following tactics are easy ways to involve your coalition in the political process:

   - *Talk to policymakers:* Share the personal stories of your coalition with policymakers, start a petition to draw attention to your issue, write a letter to your elected officials, speak at a public meeting where your issue is being debated, or turn your coalition into an official club that can advocate for your cause (strength in numbers!).
   - *Engage the media:* Send a letter to the editor of your local newspaper, write an op-ed for your local publication, or give a statement to the press on your group's position on the issue being debated. Our group of hosts in San Francisco visited every editorial board in the city to make the case for home sharing— and ultimately won the endorsement of three of the city's four papers.
   - *Make it social:* Build social media profiles on networks such as Twitter, Facebook, and LinkedIn, as they can become powerful tools to connect the members of your coalition and engage policymakers.

(Continued)

(Continued)

- *Pound the pavement:* In San Francisco, we knocked on more than 285,000 doors and had personal conversations with neighbors about the benefits of home sharing to our community. Nothing is more impactful than one-to-one conversations, especially when you can share your own story.
- *Create great content:* Use sites such as medium.com to create great, interesting content that is authentic and impassioned. One host in San Francisco wrote a piece explaining just how toxic the ballot initiative was and received nearly 100,000 views.

Our success in San Francisco really came down to one decisive factor: the tremendous leadership of our host community. Early on Airbnb hosts created their own, independent political club—the Homesharers of San Francisco—to take this issue on independently. Thanks to our hosts' work, we defeated an extreme ballot initiative in San Francisco and protected home sharing for many years to come.

A strong coalition can be a powerful force in any political process. People and the ideas they bring to the table are the key ingredients to winning political victories and influencing change in your community.

Chris Lehane is the head of Global Policy and Public Affairs at Airbnb. Prior to joining Airbnb, Lehane provided strategic counsel to political, corporate, entertainment, and professional sports clients and spent eight years in the Clinton administration.

If a solution energizes your coalition, meet with those whom you have reason to believe support the proposed solution. Use that meeting to assign specific roles for turning the proposed solution into policy. Previous chapters have already discussed some of the roles—such as conducting research and identifying the decision maker—and future chapters will cover more, like engaging the media and identifying financial resources.

Of course, the solution need not always precede the coalition. Coalitions can form around a problem and then develop practical solutions that generate public support and lead to the desired change in policy. The problem you identify and the circumstances under which it exists will help you determine whether the problem or the solution comes first. If the coalition comes together around the problem, organize a meeting of all the coalition partners to brainstorm possible solutions, as the citizens of Steamboat Springs (described in chapter 4) did in bridging the gap between a majority of its residents and the school board.

Of course, our digital world provides more ways than ever before to "meet" potential coalition partners. For example, social media offers meaningful opportunities for cooperation. As you are looking for allies, follow the example of other successful civic advocates and use tools like Facebook, Twitter, Tumblr, Pinterest, and other sites to enlist and deploy allies.

In April 2008, the *Sun–Sentinel* reported that a University of Florida senior who was concerned about proposed changes to the state's main undergraduate scholarship program created a Facebook group named "Protect Your Bright Futures." The student, 21-year-old Will Anderson of Plant City, Florida, invited 200 of his peers to join the group and encouraged them to forward the invitation to other collegiate friends. Fewer than two weeks later, Protect Your Bright Futures had 20,000 members statewide, prompting the state legislator who suggested the scholarship changes to withdraw his proposal. Senator Jeremy Ring explained his change of heart: "You can't ignore 20,000 people."[22]

Four years later, in early 2012, the digital world erupted when the Susan Komen Foundation adopted a rule change that would cut off additional funding to Planned Parenthood. A Tumblr campaign named "Planned Parenthood Saved Me" filled the site with personalized stories about positive Planned Parenthood actions. On Pinterest, a well-known nonprofit author and adviser launched a pinboard to rally opposition to the Komen decision. Planned Parenthood supporters were urged to take to Twitter and Facebook to protest the decision, and a new hashtag—#takebackthepink—was born to brand the effort.[23] For the Komen Foundation, it proved to be too much. On February 3, 2012, Komen announced that it was reversing the change.

3. Tailor the Coalition to the Decision Maker

While you are building your coalition, think carefully about which potential partners provide you with the access and credibility that you need to convince the decision makers. The Green Tea Coalition was successful because it incorporated conservative activists, regulators, and legislators into the effort to persuade other conservative decision makers to broaden the use of solar energy in Georgia. LGBT advocates smartly recognized that state legislators in Indiana and county commissioners in West Central Florida would respond best if they heard business leaders explain why equality and the economy were tied together.

During the process of becoming acquainted with your decision makers, we suggest that you take time to understand the kinds of potential coalition partners who are best positioned to sway them (see chapter 5). If your goal is to persuade the University of Michigan president, don't bring a team of supporters from Ohio State University. A staunchly conservative state legislature would not be the best audience for the Democratic National Committee chairperson. A liberal city council might not be receptive to what Tea Party representatives have to say.

4. Don't Reinvent the Wheel

Many times, it will not be necessary to build a coalition because one already exists. The alliance you need to lower the condominium fees imposed by a board of elected condo officers probably exists within the condo association. Your local parent-teacher-student alliance (PTSA) or teachers' organization may serve as an effective coalition partner on a public school matter. Efforts to improve your city's business climate could find a friendly audience at the area chamber of commerce. If you can

---

[22] Josh Hafenbrack, "Online Political Action Can Spark Offline Change," *Sun–Sentinel,* April 6, 2008.

[23] Nick Judd, "With Pinterest and Twitter, Activists Are Out to Punish Komen," *TechPresident,* February 3, 2012, techpresident.com/news/21725/what-pinterest-and-twitter-are-doing-activists-out-punish-komen

unite with a group that already shares or could be inspired to share your passion for finding a solution to a problem, don't reinvent the wheel. Join forces and start working toward your goal.

Moreover, if you partner with existing advocacy organizations with similar interests, you inherit the power of their brand and access to their members. For example, the local chapter of the Sierra Club might be interested in your effort to stop polluters from dumping in the river. The state office of the AARP would be willing to work on your concern involving caregivers and long-term care insurance.

You should also remember that the challenge you are facing is probably not unprecedented. Another citizen or group of citizens has likely faced it before. Find those citizens' stories, determine if the group was successful, and if so utilize its blueprints. When Steamboat Springs voters went to the polls in November 2015 and overwhelmingly defeated a $96 million school construction and renovation bond issue, the board of education had a model for how to rebound from its setback—the 10 Plus 2 initiative from 20 years earlier.

5. Draft for Talent and Need

As in professional sports drafts, where some teams choose players less for their overall talent and athleticism and more because these players fill specific team needs, you may have to select some coalition partners for their expertise. If you have created a coalition around the idea that your state's legislature has not adequately funded your local college or university, find an economics professor or graduate student with special knowledge of higher education finance to give your coalition better information about how insufficient funding affects colleges and students. You would also be well advised to recruit someone who understands the politics of higher education and can direct the coalition to the most influential decision makers—and advise you how to persuade them to support your cause. If your issue requires influencing a state legislature, county commission, or city council, find savvy allies who have insights into as many of the key elected officials and appointed staff as possible.

The Florida Keys coalition we described in chapter 2 (see "Stormy Weather") offers a good example of citizens who effectively incorporated subject matter experts into their alliance. When residents of Monroe County started receiving renewals for their windstorm insurance in early 2006, with premiums that in some cases had tripled since the previous bill, they formed a coalition known as Fair Insurance Rates in Monroe (FIRM). The coalition consulted with experts such as actuaries, engineers, and meteorologists to help make its case that there was no basis for the increased insurance rates. Less than a year later, the state government rejected the proposed Monroe County rate increases, ordered that rates for the county be rolled back to pre-2005 levels, and passed legislation to address the statewide hurricane insurance crisis.

Effective coalition building must go deeper than finding the most superficially obvious partners. It takes curiosity and creativity to divine less predictable but potentially even more valuable allies. For example, since numerous states offer prepaid college tuition programs for prospective students, the many American families who have bought prepaid contracts have a giant but often unrecognized interest in ensuring the quality of their state's public institutions of higher learning. For most of the parents or grandparents who have purchased the contracts, the greatest risk is that the quality of in-state colleges or universities will decline to the point that their child or grandchild, at the time of college selection, will say, "Thank you, but I've chosen an out-of-state institution with a program and reputation superior to any in our state." University presidents looking for sources of increased financial support from state legislatures or private sources need look no further for allies than these families. On another issue, environmental leaders are forging coalitions with business leaders who understand the economic benefits of a healthy environment and with religious organizations that find biblical support for protecting natural treasures.

If you're having a hard time stimulating the creative side of your brain, start by examining what individuals or groups with similar interests have done elsewhere. If your concern is funding for universities, and you want to enlist prepaid tuition contract holders, see if counterparts in other states have had the same idea. Your efforts will have more credibility if you can cite precedents.

6. Turn Opponents into Allies

Identifying potential enemies is almost as important as knowing your friends. As Michael Corleone said in *The Godfather,* it is wise in coalition building to "keep your friends close, but your enemies closer." Although the first step in finding allies is to research and identify potential coalition partners, it is just as important to locate and analyze your probable opponents so that you can counter their arguments.

But you might also be able to defuse their opposition. Once you discover who the opponents are and why they oppose your initiative, you can determine how to turn them around and secure their support—or at least reduce the intensity of their position. In some cases, your insights into the opposition may even lead to a compromise that broadens your base of support. When sizing up potential opponents, keep these questions in mind:

- Does the opposition have its facts right? If not, how do you correct those inaccuracies without alienating them and undermining a potential compromise?
- Which individual or group in your alliance is closest to the opposition? Make that coalition member the principal point of contact in an effort to find common ground.

As you investigate and engage the opposition, remember to think long term. Although an issue may be controversial and intense at the moment, there is no reason to treat opponents with anything but respect. Respect builds goodwill that can be leveraged for your benefit. More important, it will reduce the likelihood that you will trigger a chain of old enemies to retaliate against you in the future.

7. Pick a Strong Champion to Celebrate Your Cause

Every cause would benefit from a public leader whose personal qualities and identification with the issue provide the credibility necessary to win public support. An effective champion can seize the popular imagination and bring needed attention to a cause. The most effective champions are often everyday citizens whom the public can relate to and will remember.

In 1955, that citizen was Rosa Parks, a seamstress in Montgomery, Alabama, who set in motion a public transportation boycott and launched the modern civil rights movement when she refused to move to the back of a segregated bus. In 2005, it was Cindy Sheehan, the mother of a soldier killed in Iraq, who protested the U.S. occupation of Iraq in front of President George W. Bush's Texas ranch and became a leading figure in turning public opinion against the war.[24] In 2014, many Americans learned the story of Brittany Maynard, a 29-year-old woman diagnosed with terminal brain cancer who used Oregon's death with dignity law to end her life. She had moved to Oregon from her home state of California, which had no such law. Maynard used the time before her death to partner with end-of-life choice advocates, tell her story, and urge other states to follow Oregon's example.[25] She even asked her physician and family to carry on the effort. Maynard died on November 1, 2014. Eleven months later, Governor Jerry Brown, who had spoken with Maynard before her death, signed California's aid in dying law.[26]

With champions like these, you may worry how anyone in your coalition could measure up. Stop worrying. Although Rosa Parks and Cindy Sheehan are now household names, few people other than their friends and families knew them when they first emerged into the public eye. And though their causes blossomed into larger-than-life crusades, each woman's initial goals were far more basic. Parks was tired of being asked to sacrifice her self-respect and dignity—and tired of being treated like a second-class citizen. Sheehan wanted a meeting with President Bush to express concern about a war in which her son had been killed. Maynard wanted to die painlessly and peacefully, without the suffering that her cancer would bring. People you met in previous chapters—such as Candy Lightner and Barbara Capitman—were similarly anonymous when they started their efforts.

Gaby Pacheco is another citizen whose personal narrative has helped to inspire a coalition.

Another Case in Point   The Trail of Dreams*

Maria Gabriela Pacheco, better known as Gaby, was a precocious 8-year-old in 1993 when her family emigrated from Ecuador to Miami on tourist visas. The Pachecos were eager for a safer community and better education for Gaby and her siblings—older sisters Erika, 14, and Mari, 13, and younger brother Gus, 7. When they overstayed their visas and could not secure legal residency, Mr. and Mrs. Pacheco became undocumented immigrants—people living in legal limbo whose children were part of the group of 2.1 million young people known as DREAMers.

---

[24] "Anti-War Mom Cindy Sheehan Gives up Her Protest," *CNN*, May 29, 2007, www.cnn.com/2007/US/05/28/sheehan/index.html?eref=onion

[25] "About Brittany Maynard, *The Brittany Maynard Fund*, thebrittanyfund.org/about/

[26] Nicole Weisensee Egan, "Right to Die Legalized in California Following Campaign Inspired by Brittany Maynard, *People*, October 5, 2015, www.people.com/article/brittany-maynard-right-to-die-bill-california-gov-brown

*We are very grateful to Gaby Pachecho for sharing her story and assisting us in this preparation of this case study.

Sarah L. Voisin/The Washington Post via Getty Images

Gaby Pacheco, Juan Rodriguez, and other immigration advocates attempt to deliver a petition to the White House at the end of their Trail of Dreams—a 1,500 miles-long walk from Florida to Washington, D.C. to urge support for the DREAM Act.

Seventeen years later, Gaby was one of the organizers of a 1,500-mile march from her new home city of Miami to Washington, D.C. During a pause in the walk, Gaby told her story to a crowd of DREAMer supporters.

"I consider myself to be an all-American girl," she said. "I was part of the ROTC program during high school, and after graduation wanted to enlist in the Air Force. Because of my undocumented status, I could not. But I went to college and now hold a bachelor's degree in special education. . . . There are many others like me."[27]

These personal stories of achievement over adversity became a staple of the DREAMers campaign. They conveyed the humanity of the struggle and increased the empathy of Americans for the cause.

Gaby was one of the lucky ones. Due to her superior high school grades, she attended Miami–Dade College with help from scholarships. For most of the DREAMers, higher education was just that—a dream. State and national laws denied these students in-state tuition or access to financial aid programs which made higher education more affordable. Gaby got her start as an advocate in 2005, when she founded Students Working for Equal Rights (S.W.E.R.)—an immigration youth network that, among other goals, sought in-state tuition for undocumented students in Florida.

The dream almost ended for Gaby. In 2006, when she was a 20-year-old college student, U.S. Immigration and Customs Enforcement (ICE, ice.gov) learned of Gaby's

---

[27] Gaby Pacheco, "'We Are Fighting for Our Lives' with DREAM Act," *CNN*, September 22, 2010, www.cnn.com/2010/OPINION/09/22/pacheco.dream.act/

status and outspoken advocacy for DREAMers. ICE agents came looking for her but instead found her parents and two sisters. At 6:30 a.m. on July 26, 2006, they took the Pacheco family from their home and transported them to an immigration security center. Gaby received a call from one of her sisters, who was sobbing and had a disturbing message: "They want me to tell you that we should thank you for what is happening to us."

Upon arriving at the security center, Gaby learned that an unnamed politician informed ICE of her status and activities. In exchange for a promise of silence to the media and discontinuation of her organizational activities, ICE released her family— but still left them subject to the deportation and immigration process.

Gaby admits it was a "white lie moment. I had made the decision to tell my story." Alerted to the Pacheco family's plight, members of the media were waiting at their home when they returned from ICE custody. The press attention on this aggressive enforcement caused federal and state legislators and supportive Miami and Washington organizations to help efforts to keep the Pachecos in the United States.

ICE took no immediate action. When the Pacheco family was called for its final deportation hearing in March 2008, Gaby's sister Erika was about 6 months pregnant. Gaby and her colleagues at S.W.E.R. organized a walk of hundreds of undocumented students—all wearing black T-shirts emblazoned with the word "undocumented"—from the Miami–Dade College downtown campus to the ICE center. The attention created by the marchers helped to delay the hearing. As of 2016, all of the Pachecos remain in the United States.

But Gaby was not done marching. She and her DREAMer friends were becoming increasingly frustrated as Congress continued to block the DREAM Act, a measure to give unauthorized immigrants a path to legal residency. Few states were making it easier for unauthorized students to continue their education. Some, such as Arizona, had enacted laws that certain people interpreted as giving state and local law enforcement officers the right to profile immigrants and detain them prior to federal deportation.

Gaby contemplated how to help make the cause known and supported by the American people. Having seen success with a previous march, she decided to join another one—this time from Miami to Washington, D.C. Her four-month journey with friends Juan Rodriguez, Felipe Matos, and Carlos Roa started on January 1, 2010.

On their website—trail2010.org—the foursome described the purpose of this "Trail of Dreams" as follows:

> We were brought to the United States by our families when we were young. This is the only country we have known as home. We have the same hopes and dreams as other young people, and have worked hard to excel in school and contribute to our communities. But because of our immigration status, we've spent our childhoods in fear and hiding, unable to achieve our full potential. We walk in order to share our stories and to call on our leaders to fix the system that forces people like us into the shadows, stripping us of the opportunity to participate meaningfully in society.

A march was in keeping with the tradition of American nonviolent protests. The examples of the Underground Railroad, a network of support that helped African Americans escape from slavery in the South to freedom in the North, and Dr. Martin Luther King Jr.'s march from Selma, Alabama, to the state capital of Montgomery, were inspirations to Gaby and her fellow DREAMers.

They were walking through a nation that had sharply departed from its tradition of welcoming immigrants. For most of its first two centuries, the United States had embraced the words posted on the pedestal of the Statue of Liberty—Emma Lazarus's poem, "The New Colossus":

> "Keep, ancient lands, your storied pomp!" cries she
> With silent lips. "Give me your tired, your poor,
> Your huddled masses yearning to breathe free,
> The wretched refuse of your teeming shore.
> Send these, the homeless, tempest-tost to me,
> I lift my lamp beside the golden door!"

But that spirit had largely disappeared in the last two decades of the twentieth century and the first decade of the twenty-first. Congress and many state legislatures came to view any benefits to undocumented immigrants as opening the floodgates to more "illegals" they feared would recast the cultural and political character of communities. California was frequently cited as the end result of policies sympathetic to migrants.

Surprisingly to some, the Obama administration continued a tough enforcement approach with the aggressive detention and deportation of undocumented immigrants. During President Obama's first term from 2009 to 2013, more than 1.5 million were deported—a rate of almost 1,000 per day.[28]

The Trail of Dreams marchers wanted to open hearts and minds to establish the foundation for policy change. Gaby and her colleagues saw every encounter as an opportunity to plant a seed. Along the way, the marchers came across both skeptics and allies, including

- 50 Ku Klux Klan members in a small Georgia town who held a rally to intimidate the marchers, protested the "Latino invasion," and demanded the marchers be sent back to Mexico—even though none were of Mexican descent;
- A white veteran who believed "illegal" immigrants were destroying the country–but who softened to the point he was comfortable using the term "undocumented" after Gaby explained the humanitarian purpose of the march;
- Supportive NAACP members who held a joint event with the marchers; and
- Hospitable churchgoers from multiple faiths, such as Baptists, Catholics, Lutherans, Unitarian Universalists, United Methodists, and others.

---

[28] Corey Dade, "Obama Administration Deported Record 1.5 Million People," *NPR*, December 24, 2012, www.npr.org/sections/itsallpolitics/2012/12/24/167970002/obama-administration-deported-record-1-5-million-people

The Trail of Dreams elevated public awareness about the inability of certain young Americans to pursue their dreams of self-advancement. It inspired other demonstrations and advocacy efforts around the nation. Most important, it helped to produce results.

Gaby Pacheco continued her journey even after the march reached Washington. She became the political director of United We Dream (unitedwedream.org), the largest youth-led immigrant organization in the nation. In that role, she advocated for a step that President Obama took in July 2012—when he announced that the Department of Homeland Security would no longer initiate the deportation of certain unauthorized immigrants who entered the United States under the age of 16. Two years later, the president expanded the scope of his deferral to about half of the nation's 11 million undocumented residents, which temporarily protected them from deportation.[29]

States began to enact legislation granting DREAMers in-state tuition and access to student financial aid. By 2015, more than 20 states, including Gaby's home state of Florida, had authorized in-state tuition for DREAMers.[30] Six states have given DREAMers access to student financial aid.

Perhaps most fitting, Gaby Pacheco's advocacy has come full circle. As of April 2016, she is program director for TheDream.US—a philanthropic fund that provides college scholarships to DREAMers with the goal of preparing them for careers. As of June 2015, the fund had raised $80 million—including from donors such as the Bill and Melinda Gates Foundation, former Washington Post Company CEO Donald Graham, and Facebook CEO Mark Zuckerberg.[31]

Sometimes, a cause finds a celebrity spokesperson to embrace its issues. If the celebrity is popular, personally motivated, and willing to devote the time, he or she can make a huge difference in building public support. Consider the example of the Save the Manatee Club (savethemanatee.org). In the 1970s and 1980s, the threat to Florida's unique manatee population from boat propellers and polluted waters had reached critical levels. Enter Jimmy Buffett. A Florida resident who had previously written a song with a memorable line about manatees—"Sometimes I see me as an old manatee / Heading south as the waters grow colder"—Buffett had a genuine personal interest in promoting the cause. He had the star quality necessary to be an effective champion for the endangered manatees and was able to secure political support, as demonstrated by the Florida Legislature's passage of a Save the Manatee license plate that raised millions of dollars for the cause. Finally, he motivated private contributors to lend their support through appeals at his Parrothead concerts and special Save the Manatee benefits.

Buffet's involvement gave Save the Manatee a public momentum that has helped to produce long-term results. In 2016, the club celebrated its 35th birthday with

---

[29] On June 23, 2016, in a deadlocked 4-4 vote, the United States Supreme Court upheld a lower court decision blocking President Obama's 2014 executive action.

[30] NCSL, "Undocumented Student Tuition: Overview," National Conference of State Legislatures website, October 29, 2015, www.ncsl.org/research/education/undocumented-student-tuition-overview.aspx

[31] Miriam Jordan, "Mark Zuckerberg, Wife Donate $5 Million to TheDream.US Scholarship Fund," *Wall Street Journal*, June 17, 2015, www.wsj.com/articles/mark-zuckerberg-wife-donate-5-million-to-thedream-us-scholarship-fund-1434578374

notable accomplishments and signs of progress. The State of Florida has designated the entire state as a manatee sanctuary, restricted boat use or speed where it would threaten manatees, and worked to improve water quality in manatee habitats.[32] As a result, the manatee population in Florida has increased more than 500 percent since 1991. The U.S. Fish and Wildlife Service (FWS) announced in January 2016 that it intended to elevate the manatee from "endangered" to "threatened" status.[33] While advocates, including officials from the Save the Manatee Club and several Florida editorial boards, have questioned whether the proposed FWS reclassification is premature, few dispute the manatee is better off today than when Jimmy Buffett first championed the cause.

Think carefully about who should serve as your coalition's public voice. You want someone whose personal story, celebrity, or rhetorical skills are likely to rouse public support. Just make sure that your champion is someone who can win support both outside and inside your coalition. Pushing someone to the front of the effort without first ensuring he or she has wide backing within the group can backfire. Looking back to the chapter 1 North Carolina story, several relatively new residents with impressive résumés wanted to lead the Jackson County Smart Roads Alliance in the mountains of western North Carolina. Using the ancient Scottish word common in these isolated highlands, they were seen as "foched on"—newbies who didn't know the territory or its culture. The coalition ultimately chose to elevate people like Harold and Gwen Messer so it would have local credibility.

8. Have a Simple, Direct Message—and Repeat, Repeat, Repeat

Because a coalition is a confederation of independent organizations and individuals, it always runs the risk of dissolving into a Babel-like collection of disassociated talking heads. You can mitigate that danger by formulating a clear, coherent message that every member of the alliance abides by and repeats. In Georgia, every member of the solar power coalition from lobbyists to Tea Party activists to Sierra Club leaders spoke in terms of personal freedom and free market competition.

In determining its public message, a coalition should do the following:

- Determine the most influential audience that must be persuaded—and speak using words and values that will move that audience.
- Decide the salient points and determine how best to express them.
- Select a limited number of spokespersons.
- Provide the spokespersons with the factual information needed to make the message credible.
- Exercise discipline in transmitting a coherent and consistent message.

---

[32] Noelle Swan, "Record Number of Endangered Manatees Spotted in Florida's Annual Count," *Christian Science Monitor*, March 16, 2015, www.csmonitor.com/Environment/2015/0316/Record-number-of-endangered-manatees-spotted-in-Florida-s-annual-count-video

[33] U.S. Department of the Interior, "U.S. Fish and Wildlife Service to Reclassify West Indian Manatee from Endangered to Threatened," Press Release, January 7, 2016, www.doi.gov/pressreleases/us-fish-and-wildlife-service-reclassify-west-indian-manatee-endangered-threatened

Commercial advertisers say that a listener must hear the same message 10 times or more before it penetrates. A political message is no different. Whether members of your coalition are posting on social media, talking to newspaper or Internet reporters, submitting op-eds or letters to the editor, conducting interviews on local radio or television stations, giving speeches to community groups, or just sharing your issue with other citizens, they should be saying the same thing every time. Variety may be the spice of life, but in the realm of public messaging, it is the kiss of death.

9. Be Vigilant in Keeping the Coalition Together

We all know one of the oldest stories in music: A highly acclaimed new band produces one or two hit albums and then drifts apart out of boredom. Or the albums go nowhere, and the band dissolves from the lack of initial success. Coalitions often have the same problems.

It is almost always more difficult to hold a coalition together than to assemble it in the first place. This is particularly true if the effort experiences an early setback and then loses the will or urgency to continue. In chapter 10, you will see that an initial loss is not reason for despair—politics has few permanent defeats.

But maintaining the coalition is also important in the face of success. Politics also yields few permanent victories, and triumphs are almost never achieved completely on the first attempt. Your cause requires constant vigilance to achieve the intended results. There are several keys to maintaining tenacity over the long run.

First, keep stakeholders engaged through an effective division of labor. If alliance partners believe their efforts are critical to achieving victory, they are much more likely to maintain interest in and commitment to the cause. While some broader tasks can be shared by all coalition partners—e.g., recruiting new members—other more specialized jobs should be assigned among various stakeholders. For example, a coalition partner with significant experience in messaging might take on the responsibility for media relations. Another ally that has demonstrated past fundraising success could be in charge of raising financial resources for the cause. Yet another might be in charge of mass outreach to decision makers through the organization of social media, letter-writing, e-mail, or telephone campaigns.[34] Or a particular stakeholder could be asked to reach out to a single decision maker, especially if the coalition member has a preexisting relationship with that official.

Second, organize the coalition to ensure that individual decision makers do not receive varied messages. This step is especially important when your interest in influencing a decision maker will be ongoing rather than limited to a single issue. As we noted in chapter 5, Florida's chiropractors were very skilled in matching each member of the Florida Legislature with a chiropractor from his or her district. Over time,

---

[34] In this digital age, an increasing number of online tools exist to connect coalitions with decision makers. For example, Rocket Lobby (rocketlobby.com) gives users in all 50 states the one-stop ability to identify their state legislators and call, email, or request appointments with those officials. Citizens can then anonymously rate the responsiveness of those lawmakers much like people rate restaurants on Yelp or products on Amazon.

the legislator and the chiropractor built a strong personal relationship, and when an issue affecting chiropractors arose, the legislator heard one message from one person he knew well.

Third, a partial achievement of the goal is not a defeat but a victory on which to build. The glass is half full. Don't celebrate a first accomplishment and then disband. Use an achievement as your springboard to even greater success.

Fourth, the transparent exchange of ideas and data is the lifeblood of any coalition. Don't compartmentalize or play favorites. Provide each member of the alliance with the same information—as did the organizers of the Steamboat Springs initiative in building support for educational enhancements. Elicit coalition members' thoughts and consider their ideas. Hold regular listening sessions with your allies.

Fifth, lack of growth is death. A coalition that is not continuously expanding is one that is foundering. As circumstances change, through victory or defeat, some coalition members will move on to different issues. Make sure that other individuals and groups are aware of your campaign, and treat them as candidates for recruitment.

Sixth, coalitions need new mountains to climb in order to stay together. In the same way that lack of growth is death, the failure to redefine goals and renew purpose regularly is also problematic. Have ongoing conversations with your colleagues about how the coalition needs to evolve, and take on the next challenge. Don't quit because you have successfully scaled Mount Kilimanjaro. Aconcagua, Denali, Elbrus, Vinson, Kosciuszko, and Everest await.

CHECKLIST FOR ACTION

- ☐ Define the problem to attract the widest possible coalition.
- ☐ Build the coalition around a solution or a problem.
- ☐ Tailor the coalition to the decision maker.
- ☐ Don't reinvent the wheel.
- ☐ Draft for talent and need.
- ☐ Turn opponents into allies.
- ☐ Pick compelling champions.
- ☐ Have a simple, direct message—and repeat, repeat, repeat.
- ☐ Keep the coalition together.

8 All Your News Is Fit to Print

Engaging the Media[1]

> "If a tree falls in a forest and no one is around to hear it, does it make a sound?"
>
> —Philosophical riddle

Case in Point   **The Street Doctor**

By Tom Fiedler*

If you encountered Jim O'Connell on almost any day, you might conclude that he's a media star. Television and film crews regularly follow him as he tours the back streets of Boston, usually late at night and even in the meanest of weather. He's often a featured speaker at gala events and the recipient of accolades as photographers bathe him in their flashing lights. Or you can find him featured in major newspaper articles, watch him being interviewed on popular TV news shows, or buy his memoir, which landed him a coveted interview on NPR's "Fresh Air" with Terry Gross.

But that's not the Jim O'Connell who is known by countless numbers of men, women, and children whose lives have been touched—some of them saved—by his kindness and care, yet no media was there to bear witness. In fact, media attention wasn't a consideration back in 1985 when this lanky, soft-spoken Rhode Island native completed Harvard Medical School with dreams of being an oncologist. Then his medical director called him to his office and asked that he postpone that dream—probably not for more than a year, the director said—to start up a health-care program to serve Boston's homeless.

---

[1] We are very grateful to David DeCamp for his thorough review of and insightful feedback on this chapter. He previously served as communications director for the City of Jacksonville, Florida, and as a reporter for the *Tampa Bay Times*, *Florida Times-Union*, and *Journal Gazette* (Fort Wayne, Indiana). DeCamp is now the manager of corporate and marketing communications for Crowley Maritime Corporation (crowley.com).

*Our thanks to Tom Fiedler for writing this Case in Point and providing much of the expert advice in this chapter. Tom worked for the *Miami Herald* for more than 30 years as an investigative reporter, a political columnist, and an editorial page editor; he was executive editor from 2001 to 2007. He currently serves as dean of the Boston University College of Communication (bu.edu/com).

© Rick Friedman

Dr. Jim O'Connell of the Boston Health Care for the Homeless Program (BHCHP) examines a patient. Thanks to a fundraising effort propelled by media engagement, BHCHP raised the funds for a dedicated facility equipped to provide medical, dental, and mental health care to Boston's homeless community.

"I agreed to do it because I thought it would be like spending a year in the Peace Corps, except it would be in Boston," he said.

Days later, prominently wearing his new stethoscope given to him at medical school graduation, he arrived at the makeshift clinic, summoned the staff, and prepared to give orders. The head nurse—a drill sergeant of a woman—stopped him cold. She stripped away the stethoscope and pointed to the adjoining room where tubs of warm water spread across the floor and a half-dozen disheveled people sat along the walls. "You'll start by washing their feet," the nurse told him. And he did.

That "one year" has stretched to three decades. Even today James J. O'Connell, MD, can still be found washing feet, typically those of his patients, people he calls "broken" or "brave survivors" trying to cope with life on the streets and in the shelters of Boston.

But the care he is able to provide is far beyond what was available to him during those humble days.

That's owed to the creation of the Boston Health Care for the Homeless Program, one of the nation's first and still best programs of its kind helping this distressed group cope with disease, mental-health issues, addictions, and the stresses of surviving in the shadows and streets of urban America. The program that started with "Dr. Jim" and 7 staff in 1985 now has more than 400 medical providers and supporters working from 60 locations throughout the region to help the homeless.

How did this transformation come to be? Are there lessons in it for other well-meaning organizations and individuals who are starting with humble resources but harbor great dreams? Probably so.

Through its initial years, the program operated nearly out of public sight, said O'Connell, and it actually worked that way by design. The unfortunate men, women, and children who comprise the homeless population feel vulnerable in many ways and tend to be wary of anyone who might be seen as exploiting them for their own purposes. The process of building trust to overcome this suspicion takes time, personal engagement, and even humility, as demonstrated by washing the feet of homeless people—a critically important step in preventing disease. O'Connell recalls washing an older man's ravaged feet several times over many weeks. The man remained distant and silent during this process, seemingly ignoring O'Connell entirely despite the many encounters and refusing all medical treatment.

"Then one day," O'Connell said, "he looked at me and said, 'Aren't you a doctor? What are you doing washing my feet?'" From that day onward the man engaged fully with O'Connell and the staff, apparently secure in their presence and with dignity intact. Over the course of many years, O'Connell won similar trust from scores of homeless people living under the bridges or in the abandoned buildings that he visited regularly, always bringing a sandwich or coffee and his medical bag while asking nothing in return.

But O'Connell realized that reaching more than a handful of the estimated 7,000 or more homeless people with such a modest program was impossible. He concluded that he needed a facility capable of treating the full range of health problems experienced by the homeless, and where other physicians and researchers could learn better ways to deliver this care. And for that he needed money, lots of it. O'Connell reached out to a consultant who, after surveying the philanthropic landscape, concluded that, given the public's awareness of the Boston Health Care for the Homeless Program, a fundraising campaign might raise $300,000.

The dreamed-for facility was projected to cost $45 million.

Despite having been in operation for 20 years, "Nobody knew who we were," said Linda O'Connor, a former volunteer who became the program's development director. Clearly, something had to be done to bring the program to the public's attention in the hope that it would spur generous donors to get involved. A local public-relations practitioner told O'Connell and his team that they needed to tell the story of what they were doing. But how the story was to be framed was critically important.

"We learned that people don't give money if the message is 'X numbers of people are homeless,'" O'Connell said. "People give when they know who is delivering the care, and when they can see and feel what that care is all about."

That "see and feel" became the key. O'Connell invited journalists to accompany him on his late-night tours of homeless hideaways, often in Boston's bleakest neighborhoods. But the journalists were instructed as to how to respect the dignity of these people by following O'Connell's lead. Typically a reporter might have several encounters with a homeless individual without asking a question, taking notes or a photograph. Only when a level of trust and comfort had been reached would these tools come out and the stories of these people get told to a wide audience, most of whom were unaware of the project's work or the humanity of the people being treated.

O'Connell's goal was simple: Allow the public to become witness to this and then hope that people of good will would help through donations. They did.

Today, the Boston Health Care for the Homeless Program occupies a multistory building adjacent to the city's public hospital and is equipped to provide medical care, dental care, mental-health treatment, counseling, and more. The news media's response has been extraordinary: local TV features the program regularly, including tagging along with O'Connell through the streets. Articles have appeared in the *New York Times*, *Boston Globe*, and countless other newspapers. The program and "Dr. Jim" have been covered on the CBS Evening News and in a documentary film. NPR host Terry Gross interviewed him shortly after he published a memoir called *Stories from the Shadows: Reflections of a Street Doctor*.

"The next day we had orders for 3,000 copies of the book—except that we didn't have 3,000 copies of the book to sell," O'Connell said.

The most powerful impact has come through the program's association with the Boston Red Sox. The baseball team's community relations staff asked O'Connell several years ago what it might do to help. The result has been the hugely successful "Sox for Socks" campaign, highlighted by a game to which fans are asked to bring a new pair of white socks or the equivalent in cash to be donated to the program. Each of those games has resulted in thousands of pairs of socks to be distributed to the homeless.

And as important as the footwear is, the "Sox for Socks" campaign brings a fresh wave of publicity to the program and the cause. At a recent annual dinner, former Red Sox pitching ace (and now broadcaster) Dennis Eckersley told of his personal interest in helping the homeless. He said that his brother—battling substance-abuse addictions—lived on the streets and resisted attempts to help him.

O'Connell said stories like that are increasingly commonplace because of the opioid epidemic hitting so many people. He and others on his team are daily witnesses to this epidemic and thus frequently interviewed in the news media. "The challenge for me isn't getting the media's attention, it's managing it," O'Connell says with an appreciative smile.

Managing it is largely the responsibility of Linda O'Connor and her partner Sara Pacelle, who oversee development and communication. They point out that the program's success in getting attention in traditional media—newspapers, television, and magazines—is now complemented by, even being surpassed by, success in new platforms, primarily social media. The term social media implies that this form of communication is a direct exchange between individual people, albeit through such services as Facebook, Twitter, Instagram, Snapchat, Periscope, YouTube, and many more. Traditional media filters—you give information to the media, which decides whether and how to pass the information to its audience—are absent with social media. Anyone with access to the Internet can be a publisher.

"We're controlling through social media the messages that we want to put out," said Pacelle. "We can show who we are and what we believe. We want people to see the human side of homelessness, to see the faces of the homeless, to see that they're just like you and me."

The phenomenon of social media is unprecedented. No form of communication technology has become adopted more quickly by more people than any prior form in the history of humankind. Technologist Erik Qualman, in his book *Socialnomics*, noted that, were Facebook a country measured by population, it would be the third largest in the world behind only China and India.

For young adults, the so-called Millennials, social media is the platform of choice. A Pew Research Center survey in 2015 found that 67 percent of this cohort gets news from Twitter and 74 percent from Facebook. (Ironically, neither Twitter nor Facebook produce journalism; the news cited by users typically originates on sites produced by traditional media.)

And it's not only young people who rely on social media. The Pew survey found that 65 percent of all adults use social media in some form, exponentially up from the 7 percent who used social media in 2005.

Sara Pacelle said she uses social media daily to keep the Boston Health Care for the Homeless Program engaged in the public conversation. The primary use, she said, is to help educate others on medical treatments used by, or discovered by, the medical staff in the course of their treatments. Such issues as opioid addictions, HIV, and disease related to weather exposure are often the subject of tweets and Facebook posts. Also, talks by O'Connell and other staff members are captured on video to be posted on the program's website (bhchp.org) or distributed on social media. And it's not necessarily serious.

"People really seem to respond to photos we take of the therapy dogs interacting with patients," she said.

This isn't to overlook the continuing importance of traditional media. One staff member continues to "pitch" potential stories to these outlets and maintains a strong relationship with editors and reporters. Older citizens continue to rely on TV news and the newspaper for their news diet. As recently as 2014, nearly 50 million Sunday newspapers were sold in a typical week across America, each one read by two or more people. That means as many as one-third of all Americans can be reached by newspapers. What's more, these readers tend to be more affluent, better informed, and more civically engaged that those who get their information online, according to many surveys.

Linda O'Connor has learned that the two platforms—traditional media and social media—can be complementary rather than competitive.

"Traditional media is looking to your social media to learn more about who you are and how active you are," she said.

The evolution of the Boston Health Care for the Homeless Program from its humble start to its present stature is tied inextricably to its ability to gather community support largely with the aid of the media. And, as is usually the case, community support translates into political and governmental support.

Dr. Jim O'Connell puts it all together this way: "This was the result of a community forcing the government to do something that it otherwise wouldn't have done."

PLANNING FOR MEDIA SUCCESS

The success of Boston Health Care for the Homeless Program's efforts to attract media attention was not the product of coincidence or good fortune. Under the leadership of Dr. Jim O'Connell, the program set an overall public engagement goal, determined which specific outlets could help advance its aims, created a media plan, empowered Linda O'Connor and Sara Pacelle to oversee media outreach, and utilized a variety of methods to interest those outlets in shining a light on the work of the program.

As we explain in this chapter, your media efforts should follow the same process. Make sure to understand all of the traditional and new media sources and tools at your disposal. With that knowledge, develop a message and design a media plan. Assign a member or members of your team to execute the plan using skills proven to maximize the chances of media interest. When the plan has been executed, evaluate whether your efforts were effective and apply the lessons learned to your next interaction with the media.

GETTING TO KNOW THE MEDIA

To most people the media is complex, inscrutable, and remote from their daily lives. But though the media is often perceived as monolithic, it appears in many shapes and sizes—and each of those forms plays some role in helping to bridge the distance between the everyday citizen and colossal institutions, such as the government, the business community, the entertainment world, and organized religion. Understanding the different faces of the media is crucial for citizen advocates. Your efforts to solve the challenge you have identified will be advanced if you can utilize media to present your story to readers, viewers, and listeners.

For decades if not centuries, the media existed as a kind of filter—taking in new information from a variety of governmental and private sources; straining out irrelevant data, conjecture, speculation, and rumor; and providing the public with the remaining facts as news. To a large extent, traditional media still plays that filtering role. Journalists for newspapers, television, radio, and their Internet equivalents generally gather information by investigating and scrutinizing the subjects they cover and relaying those insights to the reading or viewing public. In this sense, the news media provides a layer of accountability through which citizens can evaluate the actions of various institutions and leading individuals in those institutions.

However, traditional news sources are no longer the undisputed champions of the media world. They increasingly share space with outlets for direct communication—the so-called "new media."

Unfiltered sources are not new: Television network C-SPAN, which provides live coverage of Congress in action, and its equivalent at the state and local levels show governments in action, without explanation or filtering. For the last two decades, talk radio shows have provided citizens with the ability to call in and contribute to the conversation of the day. Newspapers have long offered readers a platform through the submission of opinion pieces (op-eds) or letters to the editor. But these outlets came with caveats. Broadcasts of Congress, state legislatures, county commissions, and city councils provide crucial transparency but minimal opportunities for interaction. Callers to talk radio shows or contributors to newspaper opinion pages present their views in the context of what a host or other listeners have said or what a newspaper or other readers have written.

What is new is the explosion in new media vehicles that allow citizens to share information and opinions directly and instantly with decision makers, potential allies, more traditional media outlets, and each other. While we strongly urge you in this chapter to build good working relationships with reporters, editorial writers, or news producers, you are no longer entirely reliant on the traditional media to present your story.

Your goal as a citizen leader is to follow the example of Dr. Jim O'Connell and his team at the Boston Health Care Center for the Homeless: Develop and execute a plan that helps you share your message through both traditional and new media. Citizens who engage media on a regular basis accept the risk of occasionally negative coverage in exchange for access to a low-cost way to communicate their message to thousands or even millions of people. Whether the problem you identified after reading chapter 1 is a statewide issue (such as public education funding) or a local issue (such as crime control), you are unlikely to persuade decision makers to address your problem unless you can rouse sufficient public attention. Nothing focuses official attention on a problem quite like the prospect of media scrutiny. Additionally, an effective media plan will alert potential allies and help you recruit coalition partners and funders needed to solve your problem.

We'll get to the question of how you can most effectively engage the media later in this chapter. First, we will look at the types of media with which you will need to interact if you want to increase public awareness about your issue. Each has unique advantages and disadvantages that you should keep in mind as you put together a media plan to focus awareness on the problem you have identified.

Before we get started, you should know some important data about where and how Americans get their news.

- In June 2013, Gallup surveyed more than 2,000 U.S. adults to determine their primary sources of news. Fifty-five percent (55%) chose television, including half of adults under the age of 50. Twenty-one percent (21%) said the Internet, which can include digital sites of other media outlets and social media such as Twitter and Facebook. Nine percent (9%) said print, especially those classified as seniors or with a postgraduate education. Six percent (6%) said radio.[2]
- From January to February 2014, the Media Insight Project, an initiative of the American Press Institute and the Associated Press-NORC Center for Public Affairs Research, polled nearly 1,500 adults and found that 75 percent of Americans get news daily, including 60 percent under the age of 30. Moreover, they obtain that news from diverse devices. The majority of those surveyed reported gathering news sometime in the previous week from television (87%), a computer or laptop (69%), a radio (65%), a paper version of a newspaper or magazine (61%), and a smartphone (59%).[3]
- In the same Media Insight Project survey, a large majority (88%) of those who did find news said they found it "directly from a news organization that reports the news, such as a newspaper, TV newscast, website, or newswire."[4]
- Those surveyed also expressed a great interest in their own communities. Seventy-five percent (75%) of respondents said they tried to keep up with news about their local town or city. Asked where they liked to find news about their local city or town, 37 percent said newspapers and 30 percent said television.
- Pew Research Center conducted a survey from March 2015 to April 2015 of randomly selected U.S. adults who have online access. The conclusion was striking: "When it comes to where younger Americans get news about politics and government, social media look to be the local TV of the Millennial

---

[2] Lydia Saad, "TV Is Americans' Main Source of News," *Gallup*, July 8, 2013, www.gallup.com/poll/163412/americans-main-source-news.aspx

[3] American Press Institute, "The Personal News Cycle: How Americans Choose to Get Their News," March 17, 2014, www.americanpressinstitute.org/publications/reports/survey-research/personal-news-cycle/

[4] American Press Institute, "The Personal News Cycle: Topline Survey Results," www.americanpress institute.org/wp-content/uploads/2014/03/AP_NORC_API-Personal-News-Cycle_Topline_March-18-Release.pdf. See page 16 for the statistics in this bullet and page 34 for those in the next.

generation."[5] The percentage of adults ages 18 to 33 who gathered news from Facebook in the previous week was 61 percent, as opposed to 37 percent who got it from local television news. Generation X members—ages 34 to 49—preferred Facebook by a margin of 51 percent to 47 percent. Even 39 percent of Baby Boomers aged 50 to 68 years chose social media, with another 60 percent selecting local television.

- In December 2015, the Center for the Digital Future at the University of Southern California's Annenberg School of Communications published its annual report.[6] The survey of 2,000 U.S. households produced some interesting results about the power of the new media. For example,

  o Sixty-seven percent (67%) of Internet users agreed or strongly agreed that going online can help people better understand politics, up from 63 percent in 2013.

  o Forty-two percent (42%) of Internet users agreed or strongly agreed that by using the Internet, people like them can have more political power, an increase from 37 percent in 2013.

  o Forty-two percent (42%) of all respondents believed that by using the Internet, public officials will care more about what people like them think, up from 32 percent in 2013.

  o Forty-one percent (41%) agreed or strongly agreed that the Internet gives people more say in what the government does, up from 32 percent in 2013.[7]

As you can see, Americans access a variety of media resources to stay informed. Your job as a citizen advocate is to meet potential allies, funders, and decision makers in whatever medium they choose—and use the opportunity to persuade them your initiative is worth their time.

Traditional Media

Newspapers. Newspapers have a long history of providing details of current and local events, and almost every community in the United States has a newspaper of some kind. Larger cities and towns tend to have daily newspapers (examples are the *Sacramento Bee, Denver Post, Buffalo News,* and *Charlotte Observer*). Smaller communities often have weekly newspapers. Daily newspapers typically cover large geographical areas and thus a wide range of reader interests. Your "pitch" should mirror this broad coverage. In contrast, weekly newspapers usually have a narrow

---

[5] Amy Mitchell, Jeffrey Gottfried, and Katerina Eva Matsa, "Millennials and Political News: Social Media—the Local TV for the Next Generation?" *Pew Research Center*, June 1, 2015, www.journalism.org/2015/06/01/millennials-political-news/

[6] Jeffrey I. Cole, Harlan Lebo, Michael Suman, Phoebe Schramm, et al., *Surveying the Digital Future: The 2015 Digital Future Report, Year Thirteen* (Los Angeles, CA: University of Southern California, 2015), www.digitalcenter.org/wp-content/uploads/2013/06/2015-Digital-Future-Report.pdf

[7] Public Affairs Staff, "Center for the Digital Future Study Finds Increasing Importance of Internet's Role in Politics," *News from the USC Annenberg School for Communication and Journalism*, December 9, 2015, annenberg.usc.edu/news/centers/center-digital-future-study-finds-increasing-importance-internet's-role-politics

audience and view the news through a more parochial and personal lens. Adjust your approach accordingly.

Whatever their differences in scope and approach, most newspapers are organized along similar lines. A publisher has overall command, with ultimate oversight over the three main elements of the newspaper. The business side is primarily responsible for generating revenues through newspaper circulation and advertisement sales, as well as for managing costs to maintain a profitable and thus sustainable news organization. The news side consists of editors and reporters who produce news articles. The editorial side conveys the newspaper's opinion on relevant issues of the day. For your purposes, you need be concerned only with the news and editorial functions.

The news staff generally has two types of personnel: reporters, who investigate and write the news stories that appear in the newspaper, and editors, who decide which subjects the newspaper will cover and carefully review and revise the articles that reporters submit for publication. Reporters are usually organized into "beats." For example, at your daily newspaper, one reporter may be assigned to the police beat, to cover crime; another reporter has the schools beat and is responsible for education coverage; yet another follows municipal government on the City Hall beat; another handles investigative matters; and so on. Pay close attention to which reporters are assigned to the various beats at your college or local newspaper: The reporter who covers your issue can be a valuable ally in introducing your cause to a wider audience.

Please keep one caveat in mind. As newspapers have struggled financially, the beat system has suffered organizationally. Due to staff reductions, many publications no longer have the specialization of years past. Reporters are more flexible and versatile in what they cover. Because your goal is to influence government, you should be able to find a potentially interested journalist if you focus on those reporters who are regularly covering the state legislature, mayor, county commission, or city council. Alternatively, look for one who has covered the subject matter of your citizen initiative. If your goal is to persuade the city government to offer more daytime options for homeless residents in your urban core, see if you can find a reporter who has covered downtown revitalization or the local impacts of the housing crisis.

When you begin your efforts to attract newspaper coverage of your issue, you will first approach a reporter who can produce a news story. But newspapers also have editorial boards that publish pieces giving the newspaper's stance on a particular subject (so-called editorials) and also pieces from professional columnists who analyze and comment on local, national, or international news. Individuals are also given a chance to publish their own opinions (in op-ed pieces or letters to the editor). A newspaper's reporting staff and editorial board are separate and independent entities, a structure that you can use to generate both news and editorial coverage of your initiative. Also keep in mind that many newspapers have local columnists who write twice-weekly or even thrice-weekly columns on regional news, politics, and compelling human-interest stories. Because community leaders and elected officials typically pay close attention to these columns, you should build a working relationship with key columnists and persuade them to take an interest in your cause.

As you strategize about your media plan, be mindful of the changing influence of newspaper coverage and its relative advantages and disadvantages as a news source. For most of American history, newspapers have been the dominant form of political and governmental media in the United States. In decades past, citizens who wanted to reach policymakers through the press had no choice but to work through newspaper reporters. But times have changed. The advent of broadcast news in the mid-twentieth century and its rapid expansion since then, as well as the more recent explosion of new media as a source of news and information, have changed the role of daily and weekly newspapers.

The shift from print to broadcast and online sources has caused economic havoc in the newspaper industry. As former readers move to new sources of information, advertisers have followed them and significantly reduced their newspaper-based marketing. In an effort to cut costs, many daily newspaper chains have either bought out or laid off significant numbers of reporters and other news employees. Daily newspaper stories are increasingly generated not by local reporters but by national news services, such as Associated Press (ap.org), Reuters (reuters.com), Bloomberg News (bloomberg.com), or state-specific resources such as the News Service of Florida (newsservice florida.com).

Despite these financial troubles, the newspaper industry continues to look for new business models that will help daily print journalism survive. Many papers emphasize their presence on the Internet and on social media sites, and with good reason. Digital impressions and advertising offer possible new revenue streams. And in the same way that Willy Sutton robbed banks because "that's where the money is," newspapers are shifting online because that's where potential future generations of newspaper readers exist. Print reporters are also making more of an effort to converse with their readers on social media, and with good reason. A December 2015 study from assistant professor Mi Rosie Jahng of Hope College and assistant professor Jeremy Littau of Lehigh University found that, among younger readers, "[j]ournalists who interact with their followers are seen as more credible and rated more positively than journalists who use Twitter solely to disseminate news and information."[8]

We should all hope these revitalization efforts flourish because newspapers offer great advantages to you in communicating your citizen message. The first is credibility. Newspapers are often seen as the medium most likely to "get it right" in terms of accuracy of reporting and fairness to their subjects. A comprehensive newspaper account will help to validate your initiative in the eyes of decision makers, possible coalition partners, and other journalists. Another advantage is breadth of coverage. Unlike television and radio reporters, who may have two to three minutes to report a story, newspaper reporters have comparatively more room to provide a comprehensive account of the news item or issue in question. Although the facts you gather in support of your initiative will be helpful to any reporter, you are much more likely to see them published in a newspaper than aired by the broadcast media. Additionally, newspapers often shape other types of news coverage. Broadcast news directors often base their decisions on where to send their reporters on national and local newspaper headlines. A front-page story can produce a ripple effect across other media outlets in your community.

Television. Television remains the dominant source of news around the globe—the 800-pound gorilla of the media world. Its dominance cuts across socioeconomic lines. But television, like the media in general, is not monolithic. It consists of several levels of which you need to be aware as you consider how to put your issue in the spotlight.

---

[8] Natalie Jomini Stroud, "Interaction on Twitter Enhances Journalists' Credibility," American Press Institute website, December 7, 2015, www.americanpressinstitute.org/publications/research-review/twitter-credibility/

You are watching national network news if anchors employed by ABC, CBS, or NBC are presenting the day's stories. But unless the problem you have identified has broad, national significance and has attracted intense interest in Congress or at the White House, you will probably not work with these networks in airing your initiative. Cable news is another form of television news coverage. Its mention immediately brings to mind Cable News Network (CNN), Fox News Channel (FNC), and Microsoft/NBC (MSNBC), but those national cable stations present the same problem as national network news. Until your initiative has controversial national implications, they will likely not broadcast your story.

The level with which you are most likely to engage is local television news. Local television stations are referred to as network affiliates when they are affiliated with one of the national television networks (PBS, NBC, ABC, CBS, Fox, and CW). Some local stations are independent with no network affiliation.

Local TV news is best known for half-hour newscasts—usually aired sometime between 5:00 p.m. and 6:30 p.m. and then again between 10:00 p.m. and 11:30 p.m.— which provide summaries of the day's local news, weather, and sports. Although local television stations in big cities have larger staffs, almost every local station has a news director, who oversees the news operation; several news anchors, who present the news on set to the viewing public; news reporters, who cover general assignments; and an assignment editor, who directs news reporters to follow up on news tips or cover planned press events.

Some local cable systems are sponsoring "Headline News"–style channels that provide local and regional news, weather, traffic, and sports 24 hours a day, 7 days a week. For example, Time Warner Cable News (twcnews.com) provides the well-known New York City station NY1 (ny1.com) as well as similar all-local, all-the-time operations in California, upstate New York, North Carolina, and Texas cable markets. Bright House Networks in the Tampa Bay area offers Bay News 9 (baynews9.com) to its cable subscribers in a six-county region. In the Orlando area, Central Florida News 13—"All Local, All the Time"—performs the same service (mynews13.com). Given the amount of airtime local cable stations have to fill, your issue might be of interest to a similar station if one exists in your community.

As with newspapers, television news offers its own set of advantages and challenges. The scope of television viewership is a major plus. Because Americans prefer television as a news source, there is no better way to reach a large audience. Television news penetrates almost every household in the nation, including those in your community where citizens live who can bring pressure to bear on decision makers. The more your issue is aired and discussed, the more likely you are to bring about positive action.

Although television remains the best way to communicate with a mass audience, that reach comes with trade-offs in the form of reduced depth and credibility. With limited time available (after commercials, 22 to 23 minutes of a 30-minute broadcast), local television reports rarely last more than 2 or 3 minutes. That is hardly enough time to introduce, never mind fully present, the challenge you have identified and the solutions you are proposing. The 24/7 local cable stations offer another opportunity for broadcast coverage, but they also present news according to a strict format that does not usually allow in-depth reporting. Local TV stations are notorious for prioritizing stories about murder and mayhem over other subject matter—hence the saying, "If it bleeds, it leads."

If your local community has one or more television stations that provide news coverage, make an effort to build relationships with each station's news director and key reporters. Like Dr. Jim O'Connell, and using the suggestions in this chapter, convince them that your citizen initiative deserves television coverage. Remember that it is your job to help them craft stories that can be told in 180 seconds or less. Television is a visual medium, so the more you can help assignment editors and reporters find the video and photographs that will help viewers see your story, the more likely they are to cover it. It is also a time-driven medium. Be mindful that you need to help television journalists assemble a story in time to make their afternoon deadline, so that your story appears on the evening news.

In her tips (See Tips from the Pros: Citizen Advocacy on Camera), award-winning television journalist and public education proponent Deborah Gianoulis explains how citizens can tell their stories on television.

TIPS FROM THE PROS

Citizen Advocacy on Camera
DEBORAH GIANOULIS

Television remains the primary source for news for most Americans. If you want to tell your citizen advocacy story to the broadest audience possible, you need to get it on TV.

As a television journalist for more than 25 years and a public education advocate, I have experience on both sides of the camera. TV reporters have little time to research and investigate the stories they report, which is an advantage for an effective advocate who can help them do their job.

One of the most successful advocacy efforts I experienced as a television journalist was a rare invitation from Jacksonville, Florida's domestic violence shelter Hubbard House.

Hubbard House was Florida's first domestic violence shelter with a reputation for being responsive to the media. In 2000, the executive director asked for a meeting with the WJXT Channel 4 general manager and news director to offer unprecedented access. They invited an all-female reporting team to spend a night inside the shelter to meet the women and children who live in terror. Hubbard House's goal in seeking coverage was to persuade leaders in law enforcement and the criminal justice system to adopt policy changes that would save lives and help break the cycle of domestic violence.

But first, Hubbard House orchestrated a full day without cameras. They wanted us to understand all of the research on domestic violence and what they perceived as failures in public policy. We visited the shelter, the courts, the sheriff's office, the batterer's intervention team, and with women and children victims.

Our night in the shelter was the "hook" to tell the story. Shortly after midnight, a woman was delivered by taxi, direct from the emergency room, still in her hospital

(Continued)

(Continued)

gown and socks, her face swollen, her hair caked with blood. As she told her story, between quiet sobs, to the Hubbard House emergency response team, we heard echoes of all we had learned about the cycle of abuse, perpetuated by fear and the ignorance of those who should be her protectors.

Hubbard House was proactive, educated us on key domestic violence issues, provided access, and clearly stated its policy goals. The result was a documentary—*Behind Closed Doors*—which prompted the Florida Supreme Court to change the judicial code of conduct and require domestic violence training for judges. Law enforcement agencies throughout the country began using the video to educate police officers. WJXT was awarded a national Peabody Award for exceptional local reporting.

Of course, not every story is made for a long-form TV documentary. Most of the time, your goal will be to inject your issue or cause into the daily news cycle. The keys to success in this mission are to be brief, credible, prepared, and alert to opportunities where you can provide a compelling visual in support of your cause.

After I left journalism, I became a public education advocate. In 2009, the Duval County School System was struggling from the budgetary impacts of the Great Recession and state-imposed mandates on the use of existing funds. We formed Save Duval Schools to work for better funding and more local control of public schools.

Telling that story on television was a major part of our strategy. We recruited parents and students to be the face of the budget cuts. For example, while budget cuts were forcing the school system to dismiss music teachers, the state required the purchase of new music books. Save Duval Schools worked in tandem with the Duval County School Board to raise the challenge at well-attended community meetings—which were covered by the television media when we recruited dueling high school bands to highlight the importance of music education.

Similarly, when a highly controversial teacher evaluation bill opposed by teachers and parents passed the Florida Legislature in 2010, Save Duval Schools mobilized students, educators, and parents for media interviews to promote a public rally that would be held two days before the Florida governor's deadline to sign or veto the bill. Hundreds showed up and marched across the pedestrian path of a major downtown Jacksonville bridge during rush hour, chanting "Hey, Hey Governor Crist, veto Senate Bill 6!" With "live" cameras rolling, motorists honked in support. The video of the rally went viral. Two days later, the governor—who needed educational community support for a United States Senate bid—vetoed the bill.

Save Duval Schools set out to raise awareness and direct average citizens to take action that would influence policymakers. As a result of persistent television outreach and resulting coverage, citizens were motivated to attend community meetings and ultimately rally toward a clearly defined goal.

Television news is unlike any other media outlet. It challenges you to present your message in a succinct, clear, and visually compelling way that TV journalists can report in their limited airtime. But if you can master this medium, you will significantly increase the number of decision makers—and people who can influence decision makers—who are aware of your cause.

For nearly 25 years, Deborah Gianoulis was an anchor on WJXT Channel 4 (news4jax.com) in Jacksonville, Florida. During her time at WJXT, Deborah helped to lead the most-watched news team in North Florida. She later became a public schools advocate and ran for the Florida Legislature on a pro-public education platform. Deborah currently serves as president and CEO of the Schultz Center for Teaching and Leadership (schultzcenter.org), which provides professional development and leadership training for educators, and professional learning services across all sectors: public, private, and nonprofit.

Radio. Radio may seem an anachronism—a throwback that once filled the role that television now plays in our media culture. But it remains a potent medium. According to Nielsen Audio, 91 percent of Americans over the age of 12 listen to radio at least once weekly.[9] While that finding is a decrease from the 96 percent who listened weekly in 2001, any source heard by 9 out of 10 Americans is worth including in your messaging plan.

As a citizen advocate, you should strive to tell the story of your cause on radio news. When you design your media strategy, keep the changing radio news listenership numbers in mind so you can plan and target accordingly. Between 2010 and 2015, morning drive-time broadcast listenership of National Public Radio (NPR) dropped 11 percent. The NPR flagship morning news program—*Morning Edition*—saw a 20 percent decrease in listenership among people under 55 years old. Afternoon drive-time listenership lost 6 percent of its audience.[10] Although more Americans are listening to public radio podcasts, this may not compensate for the loss in broadcast listeners—an especially significant problem for local stations that depend on contributions from listeners for a serious portion of their financial support.

However, none of these statistics should cause you to cross radio communications off your list of media tasks. The same study that showed a decline in NPR listenership for those under 55 years of age saw an 18 percent spike among those aged 65 years or older. Radio also tends to be a medium that attracts opinion leaders and decision makers. Because you have ample reason to persuade both of those audiences, citizen engagement with radio is well worth your time.

Radio news generally falls into four categories:

- Public radio, often associated with National Public Radio (npr.org);
- National and state radio news networks, which sometimes have local stations;
- National, state, and local radio news/talk programs;
- Satellite and Internet radio.

Given that your goal is most likely to reach decision makers at the local or state level, most of your efforts will probably be focused on the first two categories, with some attention to the third if you have an influential local news/talk show.

---

[9] Nielsen Audio, "Audio: Weekly Radio Listenership," *Pew Research Center: News Media Indicators Database*, www.journalism.org/2015/04/29/audio-fact-sheet-2015/

[10] Tyler Falk, "Drop in Younger Listeners Makes Dent in NPR News Audience," *Current*, October 16, 2015, current.org/2015/10/drop-in-younger-listeners-makes-dent-in-npr-news-audience/

You probably know the first category, public radio, from national programs such as *All Things Considered* (npr.org/programs/all-things-considered), the *Diane Rehm Show* (thedianerehmshow.org/), and *Fresh Air* with Terry Gross (npr.org/programs/fresh-air). Far more central to your citizen advocacy is the network of state and local public radio affiliates around the nation that add community news and programming to these better-known NPR shows. These state and local stations often have a news director and staff who provide a steady diet of regional news updates throughout the day. They may give you an opportunity to have your issue aired if you pitch your story successfully, so take the time to learn the names and contact information of your state and local public radio news personnel. In her tips (Tips from the Pros: Cut Through the Static—How to Stand Out on Radio), award-winning radio journalist Judith Smelser offers advice on turning those contacts into on-air stories featuring your advocacy initiative.

TIPS FROM THE PROS

Cut Through the Static—How to Stand Out on Radio
JUDITH SMELSER

If radio journalists seem a little harried these days, it's because the radio news landscape is changing before our eyes and ears. While many people still flip on their car radios to listen to NPR or their favorite AM talk station, others are changing the way they access audio content and the way they consume news in general. Much of that change is happening in the digital space.

That means radio-exclusive journalists are largely becoming multimedia journalists. Most radio reporters still produce audio news as their primary product, but many are also expected to write for and provide photos (and sometimes video) for their organization's website and engage with audiences on social media.

So, they have a lot on their plates. They also have in-boxes overflowing with story pitches—I know I did during the decade I spent as a public radio reporter, editor, and news director.

If you want to cut through the noise, here are some questions to ask yourself before you hit "send" on a pitch to a radio journalist. Some of these are audio specific, some aren't, but all of them will play into the split-second decision that determines whether your message gets deleted or turned into a news story.

1. Why now?

Why is your cause or organization relevant at this particular moment in time? If a reporter asks you about the news "peg" for your pitch, this is what she means. Can you relate your pitch to a piece of legislation coming up for debate? A prominent court case? A business merger? An environmental disaster? New economic figures?

2. What's about to happen?

Radio and digital platforms both operate in real time. If you tell me about something your organization did last week or a school board vote that happened yesterday, it's not news anymore. Instead, tell me something that's happening in the next week or two . . . and how you can help me preview it.

3. What's the story?

Unlike a broad topic, a *story* is something specific that's happening now. The fact that your organization or cause exists is not, in itself, a story.

4. Is it news or a PSA?

If you want to get the word out about a community event, art opening, festival, or performance, your first stop should not be a radio station's news department, since these types of happenings would rarely be considered news. Instead, find out whether the station accepts public service announcements (PSAs) or if it has an on-air or online community calendar. If not, you could always go the route of paid advertising (or underwriting, in public radio parlance).

5. Why should the audience care?

Why is your story important to someone who doesn't have a direct stake in the cause or who's not already interested in the subject? Why is it important to people in the reporter's geographic coverage area? It can't be too parochial, but if you're pitching a local station, it must have local and/or regional relevance. If you're pitching a national program or network, it must have national significance.

6. Who are the characters?

Every story needs compelling characters. Audio journalism especially thrives when it amplifies the voices and stories of real people, not just talking heads. Offer to put the reporter in touch with well-spoken real people who exemplify your cause.

7. What are the sounds?

TV journalists use pictures to tell their stories; audio journalists use sound. The best radio pieces paint audio pictures, taking the listener on an aural journey to places where the action happens in the story. That could be a family's kitchen, a hiking trail, a factory floor, a classroom, a farm, or a protest, for example. Here are a few sound-specific tips for dealing with radio journalists:

- Tell the reporter about the sound-rich action in your story and when and where he needs to be to record it.
- Sometimes, a reporter will be happy to do interviews over the phone, but often she will need high-quality sound that can only be achieved through an in-person recording. Alternatively, she may ask you to record yourself using a smartphone and send her the audio file.

(Continued)

(Continued)

- Don't be surprised if the reporter asks to meet for an interview in a location with relevant ambient sound in the background.
- Some stories may require the reporter to get creative when it comes to audio pictures. Be receptive if he asks for a descriptive tour of your kitchen or a family photo album.
- Every room has a sound, even if it seems quiet. There may be an air conditioner whooshing, a computer humming, or fluorescent lights buzzing overhead. Audio producers call this "room tone." Often, a reporter will ask to record a couple of minutes of that tone on its own, to aid in mixing the final piece. We always feel a little silly when we do this, so please be understanding.

8. What are the visuals?

As I mentioned earlier, it's not just about audio anymore! Most radio journalists will spend time taking pictures for the digital versions of their stories. Some may even want to shoot video. Like audio journalism, good photojournalism needs action, so tell the reporter what colorful visual opportunities exist as part of your story. That said, do *not* pitch a radio reporter as though she were a TV reporter. Audio still comes first.

The more you work with radio journalists, the more you'll get a feel for what they need and what the audio medium needs. If all goes well, those relationships will benefit you, your cause, and the listening public . . . whether they're listening on the air, on their phones, or on some newfangled gadget that's yet to be invented.

Judith Smelser spent nearly 15 years as an award-winning radio reporter, editor, and news director for news organizations around the world. Most recently, she led newsrooms at Colorado Public Radio and at WMFE-FM in Orlando, Florida. In 2013, she launched Smelser Editing & Consulting (judithsmelser.com), advising news operations on editorial content, organization, and strategic planning, and providing journalists with management and leadership coaching, training, and story editing services. She is also the author of Scribbles & Scruples, a blog about the craft and conundrums of modern journalism (scribblesandscruples.wordpress.com).

The second radio news category consists of national and state radio networks that provide regular news updates throughout the programming day for stations that pay for their services. If you listen to your favorite FM station and hear a brief news report at the top or middle of the hour from ABC Radio News or the Florida News Network, you are hearing one of these quick national or state news broadcasts. As is the case with network television news, you are unlikely to interact with the producers of these types of radio news unless your issue is controversial or of statewide interest.

Some national radio networks still have local news operations that cover government and politics. For example, Cox Radio (coxmediagroup.com) has news/talk stations in places as far-flung as Atlanta, Jacksonville, Dayton, and Tulsa. CBS Radio (cbsradio.com) has stations in markets such as Chicago, Detroit, Minneapolis, San

Francisco, and Los Angeles. Although the number of all-news radio stations dropped from 37 in 2012 to 31 in 2014,[11] they should continue to be on your list of potential media opportunities. Again, look to see if your media market has a local all-news or news/talk station with a staff of reporters who might be interested in your story.

At least in public perception, much of the radio news landscape is defined by the third category: news/talk programs. As of Pew Research Center's 2015 State of the Media report, this format remains popular, with an 11 percent share among listeners over the age of 12—second only to country music.[12] In the past two decades, national talk show hosts on both the right and left have become household names. More important for your purposes are the local radio news or talk shows that exist in media markets across the country. Although the programs in this medium do not present the news so much as they comment on and foster conversations about it, they attract listeners who, in effect, use the shows as a source of news. Some of these local public affairs shows utilize a straightforward news analysis format, such as *First Coast Connect* (news.wjct.org/programs/first-coast-connect). Others have a certain ideological or political perspective that infuses the program. See if your community has a radio news/talk show and determine if you can use it to shape discussion of your issue once it has been introduced into the public arena. Remember how vital it was to the Georgia Green Tea coalition when national consumer radio personality Clark Howard and conservative radio commentator Erik Erickson came out in favor of solar power. In his tip (See Tips from the Pros: Talk to Me. Quickly.), broadcast host Michael Smerconish offers advice on how to make your approach.

TIPS FROM THE PROS

Talk to Me. Quickly.
MICHAEL A. SMERCONISH

In a typical week, I'm responsible for originating 15 hours of live radio, an hour of cable television news, and a newspaper column of roughly 900 words. I also host a website, which I use to give platform to nonideologically driven thinking. I am a content provider. And I am always looking for good subject ideas, which is well known to many who seek my attention.

Every day brings a mailbag full of books to my radio studio, which publishing houses send unsolicited in the hope that I will interview the authors. My e-mail address receives requests from both friends and strangers seeking to introduce me to issues and possible expert guests. The volume of the solicitations I receive in addition to my daily reading of a wide range of source material requires that I make swift

(Continued)

---

[11] See a list of these stations at journalism.org/2015/04/29/audio-fact-sheet

[12] Nancy Vogt, "Audio: Fact Sheet," *State of the News Media 2015* (Washington, DC: Pew Research Center, 2015), www.journalism.org/2015/04/29/audio-fact-sheet/

decisions on how to parcel my programming time. So here is my advice for getting the attention of people who, like me, can give you the access you need to promote your cause.

First, know your intended audience, and then target the individual or outlet that can spread your message. Realize that the media world today has become a very stratified place. In 1973, an LGBT pioneer named Mark Segal stormed the set of Walter Cronkite delivering the CBS Evening News because, at the time, 60 million Americans were routinely tuning into the show. Today, no one program holds such a command. We've fragmented into hundreds of different audiences. So decide who or what outlet commands the attention of people you need to reach, and apply your focus accordingly. Is it a talk radio host? A TV commentator? Maybe a blogger? Perhaps a well-traveled website? The point is that citizens and consumers are exercising choice. You must be selective.

Second, having identified your target, summarize your purpose and focus your message. If you cannot explain your mission and interest me in learning more in a single, short paragraph, you have not sufficiently fine-tuned your thinking.

A radio listener recently stopped me in Las Vegas where I was covering a presidential campaign debate. He told me he was in town for a trade show of professionals and that there was something urgent I needed to share with my audience. I gave him my personal e-mail address and invited him to send me a "paragraph" summarizing the issue.

The next day, I received a voluminous explanation. My eye moved to the final graph: "Longer than a paragraph, I acknowledge, but it is a complicated situation with lots of colorful story lines and both economic and political dimensions. It is an important topic, one that could really use a fair and balanced look. I believe that digging in to this space will prove interesting and rewarding."

Too late.

Because he could not condense his thinking in the introductory note, I had no confidence he could do so verbally if I gave him access to the airwaves. Interest your target first. Then supply the details. But don't overwhelm before you've grabbed attention.

Third, both in your introductory communication and in any follow-up, tell a story. Think Larry David, not Barack Obama. I've only met the former once. But I've interviewed the latter seven times. Here is what I have noticed: No one ever stops me to comment on those conversations I've had with our 44th president, but they do engage me to discuss subject matter I've addressed that is Seinfeldian.

Remember season four of Seinfeld, when Jerry and George were at Monk's Café trying to come up with a show pitch for NBC? And what was the solution? A show about "nothing." There was genius in that. People love to talk about what TV they're binge watching, how to approach their teens regarding drinking and drugs, and whether you'd want life on another planet to be religious.

The content I have provided over the years on radio, on TV, and in print that has had the most lasting impact has not been the political subject matter that exacerbates the polarized divide but, rather, that which draws on our common bonds—the everyday life experiences in which we are all invested. Try to relate to them. Advance your cause by telling me a story in a way that can have broad appeal preferably in a subject area where we all have skin in the game.

The Michael Smerconish Program is heard daily on SiriusXM's POTUS Channel, 124. *Smerconish* airs on CNN Saturdays at 9 a.m. ET. Michael Smerconish is a Sunday columnist for the *Philadelphia Inquirer*.

Regardless of the form of radio that is appropriate for your initiative, keep in mind that it has its own pluses and minuses as an information source. Its wide scope is a major advantage. However, it is not always ideal, especially in terms of reach, depth, and credibility. As evidenced above, radio faces ratings challenges. Like television, it has limited airtime available to give to the problem you have identified and the solutions you are proposing. Unless you can convince your local public radio or news affiliate to produce a comprehensive feature story on your subject, your chances of more than succinct radio coverage are slim. Finally, although NPR and its affiliates and other national and state public radio and news networks win high marks for credibility, some news/talk programs do not because they come with an inherent political bias. Of course, that can also work in your favor. If you can find a talk radio host who has particular influence with the decision makers you want to influence—such as a popular conservative to whom Republican lawmakers listen—you may want to see if you can convince that host to champion your cause on air.

As you organize the media effort for your initiative, plan to visit your local public radio affiliate and any news or news/talk radio stations in your area, and make contact with key reporters, anchors, and hosts. See if your community or state has a radio news station or network not affiliated with NPR that may provide coverage of your initiative. Build a team of supporters who can call into local talk radio shows and create buzz about your concern.

Multicultural Media

Increasingly, our nation's unique diversity is reflected in the news media. Throughout the United States, Hispanic, African American, Asian, Creole and other multicultural newspapers, radio stations, television stations, and websites are integral members of the media. In New York, Los Angeles, Houston, Miami, Chicago, and other major media markets, Spanish-language television and radio stations—either independent or affiliated with a major network such as Telemundo (telemundo.com), Univision (univision.com), and Black Entertainment Television (bet.com)—consistently have some of the largest audiences and highest ratings. The larger Hispanic media markets often see even more specialization with individual radio stations appealing to particular nationalities, such as Cuban, Mexican, Puerto Rican, and Columbian individuals.

African American networks, such as Black Entertainment Television, and local African American newspapers and broadcast stations also hold significant sway. In some areas, specific groups (for example, Haitian Americans in South Florida) have media outlets of their own in which they can discuss community issues.

If your community enjoys this kind of media diversity, include these news sources on your outreach list. Analyze your issue to determine if it will particularly affect the communities those outlets cover, and build relationships with news personnel. Your outreach will make a difference with key segments of the overall audience you hope to reach.

The New Media

When we wrote our first version of this book, the digital world was growing but still in its childhood as a platform for news and messaging. Since then, its growth as a news source and messaging platform has been explosive.

You're already well aware that many traditional news outlets have transitioned to an online model that allows news consumers to access their products via home computer, laptop, tablet, or smartphone. Some of the statistics we have already cited in this chapter tell the story of how more and more Americans use technology to access news. As you are working to persuade newspaper, television, radio, and other more traditional news outlets to cover your citizen advocacy efforts, just know that much of their journalistic mission is now focused online. Package your initiative so it can be told across the various platforms that these reporters now use.

Internet-Only Media. While traditional news sources have molded their long-standing print, television, and radio products to exist in an online world, some outlets have sprung to existence because of the digital revolution. Six or seven years ago, these innovations were known as blogs. Most followed the same format: A blogger posted a story or opinion on a subject and invited fellow bloggers to respond with comment. This invitation usually led to a stream of back-and-forth on the issue posted and may have even produced online discussion of other subjects.

Blogging still exists, but like everything in the dynamic media world, it has in some cases evolved into the more concrete format of a news website that, in many markets, competes with print journalism on a relatively equal basis.

For example, FloridaPolitics.com describes itself as "a statewide, new media concern covering campaigns, elections, government, policy, and lobbying in Florida." Its reporters write succinct stories that are published online and distributed through social media. Another online news analysis and discussion application, MetroJacksonville.com, also started as a blog. But it now contains daily original content, long-form stories about local history and public policy issues, video (tvjax. com) and audio interviews, and an electronic forum in which readers can discuss the issues of the day. National examples include HuffingtonPost.com and slate.com.

These new digital outlets are important to your initiative for three reasons. First, because they thrive on maximizing their digital impressions and being first to a story, these publications are hungry to report stories like yours. Second, given the decline in newspaper staffing, digital sources are assuming more of the responsibility for original reporting, some of which the traditional press later picks up as newsworthy. Third, these new media concerns are designed in a way to attract the attention of Internet search engines. If someone searches Google, Bing, Yahoo, or another search engine for a particular issue, he or she is likely to encounter new media sources that reference that issue.

Please note that some of these new digital outlets are ideologically based. For example, the left-leaning Daily Kos (dailykos.com) advertises itself as "at once a news organization, community, and activist hub."[13] RedState (redstate.com) calls itself "the most widely read right of center site on Capitol Hill, . . . highly respected and cited in the media, and . . . one of the most influential voices of the grassroots on the right."[14]

Although the new digital news sites sometime blur the line between reporting and commentary, decision makers and other opinion leaders are increasingly paying attention to these new outlets as a way to keep a finger on the pulse of public opinion.

---

[13] Daily Kos, "About Daily Kos," www.dailykos.com/masthead#dk

[14] RedState, "About," www.redstate.com/about/

Don't ignore the new digital culture as you seek to raise awareness about your initiative. Take advantage of its growing influence by forming relationships with these online news sources and working to have your story told. In so doing, you may help to build a core of committed online allies who can help spread the word about your challenge and proposed solutions.

TIPS FROM THE PROS

Engaging the New Media
SARAH RUMPF

The explosive growth of the Internet has revolutionized nearly every aspect of our lives, and the news media is no exception.

According to the American Press Institute, one-third of Americans prefer to stay up to date on the news throughout the day, and over half of them use their cell phones to follow the news. Many of the biggest media companies now operate chiefly or even exclusively online.[15]

Today, major stories frequently originate not with a major television network or newspaper but on Twitter or on a website. You can always start your own blog or tweet your thoughts directly, but to maximize your impact, you're almost always better off trying to get an established new media journalist to pick up your story.

Accordingly, strategic outreach to new media journalists is an essential part of any modern advocacy work. The new media often gets criticized for an overreliance on clickbait (content designed to generate views) and viral content (which readers share widely on social media). Some of that criticism may be fair, but you're going to have to do more than simply e-mail out your press releases and hope for the best. Here are a few tips:

Follow and learn the trends

On Twitter, what are the main search terms—aka "hashtags," which lead with the # sign—driving the discussion? For example, a lot of the political chatter in Texas is found under the hashtag #txlege (short for Texas Legislature, but often representing any Texas political topic) and in Florida, #flapol and #sayfie (after Sayfie Review, sayfiereview.com, a news aggregator website) are the most popular. Criminal justice reform advocates should check out #cjreform, and there is a long list of hashtags used by both the pro-life and pro-choice sides of the ever-contentious abortion debate. Searching with the hashtags most related to your issue will help you identify who is writing and talking about it online.

(Continued)

---

[15] American Press Institute, "How Americans Get Their News," *The Personal News Cycle* (Chicago, The Media Insight Project, 2014), www.americanpressinstitute.org/publications/reports/survey-research/how-americans-get-news/

(Continued)

What are the websites, blogs, and Facebook groups that are most influential in your state or subject matter? What topics are they frequently covering? Is your issue already getting a lot of attention, or being ignored? If you're not getting much media attention yet, what similar topics are getting covered?

Know who the influencers are

Who are the top new media reporters covering your issue or similar ones? Are there elected officials who have publicly expressed a specific interest in your issue or have worked on legislation? Are there other citizen activists involved in your issue who already have a large social media following?

Study what these people write and say, with whom they interact online. You should be able to identify not just those who are already on your side (or at least leaning your way) or who are your opponents but also the commentators who remain neutral and are still an important part of the discussion.

Know your targets and tailor your pitch personally for them

Most reporters have more story ideas floating around than they'll ever have time to write. It is blatantly obvious when someone hasn't actually read my work and is just blindly sending out pitches, and that usually kills any enthusiasm I might have for that person's story.

If you can, make a specific reference to something the reporter has covered that relates to your issue (e.g., "I enjoyed your recent article about [topic]" or "I see you frequently write about [topic]"). Make it clear that you're not just spamming a thousand reporters but that you personally wanted to reach out to this individual reporter.

Ideally, sending your pitch by e-mail is best for your first contact because it is less intrusive than a phone call, puts the information in writing where the reporter can review it, and is private, unlike trying to reach someone with a public communication on Twitter. If you can't find an e-mail address for a specific reporter, many media websites have submission forms for tips or a dedicated contact person.

Keep your pitch straightforward and informative

Obviously, you're passionate about your issue, and expressing your opinion on why this story is important is fine. However, it's best to avoid hyperbolic language and be extremely judicious with the caps lock and exclamation points.

You don't have to tell the entire story in your first communication but you should provide an outline of what the important bullet points are. Describe any evidence you can share: photos, video, quotes from the people involved, or audio clips, for example. Provide links to other sites that support your argument. Online journalists are still journalists, and a story with original photos and on-the-record quotes is an easier sell.

**Understand how original
and exclusive content drive traffic**

The business model for most online media companies is traffic driven: for example, how many unique and repeat visitors a site has, how long they spend on the site, or how many times a story is shared on social media.

In today's hyper-competitive media environment, there is a lot of value in being first with a story. Because online stories can include links to other sites, whoever breaks news will reap ongoing traffic benefits as the reporters who follow the coverage link back to the original story.

If you are able to offer a reporter an exclusive on a story, that usually helps draw interest. Make sure to specify the terms of the exclusive: what information you are giving to them first and how long you'll wait before sharing it with others.

Even if you can't offer an exclusive, do your best to highlight what's interesting, controversial, unique, or otherwise creates the potential for a viral story.

Sarah Rumpf is a journalist living in Austin, Texas. Originally from Orlando, she's a proud alumna of the University of Florida who practiced law and ran her own campaign consulting practice before becoming a full-time writer. You can find her work at *National Review, Independent Journal Review, Opportunity Lives, Legal Insurrection, The Daily Beast, Heat Street,* and many other places. Follow Sarah on Twitter:@rumpfshaker.

Social Media. Though the shift to online news is a game-changing development all of its own, the even more revolutionary transformation has been the monumental growth in social media. Social media has become so influential, so fast, that we almost take it for granted. Think about it. If you take a break from reading this book (which we don't encourage), chances are that you will, without even thinking about it, pick up your smartphone, turn on your personal tablet, or log on to your laptop and see what others are posting on Twitter, Facebook, Reddit, Snapchat, Instagram, Flickr, Periscope, and numerous other social networking sites. You might share and comment on a news article you find interesting. You can provide your thoughts on virtually any subject under the sun. No longer are you trying to persuade a journalist to communicate your message. In the social media age, you can say what you want, when you want.

Because of the communications autonomy that social media offers, its use has become widespread. As is usually the case, the numbers tell the story:

- According to the Pew Research Center in 2015, "Nearly two-thirds of American adults (65%) use social networking sites, up from 7% . . . in 2005."[16]
- Similarly, the December 2015 report *Surveying the Digital Future*, cited previously, found that nearly 60 percent of adults visit social networking sites at least once daily. This includes 87 percent of people between the ages of 35 and 54 and 96 percent of those between the ages of 18 and 34.

[16] Andrew Perrin, "Social Media Usage: 2005–2015," *Pew Research Center*, October 8, 2015, www .pewinternet.org/2015/10/08/social-networking-usage-2005-2015/

- Pew's continually updated tracking of social media use shows that "66% of social media users (39% of American adults) have engaged in . . . civic or political activities with social media:

  o 38% of those who use social networking sites (SNS) or Twitter *"like"* or *promote material related to politics or social issues* that others have posted
  o 35% have used social networking sites to *encourage people to vote*
  o 34% have used the tools to *post their own thoughts or comments on political and social issues . . .*
  o 31% have used the tools to *encourage other people to take action on a political or social issue.*"[17]

As you can see from those numbers, social media offers tantalizing possibilities for sharing your message. Also, elected and appointed decision makers and their staff tend to be active on social media sites, so these provide another method for interacting directly with officials. Many find that social media is a way to build relationships with reporters from both traditional and online outlets. And especially since influencers are present, you have an opportunity to try to build messaging momentum.

Social media has proven that it has the ability to change the course of events. In the so-called "Arab Spring" of 2010–2011, popular uprisings primarily led by young people concerned about human rights, political corruption, and economic distress erupted across North Africa and the Middle East. These movements overthrew dictatorships in Egypt, Libya, Tunisia, and Yemen. Heads of government either stepped down or were fired in Iraq, Jordan, Kuwait, and Sudan. Other regimes had to offer concessions to their citizens, like Algeria, which ended a nearly 20-year state of emergency. For the first time in human history, one of the main tools that protestors used was social media. According to a June 2011 study—the Arab Social Media Report by the Dubai School of Government—nine out of ten Egyptians and Tunisians used Facebook to organize or publicize protests.[18] On Twitter, hashtags such as "#Egypt," "#Jan25," and "#Libya" received close to one million mentions in the first three months of 2011. A team of University of Washington researchers analyzed more than three million tweets and large amounts of YouTube data. They found that during the zenith of the protests, the rate of tweets about the need for change in Egypt grew ten-fold to 230,000 per day, while key protest videos earned more than five million views.[19]

Here in the United States, social media has proven highly effective in raising awareness. You probably recall the successful "ice bucket challenge" campaign to educate the public about amyotrophic lateral sclerosis (ALS), also known as Lou Gehrig's disease. Inspired by a Boston College student suffering from ALS and his friends, millions of people videotaped themselves dumping buckets of ice on their heads and

---

[17] Pew Internet Project, "Politics Fact Sheet," *Pew Research Center*, www.pewinternet.org/fact-sheets/politics-fact-sheet/

[18] Carol Huang, "Facebook and Twitter Key to Arab Spring Uprisings: Report," *National*, June 6, 2011, www.thenational.ae/news/uae-news/facebook-and-twitter-key-to-arab-spring-uprisings-report. Arab Social Media Report by the Dubai School of Government.

[19] Catherine O'Donnell, "New Study Quantifies Use of Social Media in Arab Spring," *UW Today*, September 12, 2011, www.nytimes.com/2014/08/18/business/ice-bucket-challenge-has-raised-millions-for-als-association.html

then challenging other family and friends to do the same or donate to ALS research. As of late August 2014, more than one million bucket-dumping videos had been shared on Facebook. The campaign was mentioned more than two million times on Twitter. The ALS Association received $12 million more in donations than it had the year before and nearly 300,000 new donors.[20]

Although not every messaging effort will be as history changing as the Arab Spring or go as viral as the ice bucket challenge, yours can still have significant impact if you think carefully about your social networking strategy. In their respective tips, Laura O'Shaughnessy and Ben Weiss of SocialCode and Steve Ziff of the National Football League's Jacksonville Jaguars provide guidance on how you can maximize your social messaging opportunities.

Of course, the biggest challenge with a medium that allows anyone to write anything is believability. The 2015 report of the Digital Future Project found that only 15 percent of Internet users believed that most or all of the information on social networking sites was accurate.[21] As you look for ways to tell your story via social media, take pains not to sacrifice your credibility. The opportunity to present information to the public without any filter comes with a risk, as you no longer have a professional intermediary with subject matter experience to separate rumor from fact. You have a responsibility as a direct communicator to make sure that whatever you post, forward, or like has factual support.

TIPS FROM THE PROS

Social Messaging Strategies
LAURA O'SHAUGHNESSY AND BEN WEISS

At SocialCode, we have helped social platforms transform from sideshows to marketing monsters that drive awareness and action better than any other media channel. We have seen social platforms drive the same transformational benefits for all organizations, whether Fortune 500 brands, nonprofits, political candidates, advocacy groups, or universities. Based on our experience, we have outlined quick tips on effectively marketing your organization on social channels.

(Continued)

[20] Emily Steel, "'Ice Bucket Challenge' Has Raised Millions for ALS Association," *New York Times*, August 17, 2014, www.nytimes.com/2014/08/18/business/ice-bucket-challenge-has-raised-millions-for-als-association.html

[21] Jeffrey I. Cole, Harlan Lebo, Michael Suman, Phoebe Schramm, et al., *Surveying the Digital Future: The 2015 Digital Future Report, Year Thirteen* (Los Angeles, CA: University of Southern California, 2015), www.digitalcenter.org/wp-content/uploads/2013/06/2015-Digital-Future-Report.pdf

(Continued)

Create content

The first step for your organization is to start posting information about your mission. Think about taking pictures, linking to relevant articles or making short videos to tell stories about your cause. And for those thinking video requires Hollywood-caliber production, we often see the best results from iPhone videos that are simple and clear.

Pay attention to how many people are engaging with your different kinds of content (videos versus photos, more educational versus more action oriented) and make more of what people like and less of what they don't.

Remember, you don't need to be everywhere. Limited resources are always a factor, so choose the platforms on which your content will have the greatest impact. Study conversations on social channels about similar organizations or topics and see which platforms are working best. Then, once you have begun distributing messages, encourage your constituents to join, engage, and share as the best way to connect and stay current with your organization.

Tailor the message to the platform you choose

Since people expect authenticity on social media, tailor messaging and style for the platforms on which you choose to communicate. For example, Twitter is excellent for connection during real-time events and extending event impact. Pinterest, however, is defined by longer-form messages that inspire action and help people plan for life events.

Inform all strategy with insights from social platforms

Social media is about more than just educating the public and getting people to take action. Social platforms are powerful learning engines. Learn what types of photos, articles, and videos resonate best with people that matter to your organization. Study your advocates and detractors, and then use these learnings to improve your messaging in other channels, such as brochures and television ads. The gold mine of information you learn on social platforms should influence the way your organization approaches its strategic goals.

Consider paid media

Why advertise? Understand that there is so much activity happening on social platforms that a limited number of people will see the messages that you post without your paying for their distribution or promotion. When a message is really important, it must be spread more broadly, and that means you need to pay to reach more of the right people.

Before you buy ads, though, first consider who you want to reach and what you want them to do as a result of the ad. Remember that people self-identify tons of privacy-safe data about who they are, what zip code they live in, and what they care about. Most important, groups can also integrate their own campaign data (e.g., people who signed up for an e-mail list) as well as privacy-safe data around people's offline activity (e.g., the causes to which people have donated).

All of these data allow you to—when possible—create key clusters of people based on their unique characteristics. Then you can target these groups with paid messages addressing their needs and encouraging action in a way that's more personalized. This audience-specific messaging is MUCH more effective than a one-size-fits-all message. For example, SocialCode recently managed a campaign for a children's nonprofit called Horizons. A cornerstone of our strategy was grouping Horizon's audience into segments, such as existing donors and people who donated to children's charities in the past. We then educated people about the cause for several months with personalized content before helping the organization drive $1 million in donations on its first annual "Giving Day."

Laura O'Shaughnessy co-founded SocialCode (socialcode.com) to provide the world's most valuable brands with tools to build valuable communities over social media. She continues to work closely with clients to develop innovative ways to achieve social advertising goals. Prior to SocialCode, she ran business development and product strategy for the Slate Group, focusing on advertising product development and strategic partnerships. Laura holds an MBA from the MIT Sloan School of Management and a BA in economics from the University of Chicago.

Ben Weiss is the platform strategist at SocialCode. He is responsible for packaging recommendations, insights and case studies across verticals, helping clients and partners achieve their goals efficiently and building thought leadership in the industry at large. Ben also leads SocialCode's beta team, a pipeline for spreading early product knowledge, driving comprehensive product understanding and building data-driven documentation.

TIPS FROM THE PROS

Social Media Success Is All about Personality
STEVE ZIFF

 At its roots, social media has always been a peer-to-peer connection. So it's no surprise advertisers are latching on to the platform. It's where the masses live today.

The tricky part of social media is that the role of curator now lies with each individual. Unlike a traditional print ad in a magazine, content surrounding an advertising message in a social media setting is no longer predefined. Now an individual's social media stream is filled with all of their competing interests, in no discernable order, at no specific time of day.

How can an advertiser break into a feed and capture attention? With a little personality.

(Continued)

(Continued)

Approaching social media as a human-to-human interaction automatically gives it personality. Your audience is smart. They know there's a real person behind the wall. Begin by defining that social media manager role within your organization to ensure a consistent voice across all platforms.

Content is king in any social media platform. Let people into your world. For the Jaguars, our personality takes shape through the access we provide to our players, coaches, and the inner workings of our organization.

The Jaguars are a larger-than-life brand, so our content extends beyond the Xs and Os you see on Sunday afternoon. By giving voice to what's behind the helmet, we believe fans will naturally draw closer to the team and its players.

Finally, accept that it's nearly impossible to create something viral. What qualifies as interesting is in the eye of the beholder, or in this case, the social media user.

Create content that you believe is unique to your brand. Your followers will tell you if it's interesting or not. Track that data and use it to tinker with your social media voice until it raise the conversations you seek.

Steve Ziff joined the Jacksonville Jaguars (jaguars.com) as the vice president of marketing and digital media in September of 2014. He is responsible for all areas of content, marketing, creative, and digital media, including gameday presentation and production. Prior to joining the Jaguars, Ziff worked for the San Diego Padres as the senior vice president of sales and services, responsible for the sales and development of ticketing, premium seating and suites, and all non-ballpark events and concerts. He previously served as the senior vice president of marketing and brand strategy for the Florida Panthers.

Podcasting. In this era of direct communications, podcasting is an increasingly popular way of telling your own story. In simple terms, a podcast is like a personal audio program that you record, produce, and arrange for distribution to the audience you are trying to reach. Podcasting can help you share your citizen advocacy story directly with the public—including decision makers and people who can influence decision makers. A well-received podcast can also help to establish your bona fides on your initiative and build credibility with stakeholders.

While the first podcasts began to appear at the turn of the millennium, the explosion in podcast-friendly smartphone apps on the iPhone, Android, and other operating platforms has made downloading and listening to podcasts easier than ever. In 2015, Edison Research released survey results showing that 33 percent of Americans aged 12 and up had listened to a podcast at least once. At least 17 percent had listened in the previous month, and 10 percent in the previous week.[22]

Chris Giliberti, chief of staff at digital company Gimlet Media, described podcasting as the next evolution of the "oral storytelling [that] has served a critical role

---

[22] Edison Research, *The Podcast Consumer* (Somerville, NJ: Edison Research, May 2015), www .edisonresearch.com/wp-content/uploads/2015/06/The-Podcast-Consumer-2015-Final.pdf

as the sole means of abstracting experiences and emotions in narrative form."[23] He points to increasing investor interest in podcasts, improved podcast content and talent, and expanded distribution opportunities as reasons that he believes "podcasting will become the most important storytelling medium."

Though some think of podcasts in terms of radio networks and stations making their programming available in podcast form—shows like *This American Life* and its spin-off, *Serial*—podcasts are a very accessible and entrepreneurial tool that virtually anyone can utilize. Expert podcasters Margie Omero and Kristen Solis Anderson explain in their tips (see Tips from the Pros: Podcasting for Citizen Success) how you can create interesting, informative, and popular podcasts.

TIPS FROM THE PROS

Podcasting for Citizen Success
MARGIE OMERO AND KRISTEN SOLTIS ANDERSON

While podcasting has been around for more than a decade, attention the last few years has grown enormously. Much of this focus has been on the tip of the podcasting pyramid, in shows that feature celebrities or former public radio journalists. But the long tail of the podcasting world, like the long tail of the blogging world in years past, is an incredible format. With a relative minimum of expense, you can create your own podcast and directly educate decision makers, opinion leaders, and interested members of the public on your mission.

Our podcast is about political polling. We began as casual Washington acquaintances who were pollsters on opposite sides of the political spectrum. After a joint media appearance discussing the 2015 State of the Union address, we came up with the idea of creating our own content through a podcast, and built a platform on which we could dig far deeper into polling than even the longest news segment or radio show ever could. At the time, there was no other podcast about public opinion research generally or polling specifically. No other show was cohosted by a bipartisan team of women. So we planted a flag for *The Pollsters* (thepollsters.com).

In our first year, our audience has grown exponentially, and our podcast is a regular top-rated political show on iTunes. Although many shows benefit from

(Continued)

---

[23] Chris Giliberti, "6 Reasons Why Podcasting Is the Future of Storytelling," *Forbes*, March 31, 2016, www.forbes.com/sites/under30network/2016/03/31/6-reasons-why-podcasting-is-the-future-of-storytelling/#246ef4da2120

(Continued)

production help or the backing of an existing media platform, *The Pollsters* runs with a skeletal crew—us! So we have a good perspective to help other nascent podcasts.

If you worry that creating, producing, and airing a podcast is beyond your technical abilities or financial means, think again. Podcasting is often the ultimate DIY activity. If you have two hosts and guests, you may want a mixer and digital recorder, along with your microphones, like we do. But many podcasts easily run on a single mic hooked up to their laptop. We use a free editing software (Audacity®—audacityteam.org) and a low-cost automated audio sweetener (Auphonic—auphonic.com). Our media host (Libsyn—libsyn.com) sends the show to podcast apps and has a helpful beginner-friendly support team. Find a place with good acoustics, like a sound booth or even a closet, and you're good to go.

But once you have these basics down, your goal should be to build a podcast with a dedicated and growing audience. Below are some tips for launching your own effective podcast, with an eye toward advancing the public dialogue on the issue or cause you are advocating.

1. *Identify a beat and a format*. You should be able to describe your show in one sentence. Are you focusing on a single issue, region of the country most impacted by your concern, or branch of government that can do something about it? Do you have regular interviews? A cohost? A specific point of view? Your show's title, cover art, intro, and description should all very clearly explain what your show is about.

2. *Provide a service*. A podcast in which you say what's on your mind may be rewarding and interesting, but it's not always the best way to build a new audience of listeners. Provide a clear service, like explaining how your local or state government oversees transportation policy, interviewing teachers around the country about their jobs as a way of highlighting public education issues, or going "beyond the news" to study a topic in more detail. Jennifer Briney of *The Congressional Dish* (congressionaldish.com) reads bills that pass and distills them for her audience. Both left-leaning and right-leaning women's organizations, e.g., MomsRising (momsrising.org/page/moms/radiopage) and the Independent Women's Forum (iwf.org/podcast) have regular podcasts during which they talk through their issues. The Boy Scouts (scouting.org/RSS Feeds/Scoutcast.aspx), PoliceOne (policeone.com/columnists/Policing-Matters), and the Fort Worth Independent School District (fortworthisd.granicus.com/ViewPublisher.php?view_id=2) all have regular shows, and think tanks such as Brookings (brookings.edu/research/podcasts/brookings-cafeteria-podcast), AEI (media.aei.org), or even the local Illinois Policy Institute (illinoispolicy.org/radio) have podcasts as another way to push out their messages. But honestly, there is a lot of room in this space for more stories about civic engagement—why not yours?

3. *Identify your target audience*. Who are you trying to influence through the podcasts? Who do you think would most enjoy your show? Are you creating

a new way for your organization to connect with its existing members and stakeholders, or do you want to grow its support base? Do you have existing followers or e-mail lists, or are you creating a new audience more or less from scratch? Are you appealing to insiders and experts or to those who want more "explainers"? Having a clear picture of your listeners will help you better find them and talk to them.

4. *Familiarize yourself with the space.* As best you can, familiarize yourself with the podcasting space. It'll help you flesh out what you like and don't like, and to what listeners seem to respond. There is also a whole niche of podcasts about podcasting, and these can be invaluable resources as you're just starting out (see podcastjunkies.com). As *The Pollsters'* resident podcast junkie, who also has a long commute, Margie has dipped her toe into hundreds of shows over the last year.

5. *Don't overthink the hardware or the audio extras.* The technical piece can be overwhelming, but online guides and how-to videos by podcasting experts such as Ray Ortega (thepodcastersstudio.com), Cliff Ravenscraft (podcastanswerman.com), and Daniel J. Lewis (theaudacitytopodcast.com) will help you get started. Even once you master your setup, there are endless ways to improve your audio and format, like adding music, pulling in outside audio clips, creating robust shownotes, or making extensive edits. These are all great enhancements, but if they get in the way of regularly creating solid content, or if editing and production are simply not your thing, then try to find a simpler work flow. Get your content right first, and add the extras later once you get into your groove.

6. *Plan content.* Few people want to hear someone's stream of consciousness. While you don't need to be 100 percent scripted, having your show planned out with talking points or interview questions at the ready will improve it enormously. At *The Pollsters*, we have a weekly script that includes all of the polls we want to discuss—including charts—laid out in one document, with our topic areas clearly labeled, so everything is in one place. We even have some of our jokes set in advance. As a bonus, more planning usually means less editing.

7. *Prepare for regularity.* Podcasting takes time and work, and audiences typically respond best to regularity. What kind of podcasting schedule works best with your schedule? Or with your content? Podcasting can be like exercise—you have to build the time into your schedule, rather than wait for free time to simply arrive.

8. *Engage your audience.* Be open to criticism and suggestions from your audience. When our listeners said we crumpled our paper too much, we rearranged our sound booth and worked to reduce the noise. We've also read out reviews on the show, given listeners "micro-assignments," answered Twitter questions, and asked listeners to vote in a Twitter poll about our format. And many of our best guests have been listeners who reached out to us. Podcasting is an intimate medium, and many listeners expect to be able to reach you. An engaged audience also feels invested in your success, and part of the community you're building.

(Continued)

(Continued)

9. ***Promote across channels***. You need not be on every social network, but it helps to promote your show on as many as you can comfortably manage. Twitter, Facebook, LinkedIn, Instagram, YouTube, or your existing e-mail contact list are all good places to make sure people know about your show. We stuck with the channels on which we each already had an individual presence (Twitter, Facebook, LinkedIn, and our e-mail lists), although a good next step would be developing YouTube and Instagram content.

10. ***In fact, tell everyone***. But don't just leave the promotion to Twitter and Facebook. Tell people when you or your organization hold in-person events, tell your family and friends, and add your show to your e-mail signature. Join the podcasting subReddit or She Podcasts or any of the many online podcasting communities, or promote your show on an online community focused on your issue. There are now podcasting conferences around the country you could attend. And many of our best promotional breaks have occurred when we simply let people know about the show, and they featured us.

11. ***But be patient and remember your goal***. "Building an audience" is the podcasting holy grail. Even people with top shows want to know how to grow their audience further. And while there are some insider tricks to increasing discoverability, like soliciting listener reviews on iTunes, the best way to build an audience is to have great, consistent content and tell the people you'd think would be interested. Even with that, remember about half of all shows have fewer than 200 downloads per episode. Starting a podcast shouldn't be just about the numbers, but about your goals—getting out your message, finding your tribe, and deepening your community ties.

Margie Omero and Kristen Soltis Anderson are cohosts of *The Pollsters*, a weekly podcast. Ormero is the Executive Vice President of the Public Affairs Practice at PSB Research (psbresearch.com). She manages all facets of qualitative and quantitative research for Purple's clients, including everything from methodological design to business development and strategic analysis. Her clients include some of the world's biggest brands, as well as nonprofit and advocacy groups. Anderson is co-founder of Echelon Insights (echeloninsights.com), an opinion research, data analysis, and digital intelligence firm. She is also a columnist for *The Daily Beast*. Previously, Anderson served as vice president of The Winston Group, a Republican polling firm in D.C. In 2013, Anderson was named one of *Time* magazine's "30 under 30 Changing the World."

DESIGNING AND IMPLEMENTING YOUR MEDIA PLAN

With some basic planning and a better understanding of how to attract press interest, you can engage the media to advance your citizen agenda and promote solutions to the challenges you have identified. Try the following steps:

1. Know Your Goals, Message, and Media Audience

The worst possible way to engage any media is a backward "Fire . . . Ready . . . Aim" approach. Before you even begin to think about which reporters you might contact, you need to decide how you want the media to benefit your cause. Are you simply trying to bring an issue to light because a decision maker is keeping it in the dark? Are you trying to sway legislators in advance of an important decision or vote? Do you want to identify others who share your concerns and build a strong coalition? Is your goal to alert the general public about a problem that people should be aware of but are not? Do you hope to build support for a particular piece of legislation that would solve your problem? Are you belatedly attempting to rebut the public arguments your opponent has already made? Think carefully about what you want your media campaign to accomplish, and stay focused on that goal in all of your upcoming interactions with the media.

But simply articulating a media goal is not sufficient. You must also develop a basic message, one that can be summarized in a single sentence. Because you want to share this on social media sites such as Twitter, have a version of the message you can share in fewer than 140 characters. For example, assume that a wave of violent nighttime muggings has spread through your college community, and students are afraid to walk through campus after dark. Angered by what you feel is a lackadaisical response from local authorities, you want to use the media to stir public outrage and force action. Your every interaction with the media must drive home the same message: The crime spree has put students, faculty, staff, and community members who walk across campus at risk, and local law enforcement officials must eliminate the danger. In their tips (see Tips from the Pros: The Right Message), J.J. Balaban and Pia Carusone explain how you can develop a similarly focused and memorable message for your advocacy initiative.

After you develop your basic message, consider which members of the media are best suited to help you convey it. As we explained in chapter 5, Marshall McLuhan, who many have called the father of the electronic age, captured this concept in a now-famous phrase: "The medium is the message." Some stories are visual in nature—a house crushed by a fallen tree, a hurricane battering a beach, a SWAT team storming a suspected crack den, a rat-infested government apartment complex. These stories make compelling television.

However, other important stories lack a live, visual dimension. For example, it may be hard for television to present a comprehensive account of a major government decision or conduct an investigative report into government misspending. These stories could be page-one features in your newspaper, but they may do little to excite a television viewer's interest. How is your story best told? Is it visual? If so, a television journalist is likely to be receptive to doing that story. On the other hand, if telling your story requires a reporter to dig through government records or to privately interview many people who don't want public attention, it may be best suited for the newspaper or the Internet.

TIPS FROM THE PROS

The Right Message
J.J. BALABAN AND PIA CARUSONE

At the core of any persuasion effort is a message. In a political campaign, that message is communicated directly by the candidate and his or her surrogates, or by ads on TV, radio, or computer, or through mailings. Few citizen advocates will have the money to run thousands of television ads, but the principles that guide formulating the message of candidate Jane Doe also apply to citizens' groups that, say, are trying to persuade a city commission to increase after-school initiatives.

Keep it simple

Elected officials are busy. "Normal people" are even busier with their jobs or taking care of their children; they spend a shockingly small amount of time thinking about politics. If your aim can't be communicated with a pithy message and the thrust of your argument for achieving that aim can't be summed up in a minute, it's difficult to get the attention of most people for much longer. This doesn't necessarily mean a slogan. The corrosive long-term impact of economic inequality on the health of the middle class is time consuming to explain and difficult to comprehend. Advocating for "raising the minimum wage" is something that is easier to rally behind because it's specific and concrete and something most voters understand.

Avoid jargon

Most people have no idea that they live in Ohio's Third Congressional District or Arizona's Fifth Congressional District. Most people don't know what a "veto override" is or what the meaning of the acronym "CHIP" is. If you use jargon, activists, journalists, and insiders will understand you, but you probably won't expand your base of support because most people won't understand what you're talking about.

Beware of the conventional wisdom

Every serious political candidate for Congress or Senate will take a poll at some point not just to learn her or his standing with the voters but also to measure public sentiment on various issues. Contrary to conventional wisdom, most candidates in our experience won't change their opinions based on the poll, but polling does provide crucial insight on the political environment. For example, if the issue that voters are most concerned about is public safety, it may not be the best time to advocate for eliminating mandatory minimum sentences. The conventional wisdom is often wrong, and the only way to know that is to poll. You are better off spending $25,000 to take a poll than $100,000 lobbying for a proposal that is fundamentally unpopular.

Aim for the heart more than the head

Because of the way our brains are wired, the most memorable messages invariably contain an emotional appeal. It was one thing to argue against segregated buses in the 1950s South by appealing to abstract concepts of fairness. It was much more powerful when Rosa Parks refused to yield her seat, because people were able to connect with her on an emotional level. Similarly, those advocating recently for marriage equality have found the emotional appeal of hearing gay and lesbian couples talk about why it's important to them to be able to marry just like heterosexual couples is more effective in changing minds than philosophical arguments about civil rights.

Make sure your message targets the right audience

If the decision makers have a particular worldview, it's important to make sure that your pitch is suited to appeal to that perspective. For example, arguing that we should eliminate mandatory minimum sentences because of the disproportionate impact on certain demographic groups is not as likely to convince conservative Republican legislators as presenting data which shows taxes increasing from the cost of building more prisons to house people incarcerated under the rules.

J.J. Balaban and Pia Carusone are partners at The Campaign Group, a media consulting and ad-making firm (CampaignGroup.tv). J.J., who is based in Philadelphia, has helped create television and radio ads for campaigns in 35 states, 60 congressional districts, and 115 media markets. J.J. served as a congressional press secretary and worked on various political campaigns prior to joining The Campaign Group in 2002. Pia Carusone, who leads The Campaign Group's Washington, D.C. office, served as chief of staff to U.S. Rep. Gabrielle Giffords and was recognized on the floor of Congress for her leadership after the Tucson shooting. She is the former assistant secretary for public affairs at the Department of Homeland Security and the first executive director of Giffords' gun violence prevention organization, Americans for Responsible Solutions.

2. Distribute Your Own Message

Most media outlets serve as a filter of sorts between newsmakers and the general public, and below we'll provide some best practices in working with them. But as discussed earlier in this chapter, they are no longer the only game in town. The Internet has given citizens more direct access to making, reporting, and reacting to news than at any other time in history. Take advantage of these unique opportunities. Before you do anything else, put your citizen advocacy effort in a position to communicate directly with the public at large and any specific decision makers, potential coalition partners, and funders. Though strategist Chris Talbot explains in detail how you can build an effective digital platform for your citizen advocacy effort in his tips (see Tips from the Pros: To Win Digital, Be Flexible, Mobile, Versatile—and Real), here are initial suggestions:

- Develop a memorable website that can serve as the go-to nerve center for your digital campaign. If you can't afford to hire a web designer to build your site, ask appropriately skilled volunteers who care about the cause and might be willing to create one for free as their contribution to the effort. Update website content as often as possible to prevent it from becoming stale. If possible, make sure your site has the functionality to organize volunteers, capture e-mail addresses and send communications, receive political contributions, and empower supporters to contact decision makers.

- Determine which social media channels are used by key decision makers, prospective allies, and reporters. If you aren't already on the necessary sites, sign up for Twitter, Facebook, LinkedIn, Instagram, YouTube, Periscope, Snapchat, Reddit, or whichever social network can help you put messages, photographs, news clips, and other persuasive information in front of those key opinion leaders. Assign someone in your cause to oversee the social media so he or she can grow your list of followers and friends. Look for hooks to reinforce your message, and rebut any misinformation or attempts from the opposition to undermine your efforts.

- As your effort progresses and you build supporters and other interested citizens, capture as many of their e-mail addresses and cell phone numbers as possible. Grow your list as organically and quickly as you can. Regular e-mail updates to the people signed up will keep supporters engaged and may help you land interested but not yet committed citizens as they follow you.

- Remember that any blast e-email will likely find its way to your opposition and the media. Apply the "front page" test before you press send: How would you feel if you read about the e-mail on the front page of the newspaper?

TIPS FROM THE PROS

To Win Digital, Be Flexible, Mobile, Versatile—and Real
CHRIS TALBOT

Digital media has become the most ubiquitous communication platform in America (and on the planet as a whole). Yet most citizen advocacy efforts still don't take full advantage of it. Harness its potential to build movements and move messages that lead to real, lasting change.

Know thy format

"Online Media" used to mean e-mail marketing and Google ads. Today there are a plethora of different formats that comprise digital media. Preroll ads, which look like TV ads and appear before the online content you are seeking, can disrupt an audience with a powerful message, generating awareness and persuasion. Social media imagery and "native" advertising (e.g., ads that are made to look like Facebook posts or Twitter tweets) can help build an army of enthusiastic supporters to carry your ideas on through their own communities. Viral videos capture the imagination of the press and generate untold millions in earned media value. Basic text ads and e-mails, while no longer sexy, still get the job done, turning supporters into avid donors and active volunteers. With so many digital options, knowing which arrow to choose from the quiver can make the difference between victory and defeat.

Be yourself (authentic, and you)

Online media provides a more intimate experience than those of most traditional media. Consider that online content is almost always consumed less than 12 inches from your face, and in social media the user is not just a viewer of that content but indeed an active participant in its creation and discussion. Smart advocacy campaigns play into the nature of online media by delivering fresh, personal content. It should be less formal than the content provided by other media packages, and more emotional—making it more likely to be discussed and shared. Focus on videos, images, and dialogue that convey the personality of your cause or your supporters. And don't be too concerned with hiding the warts: authenticity possesses premium value in such an intimate channel. Moreover, if you try to hide it—and fail—your content will fall flat.

Bet big on big data

Big data refers to data sets so large and complex that just recently have our processing applications begun to make sense of them. Big data analysis is disrupting all industries and marketplaces, and politics is no exception. But you don't need a seven-figure technology budget to take advantage of its potential. Data modeling done by third parties (or at the state or national level) can help you build a custom audience of unique individuals for your messaging campaigns—using millions of data points about your targets to craft an optimal set of recipients. Imagine the benefits of not wasting any resources communicating with voters and influencers who are not interested in your effort. This new efficiency allows your investment with the true target audience to go further—in leaps and bounds.

Mobile is massively mainstream

When we speak of "going online," most people conjure up images of desktop and laptop computers with the full arrangement of keyboards, mice, and features. But today more than half of all time spent with digital media takes place on a mobile device, and the gap is growing. Nearly all digital activity is shifting to smartphones, with consumer behavior leading the way. Consider the social networks that are nipping at the heels of Facebook and Twitter: Instagram and Snapchat are not just mobile-ready networks—they are mobile-only. The implications could not be more important for your campaign. Here are a few mantras to follow:

(Continued)

(Continued)

- Build responsive websites that are appealing and effective across devices.
- Create brief, catchy content that stands out quickly in a busy feed and can be digested on the go.
- Design images and videos that are up close and personal: they will mostly be seen on a screen surface of 4 inches or less.

Don't get comfortable

Two years ago, most of the digital insights above would have been irrelevant (indeed, some of the social networks mentioned didn't even exist). And two years from now, much of this advice will likely be outdated. Everything about digital is changing at breakneck pace: the devices, the data speeds and pricing, the platforms and privacy settings, and Americans' expectations and usage of digital media. It's imperative to understand that today's best digital strategies won't last for long. You must always be learning, always be testing, and always be ready to update your approach to meet the digital world of tomorrow.

Chris Talbot is a nationally recognized expert on digital marketing in politics and public affairs. As the principal and founder of Talbot Digital (talbotdigital.com), he provides digital strategy for political organizations, corporations, nonprofits, and the federal government. Recent clients include Maryland Governor Martin O'Malley, Senator Jeff Merkley, The Aspen Institute, Boeing, and the State Department. In 2012, he was named a "Rising Star" by *Campaigns & Elections* magazine.

3. Do Your Homework

Once you have settled on a message and analyzed which medium—it could be more than one—will help you communicate that message effectively, identify specific media members who can best help you talk to the public at large.

For example, if you have decided to target print sources, try to identify reporters who are likely to be most receptive to your concerns. Many outlets list reporters and their assignments on the Internet. If you can't find them there, look for recent stories on your issue and identify the reporter assigned by looking for the byline. If all else fails, telephone the newsroom and simply ask which reporter covers the issue. You can repeat the same process to discover which member of a newspaper's editorial staff is responsible for writing about your issue.

The setup for broadcast reporters is similar, although only a few are as highly specialized as their print counterparts. Moreover, most television and radio stations have limited news personnel. In most cases, you'll want to start with the news director or assignment editor and have that person guide you to the correct reporter. If your local television stations are among the few that still broadcast editorials—a station's position on an issue usually presented by its general manager or editorial director—contact the stations and arrange a meeting with the appropriate personnel.

As for the Internet, you may find web-based publications such as those mentioned above that seem open to writing about your issue. And you should look for social media search terms or trends that offer opportunities to magnify your message.

4. Walk a Mile in the Media's Shoes

After you have identified the media outlets you want to approach, take time to think like its reporters before you make contact. Put yourself in the place of a journalist who is learning about your issue for the first time. Ask these questions: What makes this a story of community interest? How would I tell it? Why is this newsworthy? Why should other people care? If you can't answer these questions on your own, you're going to have a hard time convincing a reporter that your story is news.

Don't limit yourself to questions a generic journalist might ask. Review this particular reporter's previous stories on the subject, if they exist, and see if you can detect a common thread. Imagine, for example, you wanted to expose a property insurance company that is illegally denying claims. It would help to know if the reporter you want to target has previously investigated insurance claims practices of any kind.

If you have thought through the general and specific interests in your story, you're ready to approach the reporters who can help you convey your message to the public. But don't go empty-handed. Instead, rely on a phrase that is a fundamental precept of journalism: "Show me; don't tell me." To focus the news media's attention on your issue, gather supporting information, line up contacts, or provide helpful leads. The more tangible information you can provide, the more likely the reporter will write your story. For example, in the case of the campus safety issue mentioned earlier, if you were able both to put the reporter in touch with robbery victims who could describe their harrowing experiences and to provide minutes from public meetings that demonstrated a heel-dragging response, you would enhance the reporter's interest in the issue.

Don't wait until you're about to engage the media to collect supporting information. As you employ the research methods described in chapter 2, consider how the data you have already gathered might be useful to a media member. But don't just focus on the past—envision and pursue new lines of research that could result in positive coverage.

Especially when you are working with television and radio reporters, it helps to take this proactive approach one step further and create the powerful visual images and sound they need to tell your story. You should not manufacture news. But it makes sense to present your concerns in a setting that is visually or aurally compelling. For example, if you want to focus attention on your state's chronic underfunding of its transportation infrastructure, bring broadcast reporters to crowded roads and highways so they can film, record, and talk with motorists forced to wait in gridlocked traffic. Walk them to nearby bus stops and introduce them to riders tired of long waits for public transit to arrive.

Finally, as you stick carefully to your basic message, think about which applications of that message might catch a media member's interest. The media values the good of the many over the good of the few—or of the one—and reporters are most likely to take up the causes of people to whom most others in their audience can relate. They are not inclined to act as an advocate for an individual whose concerns aren't widely shared by others. For example, a job seeker who loses out to a rival isn't likely to persuade a TV reporter to make that story the subject of the evening news. But if that job seeker was rejected because of his race, gender, age, or sexual orientation and not his qualifications—and there is evidence to that effect—that's newsworthy. Suddenly, this isn't about one person's grievance; it's a matter of group discrimination, which most people won't tolerate.

5. Make Contact

Become a person to journalists, not just the faceless author of a text message or a voice mail. Once you've identified the reporters most likely to be interested in your issue, find a way to communicate directly with them. An e-mail may crack the door, but barely. A phone conversation is better, perhaps followed by an e-mail. Best of all is a face-to-face meeting followed by an e-mail summarizing your key points.

Don't stop with reporters. Find out who oversees the reporters who cover the subject area in which you're interested. Again, send an e-mail, make a phone call, or, if possible, schedule an in-person appointment. Remember to be specific about the subject and emphasize why you believe your story is newsworthy. Building independent relationships with editors is important for another reason: Individual reporters come and go, frequently moving from beat to beat. Editors are more likely to stay in one place and can be the key to an ongoing relationship. However, as you are building relationships with editors, take great pains never to seem as if you are going over a reporter's head. Most journalists try hard to be fair, but they are human. Alienating them either purposely or inadvertently is never a good idea.

As you discovered in chapter 6, timing is everything—and that precept is no less true when you are dealing with reporters. It used to be that the pace of a news reporter's day generally accelerated as the day went on. So if you wanted to make initial contact with a reporter, you did it during a "slow" part of the day. For most reporters, the later in the day it was, the more hectic things became as deadlines closed in for the evening television news, the drive-home radio, or the next day's morning newspaper. But in our current 24 hours news cycle, the fierce competition for media outlets to be first in reporting a story means that reporters and broadcasters are almost always in a rush. They follow the admonition of fictional stock car driver Ricky Bobby: "If you're not first, you're last." Because of that hurry, there are fewer "slow" parts of the day, and earlier is always better for media. It is also better for you because an earlier-in-the-day story on your issue could force other outlets to cover it as well, and gives you more time to boost that story's reach on social media.

Think also in terms of when your story would receive the most (or least) attention. Weekday news will normally have a larger audience than weekend coverage, especially on broadcast outlets that don't have the equivalent of a Sunday newspaper. Because readership, viewership, and listenership have traditionally been down at the end of the week, government officials and companies often release bad news late on Friday.

Timing is also a question of context. If a reporter is not able to cover your initiative right away, don't worry. Be patient. Some matters require lengthy investigation. For other matters, at least in the opinion of the news media, the timing isn't right for your story to be told. This example may sound familiar: Some citizens warned for years that punch-card ballot machines disenfranchised many voters in every election. They had the data and the evidence to back up their allegations and to support their demands for new machines. But only when the result in the 2000 presidential election was too close to call in Florida were those machines discredited and ultimately replaced.

6. Take Multiple Bites at the Apple

Even when a reporter has written or broadcast your story, don't consider your work done. That initial media coverage is usually just a launching pad for additional press interest. When the daily newspaper publishes a story about your initiative, immediately contact local radio and television stations and other interested sources to provide copies of the article. If you can also provide them with facts, people to interview, and compelling audio and visual depictions of your message, your story may start off in the morning news cycle and end up on the evening news and all over the Internet. The reverse is also true. In this era of new media, your first hit may occur on an Internet site before more traditional sources pick up the story.

Additionally, don't forget that media outlets often offer more than one avenue to print coverage. Once your story becomes news, ask for a meeting with the editorial editor. Persuade him or her that the newspaper should adopt your position as its own. If you are successful, the paper may produce a favorable editorial that validates your cause as you seek allies, funding, and even more media attention. Similarly, contact your local TV stations if they still broadcast editorials.

Finally, take advantage of opportunities to argue your case using your own words. In addition to publishing the opinions of syndicated columnists (writers such as George Will, Kathleen Parker, and David Brooks) whose work appears in newspapers across the nation and world and those of local columnists who write primarily for a particular newspaper, newspaper editorial pages often reserve space for op-ed pieces in which policymakers, community leaders, and everyday citizens can express their views on a particular issue—usually in about 600 words. Once your initiative has become a news story, a published op-ed in which you argue your position can not only extend the life of the story but also generate public discussion. Conversely, if reporters have not yet paid significant attention to your cause or issue, an op-ed can help you present it to the public directly. If the newspaper won't publish your op-ed, drop down to the shorter letter to the editor (from 150–300 words) to express your views. Of course, the daily newspaper is hardly the only place that will publish your opinion. Many Internet media outlets welcome citizen opinion columns and encourage you to submit them. Some sites, such as Context Florida (contextflorida.com), are devoted to nothing but op-eds.

7. Stay Credible at All Costs

Do not exaggerate, lie, or deceive. Chances are that a good journalist will discover the deception, and your credibility will be damaged. When that happens, your ability to engage the media effectively on this or any other issue will be seriously curtailed. While a response of "no comment" does not advance your message and should generally be avoided, it is preferable to misleading comments. If you inadvertently provide inaccurate information, contact the media member immediately upon discovering the inaccuracy to correct your error.

Additionally, remember that you are pursuing this initiative to be a good citizen, not to supplement your income. News isn't for sale. Those outlets that do pay, such as supermarket tabloids, generally have little credibility with the public, just as a paid police snitch has limited credibility with a jury. Conversely, do not offer to pay journalists for reporting on your issue. Stay focused on the news value of the cause you are advocating.

As you design your plan, know that you stand on the shoulders of citizen advocates and organizations that have gone before you. In his tips (see Tips from the Pros: The Dos and Don'ts of Advocacy Storytelling), Paul Anderson describes tried-and-true strategies you can use to engage the media and share your compelling story.

The Dos and Don'ts of Advocacy Storytelling
PAUL ANDERSON

DO make your media strategy a key component of your overall advocacy plan from the beginning, and plot a narrative arc as you map out the rest of your tactics. Good communications is all about telling a compelling and relevant story to the people you want to motivate, and it rarely just happens as your effort unfolds. Be deliberate.

DON'T assume the media will be interested just because you believe something is important. Media channels are facing ever-greater pressure to attract eyeballs, even as newsroom employees are being cut and deadline pressures increase. Put yourself in an editor's desk chair and don't waste his or her time.

DO decide on a target audience for your message and approach the right media outlet for reaching that audience, be it a newspaper, TV station, or social media. Be sure you research the media outlet's staff members and their prior coverage, so you can approach the right reporter or editor and make your pitch relevant.

DON'T do a shotgun-style press release and expect all the media to cover your story the way you want. The worst request to make of a reporter or assigning editor: "Will you help give us 'surround-sound' coverage? We're giving this story to every media outlet in town and want you to help us get people interested." Make it clear that you are reaching out with careful intent and that this is a story that will matter to a specific media outlet's audience.

DO craft a message that will resonate with your target audience and also interest a channel manager enough to cover your story. Focus the message on what's in it for the reader/viewer/listener; don't make it about you or your organization. If you can afford it, do some research to test your message and refine it. Even the weightiest subject needs some pizzazz to grab and hold people's attention, so think in tweet length (140 characters or less) and use a snappy hashtag.

DON'T make an "ask" that's so vague or generic that no one can engage even if they want to support you. Be specific when you devise your call to action—Call this number, or Go to this website—and be ready to handle those responses, whether it's having staff on your phone bank, someone checking your e-mail account, or a content strategist updating your weblink or checking your social media accounts. Horror of horrors: An unanswered call or broken link could prompt a potential supporter to call the media outlet and complain about you!

DO consider allocating some of your budget, if you can afford it, to "paid media"—advertising, event sponsorships, promoted social media. Done right, paying for attention can be surprisingly affordable and effective at reaching your targeted audience.

DON'T engage in media tactics that might backfire. If you're inviting the press to cover a rally, make sure there's a crowd with signs and noise. Or if you promise to make news at a press conference, be sure you've got something newsworthy to announce.

And finally, DO tell the truth. If a reporter or a supporter discovers that you have offered misleading information on even the smallest fact, your credibility is shot and your cause suffers. And know that exaggeration is lying; claiming to have 1,000 petition signatures if you only have 500 will likely be discovered and do lasting damage.

DON'T speculate. If you don't know the answer to a reporter's question, admit that and say you'll get back with the answer. If you guess and guess wrong, you haven't told the truth—see tip above.

Paul Anderson is a former journalist for the *Miami Herald*, Knight Ridder, Inc. (now McClatchy), and the *Congressional Quarterly* (now *CQ Roll Call*). He served as communications director for U.S. Senator Bob Graham and managing director of public affairs for the U.S. Government Accountability Office (gao.gov) before joining the AARP (aarp.org) as senior vice president for integrated communications and marketing. He is active in his community outside Washington, D.C.

CHECKLIST FOR ACTION

☐ Understand traditional and new media sources and tools
- Newspapers
- Television
- Radio
- Multicultural Media
- Internet-only Media
- Social media
- Podcasting

☐ Design and implement a media plan
- Know your goals, message, and media audience.
- Distribute your own message.
- Do your homework.
- Walk a mile in the media's shoes.
- Make contact.
- Take multiple bites at the apple.
- Stay credible at all costs.

9 The Price of Progress

Finding the Resources to Support Your Initiative

"Money is a terrible master but an excellent servant."

—P.T. Barnum

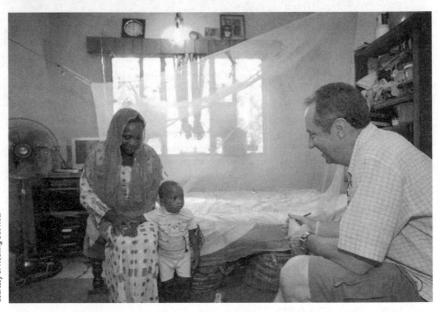

Courtesy of Nothing But Nets

Nothing But Nets co-founder Rick Reilly visits the recipients of one of the almost 10 million mosquito nets funded by the organization since 2006.

The campaign to save children in Africa started in Italy with a writer from Denver. Rick Reilly, who was best known for his wry back-page *Sports Illustrated* columns, had found an activity even more exhausting than the sports he usually covered: shopping alongside Venetian canals with his teenage daughter. At the end of that tourist marathon, Reilly returned to his hotel room and collapsed on his bed, with only

*We are grateful to columnist Rick Reilly and Elizabeth Gore of the United Nations for their contributions to this Case in Point.

enough strength to turn on television and tune into a British Broadcasting Company documentary on malaria in Africa. Expecting to be asleep within seconds, Reilly was instead captivated by a single sentence: "Up to 3,000 children die needlessly each day of malaria—and all they need is a net."[1]

Reilly's mind immediately flashed to all of the sports that use nets: tennis, basketball, soccer, hockey, and lacrosse. He envisioned Wimbledon finalists shaking hands across the net. He saw blaring red sirens when hockey pucks slipped past the goalie into the net. He saw Michael Jordan launching a perfect shot ending with a swish. And then it hit him: What the children of Africa needed was nothing but nets.

Before rushing to his keyboard, Reilly did some research. He found that malaria killed between one and three million people each year, primarily in Africa. A child somewhere in the world died of malaria every 30 seconds. Scientists had developed a new device that reduced the incidence of malaria by 50 percent or more: It was an inexpensive insecticide-treated net, easily installed over a bed, and it killed or repelled mosquitoes for three to five years.

In April 2006, Reilly located an organization already deeply involved in reducing the malaria toll: the United Nations Foundation, which had been established in 1998 with money donated by CNN founder Ted Turner. Since 2001, the UN Foundation had collaborated with five private organizations and the U.S. government to raise and distribute $29 million to fight malaria. But it had not found similar success with the public at large. In partnership with Reilly, the UN Foundation created a new fundraising entity called Nothing But Nets. Through the foundation's fast website—it could be navigated in 41 seconds— people could make donations for insecticidal bed nets quickly and easily. Even better, the UN Foundation agreed to purchase and coordinate delivery of all the nets funded by Internet contributions. In other words, 100 percent of all donations would go straight to saving lives. All each donor had to do was visit the site, complete a short contribution form, enter a credit card number or send a check to the UN Foundation, and more nets were on their way to Africa.

Nothing But Nets was unveiled to the world in Reilly's column on May 1, 2006. He reminded readers how much they used nets and urged them to skip buying the latest Beastie Boys album, dining out, or joining a fantasy bowling league and instead contribute $20 to fighting malaria.[2] In subsequent media appearances, Reilly made appeals for Americans to forego a Britney Spears CD and instead donate to the cause.[3]

The public responded. Within a few weeks, Nothing But Nets had raised nearly $1.6 million from thousands of donors. The average contribution was $60.

Nothing But Nets soon attracted a large and diverse organizational following. The National Basketball Association (NBA) and United Methodist Church were the initial partners. Major League Soccer, the Union for Reformed Judaism, and the

---

[1] Donald G. McNeil Jr., "A $10 Mosquito Net Is Making Charity Cool," *New York Times*, June 2, 2008, www.nytimes.com/2008/06/02/us/02malaria.html?_r=0

[2] Rick Reilly, "Nothing But Nets," *Sports Illustrated*, May 1, 2006, www.si.com/vault/2006/05/01/8376263/nothing-but-nets

[3] Randy Harvey, "The Morning Becomes Hectic: Raiders, Jay Leno," *Los Angeles Times*, September 17, 2008, latimesblogs.latimes.com/sports_blog/2008/09/sports-editor-t.html

Lutheran Church in America joined the team as well. As a tangible demonstration of their commitment to helping children, the Methodist and Lutheran churches—two of the largest Protestant denominations in the United States—each pledged to raise $100 million. The Gates Foundation agreed to match the first $3 million, which was quickly fulfilled.

But as grateful as the leaders of Nothing But Nets were to receive these large contributions, they were touched and awed by the innovative methods that many supporters used to generate funds. These included the following:

- At the April 2008 United Methodist general membership meeting, church leaders auctioned off a basketball signed by all the church's bishops for $430,000.
- Advocates organized Nothing But Nets teams to fundraise through athletic competitions and other activities. These "Netraisers" generated more than $150,000.
- At Howard University, in Washington, D.C., the African Student Association raised $2,300 through a fashion show.
- Yoni D.P. Rechtman, a seventh grader in Brooklyn, New York, organized a "mitzvah project" basketball tournament, which raised $1,900.
- Georgetown University students, in Washington, D.C., created a Netraiser Team appropriately named "Operation Bug Off." In advance of World Malaria Day on April 25, 2008, the Hoyas held seven events, including a 5K race, a trivia night, a bar night, a three-on-three basketball tournament, a restaurant night, and two pizza nights that together raised over $2,000.
- Seven-year-old Katherine Commale of Hopewell, Pennsylvania, may be the most valuable player. Upon seeing the same documentary that had stirred Rick Reilly in Venice, she told her mother, "We have to do something." After building a diorama of an African family in a hut, with the children protected from swarming mosquitoes by a net over their beds, Katherine cultivated interest among her elementary school peers. Her presentation to neighborhood churches raised almost $2,000. Katherine and friends made presentations to churches and crafted hand-decorated gift cards that read, "A mosquito net has been purchased in your name." In total, her team— named "One Bed Net at a Time"—raised $73,000 for the purchase of mosquito nets.
- In later years, NBA superstar Stephen Curry of the Golden State Warriors championed and raised awareness for the cause—even traveling to Africa on his vacation to hang bed nets in Tanzanian refugee camps.[4] Curry also agreed to donate three nets for every three-pointer he made.[5] In the 2015–2016 NBA regular season, Curry set a league record in making 402 shots from behind the arc—which translated into 1,206 nets.

---

[4] Rick Reilly, "Net Gain," *ESPN*, August 6, 2013, espn.go.com/nba/story/_/id/9543252/stephen-curry-hands-mosquito-nets-prevent-malaria-tanzania

[5] Chris Stone, "Editor's Letter: The Return of Rick Reilly," *Sports Illustrated*, March 7, 2016, www.si.com/nba/2016/03/01/stephen-curry-golden-state-warriors-nothing-but-net-rick-reilly

Six months after his column appeared, Reilly visited villages in Nigeria and saw the results of the initiative—in his words, "nets like crazy." The numbers also tell the story. Since its creation in 2006, Nothing But Nets has generated nearly $60 million, delivering almost 10 million bed nets.[6] The World Health Organization estimates that millions of cases have been averted, and 6.2 million lives saved. In some countries, the malaria death rate has been cut in half. Malaria has fallen from the top killer of African refugees to the fifth leading cause of death.[7] That's something from Nothing But Nets.

THE MOST POPULAR LABOR-SAVING DEVICE

An oft-repeated political maxim holds that "money is the lifeblood of politics." Although success in the political system depends on much more than the size of your wallet, virtually every advocacy effort—from a statewide ballot initiative to an attempt to convince county government to clean up a local park—requires at least some financial resources to succeed.

The good news is that the amount starts small and increases only as you aspire to more complex goals or move up the political and governmental ladder. For example, if your objective is to reform your condominium association bylaws, the necessary budget may be as small as the funds needed to pay for the printing costs of flyers or petitions, refreshments at meetings, and any advertisements necessary to build and demonstrate support for your position. In that situation, where you are trying to persuade neighbors to adopt policy changes, you will spend mostly time and energy rather than money. As initiatives affect more and more community members (residents of a municipality or citizens of an entire state, for example), the cost of victory escalates. This is especially true when an election is involved, and voters will decide the fate of your issue or candidate. As evidenced by the huge sums that candidates are raising and spending in this 2016 voting cycle, elections are expensive. If you have to put your initiative on the ballot or run a political candidate who has promised to champion your concern, you'll have to find enough financing to succeed.

But you will need to have or identify resources under any circumstances. Let's assume for the sake of argument that your goal is to have city government invest in a bike-share program so that citizens can rent bicycles and return them to various locations around the community. More than 70 other cities in North America sponsor bike sharing, so you figure it is a no-brainer for the city council to add your community to the list.[8] Not so fast. Facing a potential budget deficit and with other funding requests before them, skeptical council members resist your suggestion. Now you will definitely need money—to launch a citizen advocacy effort that aims to persuade a council majority to support the bike-share program, to raise private dollars and put nongovernmental skin in the game as part of a public-private partnership, or to identify a public funding source that council members can tap for your proposed investment.

---

[6] E-mail from Rick Reilly to Chris Hand, November 18, 2015.

[7] Nothing But Nets, "Our Impact," *NothingButNets.net*, 2013 www.nothingbutnets.net/new/saving-lives/our-impact.html

[8] To view the list of cities that have bike-share programs, visit bikeshare.com/map

In short, don't assume that you are destined for success just because your idea has merit or you are operating from the best of intentions. The political graveyard is littered with worthy candidates and ideas that didn't have sufficient financial backing to win. This chapter will help you prevent your initiative from suffocating from a lack of resources.

PAYING FOR YOUR ADVOCACY EFFORT: A USER'S GUIDE TO SUCCESSFUL FINANCING

For many of you, this first effort to make democracy respond to your concerns will also be your first attempt at raising money for a cause. If you feel nervous, you're not alone: The idea of asking for financial contributions makes even the most experienced politicians suffer anxiety pangs. Calm your nerves by thinking of fundraising in a larger context. Financial contributions are one way that citizens participate in our democracy, and asking someone for money is a way of asking that person to fulfill a civic duty. Although some may choose to participate in other ways, those who view monetary contributions as civic engagement will appreciate the opportunity.

Asking for financial help is also a good way to measure your chances of success. It is one thing for friends and potential supporters to applaud your efforts and express verbal support but quite another for them to put their money where their mouths are. Finally, the fundraising process gives you additional chances to argue your case with individuals or entities that may later be in a position to influence the decision maker you have targeted. Even if these people and groups give little or no money, they will remember the initiative.

Past fundraising experience is helpful but not decisive. If you methodically follow the steps in the next section, you should be successful in generating the necessary resources. As you follow these steps, keep an open mind. Many of the best innovations in political fundraising occurred because fundraisers were struggling with traditional methods and were forced to think creatively.

1. Determine How Much Money You Need

Many citizen campaigns have unraveled because they did not gauge their financial needs adequately at the start of the effort. Don't make that mistake. Schedule a brainstorming session with your core supporters to answer the following questions:

- What are your goals?
- Are those goals realistic, or have you exceeded your reach?
- Having established realistic goals, have you conducted a hard-nosed and itemized assessment of the funds required to achieve those goals? In other words, how much money will be required to succeed in this citizen effort?
- If the answer to the second question is no, and the answer to the third question is that you don't know, begin your assessment by thinking about each of the major citizen skills identified in this book. Assess whether conducting research, surveying public opinion, building coalitions, engaging the media, or other tasks will cost money.

Here are other questions to consider:

- Does meeting your goals require you to participate in an election? In other words, will you have to put your initiative on the ballot for voter approval or back a candidate (or a slate of candidates) who will advocate your position once elected?
- If you are running a formal campaign in which a candidate or an issue will appear on the ballot, does the election authority levy any costs? Is there a qualifying fee or any other fee?
- What goods or services will you have to purchase? Are all of those items absolutely necessary? How much will the truly essential items cost?
- Can you identify anyone to donate ("in kind") any of these goods or services to the campaign or initiative so that you don't have to pay for them?
- Do you really need to hire any paid staff members? Which campaign roles can instead be filled by unpaid volunteers?
- If your advocacy effort does not involve an election, will persuading the elected or appointed decision makers with jurisdiction over the issue require you to establish and finance a citizen advocacy organization or to join forces with a like-minded organization that already exists?
- If you do have to fund a persuasion effort to convince decision makers, can you name people or organizations that would have an interest in funding that campaign?

When it comes to fundraising, history can signal what will and will not work:

- What have similar efforts had to raise and spend in the past, and how did they raise and spend their funds?
- Have you spoken with the organizers who led those efforts to determine whether they would make different spending choices if they could do it all over?
- In retrospect, what expenditures would they prioritize if they had another opportunity? Has the cost of goods or services increased since then?

The most critical questions of the entire process are these:

- What is the time frame for your advocacy effort?
- When do funds need to be available for priority spending items?

In many campaigns and citizen efforts, the bulk of expenditures—and usually the most important ones, like paid media—are made in the closing weeks or even days of the race. If money has not been reserved for these items, the campaign will run out of gas within sight of the finish line. And if you are running an electoral campaign, keep in mind that campaigns no longer build just for Election Day. In many jurisdictions, it is now common for more than half of voters to cast ballots *before* Election Day through early voting or vote-by-mail opportunities. Candidates or initiatives that require voter approval must now raise and spend money on voter communications earlier than ever to avoid missing a large chunk of the electorate.

The law of supply and demand also applies. If a campaign waits too long to raise money, it may miss out on opportunities to secure the highest-rated television time, the most competent petition gatherers, or other critical resources.

Early fundraising is also critical because it signals viability. Since the 1980s EMILY's List (emilyslist.org) has been raising money for pro-choice, Democratic women candidates in congressional and gubernatorial races. (The organization's name derives from an apt slogan: "Early Money Is Like Yeast"—it makes the dough rise.) When any advocacy effort raises early money, it is easier to convince other potential donors that their contributions will go to a campaign primed for victory.

2. Develop a Fundraising Plan

Thomas P. "Tip" O'Neill of Massachusetts, who served as Speaker of the U.S. House of Representatives from 1977 to 1987 and enjoyed a 34-year congressional career, was a noted storyteller. In his autobiography, O'Neill recounts his very first election, a race for the Cambridge City Council. Although O'Neill ran hard, he lost by a narrow margin. The day before the election, O'Neill ran into his neighbor and former high school teacher, Mrs. O'Brien. During that time, O'Neill had consistently shoveled his neighbor's sidewalk after heavy snows and helped her with various other household tasks.[9]

When Mrs. O'Brien encountered O'Neill, she said, "I'm going to vote for you tomorrow even though you didn't ask me." He was surprised. They had known each other for decades, he reminded her, and he had been a devoted neighbor during that time. He didn't think he needed to ask for her vote. Her response was simple: "Let me tell you something: People like to be asked."

Successful fundraising operates on the same principle. The advocacy efforts that raise the most money are those that ask for money frequently and in a variety of different ways. Every fundraising effort should, at a minimum, include the following steps.

First, develop a list of the initial supporters of your cause. Start with your own individual and organizational contacts and ask them for financial support. This includes your personal circle—family, friends, and close contacts will give to the initiative because they trust and want to help you. If you cannot raise enough from this core group to support the campaign during its initial phases—at least 60 days— you may need to reconsider whether the advocacy effort is feasible. But if you are successful, you can build outward from those initial contacts. Designate your strongest initial supporters as members of the finance committee, and brainstorm with them to create an even bigger list of donors who may be interested in the initiative. Ask them to raise money for your effort from their own contacts, relationships, and networks. They should apply a basic fundraising rule: the best prospective donors are those who aren't in a position to say no when you call. If they are successful, the new contributors they recruited can reach out to their contacts, relationships, and

---

[9] Thomas P. "Tip" O'Neill with William Novak, *Man of the House: The Life and Political Memoirs of Speaker Tip O'Neill* (New York: Random House, 1987).

networks for even more potential donors. The goal is to have this process of soliciting new contributors who then find even more new donors take on a life of its own and become self-perpetuating. Meet frequently to continue brainstorming and discussing opportunities.

Second, look for individuals or groups that may have an economic interest in your success. For example, if your goal is to put your county on a program to reduce greenhouse gas emissions, companies that produce alternative fuels (such as ethanol) or specialize in "clean" technology may want to contribute to your cause. If potential customers in your area are more likely to patronize a "green friendly" business, you may also receive contributions from companies wanting to establish that reputation. Similarly, if your initiative seeks to give commercial property owners the same tax benefits given to residential owners, businesses that own commercial property, as well as real estate agents who broker its purchase and sale, will have every incentive to make sure that you are well funded.

Third, consider potential ideological allies. If your plan aims to create low-cost childcare options for uninsured working families, unions may want to lend a hand. If your aim is to reduce alcohol-related driving deaths by restricting local liquor sales to certain days or locations, socially conservative groups may assist you. A school-related initiative might win the support of the local parent-teacher-student association and relevant teachers' organizations.

Fourth, take advantage of low-cost fundraising tools. You and your fellow initiative leaders likely belong to clubs, neighborhood associations, fraternal and service organizations, and other groups that may provide names of potential donors. Additionally, look for previous advocacy efforts with political, economic, or ideological interests similar to your own. If the law allows it, and if the previous initiative is willing, see if you can use or purchase their fundraising lists.

Fifth, if your key supporters are unenthusiastic about calling friends and contacts to ask for checks, suggest that they host fundraising events at their homes or offices where potential donors meet cause leaders, learn about the initiative and its progress, and leave contributions. If you have an event, and the law allows, see if the main host or the cohosts will agree to donate the cost of refreshments so that the campaign does not have to spend money on food and drink.

Sixth, find a supporter with event-planning experience to oversee fundraising parties like those mentioned above. Without proper planning, a political fundraising event can easily end in failure. Additionally, a skilled and creative organizer may be able to schedule events that raise both money and awareness. For example, if your campaign is advocating the construction of a new professional baseball stadium in your community, it might work to schedule a high-profile fundraising game pitting current players against retired players. Fans would buy tickets and generate proceeds for the campaign, and media coverage would communicate a message of player support.

Seventh, use the mail. Although direct-mail fundraising is expensive (there are costs of printing, postage, and handling), it can be productive. If you take this approach, try to find accurate mailing lists for individuals and organizations with an interest in seeing your campaign succeed. Some lists can be obtained for free. Others are available for purchase from organizations that have compatible interests. Don't waste time on groups with little stake in your issue or candidate. If your goal were to preserve endangered species, the mailing lists of the local chapters of the Audubon Society (audubon.org) and National Wildlife Federation (nwf.org) would be valuable. The state dental society's list would not.

Eighth, use high-profile endorsements as a way to generate support. If your well-known supporter is willing to host or appear at fundraisers, hold benefit events, sell autographs or signed photographs, lend his or her name to direct-mail or Internet solicitations, or otherwise raise money, these efforts can have a powerful effect on the bottom line.

Ninth, invest in software that allows you to stay in close contact with donors and potential donors. The key to successful fundraising is not the initial "ask" but rather the follow-up. A contributor's promise to provide funds is of little benefit until it becomes money in the bank. Keep in touch with potential donors through e-mails, telephone calls, and written correspondence until their checks or credit card authorizations arrive. After the money is in the bank, send thank you notes and continue to keep donors engaged in the campaign. It is the polite thing to do, and it just might result in additional contributions. Constantly update financial commitments, contributions received, and donor and potential donor contact information in the campaign database you have purchased.

Tenth, ask for volunteers in addition to dollars. Quality volunteer assistance reduces your staff budget and increases the resources available to your campaign. You can "raise" volunteers in the same way that you raise financial contributions: Start with your core supporters and work outward to bring others into the cause.

Eleventh, use the Internet. The digital world is now the backbone of political fundraising—and for good reason, as it allows causes to send donors updates and solicitations almost instantaneously. In the past, robust Internet fundraising has usually been more practical for high-profile campaigns that attract significant media attention. The traditional model has involved sizeable start-up expenditures of money, time, and energy: hiring or finding dedicated volunteers to design and host a campaign webpage, purchasing and maintaining necessary computer systems and software for contribution collection, buying or renting e-mail lists of individuals and organizations that might have an interest in the campaign, updating the webpage continually, composing and distributing campaign news, and sending fundraising solicitations.

If your campaign or advocacy effort is big enough, you may have the resources and infrastructure to set up a robust donor communication program. If not, the easiest way for you to raise money online may be to focus on bringing potential small-dollar donors into the advocacy effort through more traditional methods while fastidiously collecting their e-mail addresses. For example, if you hold a fundraising event that fifty people attend, and each of them pays $25 to support your candidate or cause, you will have raised $1,250 and ensured that those individuals are now invested in your initiative. Having laid that foundation, you can ask them for funds by e-mail in the future and expect that at least some of those supporters will donate again. But we'll defer to an expert. In her tips (see Tips from the Pros: Digital Fundraising Success), digital strategist Taryn Rosenkranz offers five recommendations for effective online fundraising.

Digital Fundraising Success
TARYN ROSENKRANZ

In the movie *Field of Dreams* starring Kevin Costner, a whispering, disembodied voice tells an Iowa farmer, "If you build it, he will come." The farmer builds a baseball field, and the ghosts of the 1919 Chicago White Sox, including Shoeless Joe Jackson, do come. For many nationally known politicians, building a website is enough when it comes to raising money online. Folks literally Google the politician's name to find ways to contribute. Unfortunately, when you are trying to raise money online as an everyday American, it takes a little bit more than that to achieve optimal success. But, the truth is, if you build a successful e-mail program, they will come.

E-mail is still king when it comes to the largest source of revenue online. Building a successful digital fundraising program should focus on reaching supporters' in-boxes with smart content.

Here are my top five best practices from political campaigns that can help you to raise money for your citizen advocacy cause.

1. *Start a conversation.* It's important to send a mix of fundraising and non-fundraising e-mails to your supporters (i.e., don't just ask for money). In winning campaigns, we ask for volunteers, update the campaign contributors about the race on the ground, share articles, and ask for signatures on petitions for issues supporters care about. It isn't just a stream of endless fundraising e-mails. We tell the candidate's story and include the same narrative the campaign uses in its mail, television, and stump speeches. The same is true for whatever you are asking for in your e-mails—give them something, and you will get something back.
2. *Be authentic.* Your voice should be your voice. Make it personal and appeal to the reader. Find your voice, and use it to give urgent reasons for the supporter to give without giving up dignity.
3. *Give them a real reason to give.* We tell our campaign clients to think of fundraising like a transaction. Give campaign readers a real, concrete reason to give and why they need to give right now. The readers don't want to give to you, but they will if they have a concrete reason to do so. It's not enough to just ask; you have to tell them where donations will be put to work. For example, if you are advocating for a state initiative to fund the acquisition of environmentally sensitive and desirable recreation lands, indicate which properties from the potential donor's area are on the acquisition list and why acquiring and preserving them will make the community a better place to live.

(Continued)

(Continued)

4. ***Capturing attention doesn't always have to include a cat.*** In the 2014 elections, a number of candidates went over the top in using humor and cute cats and dogs in political e-mails. In some races, it worked. But if your persona or profile doesn't fit in the over-the-top category, find a different way. Your personal story may hit home better than any meme of a cat or dog. Garnering attention online doesn't have to be humorous. It can ask folks to take an action such as adding their name to a petition.

5. ***Include testing within your program, as it will help you to see what works or doesn't.*** Senator Al Franken can be funny because he is a professional comedian. Senator Elizabeth Warren can send really long wonky e-mails because that's her brand. Don't try to make your e-mails fit someone else's style. Test, target, and track results. You learn a lot from listening to the reactions of your supporters.

No matter what you do there are always some grievances. People will complain about the number of e-mails they receive regardless of how many they actually receive. But since in-boxes receive a lot of traffic, you may have to send more e-mails than you would prefer to make sure people see your message. The bottom line is that you can have a successful digital fundraising campaign without falling into the traps that snare so many others.

Taryn Rosenkranz is the founder and chief executive officer of New Blue Interactive (newblueinteractive.com), which has become a powerhouse firm in fewer than three years, providing digital strategy services to large organizations and party committees including the Democratic Congressional Campaign Committee (DCCC) and the House Majority PAC, as well as national groups such as the Natural Resources Defense Council. In addition, her clients include senators and congressional leadership and membership, as well as congressional challengers, mayors, and even candidates in county executive races. She has also counseled hundreds of candidates, nonprofits, and companies on online strategies, grassroots fundraising, and online advocacy. Her clients have raised $300 million collectively from grassroots efforts.

Internet fundraising has evolved to the point where online tools exist to serve your civic cause, no matter how big or small. Perhaps the most critical innovation is so-called "crowdfunding," where citizens have the opportunity to invest directly in the development of goods, products, initiatives or projects they support. These crowdfunding efforts are usually launched by the individuals or organizations seeking financial help, and tend to be facilitated by online platforms. Some of the best-known crowdfunding sites include kickstarter.com, gofundme.com, indiegogo.com, rally.org, and rockethub.com.

As local government revenues have stagnated or decreased in recent years, many communities have turned to crowdfunding to ease funding shortfalls for needed initiatives. Below, Jersey City Mayor Steven Fulop tells the story of how his community employed this technique to address its transportation challenges.

Another Case in Point	Following the Crowd in Jersey City
	By Steven Fulop

The Citi Bike bicycle sharing program, which came to Jersey City in September 2015, connects seamlessly with the corresponding New York City system that is pictured here. More than 19,000 bike trips were taken on Citi Bike Jersey City in its first month of operation.

Jersey City—soon to be the largest city in the state—sits across the Hudson River from Lower Manhattan and is home to a quarter million citizens. For all of those advantages, the long-time perception of our city was not good. Jersey City wasn't thought of as a place of good government. Crime was up. Spirits were down. Corruption was rampant. Our city's budget was in shambles.

But these perceptions are giving way to a new view of Jersey City. A big reason for that progress is the engagement of our residents, facilitated by our ability to use new tools to harness their desire for participation in Jersey City's success.

Like other communities, Jersey City is home to an increasing number of young people—such as Millennials. One of the challenges we faced is how to help these young people—and everyone else—get around.

Right now, our transportation system is congested and in disrepair. According to the American Society of Civil Engineers (asce.org), New Jersey roads are the sixth worst in the nation—a status that costs the average driver an extra $600 or so a year in wasted fuel and car repairs. Meanwhile, the Port Authority Trans-Hudson Corporation (PATH) light rail system, which connects us to Manhattan, is often packed door to door.[10]

---

[10] Port Authority of NY & NJ, "About PATH," www.panynj.gov/path/

Jersey City cannot fix these road and rail problems alone. They require state and federal participation. So we focused on a form of transportation on which we could have a huge impact: bicycles.

Our problem was that we didn't have the funding needed for new bike racks. So we harnessed the power of a new concept: crowdfunding.

Crowdfunding, made popular by sites such as GoFundMe (gofundme.com) and Kickstarter (kickstarter.com), are obviously more associated with obtaining seed funding for new technology products. But local governments are starting to think of crowdfunding sites as a way to address pressing community needs.

That's why, when we were looking at ways to fund new bike racks, we looked at crowdfunding. Together with local advocacy groups, including Bike JC (bikejc. org), Sustainable Jersey City (sustainablejc .org), and the Jersey City Art School (jcartschool.com), we worked with ioby.org, a crowdfunding platform. Our goal was to raise $20,000 over six weeks and to supplement those private funds with $16,000 in public funds.

We actually raised $38,000—enough to purchase 275 bike racks that had been designed by two local artists. And better yet, we also did some crowdsourcing to collect ideas from the citizens who donated funding. Each contributor had the right to vote—by dropping a pin on a Google map—on where he or she wanted a rack. All groups involved felt it was important to give residents the ability to decide where these racks were deployed. That way, people weren't just making a "donation" to their city; they were making an investment in their city and shaping the return on that investment.

Today, bike use in Jersey City is exploding. In September 2015, we became the first big city in New Jersey with a bike-share program, Citi Bike, which connects seamlessly with New York City's bike-share system. More than 19,000 trips were taken on Citi Bike Jersey City (citibikejc.com) in the first month, and over 1,000 people signed up for the bike-share system.[11]

Simply put, our shift towards more sustainable transportation would not be as pronounced without crowdfunding and crowdsourcing. This project illustrated that success is possible when cities and community organizations work together both to advance the quality of life in our city and to raise real money from the community for a significant project. We look forward to similar efforts for other sustainability projects in our city.

This approach can also work for other communities. The opportunity for the cities of the twenty-first century to thrive lies in using emerging technologies to escalate citizen engagement and feedback. It is not enough to keep residents informed on Twitter, Facebook, or other social media platforms. Millennials want more. They are eager to serve their communities though technology that brings about change far more rapidly than in generations past.

In Jersey City, we will be using crowdfunding and crowdsourcing not just to raise funds for future needs but also to learn where and how government resources should best be used.

---

[11] Terrence T. McDonald, *Jersey Journal*, October 27, 2015, www.nj.com/hudson/index.ssf/2015/10/more_than_19k_trips_taken_on_citi_bike_jersey_city.html

This is just the beginning. We're excited to see what the "crowd"—also known as our community—comes up with next.

On May 14, 2013, Steven Michael Fulop was elected the 49th mayor of Jersey City, New Jersey. He previously served eight years on the Jersey City Council. The son of Romanian immigrants, Mayor Fulop is a first-generation American, a lifelong New Jerseyan, and a triathlete. After graduating from Binghamton University, he joined Goldman Sachs, the investment banking firm, working in Chicago and later in Manhattan and Jersey City. On the morning of September 11, 2001, Steve was working in lower Manhattan when he saw the first plane strike the Twin Towers. A few weeks later, he decided to put his career at Goldman Sachs on hold and join the United States Marine Corps.

Jersey City is not alone in its use of crowdfunding to invest in community needs. Recovering from a rare municipal bankruptcy, Central Falls, Rhode Island, raised $10,000 through crowdfunding to clean up its major municipal park.[12] Naperville, Illinois, relied on crowdfunding to install a historic statue.[13] In San Antonio, Texas, community leaders like the San Antonio Parks Foundation (saparksfoundation.org) and residents of the rapidly growing Irish Flats neighborhood hope to raise some of the dollars needed to redesign and revitalize city-owned Maverick Park through a crowdfunding campaign.[14]

Some of the same funding innovations that have built bike racks in Jersey City and filled funding gaps in other cities can work for you as well. New civic crowdfunding tools can help local governments and civic advocates raise money for important projects that might otherwise go unfunded. As Mayor Fulop explains, Jersey City worked with ioby.org. Other communities have paired with citizinvestor.com. The National Parks and Conservation Association (NPCA) gives people the opportunity to invest in park improvements through fundyourpark.org. Spacehive.com primarily operates in the United Kingdom. Neighborly.com helps citizens invest directly in community capital initiatives.[15] As was the case in Jersey City, crowdfunding technologies like these simultaneously generate financial support and encourage citizens to become active community participants.

The Internet can also be a robust tool for recruiting volunteers who expand your resources and lower your costs. Websites such as VolunteerMatch.org, Network for Good (networkforgood.org), or Idealist (idealist.org) match eager volunteers with like-minded causes. Additionally, the rise of telecommuting allows volunteers to help from home with conducting research, drafting press releases and other campaign communications, developing potential volunteer and donor lists, and performing other tasks that conserve resources for your advocacy effort.

---

[12] Denise Fedorow, "Civic Crowdfunding," *The Municipal*, June 2, 2015, www.themunicipal.com/2015/06/civic-crowdfunding/

[13] Drew Lindsay, "Local Governments and Nonprofits Test Crowdfunding for Civic Projects," *The Chronicle of Philanthropy*, January 7, 2015, philanthropy.com/article/Local-Governments-and/152005

[14] Jen Kinney, "San Antonio Crowdfunds for 'World-Class' Dog Park," *Next City*, February 18, 2016, nextcity.org/daily/entry/san-antonio-park-public-space-design-dog-park-crowdfunding

[15] Anusha Alikhan, "Neighbor.ly Expands Crowdfunding Service for Civic Projects with Knight Foundation Funding," *Knight Foundation*, June 18, 2013, www.knightfoundation.org/press-room/press-release/neighborly-expands-crowdfunding-service-civic-proj/

3. Establish a Finance Infrastructure

Poorly led and unorganized finance operations are doomed to failure. As you create yours, make sure that trustworthy and competent people hold the key positions and that each of them has clear lines of authority. Before former Rhode Island Auditor General Ernie Almonte guides you through some of the key requirements of effective citizen advocacy finance management in his tip (see Tips from the Pros: The One B and Five Cs of Financial Management), we first want to stress four vital principles for your fundraising efforts.

First, don't mess around with the bookkeeping. Campaign accounting is inherently complicated, and mistakes can put a candidate or initiative in serious legal and political jeopardy. It is critical that you appoint a competent and trustworthy treasurer to be accountable for money management. If yours is a formal political campaign or citizen advocacy organization, most jurisdictions require campaigns to appoint a treasurer. The treasurer also works closely with the initiative leaders and staff to record all donations and report them in the legally required manner.

Even if you are not required by law to have a treasurer, appointing one is a good practice. And don't be penny wise and pound foolish. If you need to hire a qualified treasurer to make sure the books are properly managed, do it. For small grassroots campaigns that cannot afford to pay staff, ask someone to serve whom you would trust with your life—or whose strong integrity can be verified by others.

Second, as Ronald Reagan said, "Trust, but verify." Buy personal-warranty insurance against the risk of inappropriate behavior. Ask Dennis DeConcini, former U.S. senator from Arizona, why this matters. His treasurer stole hundreds of thousands of dollars from the campaign coffers.

Third, know the law—or enlist the help of someone who does. Campaign or advocacy organization financing is heavily regulated at the federal, state, and local levels. It is very important that you comply with the spirit and letter of those laws, rules, and regulations. Otherwise, you will be subject to legal punishments, which could include fines and, in some extreme cases, disqualification. Furthermore, the media will often report finance violations, and this negative press coverage will cast your initiative in an unflattering light. So it is in your interests to find an attorney with the necessary legal expertise to serve as your advocacy initiative's legal adviser and help you navigate the often tangled web of finance laws and regulations. Sound legal advice will help you avoid common pitfalls. If you don't have sufficient funds to pay for an attorney or have a supporter from within your ranks who is an attorney to act in that capacity, see if you can find one who will volunteer or donate his or her time. If you live in a community with a law school, this person might be a law school professor who is willing to advise you on the campaign's financial and legal issues.

Fourth, if you do have to provide public information on your advocacy fundraising, don't view disclosure deadlines and reports simply as operational requirements imposed by law. In truth, fundraising reports are opportunities for you to share news about campaign progress. If you raise substantial amounts of money during a fundraising period, media outlets will view that achievement as tangible evidence of your campaign's strength. Conversely, if you don't have success in a fundraising period, you'll need to present that data to the media in a way that minimizes any harmful public perception.

In campaign or advocacy financing, few things demoralize the staff more than having what you thought was a successful fundraising period only to read in the newspaper that you raised "less than expected." When it comes to political contributions, you should set expectations carefully. No sane professional football coach would guarantee a Super Bowl victory in his first year, and you shouldn't promise the moon and the stars in political fundraising. Keep your expectations at a level where you can surpass them.

Money raised and spent is the immediate focus of any disclosure report, but reports provide you with other opportunities to share good news about your initiative. Especially in local campaigns, the sheer number of people who have made contributions, regardless of the amount, can be a critical sign of community support. Your goal should be to collect donations from as many different individuals, organizations (if legally permissible), and interests as possible. Pay particular attention to contributors whose support will create positive buzz for the campaign. These include well-respected community members, significant numbers of donors from a highly regarded profession or occupation ("Small business owners support our campaign"), members of a particular demographic ("More women gave to our campaign than to the other side"), or geographic group ("At least one person from every precinct has contributed").

TIPS FROM THE PROS

The One B and Five Cs of Financial Management
ERNIE ALMONTE

Congratulations. You've made the decision to shape public policy or lead a campaign to champion a public cause. Unfortunately, without a financial plan and the funds to deliver your message, you might as well just put this idea on your bucket list. You're not ready!

Before telling the world about your mission, you must develop a finance plan, which requires Budgeting (the one B) and the five Cs (Cash flow, Compliance, Communication, Competence, and Collaboration).

Budgeting

As you would with your personal finances, you must know how much money is coming in and how much is needed to pay your expenses. A budget will help you take control of your finances, outline spending priorities, and plan for recurring and unexpected expenses. Running an organization without a budget is like driving down a dark back road with your headlights off—something bad is likely to happen.

A budget should include all expected contributions, loans, matching funds, and any other cash to be received by the organization. It should also include all expenses, broken down by month and listed according to when the expenses must be paid. Bonus tip: If your cause requires a voter referendum, create a weekly budget for the two months leading up to Election Day.

Your budget should be prepared around your strategy and reflect key strategic decisions, such as fundraising plans, organizational priorities, the best time

(Continued)

(Continued)

to pay for advertising, and how much to spend on professional advisers. Don't forget to revisit your budget at each high-level organization meeting—compare your plan against actual income and expenses. Consider purchasing software to help you build a budget and track your progress; be sure to select software that helps you comply with laws, regulations, and any filing requirements.

The Five Cs

Cash flow. The timing of income and expenses is critical, so plan ahead. The ability to raise necessary funds at the right time will greatly improve your chances of success. I've seen many organizations fail because they lack available cash to pay for priorities on a timely basis. Late payments could cost the organization in many ways: late fees, inability to hire professional advisers, higher prices, and, worst of all, inability to execute according to your plan.

Compliance. In any organization, noncompliance with laws and regulations can lead to the perception that you lack the ability to manage and are therefore unqualified to speak on behalf of your cause.

Appoint someone to oversee your organization's registration, form filing (including deadlines), and closing out of any election-related responsibilities. Personal loans to your organization must comply with laws and could affect your ability to receive matching funds. I've found election offices and the Secretary of State are extremely helpful in providing compliance information.

Communication. Clear communication is critical, whether you're talking about the issues or your organization's finances. In my experience, the media always asks how much cash was raised and how much cash was on hand. Reporters want these questions answered every time they call. You must have the answers readily available.

Communication gives you the ability to control the message. Savvy messaging about a strong quarter of fundraising will encourage others to donate to your cause and show the opposition that you're a legitimate policy leader.

Competence. Hiring the right professionals to oversee the financial plan is another important piece of the puzzle. Take your time and make smart decisions, but also be willing to make changes when necessary.

Taking out insurance bonds on the people who will handle your finances will help reduce risk. Even though you've conducted a rigorous interview process before hiring finance personnel, fraud is always a possibility. The bond will provide coverage in case of fraud, allowing you to be reimbursed for any missing funds.

Engaging competent individuals does not exempt you from oversight. You must hold your leadership accountable and ask challenging questions regarding finances and other areas of your organization.

Reputational risk is real and costly—to you personally and to your organization. As the leader, you should seek ways to manage the overall risks of your organization. This includes an honest assessment as to whether you are the right person to lead this organization.

Collaboration. Collaborating with others can provide necessary information and potentially reduce expenses. Sharing expenses with other advocacy efforts can free up cash for priority needs. High-level volunteers can often provide valuable input without tapping your cash reserves. Coordinating with organizations with similar goals can help leverage the delivery of your message at no cost to your advocacy effort.

Ernie Almonte CPA is a partner at RSM US LLP (rsmus.com), the fifth largest U.S. accounting, tax, and consulting firm. He is the former Rhode Island auditor general, the former Department of Defense Audit Advisory Committee chairman, the former American Institute of CPAs (aicpa.org) chairman, and a former candidate for R.I. general treasurer. He has more than 35 years of financial and consulting experience.

4. Be Creative

Although advocacy fundraising has certain basic tenets you should follow, it does not have to be a rote and tedious process. As anti-malaria advocates did through Nothing But Nets, brainstorm ways to be innovative. Creative approaches to raising money can invigorate your effort and attract the interest of potential donors. Just ask Sean Tevis.

Another Case in Point   Comic Relief

Two years after Rick Reilly started his effort to buy mosquito nets, Sean Tevis launched a quixotic political campaign. Arlen Siegfried was a senior and respected Republican member of the Kansas House of Representatives—a Goliath in the politics of the Sunflower State. In 2008 his reelection to a fourth term seemed assured. And then his David appeared in the form of Tevis, a 39-year-old web designer who had not run for office since high school. He didn't have a great deal of name recognition or financial support in the suburban Kansas community in which he was running (Olathe—birthplace of the cowboy boot). He was running as a Democrat in a district in which Republicans outnumbered Democrats almost two to one. At first, Tevis ran a traditional campaign. He spent the first weeks of his campaign asking friends and family for financial contributions and knocking on doors for support. But the people being asked, like many Americans, were drowning under high gas prices and mortgage payments and lived in fear of losing their jobs. Tevis's efforts raised $1,525—a drop in the bucket compared to the resources his opponent would have. Tevis was a realist. He recognized that he had to do something to enhance his name recognition and to finance the campaign. So Tevis turned back to what he knew best and designed a campaign website that he hoped would turn heads.

On July 16, 2008, Sean launched his website: seantevis.com. Some of the features were standard political fare. The front page showed a serious man making direct eye contact with site visitors. The easily navigated page had two hallmark messages: "Let's Make Government Work for US" and "No Sales Tax on Food." From there, the viewer was led to crisply written positions on three issues: no tax on food, best schools in the U.S.A., and transparency in government. The other drop-downs implored visitors to join the campaign, make direct contact with Sean, read Sean's succinct biography (concluding with "He loves Olathe"), and take advantage of the opportunity to donate to his campaign. But what set Tevis's website apart was his commitment to innovation.

He tells the story of his campaign in a comic strip. In one of these comics, stick-figure candidate Sean receives advice from a bearded stick-figure strategist. At one point, as Sean frets about the need to raise money, his bearded strategist consoles him. "Relax," he says. "You just need 52 people who can contribute $500." A dispirited Tevis replies, "I know **two**." Then, he hatches a new plan to raise the needed campaign funds. Rather than ask for $500 from each supporter, he will ask for $8.34. Why that small amount? Tevis had been told that the cost to run as a challenger for a Kansas House seat was $26,000. So with the $1,000 total contribution from his two big supporters, he decides he needs about $25,000. Most candidates would try to follow the bearded stick figure's advice and seek $500 to $1,000 from 25 to 50 supporters. By Tevis's calculations, if he could get 3,000 contributors the cost would be only $8.34 per donor. Moreover, targeting large numbers of small donations from everyday people would also highlight his decision to forgo donations from lobbyists—and serve as a contrast to his opponent, who was accepting lobbyist contributions.

Tevis's page also featured his own blog—a day-by-day diary of what it is like to run for public office the first time. This blog made his efforts both accessible and authentic. But the best website that nobody sees is like the tree falling in the forest with nobody around to hear it. So Tevis sent his website to a network of 200–300 fellow web programmers and asked it they would link to it from their sites. The results were stunning. In a week, almost 10 people per second were visiting his site. In 35 days, over 750,000 individuals had visited. More than 6,200 visitors contributed in excess of $100,000— 18 by check and the rest through credit cards. In that same period, Tevis received almost 3,000 e-mails of support and encouragement. His creative efforts won the attention of state and national news outlets including the *Los Angeles Times*, *Wall Street Journal*, and National Public Radio. On Election Day 2008, Democrat Barack Obama lost Kansas by 57 percent to 41 percent. Sean Tevis didn't win either—but he almost did. Of 10,000 votes cast, a mere 425 votes separated him from his opponent. Goliath, beware.[16]

Rick Reilly's crusade to save African children from malaria and Sean Tevis's near-victory in a seemingly impossible electoral challenge show that ingenuity can generate the financial resources an advocacy effort needs to succeed. Put on your thinking cap, brainstorm with your allies, and find innovative ways to interest potential donors in making contributions to fuel your citizen initiative.

5. Demonstrate Financial Credibility to Decision Makers

Though the financial resources you raise for your citizen advocacy effort are important in themselves, they are not the only funds that may be necessary in the process. If you are asking government officials to take action that will involve public dollars, you are likely to be asked two questions: "Does this cost anything?" and "How do we pay for this?" Without good answers to those questions, you are likely to see your credibility damaged and your chances of success diminished. You are more likely to win agreement if you can guide the decision maker to funding.

---

[16]Stephanie Simon, "Politics Is National in Local Web Campaign," *Wall Street Journal*, July 29, 2008, www.wsj.com/articles/SB121729442687591943; Maria Carter, "Internet Cartoon Pays Off for Kansas Candidate," *NPR*, August 12, 2008, www.npr.org/templates/story/story.php?storyId=93346096; P.J. Huffstutter, "Kansan Sticks It to Election System: A Simple Online Comic Strip Raises Heaps for His Democratic Bid," *Los Angeles Times*, July 28, 2008, articles.latimes.com/2008/jul/28/nation/na-candidate28; Mike Hendricks, "Web-Savvy Loser Has Much to Teach Other Candidates," KansasCity.com, November 6, 2008. See also, for a reproduction of the cartoon described, Giles Bowkett's blog from Friday, November 7, 2008, "Web 2.0 Increases Freedom, Not Threatens It," gilesbowkett.blogspot.ca/2008/11/web-20-increases-freedom-not-threatens.html

Some of that funding may be money that you provide or locate. As governments at every level continue to struggle with budget challenges, many elected officials want to see private investment or partnership from other levels of government before they agree to supplement it with their fiscal support. What skin are you and your allies willing to put in the game? Make an acceptable answer to that question a precondition of moving forward with your citizen initiative. Let's say your cause is to add tennis and basketball courts to a currently passive neighborhood park. If you are going to ask your county or city government to pay for those courts, are you and your fellow neighbors willing to meet a condition that you raise the money to maintain the new facilities? Do you have a plan for generating those funds? Are grants available from advocacy organizations like the United States Tennis Association (USTA, usta.com/About-USTA/USTA-Awards/grants) or the National Recreation and Park Association (NRPA, www.nrpa.org/fundraising-resources)? What about a state government agency such as the Washington State Recreation and Conservation Office (rco.wa.gov/grants/yaf.shtml)? If you can't answer yes to these questions, then you may have a harder time persuading public decision makers to invest in the project.

Credibility isn't just a question of your willingness to put up private funding. You should also aid decision makers in identifying a public funding source for the proposed initiative. Because few elected officials like raising taxes and many would rather avoid spending cuts that may upset part of their constituency, help them generate alternatives. Does the government budget have available funding that is not otherwise assigned, such as unspent appropriations or earned interest? Is your initiative eligible for federal, state, or philanthropic grants? Diligent citizen advocates who can bring the decision maker a potential funding source to pay for a proposal are much more likely to win support.

Your first step on the path to fiscal credibility is to understand and successfully navigate the budget process of the government you are seeking to persuade. In his tips (See Tips from the Pros: Mastering Local Budgets), municipal budget director Tom Greene explains what you need to know to make elected and appointed decision makers open to funding your initiative.

TIPS FROM THE PROS

Mastering Local Budgets
TOM GREENE

If your citizen advocacy goal is to persuade county or city officials to improve a park, open a fire station closer to your home, or increase library hours, then you will be asking those officials to spend public money. Understanding the process through which they make those fiscal decisions, and knowing how to make your cause an attractive investment prospect, will greatly enhance your chances of ultimate success.

(Continued)

(Continued)

Learn the Budget

The first key to convincing decision makers that your initiative is worth funding is to speak their same budget language. Don't worry if that feels like a daunting challenge when you pick up the typically thick budget book. With a few quick pointers, you too will be able to open your community's budget and better understand where your money goes, how your city or county invests those dollars, and how you can identify funding opportunities for your initiative.

Before any discussion of influencing a local government budget, you must understand several fundamental budgeting concepts:

1. Budgets are about priorities.
2. Local governments have limited resources.
3. An annual budget is the plan for how a local government will invest limited resources.
4. Local governments are generally required to have a balanced budget (i.e., budgeted revenues must be equal to or greater than budgeted expenses).
5. In most localities, the mayor or city manager (executive branch) proposes the budget, while the city or county council/commission (legislative branch) revises that proposed budget and enacts a final budget.

Your mission is to convince the mayor or city manager (the chief executive officer) and members of the city council or commission (the governing body) that your idea is a worthy endeavor and should be included in the local budget.

Know the Difference between General and Capital Spending

One of the first issues you will encounter as you read your city's budget is that there are many different funds. There is a good reason for this. Local governments practice what is referred to as "fund accounting," which means that different funds are established to account for the revenues and expenditures of providing different services. In most cases, the two funding sources of greatest importance to your initiative will be the so-called General Operating Fund, or "General Fund," and the Capital Improvement Plan, or "CIP."

The General Fund is typically where a local government collects ad valorem revenue from property taxes as well as other general taxes such as sales taxes and utility taxes. It also funds traditional governmental services such as public safety (police and fire protection), parks and recreation, libraries, and codes enforcement services.

Another potential funding source is the capital improvement budget or Capital Improvement Plan, often referred to as the CIP. The CIP may fund the acquisition of parklands, the construction of city facilities like libraries, playgrounds, and recreation centers, or major infrastructure creation and maintenance such as resurfacing roads and streets or replacing water and sewer pipes, to name a few.

CIP funding can come from various sources such as grants, borrowing, or transfers from operating funds such as a water utility. Some communities have dedicated funding sources that provide annual resources for capital improvements. For example, Pinellas County, Florida, has a 1 percent sales tax known as the Penny for Pinellas.

Let's use libraries to show the difference between General Fund and CIP expenditures. If your goal is to increase hours at your neighborhood library, the dollars needed to pay for additional staff time and other related expenses would come from the General Fund budget. But if the mission is to build a new library branch or renovate an existing library facility, the CIP budget is the likely source.

Now that you know these basic principles, it's time to take your proposal to the elected and appointed officials who will decide whether your proposed initiative becomes part of the budget. But before you make your case, you have some assignments to ensure you can answer the questions those decision makers are sure to ask.

Respect the Zero-Sum Game

Elected officials are particularly aware that every dollar spent as part of a county or city budget is a dollar that could have been spent somewhere else. If they are saying yes to you, they may be saying no to someone else. These budgeting trade-offs are particularly challenging during periods of economic downturns when local budgets are strained. Be sensitive to this dilemma and give officials every reason to choose your proposal over others.

An Investment—Not an Expense?

Anyone can ask for money for a pet project, but those who are successful in securing funding discuss their initiative in terms of the investment. It is much easier for local officials to make an investment that has a tangible return than to just spend limited resources because someone asks. Take time to develop the story of why your investment is needed and how it will provide significant return to the residents of the community.

Skin in the Game?—The Case of the Warehouse Art District

If you and your advocacy allies have "skin in the game," the probability of success is exponentially increased. Quantify, to the extent possible, the funding commitments you have from the private sector and other levels of government (e.g., grants) when you ask local decision makers to support the investment. Their comfort level in your proposal will grow if they know other investors have endorsed it with their wallets.

In St. Petersburg, our thriving arts community is an extremely active economic driver. Recently, a group approached the city and asked for an investment to acquire a building. The building will provide cost-effective warehouse space for local artists in a cooperative setting to act as a catalyst for growing the business of the arts in our city. The Warehouse Arts District, Inc. had already raised $250,000 toward the purchase of the building, and was seeking $75,000 in city funding to complete the transaction. In light of the private support for an initiative that would help grow the arts business in our city, Mayor Kriseman recommended and the City Council quickly approved this investment.

(Continued)

(Continued)

Be Transparent about One-Time Investments vs. Recurring Expenses

Nothing hurts a citizen's credibility like selling decision makers on an investment that will cost $100,000 today—but forgetting to tell them it will also require $25,000 annually over the next decade. Carefully consider this concept as you advocate for your initiative. For example, if you want your city to construct a new playground, there will most assuredly be a one-time expense for the initial construction. But what is the cost of operating and maintaining the playground in year two and beyond? Conversely, a true one-time investment, such as the down payment assistance discussed above for the Warehouse Arts District, does not include any ongoing expenses. Know the difference, as local officials will be keenly interested in how today's funding decisions impact tomorrow's financial realities.

Tom Greene is Director of Budget and Management for the City of St. Petersburg, Florida (stpete.org). For 15 years, he has been involved in public finance both in the private sector, as an investment banker, and in the public sector. Mr. Greene served on the staff of United States Senator Bob Graham in Washington, D.C., and Tampa, Florida, where he worked as a senior policy advisor on issues ranging from agriculture, appropriation, banking, and budgeting. Mr. Greene earned a master of arts from The George Washington University, Graduate School of Political Management and a bachelor of arts from the University of South Florida.

As explained earlier in this chapter and in Tom Greene's tips, your chances of securing the necessary financial support for your advocacy goals increase substantially if you can leverage outside resources. In her tips (see Tips from the Pros: Thinking Outside the Fiscal Box), LeAnna Gutierrez Cumber provides expert guidance on the types of innovative funding that might be available to assist your cause in its budgetary needs.

TIPS FROM THE PROS

Thinking Outside the Fiscal Box
LEANNA GUTIERREZ CUMBER

While finding government funding for a citizen initiative has never been easy, economic and political conditions over the last decade have made the challenge harder than ever.

The major global recession that started in 2008 had a devastating impact on federal, state, and local revenues, leaving most governments in a cost-cutting mode that left little room for new investments. Then, in 2011, Congress abolished earmarking, a process by which members could steer federal dollars to specific projects located in their states or districts. Although earmarked funds actually accounted for a very small percentage of the overall federal budget, the process became politically untenable due to public controversy over projects of questionable merit.

These limitations on traditional funding sources such as annually budgeted revenues from income, sales, or property taxes have increased the need for citizens to explore non-traditional financing alternatives for their advocacy goals. In some cases, these atypical approaches are the only way to fund a citizen initiative when no regular governmental funding is available. Even when governments have some dollars to invest, they are much more likely to choose your project over others if you can leverage funding you have already brought to the table. For example, if you are asking your city council to fund a local museum exhibit, you will help your case if you can tell councilors you have won a National Endowment for the Humanities grant (neh.gov/grants) to cover part of the cost.

If you're looking for a substitute or a supplement to the usual governmental budgeting process, the tools at your disposal include grants and innovative financing options such as low interest or subsidized loans, loan guarantees, and private activity bonds.

Grants tend to be the most attractive financing options and also the most challenging to obtain. Types of grants range from formula grants, which are allocated to state and local governments using complex statutory formulas, to discretionary grants. Your efforts will probably be directed at the latter category.

There are federal, state, local, and private resources to help you determine if grants are available for your needs:

- Federal discretionary grant opportunities can be found on grants.gov.
- Many states have grant agencies, such as the Maryland Governor's Grants Office (grants.maryland.gov), the Minnesota Office of Grants Management (grants.state.mn.us/public), or the Nevada State Grant Office (grant.nv.gov). Check your state government resources to determine what is available.
- Local jurisdictions—like the City of Carlsbad, CA (carlsbadca.gov/business/grants.asp), the City of Boise, ID (hcd.cityofboise.org/grants), or the City of Phoenix, AZ (phoenix.gov/residents/grants)—have grant offices. See if your city or county has a similar agency.
- Find private grant dollars through comprehensive websites like the Foundation Center (foundationcenter.org/findfunders) and the Grantsmanship Center (tgci.com/funding-sources). Well-known philanthropic or private grantors include the Bill and Melinda Gates Foundation (gatesfoundation.org/How-We-Work/General-Information/Grant-Opportunities), Ford Foundation (fordfoundation.org/work/our-grants), Robert Wood Johnson Foundation (rwjf.org/en/how-we-work/grants), Walmart Foundation (giving.walmart.com/apply-for-grants), or William and Flora Hewitt Foundation (hewlett.org/grants).
- Some organizations focus their grants on specific issues. For example, clothing company Patagonia (patagonia.com) and philanthropic organization

(Continued)

(Continued)

Captain Planet Foundation (captainplanetfoundation.org) provide funding for environmental initiatives. The Bob Woodruff Foundation (bobwoodrufffoundation.org/grants) supports efforts to assist post-9/11 veterans who are wounded, injured, or ill. Look for funders that have demonstrated a clear interest in your advocacy goals.

Due to the competitive nature of discretionary grants, it is often more effective to monitor the specific federal, state, local, or philanthropic agency that has jurisdiction over your area of interest for relevant grant announcements. For grant opportunities closer to home, reach out to local grant funding agencies personally to see what may be coming available in the near future.

Other forms of financing such as low interest and subsidized loans tend to fund infrastructure projects and are available on a rolling basis, in which applications are reviewed and rated as they are received. Information about these programs can be found on the relevant agency or department websites. If an innovative financing option appears to fit your project, the first step is to contact the public employee noted as the point of contact and talk through your project and available options.

When considering which, if any, of these innovative financing options make sense for your project, be sure to consider the following factors:

- *What is the timeline?* Agencies offering innovative financing tools want project completion dates to be near term. In other words, financing is usually not awarded to projects that will start far into the future. For example, child nutrition grants are awarded annually with the understanding that the funds will be used immediately. But some projects naturally have longer timelines. Large infrastructure initiatives would have extended pre-construction as well as post-construction periods. You must understand the time line for a project, so you do not seek financing for a plan that is not truly ready.
- *Do funding sources have specific requirements?* Many grants and innovative financing tools have key prerequisites. For example, environmental clearance is a prerequisite for some financing opportunities.
- *What will the project cost?* A project is unlikely to be competitive if its advocates don't know the full costs. Take care to understand a project's scope clearly and have a detailed cost estimate that will allow auditors to track expenditures.
- *Should I look for a grant or a loan?* If you cannot repay a loan, do not have collateral to pledge, and lack a revenue stream to secure a loan, a grant may be your better, or only, option. But grants are not always preferable. If attainable for your project, a low interest loan with very agreeable repayment terms may be better, especially because some loan programs provide financing terms of up to 30 years. Often, the best way to finance an initiative is to utilize both grants and loans.

Once you decide which innovative financing tool works best for you, it is important to follow several steps:

- *Meet with the awarding agency to discuss available financing tools.* These meetings are not only critical to promoting the project with the people who award it but also potentially helpful in determining the best financing structure for your initiative. The initial meeting also helps set realistic time lines for approval of a grant or loan. Therefore, staff is always willing to discuss potential projects and how innovative financing might help.
- *Determine which other public and private entities would be able to contribute to the cost of the project.* A truly competitive public-private partnership demonstrates financial commitments from a variety of sources.
- *Demonstrate local public support.* Governments are generally not interested in funding projects that local citizens do not want. Strong local support for a project will aid your efforts to find innovative financing. Significant opposition will hurt your chances to secure funds.
- *Win support from elected officials.* Your project must have not only grassroots support but also backing from local, state, and federal elected officials. This support provides the awarding agency with confirmation that a project is not being forced upon a local community.
- *Respect application requirements and deadlines.* It is imperative that you read and fully understand the parameters and deadlines that govern the grant or other financing alternatives you have chosen. Due to the competitive nature of these options, deadlines are firm and cannot be missed. Furthermore, it is critical to address the criteria described in the financing notices to the extent possible, or your application will not be competitive.

Securing innovative financing can appear to be a complicated process, but it is entirely within your reach with careful planning and persistence.

LeAnna Gutierrez Cumber has over 13 years of experience in rail and seaport development planning, fiscal planning, project funding, and government affairs. She began her transportation career as lead transportation legislative counsel to the Senate Commerce Committee Ranking Member Senator Bill Nelson (FL). She went on to work in the Office of the Inspector General of the U.S. Department of Transportation's legal and legislative office under the Bush administration. She now heads up LeAnna Cumber & Associates specializing in grants and innovative financing in the transportation sector.

When you master the process and locate innovative sources of funding, you have the tools necessary to convince decision makers of your legitimacy. As Jonathan Trichter describes, citizens in Newburyport, Massachusetts, demonstrated how fiscal credibility can be powerful in persuading elected officials that an advocacy initiative is worthy of support.

| **Another Case in Point** | **Soccer Advocates Net Goals in Newburyport** |
| | *By Jonathan Trichter* |

Christopher Futcher/iStock

Grassroots efforts by the Newburyport Youth Soccer Association (NYSA) helped encourage scenes like this in Newburyport, Massachusetts, where advocates built a full high-school-sized soccer facility and a recreational space that transforms into fields for youth soccer and other activities.

Newburyport, Massachusetts, is a traditionally blue-collar town with limited open space for large recreational fields and the sports that require them. Then, in the 1980s, three developments increased the demand for playing space even more.

First, there was an emerging interest in youth activities. Second, there was an explosion in the popularity of soccer—a sport that is relatively inexpensive and easy to learn. Third, Coca-Cola launched the first "global sponsorship" for a sport, which amounted to unprecedented support for soccer programs that expanded the sport's reach like nothing before. Consequently, more kids were going out for soccer than most densely populated urban areas could accommodate with field space. Newburyport was no different.

Nonetheless, the Newburyport Youth Soccer Association (NYSA, newburyport-soccer.com) did its best to field new leagues for children, even sharing facilities with the local high school. But by the 1980s, demand was far outstripping access to fields, and the problem was growing worse every year.

That's when the NYSA began its effort to expand the town's soccer facilities. It took 10 years and required legislation and grassroots pressure. It also required the careful collection and presentation of data and an ability to communicate a vision that all Newburyport residents could appreciate—not just soccer moms. Mostly, though, it required public and private financing of around $750,000. Without that, the project never would have succeeded.

NYSA's success offers several lessons for effective citizen engagement. Local soccer advocates defined the problem broadly, so the effort was less about one sport and more about healthy childhood development. They also honored the principle that a picture is worth 1000 words by investing in design drawings that brought the project—new fields along with recreational space and parking—alive for the public and Newburyport decision makers. And they diligently gathered compelling data, which demonstrated consistent growth in soccer participation across all age-groups—and both sexes.

But where the NYSA effort really excelled was in its financial credibility.

Many well-intentioned citizen groups have a naïveté when it comes to public funding. Costly pet projects rarely go anywhere, as elected officials have their hands full with simply balancing their operating budget. Importantly, no politician is going to stick his or her neck out for a project that may wind up only partially completed, as that is a potential political catastrophe.

The NYSA avoided these pitfalls by demonstrating available sources of money and tight controls around the budget. First, soccer advocates developed an attainable plan of finance with almost a third of the project's investment coming from its own savings, about a third from state grants, and the final third or so from a bank loan secured by NYSA's assets. Second, the NYSA ran the numbers every which way, building in reserves for any unexpected overruns. Last but not least, they prepared credible financial projections that showed how membership growth would generate future revenues. These steps left little room for financial doubt or criticism.

The NYSA's careful financial planning paid dividends. With its existing assets and revenue projections, NYSA was able to secure a direct loan from a local bank for $200K. NYSA pledged another $200K of its own reserves. At that point, NYSA could claim it would be responsible for almost 60 percent of the total project costs. It leveraged those private dollars, plus grass roots community support and flawlessly prepared applications, into three state grants in the total amount of $284K. With total funds of $684,000 on hand, future revenues and local business sponsorships were pledged to cover the remaining $66,000 needed for the project.

The only remaining hurdle was local legislative support. The proposed land for the new fields was city-owned property, so the project required mayoral authorization and council approval. NYSA's detailed and attainable financing package was critical to winning legislative passage. In the end, all the mayor and council were being asked to do was to vote on a popular plan that had community support and full funding. Because that made for a relatively easy affirmative vote, NYSA won the right to build a full high-school-sized soccer facility, another new recreational space that transforms into two fields for youth soccer and other recreational activities, and both parking and egress improvements.

Considering the economic realities many local governments face today—steep pension obligations, high debt burdens, declining revenues, and deteriorating infrastructure—funding will be at the core of whether any popular effort for a new program or public amenity can be successful. Citizen advocates who present a financially credible plan are much more likely to prevail.

The people of Newburyport owe a special debt to NYSA Field Director Kevin Winn, NYSA Treasurer Scott Signore, and Coach Larry Kiszka, whose vision is responsible for NYSA's success.

Jonathan Trichter is a principal at The MAEVA Group, a restructuring and turnaround boutique and merchant bank with an additional specialty in municipal restructuring and public finance.

CHECKLIST FOR ACTION

☐ Determine how much money you need.
☐ Develop a fundraising plan.

- Recruit core supporters—and use their contacts and networks.
- Look for shared economic interests.
- Consider ideological allies.
- Take advantage of low-cost fundraising tools.
- Organize fundraising events.
- Find a trained event planner to help.
- Use the mail.
- Make use of endorsements.
- Invest in a reliable database.
- Ask for volunteers as well as dollars.
- Utilize the Internet.

☐ Establish a finance infrastructure.
☐ Be creative.
☐ Demonstrate financial credibility with decision makers.

10 You've Won! You've Lost

Preserving Victory and Learning from Defeat

"In victory be not proud. In defeat be not depressed."

—Chinese proverb

Approximately 500 local men, women, and children marched in a 1986 protest against plans to build a 1,450-bed state prison in the heart of Boyle Heights, Los Angeles. The demonstration was sponsored by the Mothers of East Los Angeles, whose efforts helped to defeat the prison proposal.

It appeared that July 13, 1987, would be a date to live in infamy for the residents of East Los Angeles. That afternoon, the California Senate had voted 29 to 6—an overwhelming majority—to join the California State Assembly in authorizing construction of a 1,450-bed prison in the heart of one of Southern California's most

---

*George Deukmejian, former governor of California, and his former chief of staff, Steve Merksamer, helped us prepare this case study for the first edition. We also owe a debt to two Harvard Kennedy School case studies written by Pamela Varley: "No Prison in East L.A.! Birth of a Grassroots Movement" (C14-00-1541.0) and "No Prison in East L.A.! Birth of a Grassroots Movement Sequel" (C14-00-1541.1).

economically troubled communities. Prison opponents already knew that their last hope was a lost hope. Gov. George Deukmejian, who had campaigned in support of the prison, would not veto the bill. Five grueling years after East Los Angelinos had banded together to fight the addition of more than a thousand felons to their neighborhood, it seemed their efforts had ended in defeat.

But if the history of the proposed East Los Angeles prison debate proves anything, it is that the status of the battle was never as it seemed. Unbeknownst to prison opponents, the Senate's vote on July 13, was not the end but just another of the twists and turns in a roller-coaster ride more treacherous than Space Mountain in nearby Disneyland. East Los Angeles had lost but could still win, just as it had previously won but had still lost.

The roots of the debate began growing in the late 1970s, when California, like many other states, adopted tough new criminal-sentencing guidelines to keep lawbreakers behind bars for longer periods of time. California's policy worked—almost too well. Correctional officials estimated that the statewide prison population, which numbered 21,000 in 1976, would grow to 95,000 by 1991. Because overcrowded prisons could subject California to constitutional challenges for violating federal confinement standards and were breeding grounds for dangerous inmate riots, legislators ordered the construction of six new state prisons to house the overflow.

Despite the huge expense of prison construction, mandating and financing the new facilities was the easy part. Identifying communities to host the new prisons was much harder. Although Californians were generally concerned about crime and supported both the tougher sentencing guidelines and the new prisons, the NIMBY syndrome—not in my back yard—was a powerful force. It was especially strong in Northern California, which produced only 40 percent of the state prison population but was home to 60 percent of the prison facilities. Los Angeles County, which generated 35 percent of the entire state's prisoners, did not have a single state prison. To placate Northern California legislators, the 1982 law mandated that one of the new prisons be located in Los Angeles County.

After fierce debate within Los Angeles County, the California Department of Corrections (CDC) eventually decided to place the new prison on what was known as the Crown Coach site—a parcel of land that once hosted various industrial buildings—located across the Los Angeles River from the East L.A. neighborhood of Boyle Heights. The CDC initially signaled that the Crown Coach site was too small for a full-scale prison and announced that it would instead host a prisoner-intake facility. But, in March 1985, the CDC shocked East L.A. residents with the news that it had purchased land adjacent to the Crown Coach site—enough land to build a full-scale, 1,700-bed, medium-security prison.

Overwhelmingly Latino East L.A. reacted with outrage. State assemblywoman Gloria Molina and residents of the area argued that the local and state governments had repeatedly dumped unattractive public projects—such as highways, junkyards, and landfills—in their neighborhood. Even worse, the new prison wouldn't be the first in East L.A. Five other federal or county prisons were located within four miles of the Crown Coach site and held 75 percent of the total L.A. County prison population. East L.A. felt it was being forced to carry more than its fair share of what other county residents didn't want in their backyards. Worst of all, the construction of a new state prison would prevent the Crown Coach site from being included in an economic empowerment zone that could create thousands of new jobs and offer economic hope to a community that had long suffered from serious unemployment woes.

East L.A. had been unable to repel those previous projects and prisons, and many residents thought the odds of reversing the CDC decision were insurmountable. But Molina and local business and neighborhood leaders took action. They formed the Coalition Against the Prison—a group that eventually swelled to include 47 community organizations—and set out to show state officials that East Los Angeles was unified in its opposition to the Crown Coach prison.

The consensus in Sacramento, the state capital, was that the coalition's efforts were dead on arrival. Despite the odds against them, Molina and her allies refused to go away. They aggressively lobbied state legislators with personal visits and impressive briefing books to make the case against the Crown Coach site. This investment of time and energy paid off in 1985. Although the California Senate approved the prison, and Deukmejian threw his gubernatorial weight behind it in an effort to secure quick passage, maverick Assembly Speaker Willie Brown refused to play along. He held the bill until 1986 so that assembly committees could review it fully, giving the coalition more time to build opposition in Sacramento. For the moment, East L.A. was winning.

However, victory in politics can be fleeting. Allies shift constantly. Although Speaker Brown had saved the coalition in 1985, he refused to meet with members when they resumed lobbying efforts the following year. In July 1986, the assembly overwhelmingly approved the Crown Coach prison. The fight now moved to the Senate, which had previously been hostile territory for the coalition.

Molina and company had learned a thing or two since their first unsuccessful interaction with the California Senate in 1985. Although the previous member-to-member lobbying had been a good start, success depended on convincing enough senators that they had something to lose in supporting the prison: political support from across the state, especially among Latino, Roman Catholic, and women voters. Fortunately, the coalition had a weapon that reached each of those key demographics.

The weapon was the Mothers of East Los Angeles, also known as MELA. Father John Moretta, a respected Catholic priest, had organized MELA as a way to rally women to oppose the Crown Coach prison. At first, MELA focused its efforts within East L.A. Thousands of women participated in MELA neighborhood marches to raise local awareness about the issue. Many of the marchers were 30-something housewives who could help spread the word through their family, school, and church networks, and who had the flexibility to organize on a moment's notice.

In the summer of 1986, 300 MELA members descended on Sacramento. Dressed in T-shirts, wearing message buttons, and holding up masks depicting a child behind bars, they beseeched individual legislators for support, attended committee hearings on the issue, and held rallies to garner press attention. By the time of the state senate vote, it was clear that MELA had influenced the debate. The only question was whether it had changed enough minds to block the two-thirds majority needed for approval. When the vote occurred on August 14, the final tally showed 23 senators in support and 12 opposed—exactly one vote short of the necessary supermajority. Once again, East L.A. had won an important battle.

But 1986 was an election year in California, and the war over the prison raged on. Governor Deukmejian ran for reelection and highlighted his support for the Crown Coach prison as part of his anticrime credentials. Deukmejian and his team also argued that the proposed prison would provide an economic boost to East L.A. because prison jobs paid relatively high wages. The coalition against the prison gathered high-profile support from César Chávez, the United Farm Workers president and civil rights legend, and Roger Mahoney, the Catholic archbishop of Los Angeles. It even convinced the influential *Los Angeles Times,* California's largest newspaper, to withdraw its previously unconditional support for the prison and instead to demand an environmental review of the Crown Coach site before the CDC purchased the additional land needed to build the prison.

The roller coaster continued unabated for the rest of 1986. On November 4, California voters dealt the coalition a major blow when they reelected Deukmejian as governor in a landslide over L.A. Mayor Tom Bradley. The coalition's nemesis would be in Sacramento for another four years. But December brought better news. California's state auditor criticized the CDC for its procedures in selecting the Crown Coach site and questioned the state's appraisal of the property. For the first time, the coalition had official documentation to bolster its case. Then, all of a sudden, the issue appeared to become moot. The Crown Coach property owners, opting to side with the neighborhood over the CDC, announced that they would sell the site to a private industrial developer. The property was off the market, and East L.A. reacted jubilantly. The CDC could not build on what it did not own.

The coalition members then learned that elections really do matter. Riding the wave of popularity from his reelection triumph, Deukmejian ignored the damning state auditor's report and reiterated his determination to build the Crown Coach prison. In his eyes, the property sale was inconsequential. He announced that California would buy the land from the new owners, take the property through eminent domain, or simply build a high-rise prison on the smaller East L.A. parcel the state already owned. His perseverance led a *Los Angeles Times* editorial writer to wonder "why Deukmejian is so determined to continue his political *mano-a-mano* with the Eastside."[1] Whatever the reason, the governor would not give up the fight.

Any governor, but particularly the governor of a large state, has enormous power to shape the public agenda. Legislators who ignore this executive's power do so at their own peril because a governor's influence and veto pen can kill legislators' priorities and make the legislators themselves appear ineffective. California's lawmakers understood this political reality and worked to find a compromise. On July 13, 1987, just months after East L.A. thought it had dodged the bullet, the California Senate voted 29–6 to approve the so-called pain for pain legislation. The plan called for the CDC to build two prisons: a 1,450-bed prison in East L.A. and a 2,200-bed prison in Lancaster, a Republican area in the northern part of L.A. County. After both houses of the California Legislature approved the bill, Deukmejian signed it into law. The coalition had lost what seemed to be the final battle over the Crown Coach prison.

For East L.A. community activists, defeat had been snatched from the jaws of victory. The compromise bill was devastating and demoralizing. But the coalition

---

[1] Franklin del Olmo, "Is the Governor Crossing Macho Line on Prison?" *Los Angeles Times,* January 15, 1987, articles.latimes.com/1987-01-15/local/me-4490_1_los-angeles-river

and MELA did not surrender. Against all odds, and in the face of certain construction, they continued their public efforts to block the prison.

California's elected governor and legislators had repeatedly disappointed East Los Angeles, but appointed public officials had provided evidence that was helpful to the cause. Although the governor ignored the 1986 auditor's report, its findings had given the coalition's arguments new credibility around the state. After the July 1987 vote, state regulators again came to the coalition's rescue. When California conducted an environmental study of the Crown Coach site, the survey found significant soil contamination left over from the property's former industrial use. The environmental report gave the coalition and MELA additional ammunition, as the cleanup would require the state to spend more money on the site than had originally been anticipated.

The environmental study and its aftermath also consumed significant time. Deukmejian decided to retire after two terms, and Pete Wilson succeeded him as governor in January 1991. In September 1992, following more intense pressure from East L.A. residents and facing an expensive cleanup of the Crown Coach site, Governor Wilson signed a bill terminating prison construction. At long last, the coalition had triumphed.

No prison would be built in East L.A., but the Crown Coach property did not remain empty for long. In 1998, California gave the Los Angeles Community Redevelopment Agency permission to restore the contaminated site back to productive use. After another environmental study and a $3.3 million soil cleanup, Los Angeles turned the property over to Alameda Produce Market, Inc., for the development of more than one million square feet of industrial and retail space. Instead of 1,450 prisoners, the site would attract 2,500 jobs and more than $80 million in private investment. Thirteen years after its formation, the coalition had achieved its economic empowerment goals.

The highs and lows of the Crown Coach debate are common to the task of influencing decision makers: East Los Angeles activists experienced victory, defeat, victory, again defeat, and then victory. When citizens engage democracy, there are few permanent triumphs or setbacks. There is no rest in participatory democracy. Winning brings new responsibilities, and losing presents new opportunities. This chapter will help you understand what lies ahead after winning or losing.

IF YOU HAVE WON: CAPITALIZING ON VICTORIES

Nothing is more satisfying than victory in a cause that you have passionately and energetically championed. But don't let winning seduce you. Your triumph among the electorate, through the favorable action of your state legislature or city council, or your success in winning over appointed officials is not the end of your efforts. If you want this euphoric moment to be the start rather than the end of a winning streak, take steps now to preserve and extend your victory.

1. Look over Your Shoulder

It feels like you have won, but are you sure? Though you shouldn't cross the line into paranoia, you should be vigilant in ensuring that your "victory" isn't suddenly reversed. Electoral campaigns often seem like the surest of triumphs—after all, one candidate or position won more votes than the other—but recent history tells us that the Election Day results are often far from the final word. For example, the 2000 presidential campaign was supposed to end with the election of a new chief executive on November 7, 2000. Indeed, at one point during that night, the networks called Vice President Al Gore the likely next president. Later in the evening, Gore called Texas governor George W. Bush to concede defeat, and then called back to withdraw his concession as new numbers were released. The results in Florida and New Mexico were so close that the nation needed 36 more days of recounts and litigation before it had a president-elect.

In the November 2008 Minnesota U.S. Senate contest, Republican incumbent Norm Coleman and Democratic challenger Al Franken experienced an even longer delay before the election was resolved. In fact, it was not until July 7, 2009—more than eight months after Election Day—that all legal challenges were exhausted, Coleman conceded, and Franken took office. If you have just concluded what you think is a successful political campaign, don't let the fact of winning the most votes lull you into a false sense of security. You haven't won until your county or state election officials certify the results as official. Make sure that the attorney you engaged after reading chapter 9 is helping you take the steps necessary to facilitate election certification.

The risk of unexpected reversal is even greater when your victory is the result of actions taken by a state legislature, city council, or other governmental body. East L.A. residents learned this painful lesson many times, as various "wins"—the unexpected alliance with Speaker Brown, the initial triumph in the state senate, the state auditor's report, and the property owner's refusal to sell the property to the CDC—suddenly became losses. This danger is ever present at every level of government.

Felix Unger from the 1970s television sitcom *The Odd Couple* said it well: "[Y]ou should never assume because when you assume, you make an ASS out of 'U' and 'ME.'"[2] As soon as you feel certain that your cause has won, that's exactly when you are most likely to become the unwitting victim of an unexpected loss. Look in the rearview and side mirrors immediately.

2. Run through the Tape

Very little in sports is as embarrassing as a player who spikes the ball before it crosses the plane of the goal or who is stripped of the ball just as he is about to enter the end zone. You can't declare victory until you have truly cleared every hurdle in the process. It's not enough that the legislature has passed your appropriations bill. Though that is cause for momentary optimism, any good feeling will quickly evaporate if you fail to direct your advocacy energies to the governor's office and suffer a veto.

As you are assembling your citizen engagement plan, make sure to understand and carefully map out the process so you don't miss a step. And hitting the tape requires strategy and effort in the backstretch. Using the veto scenario, know that most wise public executives with veto authority prefer not to exercise it. A veto incurs the wrath of citizens and legislators who supported the measure and shows that an opportunity for compromise has been missed.

Use this executive preference to your advantage. If possible, persuade the mayor or governor early in the process to support your initiative or to include your spending

---

[2] "My Strife in Court," *The Odd Couple*, season 3, episode 19.

item in his or her recommended budget. But if that is not possible, stay in close contact with the executive's office throughout the legislative process. Determine which staff member is following your bill, and educate that person about the status and substance of the legislation. As the bill progresses toward final passage, take the temperature of the executive branch to see if it can support the bill in its current form, or if the bill needs to be modified.

A veto is not the only obstacle that could snatch defeat from the jaws of victory. For example, assume that the local university president has just approved a longtime demand for a new parking garage located close to campus. Can his or her board of trustees or the state board of higher education countermand that decision? Alternatively, assume that you have persuaded your city council and mayor to set up a special taxing district to raise funds for children's programs. Is the city government required to put the issue before voters for final approval? Finally, imagine a scenario in which you have persuaded your state legislature to enact a sales tax rebate that will help your business retool its manufacturing plants. Can your opponents use any parliamentary tactics to derail the bill after final passage? Just remember that you haven't won, even if you have won. Anticipate and have plans in place to block all of the ways that a determined opponent could try to upend your success at the last minute.

As an example of how defeat can be snatched out of the jaws of victory, consider this scenario, which is based on real events and circumstances.[3] Education advocates in a small city resist the closure of a high school that has historical significance and a reputation for excellence. It is also located in the center of the city, which benefits downtown merchants, and the school has an arts program that attracts many more applicants than it can admit. It is the only full high school in the community.

The local school board has threatened to close the school several times in the past, only to have determined opposition thwart those plans. Then comes the most recent round of school closure talks. At first, it looks like history will repeat itself. After again suggesting closure, the board again relents in the face of considerable advocacy and fundraising on the school's behalf.

But over the summer, when parents, teachers, and students who thought they had won are not paying attention, the board changes course. While it will not "close" the school—which would be hard to sell because of its historic architecture—the board will "repurpose" the high school as an adult education center.

Two lessons can be learned from this scenario. First, do not stop watching decision makers, even after you think they have decided in your favor. Second, if a policy or decision is controversial, advocates should anticipate an ongoing fight, and one that shifts ground. In other words, sometimes the tape that you need to run through moves.

3. Say Thank You

Unbelievably, the easiest post-advocacy item on your to-do list is the one most often ignored: expressing thanks to the many people who aided your success. More

---

[3] These took place in the Canadian city of Peterborough, Ontario. But they could easily have happened in the United States.

triumphant causes lose supporters over this omission than any other. No matter whether you organized a big or small effort, you can follow several simple steps to ensure that nobody becomes an enemy for lack of gratitude on your part.

First, send a mass mailing—either by mail or the Internet, or both—to every single person who played a role, no matter how big or small, in your initiative. Second, devote adequate time to appreciative telephone calls. Just as you spent hours each day dialing for allies, dollars, volunteers, or votes, invest the time to call those individuals who helped you the most—fundraisers who hosted events or collected significant numbers of donations, donors who gave substantial financial support, precinct or county leaders who organized and rallied supporters, elected officials who were particularly outspoken in their support, and others. These calls are important not only because you owe these friends your thanks but also because they will help to solidify your network of supporters for future campaigns or citizen initiatives.

Pay special attention to decision makers, not only because they deserve thanks but also because you now have an opportunity to establish a long-term, positive relationship with them. If 10 members of a city council provided the winning margin for your position, you should at a minimum call each of them and send letters or handwritten notes expressing appreciation. Meet with them individually to convey your thanks. Include them in the tangible rewards of your effort. For example, if your success was the construction of a new county park, invite them to speak at the groundbreaking ceremony, give them public recognition and gratitude, and make sure media is there to cover it. Invite the decision maker to the annual meeting of your community organization, and present that person with an award for her or his efforts.

Third, give your most diligent supporters a memento to capture the spirit of the effort and encourage long-term enthusiasm. Many Americans who helped Jimmy Carter's successful 1976 bid for the presidency still treasure the peanut pin he distributed after victory. When I was elected Florida's governor in 1978, I sent my supporters "Graham Crackers" and copies of the book—Workdays—about many of the 100 jobs I took during the campaign.

Fourth, if your advocacy effort was large enough to hire staff members, and you have enough remaining financial resources to pay bonuses, make sure to give monetary thanks for a job well done. Staff members typically work long hours for little pay, and the financial gratitude will be warmly received.

Just remember: You can't say thank you enough or to too many people. The person you forget to thank for helping you reform the middle school curriculum, block the state legislature from placing a prison in your community, or elect you to office is the person least likely to help when you seek assistance in the future.

4. Chronicle the Campaign

As philosopher and poet George Santayana wrote, "Those who cannot remember the past are condemned to repeat it."[4] Your successful campaign or citizen initiative should have a slightly different take on those timeless words of wisdom: Those who do not chronicle their success won't remember how to replicate it. With the help of

---

[4] George Santayana, *The Life of Reason: The Phases of Human Progress* (Auckland, NZ: Floating Press, 2008), 312.

others who are intimately familiar with the topic, prepare a written end-of-initiative history while the effort is still fresh in your mind. That document should answer several questions: How and why did the advocacy effort begin? Who were its leaders, and how can you contact them in the future? What key events define the chronology? What were the high and low points? What lessons were learned? Which decisions paid positive dividends, and which were mistakes? What actions would you replicate in the future, and which would you avoid? Because this successful initiative is not likely to be the last in which you will be involved, you can dust off the written history as you prepare for the next initiative.

But don't take the risk that your chronicle is shoved into a desk drawer and forgotten. Strongly consider making it public. Just as your team sought to control the narrative during the citizenship journey, you should continue to do so at journey's end. Provide the story to a media member who has been closely following the advocacy effort and encourage that person to write the "how did they do it?" article that is common in politics. But if reporters can't or won't take on that public accounting, take the initiative to publish it yourself. As we explained in chapter 8, your community likely has Internet media outlets that would welcome a detailed history complete with video and photographs. You can also post it to your website for public view.

As valuable as that written narrative is to long-term success, it isn't enough. You are sitting on a gold mine of information, and now is the time to safeguard that hard-won treasure. Over the course of the effort, you have accumulated hundreds or thousands of names, addresses, e-mails, and telephone numbers of volunteers, contributors, consultants, policy experts, and others—data that will be extremely valuable in the future. You also have a wealth of documents, research, fliers, letters, and other papers. Using the appropriate software, organize and archive all of this information so that you have ready access down the line.

Citizen advocacy initiatives are supposed to be fun, so take care to protect those items that symbolize the enjoyable part of the experience. Paraphernalia, buttons, bumper strips, slate cards, posters, white papers, vote tally sheets, photographs, videos, websites, mail pieces, and any Internet or broadcast advertisements have both historical and sentimental value. If you keep them, they will help you recapture the positive feelings that both inspired and accompanied your victory.

5. Turn Opponents into Friends

In the aftermath of your victory the advice to keep your friends close and your enemies closer is worth following. Even if the contest was tough and the debate was heated, purge any lingering anger or bitterness you feel toward your opponents. Politics should not be a blood sport, and enemies' lists are a waste of time and energy. The partisan gridlock in Washington, D.C., and in various state capitals in recent years can be attributed in part to individuals in power who care more about demonizing and crushing the opposition than working together to bolster our democratic institutions.

You are better than that. Be magnanimous in victory, and reach out to those who opposed you. Start with a phone call to the leader of the other side on the day after your victory, and, over time, work to find opportunities for common ground. If you can turn your opponent into an ally, or at least minimize long-term animosity, you are less likely to face opposition in the future. Even more important, because politics is an ever-shifting chessboard, you may need that former opponent on your side in a future battle.

Former Senate majority leader Bob Dole set the standard when he delivered a particularly gracious concession speech upon losing the 1996 presidential election to President Bill Clinton. He spoke to his supporters and a national television audience: "I've said repeatedly in this campaign that the President was my opponent and not my enemy. And I wish him well, and I pledge my support in whatever advances the cause of a better America."[5] Celebrate your victory with an outstretched hand—not a swinging fist.

6. Close the Doors Correctly

Some citizen efforts don't require as much paperwork as others. You may not need a full-blown political campaign, with the accompanying regulations, if you lead an informal coalition to convince the school board to alter elementary school boundaries or to motivate a town official to clean up your local lake. But whenever you have established an advocacy organization, whether it is to persuade the county commission or state legislature to take action, secure voter approval of a ballot initiative, or elect a candidate, you must strictly follow the legal procedures set forth for the operation and conclusion of the campaign.

In chapter 9, we said that your initiative's greatest vulnerability is in financing—in other words, legally and ethically raising, allocating, and accounting for the money you need to be successful. The second greatest vulnerability is completion—properly shutting down the official apparatus. Most states, and even the federal government when certain types of organizations are involved, have very specific procedures for winding down the affairs of the effort, and you can experience problems if you are not faithful in the execution of those procedures. These can range from the inconvenient to the serious. For example, I once received an official notice for state taxes due for a campaign that was three years in the past— long after the records were warehoused and the people familiar with them had left for destinations unknown. But that challenge pales in comparison to former candidates and campaign staff members who are forced to defend themselves against civil or even criminal charges related to paying insufficient attention to shutdown regulations. The applicable federal or state oversight body is certain to take a dim view of violations, forcing you to spend thousands of dollars in legal fees to rectify the problem.

Fortunately, you can take several steps to avert disaster. First, appoint a competent and experienced person to manage the shutdown, and ensure that she or he has plenty of assistance from trusted volunteers. Second, do not allow your retained or volunteer attorney to go home until he or she has provided you with the expert legal advice necessary for a proper conclusion to the effort. Third, make sure your treasurer, hired accountant, or a trusted volunteer has the necessary expertise to conduct a final audit of the organization's finances. Fourth, take care to adhere

---

[5] "Remarks by Dole in Conceding Defeat by Clinton," *New York Times*, November 6, 1996, www.nytimes .com/1996/11/06/us/remarks-by-dole-in-conceding-defeat-by-clinton.html

strictly to any local, state, or federal laws governing surplus funds. Violating those rules can be disastrous. Managing these tasks competently will help your candidate transition to governing, or allow you to focus exclusively on proper implementation of your initiative, with confidence that organizational matters have been resolved.

7. Keep Your Momentum

Your triumph is well worth celebrating, but it does not mark the conclusion of your efforts. Winning has given you the responsibilities of a parent with long-term obligations for leading your initiative into political adulthood. These parental responsibilities include the following:

Keep your coalition together and look to add new members and goals. You can use the same techniques discussed in chapter 7 to expand the coalition in this post-victory period and make sure it does not wither.

Engage the individuals who will execute your idea. Your county school board's decision to give free books to elementary students for after-school reading should prompt you to contact the administrator in charge of reading instruction. If the voters have passed a constitutional amendment that requires the state to expand Medicaid, you will need to contact state legislators and regulators who will be charged with implementing the expansion.

These contacts are important because your victory gives you credibility, and your advice and encouragement will help to keep the execution of policy decisions in line with your original goals. But expect to encounter bureaucratic resistance and antagonism. Your initiative may have altered a program or pattern with which officials were comfortable, and they may drag their heels in making any changes. Administrative resistance can include delays in writing the rules and regulations necessary for implementation, complaints to the constituencies affected by your change in hopes they will seek to have it repealed, or purposeful clumsiness in administering the program to cast doubt on your reform.

Treat these officials with respect, but develop a plan in advance so that you can dodge any obstacles placed in your path. Perhaps the most important part of that plan will be good communication before and after your proposal is adopted. As you are developing and advocating the initiative, keep those people who will be responsible for its implementation well informed. Seek their advice, accept their suggested changes when appropriate, and give them credit for the modifications so they feel a sense of ownership in your idea.

If you did not engage the implementing officials before your proposal was adopted, meet with them as soon as possible following its adoption to explain the intent and solicit their ideas on how to measure its success. Look for opportunities to recognize and congratulate the administrators for their good work in achieving a smooth transition.

Devise methods for measuring the implementation of your idea. Governments routinely fail to have metrics that are clearly expressed and understood, a failing that often impedes progress. Don't make that mistake. Let's assume that the county government has just approved your plan to clean up a local lake. You will be able to track the plan's success if you develop a short list of quantifiable standards. For example, what are the levels of contaminants in the water? In the past month, how many days was the lake closed to fishing or swimming? How healthy are the wildlife populations that depend on the lake? Persuade the legislators who enacted your idea and the appointed officials charged with implementing it to use those metrics to track progress. Seek agreement on who will gather, analyze, and report the relevant data. When the report is ready to be released, engage the media so that the public knows whether goals are being met or missed.

Recognize those who are helping you. Again, success really boils down to regular expressions of thanks. Say thank you early and often. Schedule an annual event to boost your cause. Present the most supportive elected and appointed officials and the most diligent volunteers with awards, plaques, trophies, or other tangible signs of appreciation. Never fail to write or call with thanks when a legislator or other government official shows interest in your citizen initiative, and make sure that constituents or voters who support your cause do the same. Reward your friends and remind your opponents that you are alive and kicking.

Reach beyond your original territory. Mothers Against Drunk Driving started in a single California town. Before long, it was a statewide, then a national, and now an international force. With each expansion, MADD became more powerful in its original town. Don't worry if you can't or don't want to go global, national, or even statewide. If you were able to win in your community, you will almost certainly find support for your cause in a nearby one.

In politics, ultimate success looks more like the tortoise than the hare. From the start of your effort, consider each successful step part of a continuum rather than the completion of your journey. After each victory, you will need to reassess whether your objective needs to be tweaked or even overhauled in support of reaching the eventual destination. Short-term triumphs are pleasing, but long-term results are what really matter. Don't be the team with a halftime lead that ends up on the wrong end of the final score.

IF YOU HAVE LOST: RECOVERING FROM DEFEAT

Defeat on the playing field is never easy, whether it is in sports, business, law, or politics, and it stings the most when you care deeply about your cause. But a loss is not the time to surrender. As the residents of East Los Angeles discovered more than once, initial defeat can serve as the foundation for future victory if you learn from the experience and refuse to go quietly into the night. Your steps for rehabilitation will include the following:

1. Try to Snatch Victory from the Jaws of Defeat

A loss is not always a loss. Take advantage of the situation if the winning side is not looking over its shoulder. Does a higher authority at your local or state government have the power to derail what appears to be a victory? Although you don't want to display a sour grapes attitude, contribute to gridlock, or obstruct simply for the sake of obstruction, the victorious campaign has the burden of securing final triumph. There is nothing wrong with championing your position until the last possible moment.

Even if you cannot stop the opposition from achieving victory in theory, you may still be able to slow down the implementation process. If victors do not skillfully engage the officials charged with carrying out policy decisions, then you may find natural allies in the bureaucratic forces that often prefer the status quo to change or in agencies that want their interests represented in the process. For example, the hopes of the East L.A. Coalition Against the Prison were dead in the water until California environmental regulators reported that pollutants had contaminated the proposed prison site. Had Governor Deukmejian preemptively addressed concerns about the property's environmental health, he may have succeeded in forcing construction of the prison. But Deukmejian paid insufficient attention to that constituency, and the consequence was the failure of his prison construction plan.

2. If at First You Don't Succeed, Try, Try Again

Some of the best ideas in American politics didn't succeed on the first, second, or even twentieth attempt. We wouldn't have direct election of U.S. senators, Social Security, the minimum wage, NASA, women's suffrage, or universal civil rights if the champions of those causes hadn't persisted. Imagine if the Steamboat Springs school construction advocates had simply thrown up their hands when voters rejected their proposed bond issue or if the LGBT community quit when Hillsborough County repealed an antidiscrimination ordinance. Defeat does not mean that you don't have what it takes to succeed, but it does mean that you need to recalibrate. Remember that politics does not bring permanent victories or losses. Certain defeat comes only when you have thrown in the towel.

3. Be Gracious

Nobody likes a sore loser, and poor mouthing will not help when you attempt to move the cause forward in the future. People generally don't remember a negative outcome. They remember how you reacted and responded. Expressions of gratitude are even more important in defeat. Don't miss this opportunity to thank and recognize your supporters just as fervently as you would have done in a winning effort. Your words of appreciation will help to comfort very disappointed people who have given freely of their time, energy, skills, and financial resources, and those words will also help to motivate them to engage in future initiatives. The process of writing, calling, or e-mailing allies will also be healing for you. A reminder of why you originally engaged in the battle can be the best medicine for overcoming a loss, and supporters can provide a healthy dose of inspiration.

4. Finish Strong

Regrettably, losing does not free you of the obligation to close your advocacy effort in accordance with the appropriate local, state, or federal procedures. Closing down will be painful, but it is nonetheless necessary. However, some of the same post-victory actions suggested in the previous section can also work to your long-term advantage—especially if the winning side arrogantly or negligently fails to implement them. Even if they did not support you, thank decision makers for taking the time to consider your position. Ask their advice on how your effort could have been more persuasive, or how you might win their support next time. Look for issues on which you might work together. Unsuccessful advocates need to build long-term relationships and turn opponents into friends just as much—if not more—than successful advocates.

5. Diagnose the Problem and Fix It

A defeat is the proper time for some serious introspection. Was your cause inherently flawed and thus unlikely ever to achieve victory? Or did you make errors that struck down an otherwise winnable idea? The typical flaws that sink an advocacy effort involve all of the skills that we have previously outlined: failure to define the problem sufficiently, inadequate research, absence of a broad base of support, efforts that start too late or too early, incomplete public understanding of your issues or (equally dangerous) overexposure to them, or a lack of financing.

Citizens wanting to live so they can fight another day should be as aggressive in gathering information as they were when they launched the initiative. Your most trusted colleagues and impartial outside observers can help you perform this necessary analysis. Talk to as many people who followed the effort as you can to find out why they think the initiative went south or what advocates could have done better. Ask a team of supporters to analyze the contest from the perspective of your opponents to understand why they succeeded. Consider preparing a post-contest chronicle much like the one we suggested for the winning side. When you try again to achieve your goal—and you should try again—you will be glad to have a reminder of what went well and what you would have done differently.

Most importantly, take heart. As President John F. Kennedy reminded the American Newspaper Publishers Association in April 1961, "An error does not become a mistake until you refuse to correct it."[6] Your challenges can be remedied before you undertake future efforts.

CHECKLIST FOR ACTION

☐ If you have won

- Look over your shoulder to avoid a reversal.
- Run through the tape.
- Say thank you.
- Chronicle the campaign.
- Turn opponents into friends.
- Close the campaign correctly.
- Keep your momentum.

---

[6] John F. Kennedy, "The President and the Press: Address before the American Newspaper Publishers Association," April 27, 1961, genius.com/President-john-f-kennedy-the-president-and-the-press-address-before-the-american-newspaper-publishers-association-annotated/

☐ If you have lost

- Try to snatch victory from the jaws of defeat.
- Try, try again.
- Be gracious.
- Finish strong.
- Diagnose and fix what went wrong.

FINAL THOUGHTS: THE JOURNEY CONTINUES

If you have read and assimilated the book to this point, it means that you have absorbed the 10 skills most vital to successful citizen leadership. You have defined the problem; conducted research on your issue; identified which officials have the power to address your concerns; measured public opinion; persuaded the proper decision maker; used deadlines, trends, and cycles to your advantage; built a coalition; engaged the news media; found ways to raise advocacy resources; and learned to protect victory and rebound from defeat. Before this journey began, many of you were spectators in the great arena of democracy. But now you have the knowledge and skills to be a robust democratic participant.

With that new awareness comes the responsibility to use your new citizenship muscles and to help others discover how to build their own strength. The health of our democracy hinges on the exercise of your rights as an active citizen. We're counting on you to be the woman or the man "who is actually in the arena, whose face is marred by dust and sweat and blood; who strives valiantly; who errs, who comes up short again and again, because there is no effort without error and shortcoming; but who does actually strive to do the deeds; knows great enthusiasms, the great devotions; who spends himself in a worthy cause; who at the best knows in the end the triumph of high achievement, and who at the worst, if he fails, at least fails while daring greatly, so that his place shall never be with those cold and timid souls who knew neither victory nor defeat." [7]

Congratulations and good luck.

---

[7] Theodore Roosevelt, "Citizenship in a Republic," speech given at the Sorbonne, Paris, April 23, 1910, www.theodoreroosevelt.org/site/c.elKSIdOWIiJ8H/b.8090921/apps/s/content.asp?ct=14605521

Index